SWAMP KINGS

SWAMP KINGS

THE STORY OF THE MURDAUGH FAMILY OF SOUTH CAROLINA & A CENTURY OF BACKWOODS POWER

JASON RYAN

PEGASUS CRIME

NEW YORK LONDON

SWAMP KINGS

Pegasus Crime is an imprint of
Pegasus Books, Ltd.
148 West 37th Street, 13th Floor
New York, NY 10018

Copyright © 2024 by Jason Ryan

First Pegasus Books cloth edition April 2024

Interior design by Maria Fernandez

The Lowcountry of South Carolina map © Gene Thorp.

Library of Congress Cataloging-in-Publication Data is available.

ISBN: 978-1-63936-567-8

10 9 8 7 6 5 4 3 2 1

Printed in the United States of America
Distributed by Simon & Schuster
www.pegasusbooks.com

To Elizabeth, who is always full of bright ideas.

CONTENTS

The Lowcountry of South Carolina Map   ix

Dramatis Personae   xi

1   In the Spotlight   1

2   At Home in the Swamp   62

3   Secrets and Sins   102

4   Buster's Law   161

5   Predator and Prey   220

6   Fixed Outcomes   279

7   End of the Line   328

8   The Trial   379

CODA   405

Works Cited   411

Notes   415

A Note From the Author   447

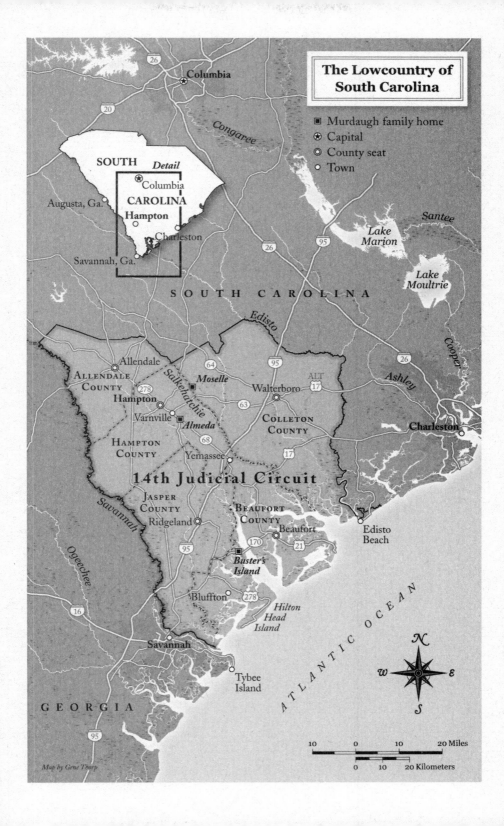

DRAMATIS PERSONAE

Within the last century the Murdaugh family of Hampton County has included five Randolphs, three Busters, two Johns, and two Richard Alexanders. Two of the Busters were truly Randolphs, and the third Buster is a Richard Alexander, but not the Richard Alexander who goes by Alex, which is not pronounced Alex, but rather Alec. Got all that?

The names alone in this story can be head spinning, never mind all the intrigue and unending wrongdoing. In an effort to reduce confusion, I offer this *dramatis personae* of the Murdaugh saga. This book focuses on four Murdaugh men across four generations, three of whom share the same name. They are:

Randolph Murdaugh Sr. (1887–1940), who enjoyed the nickname Buster when a young man but was more popularly known as **Randolph**, which is how he is referred to in the pages ahead. His oldest son, who succeeded him as an elected prosecutor and the head of the family law firm, was:

↓

Randolph Murdaugh Jr. (1915-1998), who inherited his father's name and nickname, and who was known as **Buster** nearly his entire life. His brother was Johnny Glenn Murdaugh. Buster and his wife, Gladys, had two children, including a son who succeeded him in office. This was:

↓

Randolph Murdaugh III (1939-2021), known as **Randy** to family and friends and as Randolph professionally. Randy and his wife, Libby, had four children: Lynn, Randy IV, John Marvin, and:

↓

Richard Alexander Murdaugh (1968–), known as **Alex**, a lawyer and volunteer, part-time prosecutor who was married to the former Maggie Branstetter, with whom he had two sons: Richard Alexander Jr., who went by Buster, and Paul.

IN THE SPOTLIGHT

The train rolled into Hampton County just after midnight, barreling along tracks that cut through riotous, overgrown countryside. Three men toiled aboard the train's locomotive, fueling its firebox and finessing its controls. The next station—Varnville—was at least four miles away, down a straightaway. There was no reason to slow down.

A full moon hung in a clear sky, illuminating a lush landscape divided by steel rails. The train rushed inland past pine stands and swamps and farm fields and grand live oaks festooned with Spanish moss. Every few miles the train crossed over a small creek, locally known as a branch, that fed the nearby swamps, where cypress and water tupelo trees sprung from shallow pools of black water. The moonlit scenery appeared ethereal that midsummer night, enchanting the fireman on board the train to the point he was inspired to make chitchat about it all with his companions.

The train steamed across the Lowcountry of South Carolina, a rural section of dense forestland, marsh islands, and vast estuaries that emptied into the Atlantic Ocean. The Lowcountry is flat and just barely above sea level. There is no high ground, the exceptions being small riverside bluffs and the occasional hint of rolling terrain. Much of the region is regularly overrun by water. Along the coast, seven-foot tides sweep in and out of the creeks twice a day, flushing the saltwater marshes. Inland, where the saltwater creeks dwindle and peter out, freshwater swamps pool and spill ever so slowly across extensive bottoms, replenished by rain and overflowing rivers.

The railroad's Magnolia Route operated across this part of the Low-country, providing passenger and freight car service between the seaside docks of Port Royal, South Carolina, and Augusta, Georgia, 112 miles away. The Magnolia Route was a romantic name but a misnomer; the railway's trains hauled huge cargoes of cypress and pine. Ever since the Magnolia Route opened in stages in the 1870s, sawmills and turpentine distilleries dotted the railroad line, taking advantage of the railroad's proximity to wide, towering trees within old-growth forests. Depots were built nearby to load trains with lumber and other forest products. Small communities developed around these rural factories and accompanying railroad depots, forming a line of small towns in Hampton County, each existing a few miles away from the next and each being split down the middle by the rails.

A highway ran parallel to the railroad along this portion of the Magnolia Route, providing another link between the depot towns. Any time train engineer W. W. Bartlett spotted an automobile driving on the highway he dimmed the locomotive's headlight to avoid blinding the car's driver. At full power, said Bartlett, the train's lamp shone as "bright as day." Even at a distance, he said, the headlight could reveal a fly on a man's face.

As the train traveled along the rails, toward a string of these sawmill and depot towns, Bartlett spotted an unfamiliar light flashing a half-mile down the tracks. The engineer stared ahead, puzzled. The flashing didn't seem like Morse code to Bartlett, and the signaling didn't seem frantic or panicky, either, as if someone was trying to signal an emergency. The light just flashed on, off. On, off.

The train, clipping along at thirty-five miles per hour, was closing rapidly on the flashing light. The blinking appeared to emanate from a spot beside the upcoming railroad crossing, where Camp Branch Road intersected the railroad tracks and joined the highway. From 200 yards away, Bartlett could see a car sitting to the right of the tracks, stopped at the edge of the crossing, beside an old mill. The car's headlights flashed on, off. On, off.

"[There's] somebody parked down there beside the railroad and cutting fool with the lights," the engineer thought to himself. He kept a steady speed. His crew, meanwhile, occupied the left side of the locomotive, the brakeman resting in his seat while the fireman shoveled coal into the steam engine's furnace. From their vantage points on the far side of the train, neither of these men could see the flashing headlights of the automobile.

Bartlett stared ahead, the locomotive's headlight casting an awesome beam down the tracks. As the train approached Camp Branch crossing, he watched with horror as the automobile surged forward onto the elevated crossing and stopped in the middle of the tracks, in front of the train. Bartlett released the train's deafening whistle, warning the driver and any passengers that this train was coming through, and in a hurry.

A mere thirty yards separated the train and the car. Now that the car was directly in the beam of the headlight, Bartlett could see the driver was alone. He sat behind the steering wheel wearing a white shirt and holding his arm out the window. Despite a shrieking, glaring, hulking metal machine bearing down on him by the second, the motorist did not yield. Unlike the train, he seemed in no rush.

Bartlett kept sounding the whistle, hardly giving it a rest. The whistle's scream pierced the quiet early morning air. It was a sound so sharp it prompted the fireman to turn his head in order to lessen the strain on his ears. The engineer's constant use of the whistle told the fireman and the brakeman something was wrong. They changed their positions enough to look ahead and see a car stopped on the crossing, immediately in front of the train. They saw a man sitting inside the car, waving his hand.

The fireman started ringing a bell as the gap between train and car shrunk to ten yards. The engineer, Bartlett, finally abandoned hope that this was a prank, that the waving driver would zoom off at the last minute. It was now approaching the last second, the motorist was not budging, and Bartlett needed to brace for a collision. He braked but it was too late. At about 1:00 A.M. on Friday, July 19, 1940, a horrible, violent crash occurred under a full moon in Hampton County. A whistle shrieked, a bell clanged, and brakes squealed before metal crumpled and bones snapped.

Just before this hellish scene unfolded, Bartlett peered a short distance down the track, along the beam of the train's headlight, and stared a final time at the doomed motorist. The engineer observed the white-shirted man sitting behind the car's steering wheel, making no attempt to escape. As the speeding train loomed closer and closer, the man kept waving through the car window. He was laughing.

———

Alex Murdaugh was crying.

Or at least pretending to cry. He sat on a witness stand in an old South Carolina courtroom on February 23, 2023, hunched over and fatigued, staring down a feisty prosecutor and feebly responding to the questions and accusations he posed. He blew his nose and dabbed his eyes, every action being watched intently by twelve jurors seated just a few feet away in two rows of swivel chairs mounted to the floor. Dozens of witnesses had already testified over the course of the last four weeks, but none of their answers mattered as much as the words now escaping Alex's mouth. Alex sobbed and sniffled as he recounted the day his wife, Maggie, and youngest son, Paul, were killed. Oddly, no tears appeared to run down Alex's face, noted one juror. "All he did was blow snot," said the man.

Alex had been disgraced entirely. He was a ruined man, a former hotshot lawyer and schmoozer who had lost all his money, his right to practice law, much of his family, and every bit of his reputation. His reversal of fortune was swift and complete. Four years ago he was a cocky litigator with all the trappings that came with working in a fourth-generation family law firm, including his 1,770-acre farm, a beach house, household staff, and a fleet of vehicles. He was a regular presence at college ball games, charity galas, and hunts for deer, duck, and turkey. Alex was gregarious and boisterous, having inherited acute political instincts and a natural tendency to glad-hand and slap the back of everyone in sight. Tall, redheaded, and usually quite loud, Alex came and went like a tornado in Hampton.

Now he was charged with shooting Maggie and Paul dead at the family farm on June 7, 2021. He was accused, too, of about a hundred other crimes—a stunning amount of wrongdoing, all of it undetected for years. Many of these allegations involved a long-running fraud that enabled Alex to steal millions from legal clients. A few other charges related to alleged opioid trafficking, and then a few others concerned the orchestration of a bewildering roadside shooting that sent Alex to the hospital via helicopter with a gunshot wound to the head.

Nearly all these crimes were ones of desperation. He stole clients' money to repay loans. He killed to hide the revelation of his theft. Then he ostensibly arranged his own demise to escape justice, or something like that, but something went awry.

Alex's actions trashed the family name, destroying a political and legal dynasty more than a hundred years in the making. The Murdaugh name stood for legal excellence in South Carolina, as well as law and order in the Lowcountry. Alex torched this legacy overnight, his surname becoming shorthand for predation, corruption, and squandered privilege.

Before Alex's crackup, the Murdaugh family had long held the upper hand in the Lowcountry. Beginning in 1920, three generations of Murdaugh men served as the chief prosecutors of a sprawling, five-county section of coastal South Carolina. For eighty-six consecutive years these prosecutors, known as solicitors in the Palmetto State, oversaw thousands of local criminal cases, dispensing justice, or extending favors, as they saw fit. Even after the retirement of Solicitor Randolph Murdaugh III in 2006, Alex volunteered as an assistant solicitor in the office, an unusual arrangement that allowed him to carry a law enforcement badge, which he displayed atop the dashboard of his car and sometimes dangled from his pants pocket. He tried just a handful of criminal cases, but nonetheless he preserved the family's relevance in the office and maintained relationships with cops, prosecutors, judges, and other members of the Lowcountry's law enforcement community.

Beyond serving as prosecutors, the Murdaughs also operated a small-town family law firm in Hampton with a reputation for dominance. Over the decades the firm leveraged local favor and quirks in state law to successfully sue some of America's largest corporations for multimillion-dollar awards and settlements, many of them related to vehicle accidents and personal injury. The firm hired smart lawyers who were good at sizing up wealthy adversaries. Railroad companies were sued so often by the Murdaughs and their associates that the law firm's fancy headquarters was nicknamed "The House That CSX Built." Walmart, otherwise ubiquitous in the rural South, was discouraged from opening a store in Hampton County because of liability concerns in the Murdaughs' hometown.

In this Southern backwoods, surrounded by swamps and pines and poverty, the Murdaughs lived like kings, the law being almost entirely within their control. While the family patriarchs did not rule the region by decree, the Murdaughs were about as close to country royalty as a clan could get in Hampton County. Other families were wealthier, and plenty of politicians in the state ranked higher in name recognition than the assorted Murdaugh family solicitors, but when it came to true influence, and the power to bend the law, the Murdaughs ruled supreme in their part of the Lowcountry, at least for a long time.

Inevitably the family advantage dulled. Alex failed to appreciate the decline and his crimes actually became more brazen the longer his family remained out of public office. Increasingly, Alex was living a lie. The lie almost told itself, as people in the Lowcountry expected Alex Murdaugh to be successful and wealthy, they expected him to be overbearing, and they expected him to lord over Hampton and its surrounding counties, walking in the footsteps of his forefathers and making the swamplands his own.

Alex was a pleaser and strived to meet these expectations. He started stealing and borrowing huge sums of money to bankroll his family's comfortable lifestyle. The amounts he took grew and grew until at last he was taking millions of dollars from some clients and giving them nothing. He was living precariously, regularly draining his bank accounts and then scrambling to restore the balance through assorted illegal schemes. Still he fell deeper and deeper in debt, no matter how much he pilfered. Though Alex shirked honest work, he industriously covered his tracks as he manipulated legal settlements to steer clients' money his way. Yet Alex was not on trial, at least not yet, for any of those alleged offenses. This was a murder trial. The question being posed to the jurors was simple: Did Alex Murdaugh shoot his wife and youngest son dead at the family farm?

Alex claimed he discovered Maggie and Paul's lifeless bodies when he returned home from visiting his ailing mother across town. He called 911 just after 10:00 P.M. and greeted police when they arrived at the crime scene. Alex gave an interview in an investigator's car, sobbing as he described the day's events and his thoughts about who might have killed his wife and son. He did not volunteer himself as a suspect.

Yet this was only the beginning of much pain for the family and the people of Hampton County. Little did they know that Maggie and Paul's deaths marked the start of a massive fallout that would expose considerably more wrongdoing across the Lowcountry and shed new light on suspicious tragedies from the past. Three days after the killings at the farm Alex's elderly father Randolph Murdaugh III, who served as solicitor for twenty years, died of illness at the age of eighty-one. The Murdaugh family now had three people to lay to rest. And beyond these deaths other tragedies associated with the family lingered. This included the death of Mallory Beach, a nineteen-year-old woman killed in 2019 in a drunken boat crash involving Paul; Gloria Satterfield, the longtime nanny and housekeeper for Alex and Maggie Murdaugh's family who died after falling down the porch steps of the Murdaugh's house at Moselle in 2018; and nineteen-year-old

Stephen Smith, who was found dead on the side of a road in Hampton County in 2015. A former high school classmate of Alex's surviving son, Buster, Smith may have been victimized because he was gay, according to his mother.

This conspicuous pileup of bodies attracted attention. Just weeks after Maggie and Paul were shot to death, state police in South Carolina reopened Smith's homicide case due to information gleaned in their investigation of the Murdaugh killings. Meanwhile, Satterfield's remains would be exhumed in the hope of learning more about her suspicious death, which resulted in a $4 million insurance payout that Murdaugh stole from her heirs. State investigators were also probing the law enforcement response to the boat crash that killed Beach in 2019, attempting to root out suspected police corruption that may have benefited the Murdaugh family.

Beyond reexamining two cold cases and possible public corruption, state investigators were also tasked with solving the two head-scratching and brutal murders, a case with many turns that ultimately led to Alex's arrest. All of the sordid storylines made for a media frenzy. Before the double murder trial even started, the notoriety of Alex Murdaugh had spread far beyond the Lowcountry of South Carolina, with Alex's alleged crimes and unique family legacy forming the basis of countless news reports, as well as being the subject of a handful of popular podcasts and documentaries. Now the televised trial was attracting an additional and ever-growing national and international audience. The trial proved transfixing, especially as Alex took the stand in his own defense and the trial inched, slowly but surely, toward a verdict and conclusion.

A variety of elements contributed to the story's mass appeal, including the exotic, overlooked, and overgrown locale of the South Carolina Lowcountry; the extreme duplicity of its main culprit; and the extraordinary family history that primed Murdaugh for his misconduct and propelled him toward catastrophe. As one woman who attended the trial said, it's the "layers" that made the Murdaugh saga so engrossing.

In considerable understatement, Alex testified to the complexity of his deceptions, remarking, "Oh, what a tangled web we weave . . ." This was an admission of sorts, but also a trademark attempt at control, to frame and soften his alleged wrongdoing in his own, poetic terms.

The line was a strange and obscure one for Murdaugh to quote, it being penned more than 200 years earlier by Scottish writer Sir Walter Scott. But the line could be familiar given it comes from Scott's epic poem "Marmion," about a corrupt and scheming knight who is unsatisfied with the advantages he already possesses and who recklessly pushes to obtain even more. Assorted testimonies and reporting indicated Alex was never an academic. He liked to golf, hunt, fish, attend sporting events, work the farm, and watch television, but not read many books, Scottish literature being no exception. Regardless of the inspiration for him quoting Scott, he omitted half the line, just as he'd omitted telling police crucial information concerning his whereabouts on the night of the killings, which ultimately led to his arrest for murder. To tell the full story, he should have testified, "Oh, what a tangled web we weave, *when first we practice to deceive.*"

But few people believed Alex was sharing the full story. He seemed incapable of telling the truth. Alex's credibility would become the crux of the case against him. He had lied to people for decades, and lately to police especially, right up until the moment he took the stand and admitted, finally, to being at the scene of the crime just minutes before his family was slain. Having laid his hand on a Bible, Alex promised to tell the "truth, the whole truth and nothing but the truth." He'd admit to being a thief and a fraud and a phony, but not to being a killer. Immediately he denied blowing his son's brains out of his head with a shotgun, and then denied pointing a rifle barrel at his fallen wife and obliterating the back of her head. Less than two minutes after taking the stand he stated, emphatically, "I didn't shoot my wife or my son any time, ever."

Like nearly every day of the trial, the courtroom gallery was full as Alex testified, with people packed shoulder to shoulder in uncomfortable wooden pews. Many of these court observers had stood in line outside the courthouse since before dawn to obtain their seats. Many, too, had driven hours from their homes across the South to arrive at the Colleton County Courthouse in Walterboro, South Carolina, and to catch a glimpse of the man allegedly responsible for so much death, depravity, and dysfunction. They wanted to hear Alex's explanations for themselves, as if they, too, were members of the jury and needed to decide his guilt or innocence. As everyone intrigued by this case incessantly asked: *Do you think he really did it?*

Every onlooker, whether crammed into the South Carolina courtroom or watching elsewhere on a screen, was curious to see if Alex would receive his comeuppance and be held to account, something that rarely happened with his ancestors. Although Alex's alleged criminal spree seemed absurd and unprecedented—a sprawling, multidimensional Southern gothic tale on steroids—this was merely the latest version of scandal in the swamp. Deep down in the muck, steeped in sadness, other dark secrets lay buried. When it came to the Murdaugh family of South Carolina, history had a funny way of repeating itself.

———

Nine hours after the collision at the rail crossing, train engineer W. W. Bartlett was no longer seated on his locomotive, but rather on the witness stand in the Hampton County Courthouse. Six jurors and a magistrate gathered before him at 10:00 A.M. that summer morning in 1940. A coroner's inquest was underway to determine how the motorist met his death.

The courthouse contained county offices on the first floor and a courtroom on the second, accessed via a sagging staircase lined by dingy, cracked, and partially finished plaster walls. The upstairs courtroom was plain, devoid of ornamentation, with wooden flooring. Most interestingly, the courtroom's gallery featured rows of tiered seating, which resembled playing-field bleachers, divided by an aisle. Bartlett, the first witness, related details of the collision to the jurors and a magistrate, who was standing in for the coroner.

"About half a mile down the track from Camp Branch, I noticed some kind of a light flashing on and off and just kept right on flashing . . ." said the train engineer. "The right-of-way was perfectly clear and he could have seen the train." Bartlett told how he watched in disbelief as the driver placed himself in danger. "I had no idea they were going to drive up on the track . . . I opened my sand blasts and put on the emergency brakes, but couldn't stop in time . . ."

After the crash, Bartlett explained, he climbed down to the ground with the brakeman and fireman. They walked to the front of the train, where they found a smashed automobile pinned against the nose of the locomotive. The train had carried the crippled car 900 feet from the crossing. The train crew pried the automobile off the locomotive, but no body was found within the wreckage. The fireman climbed back aboard the engine and tended the fire while Bartlett and the brakeman continued searching for the missing driver. In short order the dead man was found at the foot of the railroad embankment, closer to the crossing. The train had launched the collision victim's body 150 feet.

Following Bartlett's turn on the witness stand, his coworkers on the Charleston and Western Carolina Railroad testified to the coroner's jury. Both men also implicated the automobile driver in the tragedy. "This man drove up in the middle of the track and stopped and was looking up at the engine," said the brakeman, J. H. Montgomery. "He looked like he was waving to us and we couldn't stop and we ran right into him."

Added C. T. Billiter, the fireman: "I believe that [if] anyone here in this courtroom had been there like that they could have gotten out if they had wanted to."

After hearing the fireman's statements, the jurors began their contemplation of all the evidence. Beyond the witness testimony, the jurors read notes of a doctor's examination, which stated the deceased suffered two broken arms, two broken legs, and "numerous contused, lacerated and incised wounds." The men also viewed the mangled motorist's corpse themselves. It did not take long for the jurors to issue a finding: "Randolph Murdaugh Sr. came to his death by a blow of a moving train." Their work completed, the men exited the courtroom, stomping down the sagging staircase, past the ugly walls, out the doors, and into a square of unkempt grounds surrounded by a dilapidated fence.

Despite its shabbiness, the Hampton County Courthouse stood tall in the eyes of locals. The courthouse was the administrative center of the county, where residents took their taxes and saw their sheriff. It was a forum for settling civil disputes brought via lawsuit as well as a temple of justice, where the accused had their fates forged by juries and judges as neighbors watched in the gallery from the raised rows of seating. Chiefly, though, the courthouse was the county's social hub, a place to greet neighbors and swap gossip. A South Carolina travel guide published in 1941 did not recommend much about the county, though it did observe "community life at Hampton . . . seat of Hampton County, centers largely around the courthouse square, a big sandy lot with old oaks and a seldom-used bandstand."

It had always been that way. The courthouse is Hampton's grandest public building, a literal centerpiece built smack dab in the middle of the county. The courthouse is the physical embodiment of Hampton County, too. Governor Wade Hampton III traveled to Hampton and laid the cornerstone of the new building in 1878, the year the South Carolina legislature carved the new county out of a region known as Beaufort District. The county was formed even before the existence of a county seat, which was incorporated a year later as the town of Hampton Courthouse.

Just as Hampton Courthouse was later shortened to Hampton, the county went through a few early name changes. During its organization residents proposed calling the county Washington, Palmetto, and Coosawhatchie, names inspired, respectively, by the first US president, a ubiquitous tree in coastal South Carolina, and a nearby swamp. By the time the legislature acted, however, there was consensus to name the new county in honor of Governor Hampton, a beloved Confederate war hero. Before the American Civil War, Hampton was one of the country's wealthiest men and largest enslavers, with immense holdings of property and human chattel across the South. Hampton financed his own contingent of soldiers during the war, named Hampton's Legion, and distinguished himself through his leadership of cavalry units, including daring raids behind Union Army lines. Despite no previous military experience, Lieutenant General Hampton became one of the top officers serving General Robert E. Lee, the military commander of the Confederacy.

Hampton's fortune, mimicking the South's entire economy, turned to shambles by war's end. After returning to South Carolina he soon declared bankruptcy. But while Hampton was low on cash during the postwar period of Reconstruction, he was flush with political capital. He won election to the governor's mansion in 1876, benefiting from the support of the Red Shirts, a paramilitary force that engaged in deadly skirmishes across the state to help reestablish the political influence of Southern White Democrats and counter the rising influence of freed Blacks and their White Republican allies. Reflecting the dominant segment of public opinion at the time, *The State* newspaper in the capital city of Columbia celebrated Hampton and the Red Shirts as heroes who "redeemed South Carolina from negro rule."

Before Hampton's election, the feeling of marginalization was particularly strong in the swampy interior of Beaufort District, a hinterland of virgin cypress swamps and pinelands that pioneers seemed to skip over almost entirely during the country's westward expansion. Few pioneers wished to dwell in a land so thick with mud and mosquitoes and snakes, and those who did suffered the hardships of settling in the swamp. A decade of living under the rule of Reconstruction, as well as the rising fortunes of Blacks and carpetbaggers, hardened many locals who struggled to survive in the wake of the Civil War. The family of Maud Dowling Turner moved to

Hampton County upon its formation, when she was just six years old. She recalled her childhood unfolding during a period of pessimism and poverty:

> *Times were exceedingly difficult. Property worth millions of dollars had been ravaged in the region, most community structures had been destroyed, the patriotic investment in Confederate currency and bonds had bankrupted almost everyone, few able-bodied former slaves would help till the soil for bare necessities of food, manufactured clothing and shoes and farm tools were almost beyond the reach of all. Everything and everyone was threadbare and hungry. The work of rebuilding from scratch was the immediate task of all.*

Feelings were markedly different, however, in nearby Beaufort, an old, riverside town that Union forces seized early in the Civil War as a coastal base for maintaining a naval blockade of the South. In contrast to the sleepy interior settlements of the Lowcountry, Beaufort's dense downtown district of antebellum mansions, wood-frame houses, and waterfront stores was bustling, especially during the Civil War, when it teemed with soldiers and so-called carpetbaggers from the North as well as newly empowered Black freedmen, one of whom, Union war hero Robert Smalls, was elected to the United States Congress.

In 1868 Beaufort became the administrative seat of Beaufort District, which encompassed a large section of the Lowcountry, including the area that would become Hampton County. This decision was made after Union troops under the command of another famous Civil War general, William Tecumseh Sherman, torched Beaufort District's previous seat, Gillisonville, including the district courthouse. The move from Gillisonville to Beaufort particularly inconvenienced inland residents, placing the county courthouse, jail, and offices forty miles farther away. Beyond that, the courthouse's move to Beaufort seemed to symbolize a perceived shift in power, from Whites to Blacks, that inflamed many residents. For

these two chief reasons, one practical and one political, residents lobbied for the creation of a new county. As longtime Hampton politician
George Warren once summarized the episode in a letter: "This county
was formed in the days of Wade Hampton, was cut off from what was
then called the solidly black county of Beaufort, was made a white county
and named 'Hampton.'"

Locals decided the new courthouse should be built in the dead center
of the new county. After surveyors determined these coordinates would
place the building in the middle of a cypress swamp pond, officials
adjusted their plan, deciding to build the courthouse on donated land
located between the small railroad settlements of Varnville and Hoover's
Station. This site, still close to the geographic center of the county, was
barely settled but did boast solid ground.

Other residents donated building materials and soon the building started
to take shape. On October 12, 1878, scores of residents traveled by train
and horse-drawn vehicles to see Governor Hampton lay the courthouse
cornerstone, including an assembly of Confederate veterans and a Red
Shirt honor guard. Bands played, fireworks took flight, and a float rolled
down the street, delivering the governor to a flower- and flag-draped stage
under a massive oak tree at the edge of the courthouse square. Young Maud
Dowling stood atop a carriage to be able see over the heads of adults. She
watched and listened elatedly as her father, the Rev. William Hamilton
Dowling, a Baptist minister who fought alongside Hampton in the war,
introduced his old friend. "When the general rose to speak and placed
his arm around my father, I was overcome with pride," Dowling Turner
recalled years later. "The general's strong voice, his long mustache, both
were thrilling to me as a pre-teenage girl."

Hampton mounted a horse after his speech and inspected the assembled
veterans and Red Shirts. He laid the courthouse cornerstone and within its
recess soon was placed a small tin box stuffed with a newspaper, a Bible, and
a small wooden mallet—time capsule items to be rediscovered by a future

generation. As the ceremony finished, people picnicked and mingled. At night the residents of South Carolina's newest county celebrated with a ball.

A handsome, two-story brick courthouse was built in the months ahead, the facade of which featured a pair of curving staircases leading to a central, raised portico outside the doors to the second-floor courtroom. Underneath the portico was a ground-floor doorway that opened to a central hall flanked by assorted storerooms and offices. The ground-floor doors on each end of the hall were left open for ventilation, allowing visitors to look straight through the building.

Town planners devised a road grid that included two streets named for Confederate generals, Lee and Jackson Avenues, intersecting at the courthouse square. Shady, oak-lined Lee Avenue was Hampton's main street, spanning three blocks between the courthouse and Hampton's railroad depot. Here residents and visitors patronized the town's businesses, including its stores, hotel, bank, and newspaper.

Lee Avenue was a leisurely place, much like the rest of Hampton. In Hampton's early days, men gathered daily across from the bank at 5:00 P.M., after the last train had come through town, to chitchat. Banker Ralph O. Bowden brought an oak bucket full of lemonade to share, and the telegrapher, after closing up the train depot, stopped by with news hot off the wire, such as updates of battles won and lost during World War I, as well as the names of the fallen. A chummy atmosphere pervaded the town, or at least that's how some remember it. "Hampton seems . . . in a class all by itself. I do not believe there is another town in the South where one could conscientiously 'loaf,'" early Hampton resident Nell Paris Newman wrote in 1922. "There everyone has plenty of time to stop and talk to you and tell you yarns and jokes."

Newspaper writers from neighboring cities celebrated Hampton's slow pace and quaintness in profiles of the town. Passing through Hampton is "like having a cooling poultice laid upon a vague ache . . . its peacefulness and stillness are soothing to the jaded spirit," said the Charleston *News and Courier.* Across the state line in Georgia, the *Savannah Morning News* thought Hampton a "pretty, old town" in a "homey county." And in Augusta, also across the Savannah River in Georgia, the *Herald* penned similar sentiments: "Nobody hurries in Hampton. One can take one's own sweet time about crossing the town's main street. If you should happen to get in the way of an automobile, the driver would courteously go around you."

The *Herald* quoted a local judge who teased that only two men were ever in a rush in Hampton: one died at an early age, having run through life quickly, he said, and the other walked straight out of town. The newspaper praised Hampton for its few electric lights, which had arrived in town by the late 1920s, and cheered the town's plentiful artesian wells and water system. Altogether the *Herald* seemed pleasantly surprised by this new place of old ways, a community where people liked to linger and lag. "It is not a young and eager town, standing a-tiptoe to the sun," said the *Herald*. "Its blood is not so quick-flowing as that. It has learned wisdom and the joys of comfort. It is like a worn slipper, a favorite deep arm chair, a row of well-thumbed friendly books, a mellow old pipe."

Apart from being compared to a matted slipper, these boosterish newspaper accounts romanticized rural life. The reports did not acknowledge, however, the hardships and shortcomings of life in an isolated community. While the newspaper claimed Hampton's residents were "distressingly healthy" and its town doctors bored from "lack of work," the community suffered frequently from tragedy, especially from snakebites, stabbings, sickness, and vehicle collisions. Similarly, these articles tended to dwell on Hampton County's natural charms and overlooked the area's pervasive poverty. While the Augusta newspaper rhapsodized about the summertime blooms of Hampton's crepe myrtle trees—"like balm to a storm-tossed soul"—the *Herald* and other visiting publications neglected the perpetual shabbiness that otherwise clung to the young county.

The hometown newspaper, the *Hampton County Guardian*, occasionally did draw attention to Hampton's deficiencies, such as complaining in 1920 about the sorry state of Lee Avenue, whose unpaved roadway transformed into "a good-sized swamp" after rainstorms, discouraging people from crossing the street "for fear that he would lose his shoes or be otherwise damaged in the beautiful yellow mud that is characteristic of our MAIN street." Other times it was state authorities who sought to elevate standards, such as those at the Hampton County Jail.

The small, two-story brick jail was built in 1880, a block from the court-house, and contained an apartment on the first floor that housed the jailer and his family. The bulk of the jail's cells were upstairs, where the normally small but diverse inmate population was divided into assorted rooms and cages. Placement of prisoners was a puzzle given the jail's dizzying poli-cies. The rules dictated that juveniles were supposed to be separated from adults; inmates with venereal disease segregated from those with cleaner bills of health; men kept apart from women; and Blacks split away from Whites. No matter how the jailer divvied up the accused, and oftentimes they were mixed together, the jail was regarded as hazardously designed, a narrow central staircase being the only escape from the upstairs cells. The *Guardian* worried about inmates being "caught like rats in a trap" in a fire, bound to "suffocate or burn to death."

When the South Carolina State Board of Charities and Correction examined Hampton County's jail in 1916, inspectors found the facility to be the worst in the state, its operations wanting in almost every way. The jail had no electric light or heat. There were no beds but instead pallets on the floor. The few blankets at the jail were washed three times a year and no clothing was provided for inmates. No bathing facilities existed. Instead of toilets, some inmates used buckets with lids to collect their waste. Wooden shutters covered the windows, making for dark, stuffy rooms filled with the stench of urine and feces. Two years later these problems, including the lack of heat, remained unaddressed. An inmate froze to death one winter night, a tragedy the corrections board deemed a "shameful thing for a civilized community to allow." A year later oil lamps and stoves were provided to help heat and illuminate the jail cells, but a year after that the county stopped buying oil, forcing the sheriff himself to bring chopped firewood into the jail to keep the inmates from suffering and perishing.

Conditions were also substandard across the street at the courthouse. Much like the jail, disrepair was ignored or accommodated as long as possible; the fixing of anything would be a last resort. In the early 1920s, the Hampton County Courthouse lacked adequate heating and enough toilets. Its exterior staircases were failing. More alarmingly, so were its walls, which were cracked and separating, threatening the building's collapse. Everything, it seemed, was crumbling.

Residents serving on the county's grand jury complained so frequently, and so fruitlessly, about the courthouse in its regular reports that it threatened to cease meeting if improvements were not made. Visiting judges deplored the state of the courthouse. One judge suggested the county hold a special election to approve the funding of repairs. Another judge, J. Henry Johnson, concurred and marveled at the lack of attention given the building. "You folks in Hampton County ought to have a better courthouse. If you desire to preserve this one as a relic, why it would be a very good idea to put an iron fence around it and put a suitable bronze tablet in it." The *Guardian* chimed in and called the courthouse a "disgrace to the county." The newspaper also printed a letter from resident Fred S. Moxon, who called the building "unsafe, uncomfortable . . . and an eyesore." Moxon complained at length, too, about the state of the sheriff's office within the courthouse.

"In the first place the office is too small, and dark, there being only one window. The floor has fallen on three sides to a depth of eight inches at the base. The plastering is badly cracked, and great patches have fallen," wrote Moxon, enumerating some of the more glaring concerns. "There is no way to heat except by using an oil heater. The furnitures and fixtures consists of three tables, two of which were confiscated from gambling rooms . . ."

Finally in 1925 money was used to fix the courthouse. Workmen removed the pair of original exterior stairs and built an interior staircase in its place, making for a much plainer facade. The tin box time capsule inside the cornerstone was opened, revealing Wade Hampton's wooden mallet, perfectly intact, as well as remnants of a disintegrated Bible and early edition of the *Guardian* newspaper. The cornerstone was then repositioned slightly and reset.

Beyond the building, the grounds surrounding the courthouse had also devolved into scruff. Live oaks that once stood tall in Courthouse Square and down neighboring streets had fallen victim to the saw over the years despite assorted protests from a group of determined women. Garbage was dumped on the square, and once someone even tried to bury a dead mule outside the courthouse, though this time the ladies intervened successfully. In 1921 there was a community effort to enhance the landscaping and plantings. Volunteers accepted donations of trees, plants, seeds, lumber, compost, and even the use of a mule—this one alive—that pulled a plow and harrow. Women sold baked goods, dinners, and ice cream to raise money to buy more trees and supplies. Others solicited cash donations, some as small as just seven cents, and one as grand as five dollars. This most generous contribution to the square came from Solicitor Randolph Murdaugh, a man who spent as much time in the Hampton County Courthouse as he did his own home.

Murdaugh was a local legal tour de force, resolving or trying countless cases in which he acted as either defense lawyer, litigator, or, most commonly, prosecutor. Because he wore so many hats—he served as the area's top prosecutor while also operating a civil practice through his law firm—his hand touched almost every case to come before a judge in the Lowcountry, as well as many that never got that far. He was regarded as efficient and effective—a serious lawyer who got results. Randolph Murdaugh's reputation was so strong he never once saw fit to hang a sign outside his office advertising his name and services.

Randolph loomed large in Hampton County in part because legal happenings took on outsize importance in a community starved of much other entertainment. Whenever court was in session the courthouse square swelled with parked automobiles. Across the street at the Hampton Hotel, where farmers paused to catch up with friends, that same South Carolina travel guide observed there was "less talk about crops and the weather than about cases up for trial." Assorted judges, jurors, plaintiffs, defendants, and witnesses came and went through the courtroom, but Randolph was a constant. He often took center stage, his spellbinding argument spilling out of open windows and ringing across the square. One warm November day his oratory was so charming that a woman in a house near the courthouse called over to the town florist to place a rush order. "The price doesn't matter," she said. "What I want is the finest flowers you've got delivered quick to Randolph Murdaugh. He's making the greatest speech you ever heard!"

Randolph Murdaugh was born February 28, 1887, in the Hampton County town of Varnville to Josiah Putnam Murdaugh Jr. and the former Annie Marvin Davis. Both of Murdaugh's parents had grown up locally, his father born in adjacent Colleton County and his mother growing up just a little farther away, on the Dorchester estate in Summerville. The pair were proud Southerners; J. P., also known as Captain Joe, fought in Hampton's Legion as a member of an artillery unit and, after being injured in 1862, returned to the battlefield three months later, before recuperating fully. For her part Annie boasted a distant relation to Jefferson Davis, the president of the Confederacy. The couple married after the war, about 1867, and settled in Charleston, where they started their large family of eight children. J. P. Murdaugh worked as a cotton broker and then started a phosphate mining company and moved to St. Helena Island in Beaufort County. Living with the Murdaughs at this time was Alfred Folk, a young Black man, whose family members had been enslaved by the Murdaugh family before the Civil War. Upon the recommendation of J. P. Murdaugh, Folk was hired at the Sea Island Hotel in Beaufort, where he worked as a much-beloved clerk for forty-seven years until his death.

In 1885, J. P. Murdaugh went partially blind and moved with his family to Varnville, then just a tiny town centered around a lumber mill and a railway depot, two miles away from the new county seat of Hampton. Sanders Branch divides the towns, though it's difficult to notice any demarcation, as the creek is small and unremarkable and the towns bleed into each other. Varnville was settled before Hampton, springing up as a railway settlement shortly after the end of the Civil War. The community experimented with a few early names—Dixie Station, Hickory Hill, Varnsville, and Varn's Ville—before settling on plain old Varnville, in honor of members of the Varn family, who opened a rail depot during the Reconstruction era and operated a sawmill advantageously positioned between the cypress-laden Coosawhatchie and Salkehatchie swamps.

The Murdaughs lived in a wood-frame house at 115 Carolina Avenue, according to a family history, and J. P. loaned money to locals and bought land south of town in an area known as Almeda. Two years after the Murdaughs moved to Varnville their son Randolph was born, the first of four generations of lawyers to carry that name. Randolph attended high school at the locally renowned Morrison Academy in nearby Lawtonville. Headmaster John T. Morrison was well respected as a teacher, Baptist pastor, member of the Red Shirts, and former colonel in the Confederate States Army. For local boys interested in attending college or the military academies, Morrison's school was the natural prerequisite. This included young Randolph, who had designs to enroll at the U.S. Naval Academy in Annapolis, Maryland. He was nominated by a local congressman in 1902, at age fifteen, to attend the vaunted military school on the banks of the Severn River, close to Chesapeake Bay. Randolph, the fourth alternate among a slate of local candidates, was not admitted.

Two years later Randolph enrolled at the University of South Carolina and moved to campus in downtown Columbia, near the State House and other government offices. He played on the football and track teams for the Gamecocks, but never gave up his dreams of the Navy. At the end of his sophomore year, Randolph was again nominated to attend the Naval Academy, this time as a lead candidate. He headed to Annapolis the summer of 1906, where he passed an entrance exam, earning high marks in math but displaying a lesser mastery of geography.

But two weeks later Randolph's plans to become a midshipman were sunk. During a physical examination doctors detected in Randolph a heart defect and accompanying murmur of "great intensity." The Naval Academy's medical board disqualified Murdaugh for medical reasons, no matter that he was a college athlete. Randolph would not be deterred. He immediately secured a third nomination from his congressman and returned two months later to Annapolis for another physical examination. Nothing had changed, though, and doctors reconfirmed Randolph's imperfect anatomy. "Mitral heart murmur," reported the medical board. "Rapid and signs of enlarged heart."

With no hope of appointment at the Naval Academy, Randolph resumed his studies at the University of South Carolina, where he inspired plenty of admirers. He earned a reputation as a small but hardworking athlete, credited by one rival coach, Ralph K. Foster of the Citadel, as "one of the most apt football pupils he had ever seen." Randolph's friends bestowed upon him nicknames and ribbed him good-naturedly about his quick exits from chapel, his poor performance in biology—a class he took twice—and his dismissal from the Naval Academy. When Randolph was a senior in 1908, a write-up in the yearbook told how Murdaugh, "otherwise known as 'Buster,' is a good, well-meaning boy and somewhat of a sport. Went to Annapolis, but his heart wouldn't let him stay. Returned to graduate with us and become famous as motion maker in student-body meetings."

With a habit of motion-making, it was logical for Randolph to pursue a legal career. Following graduation in 1908 he enrolled at the University of South Carolina's School of Law, where he served as president of the student law association. He was a mediocre law student and deemed merely "proficient" by the law school upon his graduation in 1910. Apart from this lackluster academic performance, Randolph seemed to have enjoyed a memorable final year and undergone a personal awakening. As the yearbook characterized the soon-to-be lawyer:

> *"Buster," or "Old Hatchet Face" as he is familiarly known, is one of the landmarks of the campus, having been a student at this university for six years. He came here a scrawny "prep," he leaves a dignified, grisly lawyer. In all things he has proven himself faithful and persevering, from biology and third French to football. For five years he lived a quiet life, but the sixth, elated over having made his "C," he became reckless and went joy riding with George Orr.*

Law degree in hand, Randolph parted ways with his schoolmates and returned home to open a law office a block away from the courthouse in Hampton, across the street from the town bank. The young lawyer inspired confidence and soon obtained a number of local clients, positions, and professional responsibilities, including roles like general counsel for Varnville and Hampton County, president of the county legal bar, and a director of the newly founded chamber of commerce. Randolph also cultivated an interest in criminal law early in his career, assisting the local solicitor with trials, including cases of murder.

Among those who took notice of the ambitious young lawyer was Etta Harvey, daughter of a country doctor. She married Randolph Murdaugh at her parents' home in an afternoon ceremony on March 24, 1914. The couple's wedding announcement praised the "charming and accomplished" Etta as "one of the leaders of the society set of Hampton, and . . . a beautiful young woman of the blond type." Randolph was described as a "brilliant young attorney" well-known for his "large and lucrative practice." After a honeymoon in Florida the Murdaughs returned to Varnville to make their home. Less than a year later, on January 9, 1915, Etta gave birth to a little boy, Randolph Murdaugh Jr., who would later come to adopt his father's former nickname, "Buster," not to mention eclipse his legacy entirely. But for now it was Randolph Sr.'s turn in the spotlight.

The next year Randolph Sr. published a short-lived newspaper, the *Hampton Herald*, and kept up a busy civic schedule. He had entered politics since coming home, following in the footsteps of his father by serving as a Hampton County delegate to the South Carolina Democratic Party's convention. Two years later Etta gave birth to another boy—John Glenn Murdaugh—but complications ensued. She was admitted to a hospital in Charleston after the delivery and treated by her father. Yet Dr. Harvey's efforts proved insufficient. Etta died of blood poisoning on September 15, 1918, at twenty-nine years old. As Randolph scrambled to find help to raise a toddler and a newborn at the family home in Varnville, his woe deepened. His widowed mother, Annie Marvin Davis Murdaugh, one of Varnville's oldest citizens at age seventy-one, fell ill and suffered extreme nausea for four agonizing months before she, too, passed.

These deaths did not dim Randolph's star for long. A little more than a year after Etta died the *Guardian* reported that Varnville residents were "quite surprised" on Sunday, November 30, 1919, to learn of the early morning marriage of Randolph Murdaugh and Estelle Marvin. The couple's honeymoon, the newspaper's society column noted, consisted of a driving tour of the Deep South. A few months after the happy couple returned, Randolph made more news: he was running for public office, seeking to become the local solicitor.

On paper the job of solicitor didn't look too attractive: a small, part-time salary in exchange for the responsibility of prosecuting all major crimes across multiple counties without the aid of any staff. But what the elected position lacked in pay it made up for in power and prestige. The solicitor controlled the local criminal docket, meaning he handled all plea bargaining with criminal suspects and decided which cases went to trial and when they did so. The prominence of the position helped deliver clients to a solicitor's private practice, too, which provided a crucial supplemental income to their public salary. Specifically, Randolph Murdaugh was campaigning in 1920 to become solicitor of South Carolina's 14th Judicial Circuit, a political and legal domain created by the legislature four years earlier that originally included four counties spread across 3,000 square miles of the Lowcountry. Beyond Randolph's home county of Hampton, the 14th Circuit contained Beaufort County, a coastal paradise of islands and marshes and seaside farms; Colleton County, a section dominated by wetlands and defunct rice plantations; and Jasper County, the lush, untamed, and isolated southern corner of the state. In 1919, rural, inland Allendale County was created and added to the circuit, too.

Leading up to the election, the thirty-three-year-old candidate campaigned at picnics and political rallies. Randolph shouted his stump speech in front of local courthouses and bought newspaper advertisements that touted his legal experience and popularity, promising he would act as a "faithful, fearless, and competent" public servant "who cannot be influenced or intimidated to depart from his duty as solicitor." Randolph's two opponents, both attorneys in the town of Walterboro, took swipes at him in their own campaign ads, claiming the large caseload Murdaugh enjoyed at his law firm would make him too busy and conflicted to discharge his duties honorably. An endorsement of rival attorney R. M. Jefferies crowed that Randolph's opponent "has no entangling connections with corporations that might embarrass or tempt him"—a barely veiled shot at Randolph and his deep-pocketed clientele. Meanwhile candidate Heber R. Padgett published an ad that highlighted his service in the army during World War I and noted how Randolph stayed out of uniform and far from action, neglecting to mention, of course, that Randolph was medically disqualified from becoming a naval officer. "Mr. Murdaugh enjoys a large and lucrative practice, which was uninterrupted by the war," said the Padgett ad. "He does not need the office."

Voters across the Lowcountry disagreed with the Walterboro lawyers, electing Randolph Murdaugh their next solicitor by a landslide. Little did anyone know Randolph's victory was the beginning of a century-long family tradition, that he would be the first of four generations of the Murdaugh family to exercise the power of the local prosecutor's office. As Randolph assumed office in 1921, he had no script to read from, no father to teach him the trade. At the beginning, Randolph relied on instincts alone to excel as solicitor. He was slated to make his debut in criminal court in February 1921, but illness intervened—the first of many times poor health would disrupt Randolph's professional life. Three months later, however, Randolph stood tall in the Hampton County Courthouse and tried one of his first cases, convicting the former county treasurer of embezzlement. So began the career of one of South Carolina's most esteemed solicitors, who quickly earned public praise for his expedient prosecution of cases that ranged from housebreaking to hog theft to murder.

Among his first murder trials was the case of Jake Terry, whom Randolph convicted and sent to the electric chair. Terry was accused of walking into a church in the Hampton County town of Estill on the afternoon of Sunday, April 9, 1922, and shooting a romantic rival dead. Thaddeus Fulton was kneeling in prayer at the church's altar, accepting wine and bread during a communion service, when Terry walked in and fired six bullets from a pistol, hitting Fulton five times and killing him on the spot. A search posse soon cornered Terry in a swamp, where a shootout occurred. Terry escaped and kept running, but was soon discovered by police in the nearby town of Fairfax, just up the railroad. This time the police caught Terry, but not before shooting him in the hip and leg. Terry was arraigned and briefly jailed before being transported to Charleston for lifesaving surgery.

Terry survived the posse and police, but he would not outlast the solicitor. Randolph Murdaugh brought Terry to trial on a murder charge just two months later with the recommendation of the death penalty. The defendant, still convalescing, attended his trial from atop a cot, where he laid immobile within a plaster cast that enveloped his hips. Terry confessed on the witness stand to the killing and asked the jury to spare his life. The jury convicted him and denied his plea for mercy. The judge had no choice but to sentence Terry to die in the electric chair. Like almost all the convicts sent to death row in South Carolina at the time, Terry was a Black man.

Terry's injuries healed slowly, requiring him to stay within the state penitentiary's infirmary as he awaited his appointment in the electric chair. Terry found himself in a bewildering situation: he was restoring his health in order to be executed. In the end Terry did not have enough time to fully convalesce. On March 16, 1923, a police captain read him his death warrant. A famous American evangelist, Billy Sunday, visited the prison in support of Terry and prayed aloud for the condemned man. Because Terry still could not walk, prison attendants carried him to the electric chair, where he was strapped into place and given the chance to speak his last words. Terry recited the 23rd Psalm, *"The Lord is my shepherd. I shall not want . . ."* then begged God for mercy right up until the moment a fatal burst of electricity coursed through his broken body.

Just as stridently as he sought to send a crippled Black man to the electric chair, Randolph sought that same year to obtain the first conviction of a White man in Hampton County for the killing of a Black person. He succeeded, though this killer got off comparatively light when a judge sentenced him to twelve years in prison for the manslaughter. Randolph fought just as hard, too, to keep one defendant out of prison in 1923, arguing unsuccessfully to a judge that it was "un-American" to punish a man who violated Prohibition laws, as he had previously been tried in federal court.

Randolph did as he pleased in public office, indifferent to political blowback. Near the end of his first term the solicitor tried Wilson Harvey, a former governor, on charges of violating banking laws, beginning the trial by boldly insisting Harvey be placed in a dock during the reading of his alleged crimes. This irritated the former governor's attorney, Edgar Brown, a legendary lawyer and legislator recently elected speaker of the South Carolina House of Representatives. Randolph and Brown sparred for two days at the ex-governor's trial, each lawyer becoming so animated and hostile that the judge threatened both men with fines and imprisonment should they not behave themselves. Though a jury acquitted the governor, Randolph's stature seemed burnished, not diminished by the legal clash. Months later he extracted a guilty plea from the former governor, anyway, when the defendant agreed to a plea deal concerning other alleged banking violations.

People admired the urgency in which Randolph dispatched his cases and cleared the dockets in all five counties under his watch. As election time neared in 1924, a judge deemed Randolph Murdaugh "one of the hardest working, cleanest, and most capable solicitors in the entire state." This opinion seemed widespread. When it came time for the next election, no other lawyer in the Lowcountry challenged him for the solicitor's post. Solicitor Randolph Murdaugh began his second term in 1925. Just six days into the new year, a killing occurred that would demand his attention as a prosecutor until the end of his life. There was a dead White policeman in Beaufort, and two Black brothers were on the run.

———

Alex Murdaugh needed a job. Dad picked up the phone.

Soon he was speaking with Jim Moss, a lawyer in Beaufort and a long-time friend to the Murdaugh family. It was 1994 and Randolph "Randy" Murdaugh III had been solicitor for eight years. He told Moss that his son Alex was graduating law school and looking to come home to the Lowcountry. But rather than him take a job immediately in Hampton, he thought Alex would benefit from working elsewhere first, to learn the legal ropes outside of the longtime family law firm, which had grown in recent decades to include a number of other partners. "Will you take him on?" asked Randy.

It was hard to say no to a friend. It was also hard to say no to the local solicitor, especially one whose family had been in the office for nearly seventy-five years. He and Randy were about the same age and attended college together. They started their law careers about the same time in the 1960s when Randolph "Buster" Murdaugh was the longtime solicitor. Moss didn't hesitate to agree to the favor. "I'd consider it an honor, as a matter of fact," he told Randy.

Randy knew the men would be a good match because Alex and Moss had grown close over their love of football. Moss was an all-star member of the football team at the University of South Carolina, whose hopes of a professional career were cut short by injury. Alex had been a walk-on member of the Gamecocks football squad almost three decades later, in the late 1980s, and he, too, suffered a major injury, to his knee. Moss was familiar with Alex's impressive high school football career in which he played both starting quarterback and was a kicker. In one magnificent performance during the season opener his senior year, Alex caught five interceptions and booted a field goal.

Alex planned to take the job and move to Beaufort with his new bride, Maggie. He had met Margaret "Maggie" Branstetter at the University of South Carolina and soon the couple was going steady. Maggie and Alex married in 1993, just before Alex began his final year at the university's School of Law. Their wedding took place in downtown Charleston at the beautiful and historic Second Presbyterian Church, followed by a reception at Hibernian Hall, another grand old columned white building in the Holy City. After Alex graduated law school the next year the couple moved to Beaufort, eventually buying a house just outside of town on Cat Island, a neighborhood where many homes fronted the marsh on one side and a golf course on the other.

The couple had young friends who lived in town, including Alex's college buddy Cory Fleming, who was hired to work as an assistant solicitor under Alex's dad. After two years as a prosecutor he went to work for Moss's law firm, too, where he eventually became a partner and practiced for more than twenty years. Alex's friendship with Fleming would later prove crucial in perpetrating some of his largest frauds and thefts.

Alex made a strong debut as a lawyer, capitalizing on his family's long-standing social connections and his personable nature. Though his father and grandfather were known as talented trial lawyers, Alex did not have the same appetite to perform in front of judge and jury. Alex was more carefree and laissez-faire than his father, the solicitor, said Moss. Alex's best work was done outside the courthouse, obtaining cases and negotiating settlements. "His real forte with the law was he knew people," said Moss. "He was good at getting clients who had been in wrecks and stuff, especially up in Hampton 'cause he knew everybody. He brought in good cases. One led to another."

Though they had moved from South Carolina's capital city to the coast, the newlywed Murdaughs did not leave Columbia behind entirely. They returned to their alma mater frequently, especially during weekends in the fall to tailgate at football games and watch the Gamecocks at Williams-Brice Stadium. Moss would attend the games, too, and make sure to stop by a tailgate spot by the stadium gate used by members of the Hampton law firm Peters, Murdaugh, Parker, Eltzroth & Detrick. "We'd always get our last beer there and go on in (to the game)," said Moss. "Maggie was usually passing out drinks."

Moss remembers Maggie as cheerful and friendly, happy to be in everyone's company. She was well-liked and a tremendous hostess. "She knew where the drinks were, where the liquor was, the beer, the chasers," said Moss. "I thought she was a wonderful girl." Maggie embraced her new home in Beaufort and the Lowcountry. She had been born to parents with roots in Kentucky and moved around the eastern United States as a kid, graduating high school in Unionville, Pennsylvania. She transferred to the University of South Carolina about the time her parents moved to Summerville, outside of Charleston. Her new life in Beaufort was convenient, about an hour's drive from both her parents' home as well as her in-laws' house in Hampton County.

While Maggie was head over heels for Alex, some of her friends had reservations about her relationship with him. One friend recalled traveling with Maggie to Mexico following college graduation. She remembers Maggie sitting on the hotel bed one day, talking about dating Alex. The girlfriend listened politely, disinclined to "burst her bubble" and reveal her negative opinion of Maggie's boyfriend. Inside her head, however, alarm bells were ringing. "Girl, you should not go there," she thought to herself, figuring Maggie would learn the truth about Alex sooner or later.

Alex had dated another of this woman's friends at the University of South Carolina before Maggie. The relationship was tumultuous, and the woman didn't like the way Alex treated her friend. "I don't know what you see in this guy," the woman once protested. "He's a meathead . . . a knucklehead."

When it came to Alex, this was hardly a unique opinion. Alex was a bruiser, more inclined to use his fists than his brain while in high school and college. He engaged in fights constantly, especially at bars and other places where he consumed alcohol, looking to find or create conflict. By all accounts he was always the loudest guy in the room, and usually the biggest, too. If anyone bumped into him, "It was on!" said one fraternity brother of Alex. "Just routinely stirring up shit."

He and Alex were members of the Kappa Alpha Order fraternity at the University of South Carolina. Among this man's memories was the night Alex clubbed someone with a beer bottle, perhaps at the bar the Cotton Gin down in Five Points, a hub of college bars and restaurants that included fraternity brother favorites like Jungle Jim's and the Elbow Room, where one former bouncer recalled twice throwing Alex out and that bar patrons became unnerved by his tendency to engage in a creepy, "thousand-yard stare." At the Cotton Gin the blood flowed along with the beer, and paramedics and police responded to the scene. Alex avoided arrest, something he managed to do quite well for a long time. Oftentimes, said his fraternity brother and others, Alex would drop his name to police and tell them his father was one of South Carolina's sixteen solicitors. "Do you know who I am? Do you know who my dad is?" his fraternity brother remembers him exclaiming to get out of a scrape. Such an invocation was often enough to spook the cops or earn their goodwill. "In our generation, if law enforcement got involved it still went away," said the fraternity brother.

Such was the case when Jared Newman, a Beaufort County sheriff's deputy, responded to a call at the Huddle House restaurant on Hilton Head very early one morning in the late 1980s. He arrived to find high schooler Alex Murdaugh fighting with another man in a parking lot. Alex had been supposedly angered when his opponent insulted his grandfather, said Newman, who later worked as an assistant solicitor under Alex's father. The other teen didn't want to press charges, so Newman sent the boys home.

Alex's fraternity brother recalled another time that a young Alex allegedly "beat the hell" out of a fellow pledge when both were rushing, or considering pledging the fraternity. Alex then taunted the other pledge, said the fraternity brother, telling him "Bo', that's how we handle things in Hampton County if someone's talking shit." "Bo'" being short for "boy," sort of the Lowcountry equivalent of "dude." Such behavior would usually be disqualifying for a pledge except the fraternity brothers held a high opinion of Alex's older brother, Randolph "Randy" Murdaugh IV, who was already a member of the fraternity. The woman who vacationed with Maggie in college said she and her friends would pity Alex's older brother, exclaiming sentiments like "God, Randy is such a nice guy. It's a shame he has to be associated with his asshole brother."

Alex was regularly rowdy, unpleasant, and dishonest. One fraternity brother remembers him cheating in class and picking his courses based on which exams the fraternity already had on file, not unlike many other fraternity brothers. Another brother remembers Alex driving around with a flashing light atop his car, impersonating police or emergency vehicles, not caring about any consequences. "He could do what other people couldn't do. And if you were with him, you could do what other people couldn't do, because he'd get you out if it," said this fraternity brother.

Brothers said Alex derived sadistic pleasure from hazing pledges. Though he drank alcohol excessively and well before the legal age, he was righteous about marijuana use, trying to exclude any pledge who smoked pot. He bullied pledges, calling one out-of-state student "Yank" so often that when the former pledge returned the next year as a sophomore he abruptly put an end to the unwanted nickname, pointing his finger into Alex's chest and bluntly instructing him to curtail its use. As one brother who left the university said, "Alex is the reason I transferred."

Kappa Alpha Order had a fixation with the past, particularly the Civil War era. The fraternity counts Confederate general Robert E. Lee as its "spiritual founder." During Alex's time in the fraternity in the late 1980s members frequently flew the Confederate flag, sang the Southern folk tune "Dixie," and wore Kappa Alpha T-shirts that proclaimed, THE SOUTH WILL RISE AGAIN. For decades the fraternity hosted Old South parties, in which fraternity and sorority members wore a combination of period garb and formalwear as they celebrated the not-too-far-removed Southern slave-owning aristocracy. Fraternity brothers were selected to assume the characters of General Lee and the president of the Confederate States of America, Jefferson Davis, to whom the Murdaugh family claimed a distant relation. Alex was photographed at one of these parties wearing a Confederate military uniform jacket over a tuxedo dress shirt with black bow tie, a gaping smile across his face.

Alex's father celebrated the same way when he was a member of Kappa Alpha at the University of South Carolina. As the 1960 *Garnet and Black* college yearbook stated, "The highlight of the spring semester was the Old South Ball. On this festive weekend KAs from all over the state gathered in Columbia to relive the ante-bellum days of the Old South. The events of the weekend—the Sharecropper's Shindig, the Secession Ceremony, The Mint Julip [*sic*] Party, and the Old South Ball—proved their usual tremendous success."

Alex was eventually elected to the No. 2 position in the fraternity, which required him to fulfill the duties of pledge trainer. Under Alex's watch, the KA pledges botched the annual fundraiser performed by the fraternity to benefit the Muscular Dystrophy Association, according to one fraternity brother. Having neglected to raise any money for charity, Alex and the pledges devised a last-minute plan to sell raffle tickets for a videocassette recorder, an expensive piece of electronics equipment at the time. The fraternity brothers didn't have a VCR to award the winner, but they didn't need one—they were going to rig the raffle and steer the winning ticket to someone who knew better and wouldn't seek the phantom prize, said a fraternity brother. The fraternity sold the tickets and gave the money to charity, but nobody ever won a VCR. Alex's moral compass, said the fraternity brother, "was always broken."

———

Ben Heyward was sleeping softly in a chair, warmed by a fire burning in the hearth. His young children rested quietly in his lap. His wife was away for the day, planting lettuce in a field down the road. Ben had shuttered all the windows in the house, making it dark. He didn't want light, or anything or anyone else, coming inside. But fate could not be kept away. This nap, almost ended, was the last carefree slumber Ben Heyward would ever enjoy.

While Ben napped an automobile arrived and parked close to his home late in the afternoon of January 6, 1925. Ben woke up, alarmed by the intrusion. He lived in the countryside, in a one-room house on a "one-horse farm," to use his words, ten miles outside Beaufort, within the tranquil rural community of Seabrook, where tidal rivers flowed silently beside fields edged by live oaks. His ramshackle home sat within a cluster of shacks. His brother, Willie, lived behind him, across a field. Not too many cars came out here.

Ben walked to the front of his house and peered through a gap in the wall. The exterior siding was weathered and imperfect, "old boards nailed together and you could look through and see good," said Ben. He spotted a man approaching his house with a pistol. Ben grabbed his own weapon—a shotgun—and waited. The man with the pistol was policeman B. Paul Carden. He and another lawman, Hubert Randall, had motored to the Seabrook community to make an arrest at the "colored houses," as Randall called them, referring to a settlement of modest homes owned by Black families. The pair of White policemen stopped the car outside the first house they saw.

Inside the small house, the policemen believed, was Willie Heyward, a Black man accused of larceny for failing to pay another man thirteen dollars of wages. The policemen had a warrant for Willie's arrest on the misdemeanor charge. As the two policemen stepped out of the car they left a young Black companion in the automobile, perched on the back seat. Paul Middleton, fifteen, had worked odd jobs for Randall that day and was catching a ride home. The policemen's plan was to nab Willie Heyward before sunset and then bring Paul to his house while they transported the suspect to jail.

Paul watched as Carden and Randall took separate paths to the house. Randall, acting as Carden's deputy, went to the rear of the house, lighting a cigar as he prepared to stand vigil. Carden walked to the front door. Both men kept a holstered pistol on their waists. From the car, Paul Middleton witnessed Officer Carden approach the house and rap on the front door of the house. He saw the door open partially and overheard the policeman's conversation with whomever was inside.

"Are you Willie Heyward?" asked Carden, skipping an introduction.

"Yes," said Ben Heyward, claiming falsely to be his brother. He slipped the nose of a shotgun through the doorway. Carden caught sight of the barrel pointed his way.

"What you doing with that gun?" asked Carden.

Heyward responded by pulling the trigger. The shotgun roared and a volley of #4 lead shot tore through Carden's abdomen, knocking him to the ground. Paul watched from the car as Ben sprinted from the house and across a field, toward another small house. Deputy Randall called out Carden's name as he ran to the front of the first house. He rounded a corner to find Carden lying on his back at the doorstep. The policeman's intestines had spilled out of his body. He appeared dead.

As Randall assessed Carden and called for help from Paul, Ben Heyward reached the home of his brother Willie. The Heyward brothers together charged back toward Ben's house, where deputy Randall and Paul were tending to Carden. Moments later men on both sides were shooting at each other and taking cover. Randall threw his body behind a chicken house. The Heyward brothers took refuge in a nearby swamp. During a lull in the shooting Randall and Paul removed Officer Carden's limp, disemboweled body to the car. The shootout then culminated with Randall driving the car away at top speed, with Paul in the back seat, holding Carden. As the lawmen and boy made their escape Ben Heyward stepped out from a hedge in an ambush and blasted away with his shotgun, peppering the automobile with shot. One pellet struck Paul in the jaw provoking the youngster to grab Carden's pistol off the car seat and fire a few errant shots back at Ben as the car accelerated toward Beaufort.

The brothers fled into nearby woods, where they stayed the night. The next day friends brought them food. That's when Ben learned, to his horror, that not only did he shoot a White man, he'd killed a White man. And not only did he kill a White man, but a White policeman. Such facts convinced Ben he needed to start running, and fast. Ben's brother, Willie, was in a similar predicament. His arrest warrant was tied to the killing. He had participated in the shootout. And even if he did turn himself in and blamed Ben for the killing, who would believe him? Willie, too, decided he needed to run as far from South Carolina as he could.

The Heyward brothers' wives abandoned their homes the day of the shooting, fearing retaliation. They were smart to leave. An armed mob of angry White men had formed within hours of the killing, and within a few days vigilantes torched the Heyward brothers' homes and slaughtered their livestock. These actions were to be expected, for not only had Ben Heyward killed a White policeman, he killed a White policeman who belonged to the Ku Klux Klan.

The Klan had enjoyed a recent resurgence, its ranks swelling across the country in the 1920s. Within Beaufort County the Ku Klux Klan had rallied the previous spring, serving barbecue to a crowd in a grove in the town of Port Royal before an induction ceremony. At 9:00 o'clock that night a bugle sounded and three robed men rode on horseback down a parade line. A single-file procession of 100 robed men followed, the leaders of which carried a flaming cross and an American flag. At the rear of the procession marched 100 new members, each of them putting their hands on the shoulders of the man ahead of them as they became South Carolina Knights of the Ku Klux Klan.

When it came time to bury Carden, the Klan planned the funeral. A hearse left the Carden home in downtown Beaufort followed by a contingent of Klansmen and cars full of mourners. Among the survivors of the twenty-five-year-old policeman were his wife and three-year-old son. At a cemetery a few blocks away, Klansmen in full, hooded attire served as pallbearers and conveyed Carden to his grave. The funeral was officiated by a Klan chaplain and attended by an audience whose outrage over the murder was reported to be palpable.

Beyond the Klan, legitimate law enforcement officials also responded with urgency. Sheriff-elect James E. McTeer was sworn in early so he could investigate Officer Carden's murder without delay. The governor and county dangled a $400 reward for information leading to the capture of the brothers, who were soon indicted for murder. Willie Heyward, said police, was thirty years old, of medium height and build, dark-skinned, and was scarred on the side of his face. Ben Heyward was twenty-eight years old and possessed a fairer, "ginger cake" complexion and limped when he walked.

While the sheriff pursued these suspects and sough their arrests, there was little for the solicitor to do in regard to Carden's death. Plenty of other criminal matters occupied his attention instead, especially since he insisted on being very attentive to the duties of his elected position. Randolph searched alongside law enforcement officers in the pursuit of fugitives, who inevitably ran to the swamps. He helped lead investigations of suspicious deaths, including the assorted bodies found on the railroad tracks or floating in rivers. Every term of court he prosecuted sordid, shocking cases of human desperation, rage, and desire, as well as plenty of petty crime, including violations of Prohibition laws.

Emboldened by his reelection in 1924, Randolph prosecuted cases that sometimes rankled fellow prosecutors and lawyers and upset some of the traditional political establishment. After finally convicting the former governor on banking violation charges, Randolph brought murder charges against Alonzo Seabrook, a federal Prohibition agent, and another officer for killing a man wrongly identified as a liquor smuggler. Seabrook and state agent E. J. Harrington were looking for contraband liquor the night of May 24, 1925, when they stumbled upon a boat set atop blocks and undergoing repair at the water's edge. They raided the boat and startled awake its occupant, J. G. Pittman, sixty-seven, who fired a gun at his unknown assailants. Seabrook fired back, killing Pittman in his boat. Afterward, less than a quart of whiskey was found on the vessel. When neighbors angrily confronted Seabrook over the needless killing, he claimed his status as a federal agent gave him legal immunity.

The killing outraged the public and editorialists across the state. Randolph shared their disgust and charged the officers for Pittman's killing. These indictments, in turn, enraged Charleston's law enforcement community and politicians. Seabrook, the federal Prohibition officer, fielded a high-powered defense team that included federal prosecutors, Charleston's solicitor, the mayor of Charleston, and Randolph's new legal nemesis, Edgar Brown. A trial ensued, where Randolph noted that no evidence of smuggling existed to justify the raid. He questioned why a man should lose his life over the police's pursuit of a misdemeanor arrest, anyway. The judge was unmoved by these arguments. Before a jury was given a chance to deliberate the judge acquitted the officers in a directed verdict, saying the lawmen reacted appropriately in the line of duty.

Randolph vigorously tried a number of defendants accused of child molestation. In 1927 he convicted a minister who began a sexual relationship with a thirteen-year-old and later impregnated her. Four years later, he prosecuted an eighteen-year-old who raped an eight-year-old girl. When Randolph called the girl to testify she broke down in court repeatedly, unable to speak. Determined to elicit her testimony, Randolph arranged for the girl's mother to sit on the witness stand and hold her daughter while the girl finished telling about being choked unconscious by her assailant and then carried into the woods. The courtroom maneuver paid dividends; the defendant was convicted and sentenced to forty years in prison.

To see Solicitor Randolph Murdaugh in court was to be mesmerized. Writer Chlotilde R. Martin of Beaufort attended the "curious spectacle" of court in the Lowcountry one day in 1933. She noted that all courtroom participants—judge, solicitor, sheriff . . . sometimes even the defendant—seemed to be buddies. "Most of them were boys together," wrote Martin. "They fish and hunt together and swap the names of favorite bootleggers."

These friendships were suspended, though, once the judge dropped his gavel and brought court to order. The legal proceedings almost seemed like theater. "Let his cue come and each man springs into action like an actor in a play," wrote Martin in one edition of "Lowcountry Gossip," the newspaper column she penned in the Charleston *News and Courier* for more than thirty years. She continued:

The man who has just swapped the latest joke with the defendant's lawyer instantly becomes prosecuting solicitor, bristling with righteous indignation for his state's honor. Mercilessly, he browbeats his friend in the witness chair, pausing at intervals to let fly venomed darts in the directions of his friendly enemy. The innocents in the courtroom beyond are so carried away by his impassioned picturing of the heinousness of the prisoner's crime, it comes with a sick sense of shock to recall that the prisoner's family and that of his prosecutor live in the same little Lowcountry town, that the battling lawyers were school mates at the same university.

Randolph's "righteous indignation" was on display in the Beaufort County Courtroom in March of 1932 when he tried Willie Heyward, recently captured after seven years on the run. Heyward had been living in Pittsburgh, Pennsylvania, and working in a steel mill under an alias. He had been arrested in Pennsylvania, and authorities passed word to Sheriff J. E. McTeer Jr. in Beaufort that the fugitive was in custody. McTeer soon drove north to retrieve the murder suspect, taking along another man and Hubert Randall, the magistrate's constable who engaged in the shootout with the Heyward brothers as he carried policeman Carden's slain body.

McTeer's father and namesake had initially investigated this case, even taking office a few days early to get started. But he died of pneumonia a year later after driving exposed in the rain. The governor appointed his son, a twenty-two-year-old electrical engineer, to replace the sheriff. According to McTeer, the governor was at first leery of naming someone so inexperienced.

"What would you do if you had a prisoner and a mob threatened to take him from you? asked the governor in an interview.

McTeer said he would stop them.

"And what if they attacked you?" said the governor.

"I would keep shooting as long as the bullets lasted," said McTeer.

With that the governor gave the young man his blessing. For many years J. E. McTeer Jr. was known as the "Boy Sheriff." Ironically, despite his tough talk, McTeer almost never carried a gun. He preferred personal intervention and conversation in place of brute force—a tactic that some fellow lawmen found baffling. Yet the gentle approach made him popular in the community, and in particularly with many Black people on Beaufort's Sea Islands. McTeer endeared himself to the Gullah people by his interest in Hoodoo culture, a spiritual tradition developed by enslaved Black people in the South. In fact, McTeer, a White man, regarded himself as a root conjurer and witch doctor. He ultimately spent thirty-seven years in public office, outgrowing his youthful nickname to adopt the grander sobriquet of "High Sheriff of the Lowcountry."

One of the first things McTeer did upon filling his father's shoes was to review every unsolved murder within the county in the last twenty years. It put Carden's killing and the Heyward brothers at the front of his mind, and he made efforts over the years to track the men. Finally his outreach and investigation paid off, at least partially. Riding back from Pennsylvania to South Carolina's state penitentiary in Columbia, McTeer chatted with Willie Heyward, who shared details of his and his brother's escape and life on the lam. Willie told how they obtained a boat after fleeing into the woods and marsh, and rowed upriver to a railroad trestle, "where we done away with our guns." Then they made their way inland along the tracks and roads to Allendale, where they caught a freight train up to Pennsylvania. For years Willie had been working in a steel mill under an alias. His brother, Ben, he said, had moved on to parts unknown in 1927 after breaking his arm. Willie said his brother Ben shot and killed Carden.

A few weeks after the arrest Solicitor Randolph Murdaugh brought Willie Heyward's case to trial. Willie took the stand in his own defense and told of how his life was upended one winter afternoon when he was lying on his bed after chopping firewood. His wife Mary was in the kitchen and she called for him to fetch her some of the wood so she could cook supper. And then Mary said, "Willie, there is a car stopped at Ben's house."

"Nothing but an insurance collector," he replied dismissively. The blast of a shotgun a moment later, however, caught his attention. Willie hurriedly put on his shoes on and looked outside his door. His brother was running toward his house, and Willie met him halfway.

"What's the matter?" asked Willie.

"I shot a man," said Ben, explaining he had assumed Willie's identity.

Willie grabbed his gun from the house and fled into the swamp and woods. At this point, he told a jury, there was no turning back. During all the excitement, he said, he accidentally discharged his firearm. "I was scared and my gun went off in my hand," said Willie, denying shooting at the lawmen.

His lawyer asked him why he ran away.

"This boy (Ben) shot this officer and shot him in my name," said Willie. "I knew he was a White man and they were not going to wait on me to say anything at all."

During cross-examination, the solicitor employed a skeptical, condescending tone as he asked questions of Willie Heyward. Randolph used a slur, too, as he began his questioning of the defendant.

"Willie, you are not a darkey that can be scared at all, can you?" asked the solicitor.

Willie said he could, in fact, be scared. "It is according to what is coming after me."

The solicitor tried to sum things up, confirming, mockingly, that Willie essentially had nothing to do with the killing. "You are putting the entire thing on Ben?" he asked.

"I have to tell what he did," said Willie.

The solicitor asked Willie more questions, to devastating effect.

"Why in the world . . . would he use your name?" wondered the solicitor, more or less disregarding Willie's answer.

"Knowing that the sheriff's house was only four miles away," Randolph continued, "why in the world didn't you go to Sheriff McTeer and tell him what had occurred?"

Again Randolph seemed uninterested in Willie's explanation. Then he asked, "When you got to Pittsburgh . . . away from the whole thing, why didn't you write back to Sheriff McTeer and tell him the whole situation and that you were willing to come back?

"From the time you cracked down on Mr. Randall when he was carrying the dead body of Mr. Carden back to the car, you have not said a word until the officers in Pittsburgh caught you, and you did not, up to that time, open your mouth?"

Willie Heyward made no response to Murdaugh's last question. He was convicted and given a life sentence, a punishment much stiffer than any he would have faced if convicted of the petty larceny allegation that started the whole ordeal. As Willie started his prison sentence, little brother Ben remained at large.

———

It's a boy! Such was the good news shared by Alex and Maggie Murdaugh after their first child was born April 11, 1996. They named him Richard Alexander Murdaugh Jr., after his father, and nicknamed him "Buster," after his great-grandfather, the legendary longtime solicitor, who had just turned eighty-one years old. It was about as flattering and sincere a tribute as Alex could extend to his grandfather, an elected official who had served forty-six years as the local solicitor before stepping down and continuing work as a deputy prosecutor. He was a local legend, the man everyone knew to see when they found themselves in a jam. Alex had idolized his grandfather his entire life.

Alex and Buster shared a lot in common. Both men had sharp political instincts and were adept at working a crowd. Buster would shake every man's hand in the room to keep tabs on the people on his turf. Alex would glad-hand, too, and just as often give hugs and handshakes and shout out "Hey, Bo'!" 'round the clock to his friends and acquaintances. They both knew just about everyone in town and beyond. Buster had a habit of popping into holes-in-the-wall down dirt roads on his way back to Hampton from some far-flung part of the circuit. Alex had a tendency to make plenty of side visits on his way to any place. Hitching a ride with him could prove an interminable experience. "He stops everywhere to talk to people," said Russell Laffitte, his longtime friend and banker.

Buster and Alex had similar tastes, constantly filling their mouths with barbecue, alcohol, and chewing tobacco. They both played college football and liked to hunt and fish. They both earned undergraduate and law degrees from the University of South Carolina, Alex being part of the fourth generation of his family to do so. "I don't think it ever occurred to us to be anything other than a lawyer," said Buster once, speaking for the family.

Buster was so intent on Alex attending law school that the well-known solicitor would visit campus some Fridays to introduce his grandson to professors and administrators and assorted officials, said one of Alex's fraternity brothers. It worked, and Alex started law school in 1991. Not everyone was convinced the law profession was the best fit for Alex, who was easily distracted and was often unable or unwilling to focus, according to assorted friends and acquaintances. Alex's younger brother John Marvin was the rare male Murdaugh who resisted family tradition and did not become a lawyer. He named his boat *Black Sheep*, acknowledging his waywardness.

Both Buster and Alex were impossible to ignore. Buster was short, stocky, and bald and had an intimidating air about him. Buster was captivating, and, as one local lawyer said, "when he talked, everyone listened." If people listened to Buster, they merely heard Alex. He was loud, always. He was usually scattered, talking a mile a minute. "I could hear him when he hit the door," said Laffitte. Seconds later Alex would appear in the community banker's office, asking affably, "Hey bo', can you do this for me?"

Alex and Laffitte had known each other since they were boys, growing up together in their family's brick ranch homes in the Pines neighborhood in Varnville. It was a childhood of bike riding, tadpole catching, barefoot adventures, forts made in the woods, and playing outside past dusk. Laffitte was the youngest of three kids born to Charlie and LaClaire Laffitte. Across the street lived Randolph "Randy" Murdaugh III and Libby Murdaugh along with their four children, Lynn, Randy IV, Alex, and John Marvin. The friendship between the families dated back at least two generations and seemed to get stronger as time passed. Randy and Libby Murdaugh coincidentally married the same day as Charlie and LaClaire Laffitte—June 3, 1961—in Lowcountry churches eighty miles apart. Then the couples became neighbors in Varnville and raised their children alongside one another.

The Murdaugh and Laffitte families each operated major institutions in Hampton County. The Laffittes and their extended family owned Palmetto State Bank, which under one name or another had been loaning money for more than a century through a number of branches in the Lowcountry. The Murdaughs, of course, had been in charge of the solicitor's office for nearly as long and also operated an old family law firm. The Laffittes may have had a lot more money, but the Murdaughs controlled the courts, which was no small thing. "They were the law in Hampton County" said Russell Laffitte. "Very influential is an understatement."

Laffitte initially resisted the pull of banking. After high school he farmed for five years, preferring to work in the fields and forest rather than sit behind a desk and computer screen. But then he went to college, earned a business degree in 1997, and gave the family business a chance. To his surprise he liked banking. Over the years he rose through the ranks to succeed his father and become the CEO of Palmetto State Bank, which under his command controlled $500 million in assets and operated seven branches.

During this time Laffitte became Alex's primary banker, extending him millions of dollars in loans. Though the men weren't especially close socially they did a lot of business together and enjoyed an easy relationship that reflected the longtime goodwill that existed between their families as well as their lifetimes of shared experiences in a small town. The men could hardy disentangle themselves if they tried. Alex was the godson of Laffitte's father. Laffitte was the godson of Alex's father. Alex once dated Laffitte's wife in high school. Russell's mother once worked in the solicitor's office with Alex's father and grandfather, and so on . . .

Yet no matter how much money Alex borrowed, it was never enough. He kept on returning to Laffitte to ask for more, even while borrowing money from others, too. This was a lifelong habit for Alex. Mike Macloskie recalled once seeing Alex at a sandwich shop in Columbia when Alex was a college student. The Beaufort lawyer was close friends with Alex's grandfather, Buster, and had pleasant memories of meeting Alex as a boy, including a number of years when he'd see him participating in the operation of the Heritage Classic golf tournament on Hilton Head Island. The men greeted each other at the restaurant and Mike asked if there was any message he could bring home to the Lowcountry. "Tell my grandaddy that I love him," said Alex.

Sometime later, when Macloskie next spoke to Buster, he relayed the tender message from his grandson. Buster was hardly impressed. He asked Macloskie if Alex mentioned money at all.

"No, why?" said Macloskie.

"That kid asks for money so much," Buster explained, "that I need a T-shirt that reads, 'Money isn't everything, but it sure keeps your grandkid in touch.'"

———

Like father, like son. That was the consensus after a University of South Carolina football game in 1934, when Randolph Murdaugh Jr. entered the game as a substitute for the Gamecocks and evoked his dad's gridiron ghost, making nearly all the tackles. As *The State* newspaper noted about the latest star of its hometown team, "It is said that Coach Laval expects to make one of the best linemen Carolina ever had out of 'Buster' Murdaugh."

So similar were the men that young Randolph adopted the youthful nickname his father had shed since leaving campus—Buster. The nickname wasn't simply inherited but earned; Gamecocks football coach Laval bestowed the revived nickname on Randolph Jr. after he "busted hell" out of an opposing player. The kid had made a splash off the field, too. He was elected vice president of the freshman class. He pledged the fraternity Pi Kappa Phi. And he had already met his future wife, the striking Gladys Marvin, who grew up in the Lowcountry on Mackay Point plantation and who was attending Columbia College across town from the university.

Buster had grown up with his father, his stepmother, Estelle, and his brother, Johnny. Life was comfortable during Buster's childhood. Randolph Murdaugh Sr. made enough money to invest in a bank and other businesses, as well as to own one of Hampton's first cars, though it was stolen briefly one year and burned in a fire the next. Despite wheeling it out of a burning garage, Estelle and a household servant were unable to save the automobile from becoming scorched. Randolph Sr. co-owned a boat when Buster was in high school, too, and invited the governor to cruise. The family took occasional weekend trips to the beach and the adults also visited New York City.

At home, Estelle appeared the consummate host. She and Randolph entertained visiting judges for dinner during terms of courts, and she held frequent bridge parties. The bridge gatherings were extravagant affairs, at least by small-town standards, featuring elaborate lunches and an abundance of prizes, such as candy boxes and hand-painted lemon dishes. Game tables were spread throughout the rooms of the Murdaugh home, each of which dripped with decorations, including cut flowers, potted plants, balloons, and gobs of confetti.

Estelle was popular. So was her husband, Randolph. "Although a pros-ecuting attorney he has more friends than any one man in this section," said *The State* newspaper in 1936, just before Randolph won his fifth straight election, again without opposition. Out of all these admirers, Randolph had perhaps no greater friend than his son, who had spent a lifetime following his father into the courtroom, first as a child, then as an apprentice, and finally as a law partner.

The deep, harmonious bond between father and son stood in contrast to the dysfunction that dominated other families in Hampton and sometimes manifested in violence. One day in 1933 a teenager in the area of Pritchard-ville consumed five drinks of alcohol, argued with his stepmother, and blew her head off with a shotgun. He pleaded temporary insanity and said he had no memory of the incident and was acquitted by a jury. Two years later, another teenager blasted his father in the back with a shotgun—retaliation for a whipping. He pleaded guilty to the homicide and was sent to reform school. There was also the case of a doctor in the Hampton County town of Yemassee whose wife was found on the floor of their bedroom in 1932, her throat slashed seven times. Three years, one long investigation, and two trials later, Randolph convicted the doctor of manslaughter.

Randolph's appeal in the Lowcountry was so strong he could stake out the occasional progressive position or try a controversial case without alien-ating his supporters. While other solicitors demurred, he stated publicly in 1935 that women should be allowed to serve on state juries, believing "their presence would have a good influence." A year later he tried a White magistrate in Colleton County for public malfeasance, accusing the official of failing to disburse all of a deceased Black man's money to his heirs. Yet at other times, when convenient, Randolph could help keep Blacks down and reinforce the notion of White supremacy, such as his use of a racial slur in the trial of Willie Heyward in 1932. Also in 1932, during the murder trial of an Estill man accused of killing a road foreman, Randolph said that the testimony of a single White witness, who believed an unlawful murder occurred, was preferable to the accounts of six Black men, who testified the killing was justified.

Randolph's political star was steadily rising. In 1935, he was named an honorary Young Democrat in Charleston alongside South Carolina political giants James Byrnes and Burnet Maybank—men who both served as governor, US senator, and other high offices. In 1936, Solicitor Murdaugh earned the honor of an appointment to the board of trustees of his alma mater, the University of South Carolina. This was the same year his son, Buster, earned his undergraduate degree and began studying at the University of South Carolina School of Law.

Yet other parts of Randolph's life were falling apart. His younger son, Johnny, was troubled, said to drown chickens for amusement. Johnny was born into trauma, his birth supposedly difficult and a factor, if not the outright cause, of his mother's death. His father always treated him coldly and held that against him, Johnny told his stepchildren.

Johnny suffered an excessive number of blows to the head over the years, including a severe gash to his skull from a car crash when he was twelve years old. These incidents were only the beginning of Johnny's problems, and he was sent to military school in Georgia as a teenager, given the chance of a new start.

Meanwhile Randolph's wife of seventeen years, Estelle, was in poor health. Estelle entered the hospital and lingered for months before dying in February 1937 at age forty-six. Randolph Sr., rarely one to miss court, convicted a magistrate's constable of manslaughter during the week and then was at his wife's bedside when she died during the weekend. He was a widower once again.

Financial troubles compounded Randolph's grief. As the Great Depression rippled through Hampton County, it caused the closure of local sawmills and banks. Randolph lost most of his wealth when one of these banks failed. It would not be the last time his family suffered a stunning and swift reversal of fortune. Buster was enrolling at college when the hard times commenced. "When I left to go to school at Carolina, he was flat broke," Buster once recalled. "His salary as a solicitor was about $137.50 every two weeks."

To afford his college education, young Buster attended school on a football scholarship at the University of South Carolina. He worked as many as three jobs a day, each of which he scheduled around his classes. He started his typical school day at 7:00 A.M. at the South Carolina highway department. Then from 9:00 A.M. to 1:00 P.M. he attended classes. From there he headed to the state insurance commission for the afternoon. If the legislature was in session, he finished the day at the State House, working as a clerk for the South Carolina Senate.

Buster made time, too, to court his future wife, Gladys. He was hardly the only one to notice the head-turning beauty. In high school she stirred desire simply by wearing her basketball uniform. Boys watched her game carefully from the sidelines, more interested in skin than sport.

"It was during this period that girls basketball teams made the change from chaste, black bloomers to the figure-complimenting shorts and sleeveless tops," wrote Lt. Col. James Walker DeLoach in an essay about old Hampton, penned decades after his school years ended. DeLoach recalled the day he saw Gladys for the first time. She was on the visiting team and wearing that new style of uniform. "There was a red-haired girl on the Ridgeland team. Pretty. Lord she was pretty—And, she was appropriately embarrassed by our stares," wrote DeLoach. "I don't remember who won the game. But Buster Murdough [*sic*] won: He married that redhead. We thought that was in order—Buster was always a go-getter."

Buster and Gladys married on June 24, 1937, at her childhood home of Mackay Point, where her father worked as the property's manager. The wedding was held on a lawn beneath the extensive canopy of a grove of live oaks, with Solicitor Randolph Murdaugh serving as his son's best man. Afterward, Buster and his bride, a schoolteacher, honeymooned at

Niagara Falls and Atlantic City, New Jersey, before returning to Columbia, where Buster began his final year of law school.

Love was in the air in Hampton County. A month after Buster and Gladys's nuptials, widower Randolph Sr. married for the third time, taking the hand of Mary T. Hoffman. He took on a new legal partner as well months later, welcoming his son Buster to the newly rebranded family firm, Murdaugh & Murdaugh.

In October of 1939, a few months into Buster's partnership with his father, police at last arrested Ben Heyward, the alleged fugitive killer from Beaufort County. Heyward had been on the run for nearly fifteen years—seven years longer than his brother Willie. Sheriff J. E. McTeer Jr. described Ben's capture as "a long trail on a slim lead." The sheriff's dogged investigation of the case had revealed the fugitive suspect to be a veteran of World War I. McTeer reasoned that one day Ben would apply to receive his service bonus, he just needed to be patient and make the right inroads and alert the right people. Indeed, in the fall of 1939 Ben traveled from his home in Akron, Ohio to Cleveland, where he met with an employee of the American Legion who helped him file an application for the payout of benefits. The police arrived before any checks did. McTeer soon got some good news: Ben was in custody in Ohio.

McTeer immediately started another drive north with former magistrate's constable Hubert Randall, who had helped retrieve Willie Heyward in Pittsburgh seven years before that. Randall would now be able to confront the man who had shot at him and killed Officer Carden. Also riding in the car were a highway patrolman and Solicitor Randolph Murdaugh. The South Carolina policemen were smart to bring along a lawyer, as Randolph would be needed.

Heyward's removal from Ohio was temporarily delayed due to an appeal from his own lawyer, Chester K. Gillespie, a Black state legislator from Cleveland who came to be known as "Mr. Civil Rights" in Ohio for his work to promote racial integration. Through articles in the *Call and Post*,

Cleveland's newspaper serving the Black community, Gillespie publicly pleaded Heyward's case, portraying Heyward as an innocent victim of racist, unlawful southern White "mobsters" who shot at him and burned his house in retaliation for a $13 pay dispute. Heyward and his brother Willie had no choice but to defend themselves, according to Gillespie's narrative, and the men had to live for four months in the swamp before they caught a train car to Pittsburgh, where they eventually parted ways and could live without threat of violence.

Gillespie decried South Carolina as a "savage and uncivilized state" where lynchings of Black people were commonplace. Even if Heyward was protected from lynch mobs upon his return to South Carolina, said Gillespie, it would be impossible for the murder suspect to receive a fair trial given "the atmosphere of race hatred and prejudice." The party of lawmen visiting from South Carolina of course felt differently than Gillespie and his client, both about the facts of the killing and Heyward's chances of staying safely incarcerated and receiving due process. Gillespie's appeal and request for a habeas corpus proceeding, in which Heyward's detention would have to be justified beyond the indictment already issued by a grand jury in South Carolina, was denied twice, first by a circuit court and then by the Ohio Court of Appeals. Finally the decision to let Heyward go or not landed on the desk of Ohio's governor, John W. Bricker. Solicitor Murdaugh and Sheriff McTeer argued to Ohio authorities that mob rule is the exception in South Carolina, and that Beaufort County has never had a lynching. Ben Heyward, they told Governor Bricker, would receive his day in court.

Though McTeer insisted Beaufort County never had a lynching, mob violence against Black men, including their killing, had occurred in surrounding counties in South Carolina in recent decades. A mob of White men took the jailer's keys and yanked Allen Seymour out of Hampton's jail one night in December 1914. The Black man allegedly confessed to hiding in a pig pen and chasing after a White teenage girl in an attempt to steal clothing because he was freezing. A mob set Seymour free and then shot him dead in the back as he ran.

In 1917 a mob again snatched a Black man from the Hampton jail despite the inmate clasping desperately to the cell bars as he was pulled away, begging to be locked up and protected. The mob beat the suspect, who was accused of assaulting an elderly man, but spared his life. One year later a mob in nearby Fairfax in Allendale County was not as merciful, tying a Black murder suspect to a tree in broad daylight before riddling his body with bullets and leaving him to rot. Another Black man, Julius Woods, was found shot to death on the side of the road in Jasper County near Gillisonville in 1920 after he got in a scrap with a White boy. According to the sheriff, no one seemed to miss the murder victim. "In fact his own people seem to take no interest in this killing and so far can get no starting point," the sheriff wrote in a report.

Just outside of Hampton, in the tiny town of Brunson, two Black boys were whisked out of their jail cell by a mob one night in August 1921. As the sign outside of town will tell you, Brunson is famous for having the world's only octagonal town hall on stilts. In 1921 the raised town hall afforded summertime shade to its residents, so long as their skin was White. When the two Black boys objected sassily to this rule, they were jailed. After sunset the boys were sprung from jail by a small mob, brought to a swamp two miles away and thrashed.

Ed Kirkland would have gladly suffered a mere thrashing for his alleged wrongdoing. Instead, the Black man from Allendale County became the quarry of an angry mob who chased him across the Lowcountry before abusing him with a shocking amount of violence—shooting, hanging, and burning the suspected killer. Kirkland's grim demise was set in motion when he feuded with his White landlord about money and then shot him in the head in the streets of the small town of Appleton the morning of October 26, 1921. Kirkland ran but was soon caught and turned over to the sheriff, who urgently tried to transport the suspect to Columbia for safekeeping at the state prison.

Knowing that a mob had formed and splintered apart to picket nearby bridges and roads, the sheriff drove on back roads, away from town, and managed to smuggle the suspect onto a train bound for the capital. But at the Fairfax station just a few miles down the track, a huge mob of masked men invaded the train cars in search of Kirkland. The suspect bolted from his hiding place but did not get far before a fusillade of bullets cut him down. His punctured body was brought to the center of the town of Appleton, where he lay ailing in an automobile. Supposedly, Kirkland made a statement that implicated a nearby Black lodge in the murder. Hearing this, the mob drove him to the lodge outside of town, swung him from the upstairs rafters and torched the building. The fire was visible all the way to Allendale, the county seat, miles away.

No one was ever arrested for any of these extrajudicial killings or attacks. No one was charged, either, for the infamous Lowman lynchings that took place in 1926 near the town of Aiken, a wealthy inland winter colony rife with horse farms. In this case, three Black suspects—two men and a woman—were awaiting a retrial on controversial murder charges when they were plucked from jail by a mob and shot dead in a nearby pine forest. The killings sparked widespread outrage, especially outside of South Carolina. In an effort to learn about locals' feelings about the matter, the *New York World* wrote to assorted South Carolina newspapers, asking for their thoughts. The *Hampton County Guardian* obliged, stating lynching was not preferable, but nonetheless a useful tool should the courts ever falter. "We have an unfortunate situation here and it is necessary to protect the White women and girls of our county by quick justice," said the newspaper, "but the courts so far have been amply sufficient to take care of such cases."

No matter the *Guardian*'s indifference, attitudes were changing. A few months later Judge J. Henry Johnson of Allendale, an admitted White supremacist but also an admirer of law and order, took a less ambivalent stand toward lynching when holding court in Aiken, urging for the practice to go extinct. "I will say that a little band of willful men have besmirched the good name of Aiken County and of South Carolina," said Johnson. "You cannot say it was manslaughter. You cannot say it was done in sudden heat and passion. It was murder."

A shift in public opinion was evident, too, from the reaction to a 1930 lynching in Oconee County along the edge of the Blue Ridge Mountains, where another Black man was tied to a tree and shot. The *Spartanburg Herald* called the lynching a "disgrace" and out of touch with common sentiment:

> *Though it be hard to face, it is true that not until the last 15 or 20 years has there been such violent opposition to lynching. There have been days when the community shuddered in the light of the day following the lynching of a Negro, then accepted it with a half-hearted investigation. Some dared say it might be the best way. Today, if that statement is made the lips from which it falls are black with ignorance and cruelty.*

To bolster their argument of being able to afford Ben Heyward a safe and fair trial, McTeer and Murdaugh might have mentioned to Ohio authorities the case of E. F. Langford, a rural policeman in Beaufort County who was shot and killed at a picnic outside of Beaufort in June of 1927. Three weeks later, six Black suspects were being tried in Beaufort for the White policeman's murder, guarded by two militia units called in by the governor, including a National Guard machine gun company. No violence befell the prisoners, all of whom were convicted of the killing, with three of them sentenced to be executed. This recalled that strange contradiction once faced by the crippled and condemned convict Jake Terry—the absurdity of life being preserved in order to be cut short.

Arguably, the decline in lynchings was hardly remarkable, with state-sanctioned executions simply taking the place of extrajudicial killings.

As the *Guardian* newspaper noted, so long as the courts are taking care of the problem, the people don't have to resort to lynching. Like a lynch mob, justice could be alarmingly swift in South Carolina courts, with some suspects caught, convicted, and executed by the state in the span of a few weeks. And like the victims of lynching mobs, the roster of prisoners executed by South Carolina was filled overwhelmingly with the names of Black men.

In the end, the Ohio governor granted the South Carolina authorities custody of Ben Heyward and permitted his return to the South. Heyward appeared in the Beaufort County Courthouse in late 1939, where he pleaded not guilty to the murder of policeman Carden. During his arraignment, Solicitor Randolph Murdaugh made sure to acknowledge the out-of-state cooperation and endorsement he and the sheriff received. "I would like to state right here in open court, that the sheriff and myself stated to the governor of the state of Ohio that this man could get a fair trial and I want to see that he does," said Randolph Sr.

Heyward's homecoming to South Carolina was not the only arrival Randolph celebrated that fall. On October 25, 1939, Gladys gave birth to his first grandson, Randolph Murdaugh III. At first blush, Randolph seemed on top of the world. He had a new wife. He was practicing law with his beloved son, Buster, who had just made him a grandfather. The Great Depression was ending and he was flush with business. He was, once again, running unopposed for reelection for his sixth straight term, and he was also on the eve of trying one of the biggest cases of his career, hoping to finally convict policeman Ben Carden's alleged murderer. Yet all this good fortune, all this success, was rendered moot by one other development: Randolph was slowly dying.

Randolph was admitted to a Savannah hospital in February 1939 for treatment of uremic poisoning, a buildup of toxins in the blood caused by kidney failure. With his father hospitalized, Buster stepped in as solicitor at the next term of criminal court, trying five cases in a day and winning four convictions. Afterward he was thronged in the courtroom by well-wishers who complimented him on his impressive debut. The *Guardian* lauded the young volunteer prosecutor for his poise and preparation: "Despite the fact that his father lay critically ill, Monday was an important day in young Murdaugh's life. A big responsibility was placed on his shoulders, that of taking the seat at the desk of one of the state's most able prosecuting attorneys."

Randolph Sr. was discharged from the hospital, but his recovery was elusive. He stayed out of court for much of the next year, allowing Buster to stand in his place. His absence in South Carolina courts was noted and the popular solicitor was missed. "Here is hoping that you will be well enough to be with us in Beaufort next week, as I certainly have missed being with you," court stenographer J. D. Mars wrote Randolph on February 28, 1940, expressing his wish for the solicitor to heal in time for the trial of Heyward.

But even for this important case—a death penalty trial of a Black man who allegedly killed a White cop and KKK member and then escaped arrest for fifteen years—Randolph could not rally. Buster again acted as solicitor, inheriting the Heyward case from his father at age twenty-five, just like the "Boy Sheriff" J. E. McTeer Jr. of Beaufort County had inherited the cold case from his father and namesake, the late sheriff.

Buster called the case of *State v. Heyward* to trial in the spring 1940 term of criminal court in Beaufort County, his first death penalty case. The defense counsel struggled to find witnesses to testify for Heyward, citing the long lapse of time between the shooting and Heyward's arrest. To compensate Heyward took the stand in his own defense and related his version of events. Heyward's story was convoluted, and not supported by any other witnesses, sometimes differing entirely from other testimony. Nonetheless, according to Heyward, just prior to the shooting of Carden, he had been the subject of one threat or confrontation after another. A man wanted him dead, said Heyward, and he had been forced into hiding for fear of his life, refusing to emerge from his shuttered home. When Carden and deputy Hubert Randall surrounded his house without warning, guns on their hips, he panicked and assumed his enemy had come to kill him. The men never identified themselves as police, Heyward said, and he shot only after Carden began beating down his door. "If Mr. Carden had presented himself like a policeman I would not have been scared like I was . . ." Ben testified. "He had me scared almost dead."

A narrative of mistaken identities emerged from the testimony: The police first confused Ben Heyward for Willie Heyward, then Heyward mistook the police for his tormentor—a supposed Mr. Robinson. "I believed my life was in danger," said Heyward, pleading self-defense. Heyward testified about being trapped in his home, the exits blocked by armed men. There was no warrant out for his arrest and he had done nothing wrong. "I was standing in my house . . ." testified Heyward. "On my real estate and I pay tax for it."

Beyond concern for his own safety, Heyward said he feared for his two young children left alone at the house. When he heard the gunshots fired by Randall, he worried his children had been targeted. "I done believe they killed my babies," Heyward testified in response to the gentle questioning of his own lawyer. After this, the solicitor was given the chance to ask his own questions, many of them pointed. Just a minute or two into the cross-examination, the acting solicitor Buster Murdaugh became aggressive. "On that particular evening when you shot down the rural policeman in cold blood, you say, Mr. Robinson broke into your house?" he asked.

"When this man bolted my door he had me in my excitement . . ." testified Heyward. "I was excited and quite natural shot right there."

Heyward said he did not see the man's face but just turned quickly and fired. Buster was incredulous that Heyward would fire on someone who merely stepped upon his porch. According to the other witnesses, Carden did nothing more than rap on the door.

"And you have got a man in his grave today that came up to your house and knocked on the door?" asked Buster.

"He bolted in the door," said Heyward, claiming Carden tried to force his way into the home.

"And you have got a man lying in his grave that came up to your door?" repeated Buster.

"He never presented himself to me, kind sir," Heyward answered.

Back and forth it went, with Heyward parrying a slew of accusatory questions and insinuations from the solicitor. The questioning was spirited, insistent, and occasionally out of bounds, with the judge reeling the prosecutor back for asking leading questions. Again and again, Buster asked the defendant why he would shoot a gun at someone he didn't recognize.

"You did not look through the crack to see who that man was . . . ?" said Buster. "Just answer my question, did you take time to see who you were shooting at before you pulled the trigger . . . ?"

Heyward maintained he was spooked and that the tragedy could have been easily avoided. "If the man had looked like a policeman and he had presented himself like a policeman I would not have been scared," Heyward said again.

Unfortunately for Ben Heyward, a jury did not believe his version of the killing. What's more, the jury declined to recommend mercy when they convicted him of murder on March 3, 1940. A judge subsequently sentenced Heyward to die in the electric chair. While Heyward was condemned, Murdaugh was celebrated for his high-stakes performance at the capital trial. "The prosecution was brilliantly handled by Randolph Murdaugh, Jr., young attorney pinch hitting for his father, Solicitor Randolph Murdaugh, who has been ill for several weeks," said the *Guardian*.

But while Buster's star burned bright, his father's dimmed. Randolph's health problems had not improved. In 1939 there was no possibility of him receiving dialysis or a kidney transplant—both these medical innovations were still a few years away from being realized. Just like Heyward, he had received a terminal sentence.

On the night of Thursday, July 18, 1940, Randolph visited friends. On the way home, after midnight, he stopped his car beside the railroad tracks.

When a train approached he flashed the car's headlights, then suddenly drove atop the railroad tracks and stared down the train. He heard a screaming whistle and a clanging bell. He saw a bright light looming closer and closer. He cackled into the chaos, determined to have the last laugh.

CHAPTER TWO

AT HOME IN THE SWAMP

In Hampton, there's no escaping the swamps. On one side of the county sprawls the Salkehatchie. On the other side oozes the Coosawhatchie. In between sits the town of Hampton, perched just above the muck. These swamps spread across thousands of acres, surrounding Hampton with sunken, submerged forests. At the heart of these swamps are small, slow-moving rivers that drain imperceptibly toward the ocean. During heavy rains, the rivers and their creeks swell and spill over their banks and flood the nearby forest floor, replenishing the shallow, dark pools from which bald cypress and water tupelos trees grow tall.

Swamps define Hampton County, in more ways than one. The Salke-hatchie River and surrounding swamp physically define the eastern edge of the county, serving as a natural border to Colleton County. Hampton County's other major swamp and river system, the Coosawhatchie, splits Hampton County itself into northern and southern halves.

Cypress swamps were the lifeblood of Hampton County's early economy, an essential resource for the county's sole industry, logging and forest products. As home to gargantuan, centuries-old cypress trees, the forbid-ding swamps sandwiching Hampton were both isolating and enabling. Throughout Hampton's history, a handful of sawmills employed thousands of people and made a few local families tremendously wealthy.

Swamps serve as the defining image of the Hampton County landscape. Visitors to the swamp glimpse exquisite scenes: mint-green duckweed floating atop ebony water; an egret wading cautiously on spindly legs at lagoon's edge, bare cypress trees silhouetted by a winter sunset. For many visitors these sights are exotic. Cypress swamps are unique to the American South; the bald cypress tree grows nowhere else. Adventurer and naturalist Winthrop Packard was so enamored of the old-growth trees he saw in Hampton County in the early 20th century that he claimed bald cypresses were as "wonderful in their way as the sequoias and giant redwoods of the Pacific coast."

Yet the swamps can manufacture less pleasant experiences, too. Crossing the swamp's soggy turf could prove exasperating. Interlopers sink into the sticky mud and wade and swim through inky pools of unknown depths and unknown inhabitants. In warm weather, hordes of relentless mosquitoes and sweltering humidity overwhelm visitors. Overlapping choruses of unseen critters chirp and click and croak to create a swamp hum that becomes unnerving as it reaches a fever pitch. The swamps can often border on overwhelming. "Such dismal swamps are frequent in Carolina, but chiefly abound along the sea coast from Savannah to Charleston," wrote the Irish journalist David Conyngham as he trekked across the South Carolina Lowcountry in January 1865.

Conyngham was a correspondent for the *New York Herald* during the American Civil War, traveling in the company of Union Army troops commanded by Major General William Tecumseh Sherman. Before the Union troops tromped across the watery wilderness of coastal South Carolina, Sherman completed his famous "March to the Sea" across Georgia in late 1864. Leaving Atlanta, Sherman's troops wreaked havoc on factories, private property, railroads, and other infrastructure in a scorched-earth effort to disrupt the Southern economy and Confederate war effort.

After reaching the sea and capturing the port city of Savannah, Sherman set his sights north, across the Savannah River to South Carolina, where he planned to attack the state capital of Columbia after venturing upcountry from the coast. Wet weather and flooding briefly slowed the Union troops, who struggled to haul and float horses, supply wagons, and artillery over South Carolina's extensive, swollen wetlands. Sherman noted in his memoirs how this part of the Lowcountry was "cut up by an infinite number of salt-water sloughs and freshwater creeks." During heavy rainfall, the general noted, the swamps turned to "lakes of slimy mud."

As the soldiers trudged northwest, they burned Gillisonville and its courthouse before traversing the region that would, two decades later, become Hampton County. At Whippy Swamp, the Union soldiers skirmished with Confederate troops. Conyngham described the battlefield as "a dense marsh, of about one mile in breadth and several in length, well colonized by snakes and alligators." The Confederate rebels burned bridges, felled trees across causeways, and unleashed floods as they retreated across the wetlands. These measures merely delayed the Union advance.

A few miles closer to Columbia, Sherman's troops encountered Woodlands plantation near the community of Midway. Here, too, the "dark, solemn swamp" near the plantation house left the foreign newsman repulsed. "This is full of fallen trees, Gothic arches of cypress and vines interlacing their branches in strange shapes," wrote Conyngham, "while the ever-pending moss waves its funereal-looking pall over the miasmatic, poisonous air of swamp lands."

Locals, however, don't fear the swamp. At least not all of them. Hampton County natives jump from bluffs and splash into pools full of snakes and leeches. They float in small boats down dark, desolate creeks. Local ministers even baptize new believers in a local cypress pond, ignoring alligators lurking within the same waters, sometimes just a stone's throw away.

Early residents hunted and fished in the swamp, bolstering the food supply grown at home, where most families kept a garden and raised farm animals, including hogs that would be slaughtered in winter. Any animal brought home from the swamp meant a reprieve from eating the staple of salt pork, recalled J. Murry Winn in his memoir *Growing up in Hampton County*:

Fishing and hunting were fun but serious experiences . . . As we approached the water, we walked through the woods very quietly, looking for alligators. If we did not see one, we stripped off our clothes and swam. If we spotted an alligator we shot at it. Sometimes we missed and sometimes we killed the gator and dragged it home. If it was too large to drag, we went home and fetched the ax to chop off the tail . . .

Winn always carried a pocketknife, fishing line, and other tackle in his pockets during the summertime. He flipped over logs and pulled water grass to find worms, sometimes uncovering snakes instead. Other times, instead of baiting a hook, he opted to use a hoe to stir up sediment in a creek bed, forcing oxygen-starved fish to the surface, where Winn and his friends collected them in buckets.

Beyond the alligator, swamp trekkers keep an eye open for venomous snakes, especially rattlesnakes and cottonmouths. Some rattlesnakes are tough to miss, growing to six feet in length. Sheriff J. E. McTeer Jr. regarded the rattlesnake as "the gentleman of all poisonous snakes." "Give him a chance," said McTeer, "and he will warn you in no uncertain terms that you have invaded his homeland and he doesn't like it." McTeer was less complimentary of the cottonmouth, a shorter and much stouter snake that opens its mouth wide when threatened, revealing a white-skinned throat behind its venomous fangs. But while rattlesnakes range over pine forests, along wetlands, onto farms, or into nesting boxes, cottonmouths stick closer to the swamp, often sunning atop isolated stumps and branches they've staked out for themselves. McTeer did not find cottonmouths, also known as water moccasins, to be easily intimidated. "You either walk around him, or kill him, for he does not give ground," said the longtime sheriff.

These fearsome predators make their home beneath the canopy, lording over nearly every other organism consigned to the muck. Yet it's not only the alligators and snakes who have ruled over swampy Hampton County. True dominion of this isolated swath of the South once belonged to someone as territorial and unyielding as the cottonmouth, as opportunistic and vicious as the alligator. He grew up in the swamps and hardly ever left, aware there was no place else he could thrive. As solicitor, he controlled every criminal matter in five counties across the Lowcountry. He used this power, as well as his legendary courtroom prowess and likability, to sometimes do the right thing, convicting killers, rapists, pedophiles, bootleggers, and plenty more criminal types. He also abused this power to become a political boss, accumulating favors, enriching himself, and punishing enemies. He was tempestuous, crude, cunning, and vindictive. He possessed a reptilian instinct to find advantage in every situation. Sneaky and never satiated, Buster Murdaugh was always on the hunt.

———

It would be a good day to rob a bank. Buster Murdaugh was being laid to rest and almost every cop in the Lowcountry was expected to be on hand for his funeral. The tributes had been pouring forth nonstop since the longtime solicitor died February 5, 1998, praising the eighty-three-year-old for more than a half-century of crimefighting and public service, including forty-six years as the region's top prosecutor. Few people, if anyone, had put more people behind bars in South Carolina, making him a beloved figure to anyone with a badge. He was "one of a kind—a true Lowcountry legend," said Beaufort County sheriff Carl "Mac" McCleod, on the eve of the funeral. "There won't be a law enforcement officer to be found on that day."

Buster had spent a lifetime devoted to the law, learning firsthand by practicing alongside his father, the popular prosecutor who perished prematurely in an automobile collision with a train. At age twenty-five Buster was placed in charge of criminal matters in five counties, the largest jurisdiction for a solicitor in the entire state. But as any veteran cop or lawyer in South Carolina will tell you, South Carolina's 14th Judicial Circuit has always been a little bit different. Indeed, the state's top prosecutor admitted as much during one speech to law enforcement in the 1980s after a sheriff from Jasper County posed him a legal question. "Well, that's Buster's circuit," answered Travis Medlock, South Carolina's attorney general. "You know there are two types of law in South Carolina, the law on the books and Buster's law. I suggest you follow Buster's law."

The line was intended to be humorous, but it contained more than a kernel of truth. Buster ran the Lowcountry. Even the attorney general of South Carolina acknowledged that.

Up until about a year before he died, Buster still reported to the old family law firm almost daily, keeping tabs on a few cases and hosting friends for social visits. He had officially retired as solicitor at the beginning of 1987, just before turning seventy-two years old, the mandatory retirement age for public officials in South Carolina. His son Randolph "Randy" Murdaugh III was appointed by the governor to replace him for the rest of the term.

Upon his death, Buster's peers lauded his masterful performances in the courtroom. Many people believed Buster was the consummate lawyer, able to inspire respect in a judge, fear in the opposition counsel, and wonder among the jury. "He had absolute control of a courtroom. He knew so much about the law, his death is like a library burning down," said lawyer Sam Bauer of Hilton Head Island. Judge Gerald Smoak was similarly impressed, claiming Buster "dominated" the courtroom. "I learned early to try to negotiate with him instead of trying a case," said Smoak, who practiced law in Walterboro before becoming a judge. "He rarely lost."

Smoak praised Buster's "razor mind" and emotional commitment to his work. "He was tough. He really was," said Smoak. "He simply was not afraid of anyone—not the public, not the press." Despite being such a cutthroat in the courtroom, Buster had a softer side, too, said the judge, describing him as "a very accommodating and kind person who was willing to help anybody."

Buster was remembered as more than a legal luminary, but also a master politico, winning a dozen consecutive campaigns for solicitor and orchestrating scores of local appointments.

"He never failed to provide me with wise counsel," said Don Fowler, a former chairman of South Carolina's Democratic Party. "He was one of the most hardworking, dedicated public servants ever to hold office in this state or anywhere else."

Buster obviously appealed to Lowcountry voters, but in some he inspired almost divine levels of devotion. Such was the case with local resident Joseph Louis Benjamin, who wrote, "Personally, as a Black man, I can find no words adequate to express my love, admiration and respect for this man so fondly called 'BUSTER' by those who loved him. I have known him all my life and I am proud to say that he treated me with the dignity of a man without color."

Buster's obituary emphasized he was "best known as a plaintiff's attorney, he represented the poor and disadvantaged, never having turned away anyone needing this aid." One of his law partners, Johnny E. Parker, bolstered this thought, commenting that Buster "treated everybody with respect—from the highest to the lowest. I don't remember him ever speaking a harsh word to anyone in the office." Parker was one of South Carolina's most successful plaintiff's lawyers, renowned for his brilliance. He grew up in Hampton and worked as a teacher before attending law school and then was hired by Buster in 1973, eventually becoming a partner at the Peters, Murdaugh, Parker, Eltzroth & Detrick law firm in Hampton.

Buster's tutelage was of tremendous benefit to Parker, who called Buster "the most outstanding trial lawyer I have ever had the opportunity to watch. He taught me how to be a lawyer. That encompasses so many things. He was one of those people you meet in life that stands out." Parker lamented that he would not see his mentor at the old family law firm "when the doors open Monday morning." Buster's death left just one Murdaugh on the law firm's payroll—Randy Murdaugh IV, the grandson of Buster and the oldest son of Solicitor Randy Murdaugh III.

Buster was buried in the Hampton Cemetery on the southern edge of town, where the houses give way to forest and fields that abut one of the swamps. Among the mourners at his funeral was Ronnie Crosby, a young lawyer who briefly worked alongside Buster. He spoke with Alex Murdaugh at the funeral, and he encouraged him to come home, to work at the law firm and fill his grandfather's shoes. Alex liked that idea and told Crosby he was ready to return to Hampton. But the law firm did not extend an offer at that time, said Crosby, and Alex had to wait, at least a little while, to join his brother Randy IV, Crosby, Parker, and the others. Unlike the time Alex's father made a call to help Alex get a job a few years ago, Crosby said it was not "automatic" that Alex would receive an offer from the law firm founded by his great-grandfather. "The fact that your name was Murdaugh didn't get you a job," said Crosby.

Alex did get an offer soon enough, however, and moved with his wife and young son to Hampton. He and Maggie built a new home on a wooded lot, across from the cemetery, less than a mile away from the law office. Crosby was the Murdaugh family's neighbor, though their houses were just far enough apart where they couldn't see each other's homes.

Hampton is a far cry from coastal, semitropical Beaufort, where breath-taking views of the water are unavoidable. Beaufort is quaint and charming, its oldest neighborhoods full of historic homes nestled under live oaks. In Beaufort the beach is a half-hour drive away on scenic highways that stretch across an enchanting landscape of islands and marshes. Dolphins can often be seen breaching the surface of Beaufort's tidal rivers. Shrimp shacks line the road.

Hampton is more hardscrabble. Its downtown is depressed, with vacant storefronts on Lee Avenue and empty, overgrown lots surrounding the courthouse. Many of Hampton's homes appear tired and sagging, bleached by the sun. Other homes appear outright uninhabitable. Even the town's few mansions are unkept and abandoned, symbols of the town's faded glory.

Instead of beaches, Hampton has cypress swamps. Instead of dolphins, Hampton has alligators. Hampton remains a frontier town, at swamp's edge, lacking refinement. It is particularly poor. People buy cigarettes individually at the gas station, asking for a "loosie." The local auto shop sells bald tires for $20 a pop. Many cars rattle, wheeze, and sputter as they roll down the streets of Hampton.

To some this was Hampton's appeal—its rawness and purity, its aversion to anything fancy. One man who moved to town declared Hampton "the last vestige of normalcy on Earth" and as close as you can get to Mayberry, that idealized Southern town full of friendly, happy people where everyone would like to live. "If you break down on the side of the road," he said, "all you have to do is lift your hood and someone will stop and help." In the Hampton he knew, racism was absent and people got along. "It's too hot and the bugs are too bad to worry about any of that," he said.

———

Buster began his reign as soon as possible. Three days after Randolph Sr.'s apparent suicide-by-train, Buster announced he would seek to succeed his father as solicitor for the five-county 14th Judicial Circuit. A challenger for the upcoming election announced his candidacy the same day—Walton J. "Stumpy" McLeod Jr., a lawyer who practiced in Walterboro, the county seat of neighboring Colleton County. McLeod was ten years older than Buster and advertised himself as "experienced" and "mature," a jab at Buster's youth and short career as a lawyer. Buster's own campaign ads countered that he was "aggressive" and "fearless," and that, when it came to experience, the twenty-five-year-old candidate had already been performing the job of solicitor for the last eighteen months. Voters across five counties sided with Buster, overwhelmingly electing him solicitor in late 1940. He promised Lowcountry residents he would give "every-one a fair deal" and "not be influenced by friendship or personal prejudice in the discharge of his duties."

Buster especially steamrolled his opponent on his home turf, capturing more than 90 percent of the vote in Hampton County. Buster owed his victory, in part, to the legacy of his father, but also to his own impressive political instincts and popularity. Buster said hello and extended his hand to every person he spotted in Hampton County. On the rare occasion he wasn't acquainted with someone, or forgot who they were, he was observed asking around the room in a low voice to find out their identity before greeting this stranger by name and acting like an old friend. Buster treated the everyday glad-handing as part of his job; the politicking came naturally to him. He befriended people of every walk of life in the Lowcountry, from the loan shark in the tiny town of Brunson, who passed cash out the back door of his home, twenty-five cents on the dollar, to the bartenders serving moonshine in out-of-the-way honky-tonks located down long dirt roads that cut through pine trees.

Every Sunday morning Buster would be standing outside Varnville Methodist Church, gregarious and gabby, puffing on a cigar as he teased and talked sports with a group of friends. As church started, the men snuffed and stubbed out their smoking devices and slipped inside. They left behind a pile of pipes, cigarettes, and cigars on the church windowsill to be sifted through later, after the service, when the men would reignite their respective smokes. When he wasn't standing before a judge as solicitor, representing the state of South Carolina, Buster Murdaugh was just one of the boys, which endeared him to his legions of friends and supporters. As newspaper columnist Chlotilde Martin characterized Buster's contemporaries in a 1935 "Lowcountry Gossip" column, "Nobody in Hampton is very rich and nobody high brow or snooty. They are an unpretentious people, farmers, mostly, and merchants, with a sprinkling of lawyers and doctors and preachers and teachers."

Martin was enamored with the soothing isolation of Hampton and struck by the sense of self-satisfaction obvious among Hampton residents. Martin, an ever-curious journalist, was intrigued by locals' lack of interest in anything that loomed beyond the county line. "Hamptonians are a home-owning and home-loving people," she wrote. "Aware of the excitement and thrill of the big outside world, they are yet content to let it be and find their own happiness within the confines of their own town among the neighbors and friends with whom they have grown up from childhood."

That's not to say Hampton residents were so insular they resisted every innovation. The town modernized in starts and stops as it emerged from the Great Depression, eventually boasting electricity, paved roads, and sewers, at least for many residents in town. High school student Zoie Edith Mason highlighted some of this progress in her 1931 poem "Just Hampton," excerpted here:

> . . . *We have not always had electric lights*
> *But had lamps painted red.*
> *We didn't have paved roads.*
> *But had sand-beds instead.*
> *The school wasn't much account*
> *But now it's coming great*
> *Right now, the coming year*
> *There's about twenty-five to graduate.*

If Zoie had waited seven more years, she could have added a stanza about Hampton's first golf course, a private six-hole club near the town's new West End in which Buster Murdaugh became a member after returning home. Buster liked to hunt and fish, too, and stalked the Lowcountry's forests, rivers, swamps, and marshes for game. The bulk of his time, however, was spent in the courtroom or the office, at work as a private lawyer and solicitor.

Buster practiced in Hampton but lived in downtown Varnville, where he grew up with his younger brother Johnny, across the street from the train tracks, in a wood-frame home built the same year he was born—1915— after the family's previous house burned in a fire. A few years after the death of Randolph Sr., Buster moved with his wife, Gladys, and young son, Randolph III, into the home, which had a small second story and a large front porch that proved a perfect place to chat. The Murdaugh home stood less than a block from Varnville's small shopping district, where Buster's uncle ran a grocery store alongside a handful of other shops. Gladys hosted elegant parties at the home, such as luncheons for new brides that featured bites like tomato jackets, creamed asparagus on toast, and peach pickles, as well as flower arrangements of roses, lilies, and larkspur.

This kind of bounty was not accessible to everyone in Varnville. As a history of the town, *Railroads and Sawmills*, notes, "Times were not always good, people were not always fair, and not everyone in Varnville enjoyed (such) middle class advantages." Poverty abounded outside of town, such as within the isolated Horse Gall community in the Coosawhatchie Swamp. Growing up in Horse Gall during the Depression, J. Murry Winn had no electricity, telephone, or indoor plumbing. However his family did own an automobile, which they generously used to ferry neighbors to downtown Varnville to go shopping. The rides were appreciated, for Horse Gall was half a mile from a school bus stop, two miles from the community mailboxes, six miles from a paved road, and eight miles from town. "We crowded as many people as we could into the car," Winn wrote in his memoir. "I see pictures now of Third World countries with people hanging all over vehicles and I can relate to my childhood with people riding on the outside of my father's old Ford coupe."

The Winn family also had a radio. On Saturday nights the neighbors would gather at their home to listen to the *Grand Ole Opry* music show. Men talked above the country music as women either quilted or shelled the season's latest harvests, crops such as beans, peas, and pecans. Occasionally the men also gathered around the radio to listen intently to a championship boxing match, spending all day making preparations, such as checking the water levels of batteries and scraping clean metal connections to guarantee clear reception of the live broadcast. These events were not the normal peanut-shelling funfests attended by everyone. As Winn recalled: "This was one night when the ladies stayed home and the kids made little noise."

There were nine homes in the Horse Gall community, three of them inhabited by Black families and six of them by White families. Relations between the families were cordial and friendly, and Black and White children played with each other as equals. "I was taught as a child to address all elders as Mr. or Mrs. if they were white and Aunt or Uncle if they were black," wrote Winn. "If caught doing otherwise I would be punished with a whipping for sure. This was a basic rule in the community."

But there were limits to courtesy. When Blacks provided help in the White households, they ate their lunch separately at a small table, sometimes with White children. And while Winn took the bus to the White school, housed in a brick building with grades running from elementary school to high school, his Black friend Tom had to walk four miles each way to the Black school, which employed one teacher in its one-room schoolhouse. Winn once questioned his father about this arrangement. "Son, you are too young to understand," his father told him. "Later in life you will."

The homes in Horse Gall were all wooden, set atop three-foot piers of rot-resistant heart pine and covered with a roof of wood shake shingles or pieces of galvanized tin. Two of these homes had glass windows, the rest featured wooden shutters alone. At the Winn home the immaculate dirt yard was swept clean once a week. After this, the kitchen floor was scrubbed with a brush made from a wooden board punched with holes and stuffed with corn shucks. Excess water ran straight through the floor, which was "made of plank boards with cracks between them through which one could see dogs, cats or chickens that had the run of the yard and the space under the house." Beyond the chickens, Winn's family raised ducks, turkeys, geese, and guineas. "The fowl supplied eggs and meat . . ." wrote Winn. "The geese and guineas acted as security, making sharp, loud noises at any intruder to the farmyard."

The Horse Gall community existed because loggers had previously plundered this portion of the Coosawhatchie swamp of its towering, old-growth cypress trees. They cleared paths into the forest and dropped trees to make primitive corduroy roads. Over the roads they laid temporary rails that enabled them to cart out the timber via rolling trams. When the loggers moved on they took the rails with them, leaving behind paths of packed ground among the otherwise sludgy soil. As Winn summed it all up: "After the trees were harvested the steel rails were removed and the roads of the future were revealed."

A few major sawmills operated around Hampton in the county's early years, including the Big Salkehatchie Cypress Company, which opened in Varnville in 1912 after Louisiana businessmen obtained the use of fourteen thousand acres of forest in the Salkehatchie Swamp. The owners sent experienced hands, loggers, and office staff from their operations in Louisiana to open the South Carolina sawmill, which at times employed as many as 400 people. Winthrop Packard, the natural history writer who compared bald cypresses to redwoods and sequoias, observed logging operations in Hampton County swamps in 1923, marveling at the "heroic adventure" required to find and extract the thick cypress trees from this forty-mile-long stretch of the Salkehatchie, where crews laid more than twenty miles of temporary railroad. "Deer, bear, alligators, and wild turkeys still dwell in parts of this swamp where, save for the passing lumber trains and the thrashing uproar of the giant 'skidding machines,' nature is as untrammeled and primeval as in the day of the centuries long ago," he wrote in the *Christian Science Monitor*.

Packard ventured far into the cypress swamp, where the foresters wore aluminum shin guards for protection from snakebites. Some of these lightweight, metal leg fenders bore fang mark impressions wider than stretched fingers. He watched one great bald cypress after another be plucked from the swamp:

> *For a little time each day you may hear the shouts and singing of the [N]egroes at work, the chugging of engines, the toot of signal whistles, and the mighty thrashing as the skidding machines pick up 60 foot logs and slam them along a quarter mile, crashing through the still standing hardwood on overhead wire trolleys, and finally lay them gently on the long logging trains . . . Then silence falls, the lumbermen and the train with its giant logs go back to the high land and the wild creatures of the swamp come forth again and roam in peace.*

Packard praised the wood of the bald cypress tree as the "finest lumber that exists" and the "eternal wood" for its rot resistance. But for all his enthusiasm for cypress in board form, Packard seemed unconcerned about the conservation of the oldest and grandest living specimens. "Strangely enough, one does not miss these giant trees after they are gone. The hardwood trees which they dwarfed seem to take on new height and the swamp world moves on with the same patient dignity which it has shown for 1,000 years and will show for as many more to come," he wrote, acknowledging it will take ten centuries to replace what was chopped down in a few years.

Just north of the Big Salkehatchie Cypress Company's operations stood the Lightsey Brothers Lumber Company's 100-acre sawmill in the town of Miley. Before the sawmill opened in 1910, Miley was nothing more than a single dilapidated wooden building. But soon after W. Fred Lightsey and Henry W. Lightsey bought the mill site and 3,000 acres of surrounding swampland and forest, the lonely outpost in the middle of the Salkehatchie Swamp boomed, employing almost 300 people by 1930. Because of its remote location, many employees lived with their families at the sawmill in company housing. Here they were generally paid with Lightsey Brothers company scrip, a mill credit the workers could use at a company general store and company market. The mill town, almost entirely surrounded by swampland, had Black and White schools, an electric station, and a fire department, as well as a hotel for teachers and unmarried employees. The mill had built a Black church and a nondenominational White church, too, which featured services of different faiths at different times of day. Before the Great Depression, the mill was cutting fifteen million feet of lumber a year in its low-slung and weathered buildings.

In 1918 the Lightsey Brothers purchased the Hampton and Branchville Railroad to haul logs from their swampland to their sawmill. They extended the railroad to a length of fifty-two miles as they acquired more land, though the tracks never went as far as Branchville. Beyond hauling logs on steam engine trains, the Lightsey brothers operated the *Boll Weevil*, a gasoline-powered passenger and mail car that ran between Hampton and the small town of Cottageville. Some sawmill employees rode the *Boll Weevil* to and from work.

The sawmill's deteriorated warehouse buildings hinted at the thriftiness of the owners. "Nothing is wasted at Miley," noted one sawmill visitor. "Odds and ends of lumber are made into crates."

Some of the money made reusing wood scraps was squandered, however, when W. Fred Lightsey was accused of injuring a Georgia typewriter salesman in a $100,000 lawsuit filed in federal court. In one of their last cases together, Randolph Murdaugh Sr. and son Buster defended Lightsey and limited a jury award to $3,000, even though Lightsey allegedly caused the salesman the loss of use of his arm.

When W. Fred Lightsey's sons Norris and Oswald took over the business the same frugality prevailed. Hampton resident Sam Crews III remembers seeing one of the Lightsey brothers' maids scrubbing tinfoil clean so it could be reused. Crews said Lightsey Brothers employees were required to keep precise mileage records when using company vehicles and that Norris Lightsey, who managed the railroad while his brother operated the lumber business, had a habit of gathering discarded envelopes, slicing through their folds, and then stapling sheafs of the collected scrap paper together to make notepads. This ethos of cost-cutting had its reward: in 1942 the Lightsey brothers purchased Laurel Spring, an 8,000-acre former rice plantation outside of the town of Yemassee.

In late 1930 or so, the indefatigable Lowcountry journalist Chlotilde Martin visited Laurel Spring as part of her research for a series in the Charleston *News and Courier* about the trend of wealthy Northerners buying Southern plantations. At that time, Laurel Spring was owned by E. F. "Ned" Hutton, a New York financier. Hutton bought the South Carolina property in 1927, the same year he and his wife, Marjorie Merriweather Post, moved into the palatial Mar-a-Lago estate they had just built in Palm Beach, Florida.

At Laurel Spring the highlight was not the house—Martin described it as a "low, white rambling bungalow"—but rather the "desirable and picturesque" grounds, including sixteen miles of waterfront along the Combahee River. This river frontage included 2,000 acres of rice fields that, until Hutton's purchase, had been kept in production as one of the last working rice plantations in South Carolina. Ducks flocked to the flooded rice fields in droves in winter, so much so that guards were employed by Hutton along local roads to safeguard against trespassers who might spook or poach the birds and spoil an upcoming hunt. Laurel Spring, reported Martin, "is said to furnish probably the best duck shooting of any estate along the coast . . . On good days the ducks can be seen backed up for half a mile. The water seems literally black with them."

———

Johnnie Moore was in a jam. He had been selling pirated compact discs and had already been caught twice. Those transgressions resulted in fines, but on December 20, 2004, Moore had been caught a third time, and this time he was going to jail. He was arrested and charged with a music piracy offense, and four stores he owned across the Lowcountry were raided, including one in Hampton, and the alleged illegal merchandise seized.

Moore bonded out of jail and sought legal help from the Peters, Murdaugh, Parker, Eltzroth & Detrick law firm. He talked to Paul Detrick, who placed a call to his fellow lawyer Alex Murdaugh, said Moore's widow, Patricia Moore, owner of Spinbad Church Supply and Printing on Lee Avenue in downtown Hampton. The next day the police showed up again, but this time to return all the alleged contraband. Johnnie Moore paid the law firm a small sum, less than five thousand dollars, and he never had a problem again. "When you get in trouble, you go to the Murdaughs," said Patricia Moore. "If they like you, you don't have nothing to worry about."

It wasn't surprising that Alex could pull some strings. He had an over-sized presence, especially in Hampton, where he was impossible to miss. "He really did have that Andy Griffith personality—never met a stranger," said Patricia Moore. Perhaps more crucially, his father was the solicitor. Three months after Johnnie Moore's arrest, Solicitor Randolph "Randy" Murdaugh III nol-prossed the piracy charge, which was his prerogative as the area's chief prosecutor, with a note written on Moore's dismissed indictment explaining the defendant had "stopped selling such recordings."

As a young lawyer, Randy worked alongside his father as an assistant prosecutor for more than twenty years. In 1987, following his father's retirement, Randy replaced Buster as solicitor. By this time the job of solicitor was a full-time position that required the forfeiture of any private practice. In other words, unlike his grandfather and father, Randy could not be the region's chief prosecutor while also working at the old family law firm. One of his first moves in office was to hire his father as a part-time assistant solicitor. The way Randolph framed it, Buster provided indispensable, irreplaceable, tried and true help. "My father and I have a fine relationship, always have . . ." said Randy days before taking the helm. "He amazes me. He's definitely one of a kind in a courtroom. I learn something new from him every time I see him."

But the way others saw it, Buster's hire simply assured nothing would change. Though there was an official changing of the guard, the true hierarchy of the solicitor's office remained the same, said some insiders, and Assistant Solicitor Buster Murdaugh was an assistant in name only, at least for a few years. Randy's comments at the time acknowledged the difficulty of replacing his legendary father. "I've never tried to compete with him . . . got better sense than that."

Yet the torch had nevertheless been passed to some extent, and Randy celebrated his long-awaited opportunity. He had been training to become solicitor his whole life, for more than forty-seven years. "I've never wanted to do anything else," he said. "I've followed my Daddy around the courthouses ever since I was little."

As a boy, Randy would visit the Hampton County Courthouse with his father and draw jurors' names from a box. He brought his own children to the courthouse to do the same when they were youngsters, introducing the next generation of Murdaughs to the courtroom. The Murdaugh family had a habit of slowly but surely ushering their descendants into the office and family firm. Both Randolph Murdaugh Sr. and Buster Murdaugh hired their sons as assistant solicitors, essentially establishing a succession plan. As Randolph took charge of the office, he mused aloud about the possibility of his oldest son and namesake, Randy IV, becoming solicitor one day.

The new solicitor's philosophy was simple: crime is curbed by harsh consequences. He felt his job was not simply to ensure justice, but to stop illegal activity in the first place. "The purpose of prosecution is to end crime—that's the ultimate good," said Randy III. "Some crime can be stopped by a slap on the wrist—some requires incarceration. And some can only be stopped by electrocution."

He sent a handful of killers to the electric chair, including a pair of men originally convicted years earlier by his father who successfully appealed for a new trial. Randy got the same result during his tenure, and this time the murder convictions stuck. It gave him no pleasure for them to die in the electric chair in 1998. He preferred stories of rehabilitation. "It always gave me great satisfaction to keep a young person out of prison and off the path that leads to a criminal life," he said. "Putting people in the electric chair or getting them life in prison is no thrill at all."

Though he followed in the footsteps of his father, Randy possessed his mother's warm and friendly temperament. He counted plenty of people as friends, and hosted regular cookouts at the house for his friends, and also played on a softball team for years. Like his father, loyalty was of the utmost importance to him. One former assistant solicitor in South Carolina once listened to a call between his boss, a solicitor, to his counterpart Randy in the Lowcountry.

"I need a favor," said the solicitor.

"Done," said Randy. "I just have one question, and it doesn't matter what the answer is, but is it legal or illegal?"

Perhaps it was only bravado or nonsense, but the exchange left the young prosecutor slightly unnerved. The favor being requested, he said, did happen to be within the bounds of the law. But apparently it didn't need to be.

The former assistant prosecutor recalled another case, too, in which a murder suspect in Colleton County offered Randy a cash bribe of approximately $5,000, which caused the solicitor to report the attempt to police and then recuse himself from the suspect's trial for killing her husband. When discussing the attempted bribe, Randy declared, "It would take a lot more than that!" This comment, too, made the prosecutor a tad uneasy. Was it merely a joke, or did Randy have a price?

Because Randy wanted to keep the cash for his office, he would not allow investigators to seize it as evidence, fearing he'd never gain custody of it again. So the outside prosecutors trying the case in his place had to make Xerox copies of the money in anticipation of needing to present some kind of proof of its existence at trial. "Only Randolph" could get away with such antics, said the former deputy prosecutor.

Though he was fond of telling profane jokes and having fun with friends and family, Randy's demeanor hardened considerably when it came to discussing his job. In 2004, a few years after Alex moved back to Hampton to join the law firm, Randy seemed exhausted from the responsibility of processing and prosecuting the criminal caseloads of five counties for twelve straight years. He blamed much of the crime in his community on crack cocaine. In a conversation with writer Rosalyn Rossignol, he enumerated some of the reasons for his disillusionment:

> When you wake up Monday morning, see the things I see, you can't help becoming a cynic. We had another girl; Sarah was her name, too. Tortured a paraplegic man. Tried to kill him for two days. Injected him with air, put him in the trunk of a car with the motor running for forty-five minutes, shut him up in a refrigerator, stoned him, and stabbed him. Then there was two boys came down from Pennsylvania, kidnapped a retarded girl, had sex with her every way known to God and man, then killed her. A Hardeeville man cut off his wife's head and put it in bed with her, stuck it under her arm.

Rossignol's childhood friend Nell Davis was killed at her marshside home in Beaufort County on October 20, 1999, allegedly beaten and stabbed to death by her own teenage daughter and two of the girl's friends. Before fleeing they stuffed the mother's battered body in a compost bin. Rossignol wrote a book about her friend's death, *My Ghost Has a Name*, and her research for the book brought her to the solicitor's office in Hampton County, a place that appeared to her to be an abandoned storefront. The building's interior was dated and deteriorated, she wrote, and "warren-like . . . crammed with room dividers." Randy's office was messy, with towers of papers and legal folders covering his desk and floor. There were no fancy furnishings to be seen, and Rossignol reported the walls "were dingy and garlanded with brown water stains. A tightly woven carpet of faded brownish-pink, like dead rose petals, covered the floor."

Randy met Rossignol and offered a handshake. He was tall and wore a plaid shirt with big brown-and-white checkered blocks. He struck Rossignol as "bemused and self-possessed, 100 percent the country gentleman lawyer dressed down for (the) day." During the course of their conversation Randolph mentioned the long service of his father and grandfather in the solicitor's office. "So it's kind of a dynasty," said Rossignol.

"I guess you could say that," said Randy, sipping coffee from a Styrofoam cup.

While Randy toiled at the solicitor's office, his sons Randy IV and Alex upheld the family legal tradition at the law office, where it was possible to make much more money than the solicitor's salary. Alex was proving to be a good hire, generating lots of lucrative business, thanks to his affable personality and his family's long history in the community. He did not have his father and grandfather's ability in the courtroom, but he was persuasive and aggressive, and able to identify opportunity when he saw it. As Jeanne Seckinger, the chief financial officer of the law firm, put it: "He used personality more than technical skill."

Any money made from cases was always paid directly to the law firm, not to any of the law firm's lawyers. At the end of the year, following deductions for expenses and other adjustments, the money was then redistributed to the partners. This end-of-year payment acted as a supplement to an annual base salary of about $125,000, paid every two weeks. The formula was pretty simple: the more money a lawyer made through their cases, the more money they took home at year's end. As Seckinger quipped when discussing the law partners' compensation: "They eat what they kill."

It was an apt description given the popularity of hunting and fishing among the law partners. Most of the law partners at Peters, Murdaugh,

Parker, Eltzroth & Detrick were avid outdoorsmen who plowed their considerable earnings into real estate, buying up local hunting tracts and farms. Their favorite prey didn't have fur, feathers, or scales, though, but rather prey with deep pockets. The lawyers at the Hampton law firm were renowned, and feared, for filing successful lawsuits against large corporations for their alleged liability in personal injury cases, particularly transportation companies involved in vehicle accidents.

Crucial to the law firm's noteworthy success were two factors. First, the firm historically benefited from liberal South Carolina venue laws that permitted what has been labeled as forum shopping or litigation tourism. This meant a lawsuit could be filed against a company in any South Carolina county in which the company operated, even if the accident occurred in a different county or state and involved nonlocal plaintiffs. In other words, it allowed the law firm to steer far-flung cases, including some with seemingly little connection to Hampton County, to their home turf.

Second, the firm benefited from Hampton County's extremely small jury pool. In teeny Hampton County, the Murdaughs and their partners inevitably knew a healthy portion of the jury pool called into the courthouse each term of court. Visiting lawyers who lost cases in Hampton sometimes complained of home cookin'—a jury or judge predisposed to rule in favor of the local firm.

These advantages—the ability to cherry-pick lucrative cases from afar and then try them in a home court where the Murdaugh family had been in power for decades—were enhanced even more by Buster Murdaugh's hiring of a few smart young lawyers over the decades. Peters, Murdaugh, Parker, Eltzroth & Detrick was so successful at the turn of the century that the Hampton law firm attracted the attention of *Forbes* magazine, whose June 2002 article "Home Court Advantage" reported on the success enjoyed by the old Murdaugh law firm. The article noted the comparatively high number of civil lawsuits filed in Hampton County, and how the railroad holding company CSX had been sued almost fifty times in ten years by the law firm, resulting in awards and settlements that exceeded $18,000,000. CSX and others learned that trying cases against the law firm meant almost certain loss and a high jury award. It was better to settle.

The firm's hotshot lawyer Johnny E. Parker was singled out by *Forbes* for his effectiveness in the Hampton County courtroom. Parker was regarded as a top-notch lawyer, hands down, but his peers could not ignore the fact that he practiced law in a place that consistently proved favorable to plaintiffs. Parker was quick to refute claims that he and his colleagues' success was dependent on crooked juries stacked with their buddies. Hampton was like any town. "We don't live in a world where people don't have relationships," said Parker. On the other hand, after the firm won a $14,000,000 award for their client in a medical malpractice case, one Lowcountry lawyer heard Buster Murdaugh brag, "I didn't have but two friends on the jury, but they were good ones!"

Beyond finding their own clients, which was a specialty of Alex, the law firm accepted many referrals from other lawyers in South Carolina who felt they didn't have the resources, expertise, or clout to try a case themselves. Assorted lawyers made a bet that by involving the Hampton law firm they would not only win their case, but win big, or at least bigger than they would by going it alone. One personal injury lawyer in South Carolina who referred cases to the Hampton lawyers called the law firm his "big stick," and was careful to refer only the most challenging and potentially lucrative cases to them, not wanting to squander their time and talents on lesser legal matters. He said he was happy to play "second chair" knowing the case was in capable hands.

The lawyers at the law firm did not advertise their sophistication—they drank cheap beer and drove pickup trucks and wore blue jeans and greeted friends with a shout of "Hey, bo'!" But when it came to high-stakes legal matters, the provincialism faded fast, said the lawyer. "When you have to step it up and get into high-minded things," he said, "(they) led the conversation."

———

Buster and Gladys Murdaugh were on the road most weekends, visiting friends at their plantations or waterfront properties, attending Gamecock football games in Columbia, or enjoying their own cottage at Edisto Beach, south of Charleston. On the anniversary of his father's death in July of 1941, however, Buster decided to get out of South Carolina entirely. He and Gladys and their baby boy Randolph III motored south to Daytona Beach, Florida. When the Murdaughs returned home, four days later, Buster gabbed about their adventure to the society columnist at the newspaper, essentially wondering why he ever bothered to leave. "The trip was made by motor, with good roads all the way," reported the *Guardian*, "but Randolph says while Florida may be the 'Land of Sunshine' and Georgia the 'Empire State,' give him the coastal section of South Carolina every time."

As his comments made clear, Buster was disinclined to leave the Low-country. In the wake of his father's death, Buster became firmly entrenched as solicitor. In his first term he garnered praise for his high conviction rate and won the approval of a county grand jury that called for his reelection and complimented his "unselfish and untiring efforts" and the "splendid manner in which he has prosecuted and investigated criminal cases." Judges rotating through the five county courthouses of the 14th Circuit were consistently impressed by the young prosecutor, especially Buster's preparation for court and the legal command he displayed at trial. "Your Honor, please, the state's ready," he'd utter confidently as court came into session, a hush falling over the gallery.

In October 1940 Buster appeared at the Hampton County Courthouse for the first time since his father's death, disposing of fifteen criminal cases before Judge J. Strom Thurmond, who'd later become governor and a long-standing US senator. That same month Buster, acting as executor of his late father's estate, filed a $100,000 lawsuit against the Charleston and Western Carolina Railway, alleging that the company's negligence and carelessness caused the death of his father, Randolph Murdaugh Sr.

The lawsuit was typical of Buster's argumentative style—exaggerated but effective. The most convincing claims centered on the engineer's failure to signal the oncoming train within 500 yards of the crossing, as required by law; and the railroad's negligence in maintaining the Camp Branch crossing, which was bumpy and overgrown with brush. Yet a number of other allegations in the lawsuit squarely contradicted the testimony given at the coroner's inquest by the three railroad men who survived the collision. Buster's lawsuit claimed that at the time of the crash "the atmosphere at said crossing was heavily laden with fog, greatly obscuring the vision of (automobile) travelers." But during the coroner's inquest two months earlier at the Hampton County Courthouse, the train's engineer testified, "It was just a clear night and the moon was shining bright." Added the train's fireman in his own testimony: "It was very clear, and before we started out, we remarked about what a pretty night it was."

Buster's lawsuit alleged the train's engineer did not keep "a proper lookout for travelers." The engineer testified that he did see Randolph Sr. in his automobile, but "I had no idea they were going to drive up on the track." The lawsuit stated that Randolph Sr. was so distracted trying to navigate his car over the uneven crossing that he was unaware of the oncoming train. The train crew testified that it would have been difficult to be unaware of the steam train on the quiet summer night, especially since they signaled vigorously with the train's bell and whistle. "The right of way was perfectly clear and he could have seen the train," said the engineer. Added the fireman: "I mentioned something to the engineer (that evening) about what a loud whistle we had and what a bright light."

Lastly, Buster's lawsuit claimed his father "did all within his power to get the said automobile off the said crossing." The engineer, however, testified that Randolph Sr.'s automobile surged onto the tracks at the last minute, that the car was not stranded. The train's fireman was insistent the collision did not have to be fatal. "If [Randolph Sr.] had had any intent on getting out of the car," the fireman testified, "he could have done it."

No matter these discrepancies, Buster felt his family was owed for the accident. His lawsuit, which was settled for undisclosed terms, was merely an opening strike, for Buster would spend a lifetime suing the railroads.

———

It's a boy! Again!

On April 14, 1999, Maggie gave birth to her and Alex's second child, Paul Terry Murdaugh. Paul was a redhead, just like his big brother, Buster, and his dad, Alex. And just like Alex and Buster, Paul loved the outdoors. "He was 100 percent country boy," said Alex, who often found Paul peeking at him whenever he worked on a machine. "He wanted to be part of everything . . . His little head was gonna come in there, just nose in there, to see what you were doing."

Paul became a handy child to have around the farm or out in the swamps on a hunt. Whatever he put his hands on he knew how to make work. "He could hunt anything, he could catch any fish, he could run any piece of equipment, he could use any tool," said his father.

The young outdoorsman had a fascination with animals. Some he nurtured, like his hog-hunting hounds or the mother duck and ducklings who once came to live briefly in the family's saltwater swimming pool. Others he brutalized, gruesomely cutting their lives short out of sport or cruelty or for no real reason at all. Paul would have the same fate, slaughtered out of the blue, seemingly killed on a whim.

Paul and his brother Buster were said to fight constantly as youngsters, even more than most siblings. Acquaintances of the Murdaughs said Alex seemed to derive pleasure from their battles and would even pit the boys against each other for amusement. Kim Brant, owner of a carpet cleaning business in Hampton, said a number of parents in Hampton she was acquainted with expressed alarm that young Paul frequently played with weapons, used profane language, and threatened and bullied some of their children. Paul's behavior was so alarming, said Brant, that some of these parents gave Paul the nickname of "Little Dylan Klebold," a reference to one of the teenage killers responsible for the 1999 shooting massacre at Columbine High School in Colorado. One pair of these parents finally mentioned these concerns to Alex and Maggie. According to Brant, the commentary was not well received. In response, Alex immediately severed his family's friendship with the couple, as well as a business relationship, and dismissed their concerns, supposedly saying, "They're just worried my boys are gonna hurt their little faggot."

To help with the demands of two energetic boys, the Murdaughs hired Gloria Satterfield to work as a housekeeper and nanny. Gloria had two boys of her own and was a single mother, so most of her time was spent in the service of others. She wanted it no other way. Many people in Hampton remember her as a kind and hardworking woman. She was a happy person, even though she didn't have much. She didn't criticize or complain but got the job done.

Gloria drove an old, red Dodge minivan around town to the homes of Hampton families she helped with domestic work. She was in high demand, regarded as someone dependable who made other people's lives easier. Gloria once worked in Ronnie Crosby's home when the lawyer and his wife had young children. Beyond help with laundry, Gloria once taught Crosby a new way to cook turkey for Thanksgiving. Turkey á la Gloria changed Crosby's life. "Ever since," he said, "I've always pushed slices of butter under the skin."

Gloria was fond of wearing flowing, loose-fitting clothing, such as smocks or house dresses or oversize T-shirts and long skirts with a pair of sneakers. She particularly liked the color purple. Brant would sometimes see Gloria around town or when Gloria was working at Brant's sister's house. Gloria was industrious, said Brant, and "friendly and cheerful every time I ever had the occasion to see her," often singing along to music.

The Murdaughs in particular enjoyed Miss Gloria's help. She worked for Alex and Maggie for a decade and grew close to their boys. She considered it an honor to be employed by the Murdaughs and to be trusted with the care of their children and their home for so many years. "It was almost like she was family," Crosby said of her role with the Murdaughs.

With the benefit of this help, Maggie was able to dote on the boys, as well as Alex. She stayed involved in their schools and attended almost all of the boys' sporting events, cheering in the stands while Alex coached. She adored Buster and Paul, told people how handsome they were, and celebrated being their mother. Alex said he was proud of the way she adapted to their new life in Hampton. "She didn't grow up in the swamp, and in the country, riding 4-wheelers and hunting and fishing," he said. "She changed everything. She became the boys' mom . . . Her life became 'ball and riding 4-wheelers and doing those things."

Maggie's older sister Marian Proctor laughed at her sister's transformation from a girl's girl who enjoyed trading hair and makeup tips with her nieces to someone who tagged along on hunting and fishing trips. "She made the best of having two boys," said Proctor. "We used to laugh that she'd get in the deer stand with her *Southern Living* magazine, the boys would tell her she was making too much noise turning the pages . . . She just wanted to do what they were doing, she wanted to spend time with them.

"She loved her family, she loved her boys." said Proctor. "Buster and Paul were her world."

Maggie stayed busy and purposeful keeping her family in order. "She never took not working for granted," said Alex. "She might not have worked, but I promise you, she worked. She worked to make sure me and Paul and Buster had everything." Friends in Hampton said the same, that Maggie was extremely engaged in her boys' lives and always seemed to have a few projects in the works. "She wasn't sitting around doing nothing," said one friend.

Alex and Maggie may have had a bigger family except for the toll pregnancy took on Maggie's body. By Alex's account, she endured a dangerous pregnancy with Paul. "Her pregnancies were so hard," said Alex. "I would leave her in the mornings and she'd be sick. I'd come home and check on her, and she'd be sick. I'd come back at the end of the day, and she'd be sick . . . She was so sick all the time with both those boys."

Maggie was big on appearances, always dressed nicely and adorned with jewelry—"Very much a lady," according to Crosby, her onetime neighbor. Maggie possessed a dry, unexpected sense of humor, according to friends. Her sister says she was a "free spirit," and never one to worry about money. Maggie's checkbook, said Proctor, would sit on the floor of her car, buried under a pile of bills. "Organization was not her best skill," said Proctor.

Alex thought Maggie was fun, too. "She had this little playful look where she'd smile at you and bite her lip . . . it would just melt you," said Alex. Alex bragged about Maggie's versatile personality, and how she'd be able to don the most elegant gown and hobnob with wealthy people at the governor's mansion and then the next day stop by a food bank in Hampton and connect with some of the county's most destitute residents. At either place, according to Alex, people would say, "That Maggie, she's a good one. She's just a special person."

Maggie had two beloved boys, a good relationship with Alex, a nice new home with a pool, and household help. Every day was hers to dedicate as she pleased. Much of her extended family lived in Charleston, about a two-hour drive away. She was content. "They had a comfortable life. Maggie was happy," said Proctor. "It wasn't a lavish life, but it was a comfortable life. Money, it was never an issue for her, that she knew about."

Friends say that Maggie enjoyed being a member of a prominent family in town, especially when she first moved to Hampton. But marrying into a close-knit family and moving to their close-knit town carried challenges as well as perks. While Alex knew almost everyone in Hampton, Maggie knew hardly anyone, and none of them well. Because so few people moved to Hampton, she was one of the town's few outsiders. It didn't help that she didn't strike some locals as particularly friendly. Some people thought she seemed lonely. Others regarded her as aloof and secluded, or even stand-offish. "Maggie, she always had her guard up. Because she wasn't from Hampton. And if you ain't from Hampton, you ain't shit," said one acquaintance, characterizing locals' insular attitudes.

Maggie seemed resigned to the fact that Alex would always be the center of attention, and that his career at the law firm would be the main driver of their lives. She was a "great second fiddle," said one friend of the couple. "She just existed in the shadow of Alex. That's where she lived. And that's a hard place to live."

———

On August 15, 1941, eight months into Buster's first term, South Carolina prison officials executed convicted murderer Ben Heyward, bringing the new solicitor's first capital conviction to its conclusion. A South Carolina official reported Heyward, who dodged the law for fourteen years, died "calmly" after nearly three minutes in the electric chair. Heyward was the first of nineteen men Buster would send to South Carolina's death chamber. Of all criminals, Buster was particularly contemptuous of those who killed, those who stole, and those who broke the law habitually. He used a pocket-knife formerly belonging to a rapist to clip his camellia blossoms, saying the blade reminded him of his "personal responsibility for every criminal warrant issued in the 14th Judicial Circuit." His jaw would tighten when he spoke of the need for stern consequences, including capital punishment. "We're going to do everything we can to stop murders," said Buster. "Yeah, I think the death penalty is a deterrent. And another thing: I'll be damned if I'm going to put up with a thief."

Buster's pugnacious, tough-on-crime stance delighted Lowcountry law enforcement. Anything he did, really, the cops loved, such as the night in July 1947, when a crowd of more than 150 policemen, FBI agents, and some local lawyers gathered at the American Legion Hut in Hampton to celebrate the completion of a two-week police training school. Buster arranged for a barbecue banquet at Hampton's iconic hut, a large cabin made of cypress logs built in 1933 as a work relief project during the Great Depression.

The barbecue dinner preceded an inaugural meeting of the 14th Circuit Bar Association. Here, too, Buster called the shots. First he was unanimously elected president. Then he presented a leather traveling case to a guest of honor, Judge J. Henry Johnson of Allendale. It was a savvy move; Johnson was still sore over the aggressive courtroom antics and sharp tongues on display in the courtroom the day before, when Buster and another lawyer sparred bitterly during the prosecution of more than a dozen shrimpers for fishing violations. "In Beaufort yesterday I thought I was losing my grip on the bar," said the flattered judge. "Now I am changing my mind—unless this is a peace offering!"

Buster ingratiated himself with other South Carolina leaders, too. He hired State Senator George Warren to formally represent him in his lawsuit against the railroad, adding some clout to his argument for relief. Warren served a single term as the first solicitor of the 14th Circuit, just before the election of Randolph Murdaugh Sr., with whom he was well acquainted and was said to share not only office space in Hampton, but also cabinets and legal files. Warren was a close friend to Judge Strom Thurmond, who became governor in 1947. Buster befriended the legendary South Carolina politician, too, joining him on hunts, though Thurmond famously switched political party affiliations in the 1960s to become a Republican. Buster was a proud Democrat who served on the executive committee of the state Democratic Party for decades, continuing the service of his father. Beyond these men, Buster enjoyed friendships with sheriffs, state policemen, cops, clerks of court, legislators, fellow lawyers, fellow solicitors, and judges across the state—in short, most of the men who controlled South Carolina.

Buster could be just as quick to make enemies, especially when someone violated his turf or ignored him. In late 1944 he suffered both of these slights when Governor Olin Johnston pardoned rabble-rouser Sam Padgett, a man Buster had previously convicted of stabbing his stepbrother in the back. Johnston issued the pardon during his last days in office, freeing the man after he served just four months of a five-year sentence. Buster was apoplectic; not only did Johnston and the state pardon board fail to consult Buster or the judge on the case, the board and governor had for months been ignoring Buster's plea to free a different man. He published a letter of protest in the Charleston *News and Courier* ridiculing the pardon board for not seeking his input, writing, "You can well realize that if you hear only one side of a case, every criminal in the state would be released."

Furthermore, this particular criminal was notorious in the Lowcountry. Buster wrote how local police told him that Padgett "had given them more trouble than any other one man in the county: that he was constantly in some kind of trouble. Dr. Bennett, a prominent physician of Ruffin, advised the court that Padgett, through his fights and cutting scrapes, gave him more business than any other five men in Colleton County." Buster wrote how he hesitated to publicly voice concerns about the political nature of the board's conduct but "refrained from doing so due to the fact that I am by far the youngest solicitor in the state, having begun my second term in such office and am still less than thirty years of age, but conditions have become so repugnant that I can no longer remain silent." If the pardon board was serious about its work, wrote Buster, "I can give you the names of scores of criminals who are much more entitled to clemency than was Sam Padgett."

At the top of that list would be the Black man from Jasper County that Buster believed he wrongfully convicted. In 1943 a White woman accused a Black man of raping her and cutting her with a knife. Police were suspicious of her claim, thinking the cuts might be self-inflicted. But they decided to honor her complaint and arrest the accused anyway, believing the courts would settle the matter, according to a memoir by Beaufort sheriff

J. E. McTeer. Despite the defendant having a credible alibi, Solicitor Buster Murdaugh tried the unidentified Black man, a jury convicted him, and a judge sentenced him to death. For a certain angry segment of the population, the electric chair was the only punishment that fit the crime.

About the time of the conviction, McTeer recalled in the memoir, he took a leave of absence from his sheriff's post to serve in the U.S. Coast Guard during World War II. One evening he was resting in his quarters in North Charleston, just fifty miles up the South Carolina coast from his home in Beaufort, when the phone rang. Buster was on the line, telling McTeer that the convicted rapist's execution was imminent. The solicitor asked the sheriff if he believed the man should be killed.

No, said McTeer, he believed an innocent man was about to die.

"I have great respect for your judgment, Sheriff," responded Buster. "I'll stop it tonight if I have to drive to Columbia to see the governor."

The convict's life was spared, but he remained imprisoned. Then, months later, in 1945, the supposed rape victim said she was raped again, according to McTeer. Buster didn't believe her, and the woman subsequently confessed that she had made up the story and cut herself with a can opener in a bid to leave her husband. After this, Buster lobbied for the Black man's release from prison. "I moved the court for a new trial and asked that the case be dismissed," Buster later recalled. "It was the only thing I could do and live with myself." According to McTeer, the wrongfully accused man was released from prison and given an unknown amount of compensation.

The exoneration was exceptional; Murdaugh otherwise spent his time working to convict the accused, especially those perpetrating the most heinous of crimes. This was the noble but tedious work of a prosecutor, to harness the law continually to confront and resist wrongdoing. Buster did not seem fatigued by the unending manifestations of evil in the five counties he supervised, but they did keep him busy, especially the most egregious crimes that made news headlines. Apropos of nothing, a January 28, 1948, editorial in the *Hampton County Guardian* spoke of the thrill felt by

members of the press when exposing an absurd or unimaginable offense.
To illustrate its point the newspaper dreamed up a fictional murder scenario
involving a man from a well-to-do family who murders his loved ones. In
this Hampton whodunit, journalists unveiled just as many secrets as the
police. As the *Guardian* fantasized:

> *The city desk wants only the facts, the name and the address and if*
> *possible who done it two jumps ahead of the cops. We do not know*
> *what makes crime news. But we do know that things start hum-*
> *ming around a newspaper office when some no doubt obliging son*
> *or the other carves up his wife . . . I suppose every reporter dreams*
> *of the day he rounds the corner to come on a smoking pistol in the*
> *hands of a town luminary who stands over the twitching bodies of*
> *a couple of people he has just shot . . .*

This imaginary slaughter did not transpire, at least not in the short
term. But other horrific crimes did occur as Buster began his third term
as solicitor in 1948, including a spate of tragic killings within families.
One of these cases began with the disappearance of an elderly woman
outside the town of Walterboro. After eighty-year-old Carrie Carter went
missing on April 6, 1949, police questioned her brother, Wyman Hiott.
Carter was nowhere to be found at the house the two siblings shared,
but police did find a burned mattress and some of her clothing discarded
on the property.

The next morning the police returned to question Hiott, this time with
the Colleton County sheriff and Solicitor Buster Murdaugh, who brought
along six prisoners from the county chain gang. Hiott gave the authorities
a tour of his property, including a hog pen and stable. As he talked Buster
prodded the ground with a stick, which suddenly plunged two feet into the
ground. The inmates immediately started digging and soon Hiott's older
sister was unearthed from a pile of wooden fence rails, earth, and trash.

Hiott told police a host of conflicting stories—that he buried his sister after finding her dead and denied her a proper funeral out of "pure meanness." Hiott supposedly told police, too, that he buried his sister to keep her death secret and preserve the stream of income she received each month from the government. And then allegedly Hiott confessed to murdering her entirely, the seventy-year-old man becoming overwhelmed by his sister's incontinence and helplessness.

"I gave my sister, Mrs. Carter, some strychnine, as much as could be placed on the end of a knife in a cup of coffee," Hiott allegedly told police. "My reason for doing this was because she had messed up her bed so many times."

The next morning Hiott checked on his poisoned sister and brought her breakfast. "She did not eat any but was still alive at that time," he said. "Then I went out to the stable and dug the grave. I then went back in the house to her bedroom, picked her up, placed her in the grave, covering her with blankets, then paper, then dirt. At that time she was breathing a little."

Hiott's explanations were as jumbled as his sister's grave. Buster was not intimidated by the murkiness surrounding the facts. As usual, the solicitor boldly waded into the suspect's cesspool of lies and deceptions. Years later Buster explained his method for teasing out the truth. "When you've got a crime, you have to look at the whole thing and then begin pulling out the irrelevant parts, piece by piece. Once you get rid of all the tangential stuff, then you'll find the solution right there, lying open for all to see," said the solicitor. "When you know who did it and make the arrest, you just round out the evidence and plan how to present it to the court."

Buster focused on the facts, ignoring the "tangential stuff." The suspect lied when police first arrived on the scene. His story changed multiple times before he promised he was telling the full truth, that he was not responsible for his loved one's death. And a natural death seemed unlikely as Hiott's sister was found buried in a fetal position, clutching handfuls of dirt, as if she struggled to find air while soil and debris piled atop her frail body. Given these circumstances, Hiott was charged with murder, accused of killing his kin on his Colleton County farm.

In June of 1949, about 300 people packed a hearing for Hiott at the Colleton County Courthouse in downtown Walterboro. Every seat in the gallery was filled and people spilled over into aisles and stood in front of exits and the courtroom's large windows. Hiott's defense lawyer sought to move the trial out of town, complaining that publicity surrounding the death of Carrie Carter prevented Hiott from obtaining a fair trial. He introduced eight signed affidavits from people to support this point, but the solicitor had sniffed out his plan. Buster presented the judge a petition signed by 275 people—including his brother and nephew—that asserted Hiott could indeed receive a fair trial in Colleton County. A judge ordered Hiott's trial delayed to allow for the defendant's mental health to be evaluated by doctors at South Carolina's state hospital. He was eventually convicted of killing his sister and sentenced to life in prison.

Buster's father also tried several cases before a packed house in Walterboro during his twenty-year tenure as solicitor, including the unsuccessful prosecutions of at least two police officers for killing suspects unnecessarily. During another two-day trial in September 1925 people packed the Colleton County Courthouse to support a teacher, Ida Folk, who was being prosecuted for the death of a young boy who was struck by her car. The boy's family hired an out-of-town lawyer to assist the solicitor, who accused the teacher of failing to exercise "due caution" while driving, but it was to no avail. A jury was sympathetic to Folk's side of the story—that she was driving at a reasonable speed of twenty-five miles per hour and the boy suddenly darted into the street, in front of her car, and she was unable to avoid a collision. The courthouse gallery, notably full of women, cheered when the teacher was acquitted of wrongdoing.

While these tragedies were occurring in Colleton County, parallel instances of violence were occurring in neighboring areas. Back in Hampton County, Charles Mixson Jr. of Varnville shot his parents dead with a rifle on February 21, 1951. Doctors determined the seventeen-year-old Mixson, who had yet to advance beyond the ninth grade, to be sane but possessing a "dull normal" level of intelligence on par with an eleven-year-old. After the killing, Mixson wandered a field until he was arrested at 3:00 A.M. He left his parents' blood-soaked bodies to be discovered by his visiting adult sisters, who found mom crammed into a closet and dad shoved into the outhouse.

At a trial four months later, Buster told jurors that Charles's "deliberate and cold-blooded" murder of his parents was so egregious that he deserved the death penalty, no matter the young man's diminished intelligence. Too many murders were occurring within families in the Lowcountry, the solicitor complained. "I ask electrocution for what this boy has done and to deter others who might choose the same kind of action he chose to take with his parents," said Buster during his closing argument. "He knows the difference between right and wrong and therefore he is responsible for his actions." When Buster mentioned that Charles did not call a doctor in the wake of the shootings, the defendant interrupted the solicitor, yelling, "I did care about them." A jury convicted Charles of the killings but declined to impose the death penalty, leaving a judge to sentence him to life imprisonment.

Just before Charles Mixson shot his parents, another appalling family tragedy unfolded in the town of Estill, across the Coosawhatchie Swamp from Hampton. On the evening of December 8, 1948, neighbors saw John D. Bowers walk down the street to his brother's store holding a bat. He walked inside the store and declared he had "just killed his old lady." When neighbors and police went to Bowers's house they indeed encountered the battered and lifeless body of his wife, Mae. Police also found the bloodied bodies of two of John and Mae Bowers's children: seven-year-old Wayne and four-year-old Sandra. Wayne was dead but Sandra was breathing, just barely. Police rushed her to a hospital but Sandra died within the hour, succumbing to injuries suffered when her father crushed her skull with his bat.

Doctors examined Bowers at the state hospital and found him to be insane by way of an alcohol-induced psychosis that caused hallucinations. One of his doctors explained that Bowers was perfectly agreeable when sober, but "when he has whiskey in him he would act mean like the devil." After months of observation and recovery at the state hospital, doctors concluded Bowers had regained his sanity and discharged him to the state prison system. To the satisfaction of Solicitor Murdaugh and the people of Estill, Bowers was now eligible to be tried for his crimes. Buster claimed the prosecution of Bowers is "just another murder case to me. I plan to ask the jury to give him the chair and nothing less."

Sorrowful and curious onlookers filled the tiered rows of seats in Hampton County's courtroom on October 12, 1950, when John D. Bowers was tried for murder. A surviving son testified his father was constantly "raising the devil and fussing" with his mother. "I heard him threaten to kill her many times," he said, "once with a pocket knife." The Hampton County sheriff took the stand to tell how Bowers confessed to ambushing his family as they came home from a matinee, bashing away with the baseball bat as soon as he opened the front door. He slugged his wife first, then his children, proceeding from oldest to youngest, their bodies collapsing on the porch and across the threshold of the front door. "The boy was harder to kill than the girl," Bowers confessed to the sheriff.

At trial, a neighbor from Estill took the witness stand to offer confirmatory details. About 6:30 P.M. he testified he heard a dog barking and two children crying, along with a persistent thudding that sounded "like a sledge hammer you would take and pound the floor with." Bowers's attorney argued his client, who had twice previously been admitted to the state mental hospital, was insane at the moment of the crime. Buster countered this was nonsense. "He knew the difference between right and wrong. You have heard testimony to prove that," said the solicitor. "I ask you, How much mercy did he show to his daughter?"

Buster worked himself into a frenzy as he delivered his closing argument in his trademark style, which was all at once logical, exaggerated, and coercive. This was the bluster of Buster, a furious, bullying assault that shamed anyone who might dare disagree. As he erupted in the Hampton County courtroom, Buster even sought to spread culpability, declaring the jury must not just deem Bowers guilty, but also call for his execution. Should they convict Bowers but choose mercy, he explained, state law would allow Bowers to be paroled in a decade. "If he was crazy he would still be in the asylum," said Buster. "I ask you, the jury, to give him the electric chair. . . . It will be your responsibility if this man is turned loose within ten or fifteen years and allowed to roam in Hampton County."

Eight hours later the jury returned with a verdict. Bowers was guilty, said the jurors, but not deserving of execution. A judge sentenced Bowers to life imprisonment with a chance for parole. If Buster was disappointed by the jury's decision to be merciful, he would not admit such feelings. Years later he claimed he didn't become emotional over any case's outcome:

> Sometimes I'd think we had a tight case, and they'd turn the defendant loose. Sometimes I'd think the defendant was guilty but wasn't convinced I could prove it, and the jury would give a verdict of guilty. I have to assume that the judgment of twelve people is better than the judgment of one. So even when I think the jury's done wrong, I don't worry about it any more, once the verdict is read.

No sense dwelling in the past, decided Buster. Ever the opportunist, he'd rather look forward. Who knew what was around the corner?

CHAPTER THREE
SECRETS AND SINS

Rumor had it the man was a millionaire many times over, the black sheep of an old Northern family who was banished to the South for scandalous behavior. His family supposedly gave him an estate and a regular stipend on one condition: that he stay far away but call his mother daily. He rang her every morning, the story goes, since it was the only time he was sober. Like most anecdotes about the legendary Harry Cram, this tale contained just fragments of truth.

Cram would explain that he was not exiled to coastal South Carolina, but deliberately chose to live at Foot Point Plantation, the vast waterfront property he inherited from his father. He first came to the Lowcountry as a baby, just days after he was born in New York on January 20, 1907, so his father could go quail hunting. Cram resented the fact some of his first breaths were of New York's normal, neutral atmosphere and not the fetid air of the Lowcountry marsh, thick with humidity and reeking of salt and pluff mud. "I just missed three weeks being born at Hilton Head," said Cram. "I've never forgiven my mother that."

Cram's childhood was privileged and peripatetic; he traveled between continents from one killing field to another, tutors tagging along as his father, a New York attorney, pursued his passion of hunting in assorted wildernesses. In the fall, the Crams typically hunted grouse on a 40,000-acre estate and castle in Scotland before returning to Long Island, New York, to hunt ducks. By midwinter the Crams were settled in coastal South

Carolina, shooting quail. And not long after that they traveled to Florida and cast their fishing lines into the sea and inlets near Palm Beach.

On some of these travels, the Crams traveled aboard their family yacht, which towed a barge that carried a lonely cow. Harry Cram remembers the floating farm animal causing a constant stir when his family was in transit. "It was the funniest thing ever to the people on the shore who would see it," Cram said. "We had a man back there to milk the cow. My mother insisted that even if we had to be hauled all over the place, she was going to have fresh milk for the children."

Not every tutor could hack the semi-rugged and vagabond lifestyle his family embraced as they moved between rented abodes in the sticks. In autumn one year, a tutor fell off his horse and broke his leg in South Carolina, which, to Harry's delight, canceled lessons for the rest of the year. Already his education paled in comparison to his peers. When Cram's family came to enjoy Foot Point Plantation and other coastal property Cram's father bought in Bluffton, South Carolina, Cram said the local children envied his freedom. "They were jealous of me because I wasn't made to go to school . . ." said Cram. "We were off shooting all the time."

No matter his Yankee roots and childhood wanderings around the globe, Harry Cram came to be a celebrated, adopted bona fide Southerner. He built himself a home at Foot Point in 1929 when he was twenty-two years old. The modest house stood ten miles outside town on a rutted dirt road, or, as Cram put it, "at the end of nowhere." Cram deemed Foot Point his first "real home" and proceeded to throw frequent, long-running parties. Within a few years, the Lowcountry was awash with semi-scandalous tales of the improbable Cram, who had a reputation for being heaps of fun, a hell of a raconteur, and a marksman so talented he could "shoot the eye out of a bat on the wing," said his friend Tommy Heyward. Cram was described as a "constant surprise," "a figure out of an adventure novel," and a regular host of celebrations "where the guests rode hard, drank hard and played tricks on one another." His antics, both real and embellished, kept a whole community entertained. "Telling Harry Cram stories is like eating peanuts," said Heyward. "You get started and you can't stop."

Most stories about Harry Cram involve alcohol or guns, and the best stories usually involved both. There was the time he and a woman rode their horses across the state line and into the ballroom of the DeSoto hotel in Savannah, all to win a bet and collect a bottle of champagne. "You have to remember that was 1929—and back then everybody did that sort of thing," once explained a straight-faced Cram, who claimed to have removed the horseshoes from his mount to avoid damaging the hotel's dance floor.

Cram once admitted to setting loose a raccoon in the room of an ailing friend who had broken his leg while racing horses against Cram and was awaiting the arrival of a doctor. Cram was reputed to drive his forty-foot speedboat recklessly and to have once made an acquaintance guzzle inordinate amounts of Pepto-Bismol stomach medicine. One magazine told of Cram unexpectedly target shooting the dials of telephones and jars of unwanted jam when he was at home. This article related, too, a story about Cram's son Jackie wearing a coat with a bullet hole in the front and back of the garment. Jackie Cram told friends that his father had once given up alcohol and locked all the family's liquor inside a closet. After some time Cram's resolve to stay sober weakened. He became desperate to open the closet but had lost its key. His thirst growing, Cram grew impatient, pulled out a gun and shot the lock clean off the door. The bullet, Jackie added, "went through every suit in the closet." But when a novelist claimed Cram once climbed a tree and shot off the hood ornaments of cars arriving to his party, his family cried foul, disbelieving at least that particular claim: "I've never seen daddy up a tree in his life," said his son Hank. "And he's always been a great host."

In 1931 Cram's reputation was significant enough to attract the attention of roaming Lowcountry correspondent Chlotilde Martin, who included Cram among her profiles of local plantation owners published in Charleston's *News and Courier*. "Whatever it is that they have heard about him, the fact is that everybody in this section has heard of Harry Cram . . ." wrote Martin in August of that year. "He lives in a little white cottage with three servants to take care of him. He raises turkeys and has a lot of dogs that, unleashed, almost match him in energy."

Despite inheriting a waterfront plantation of a few thousand acres, spending his teens playing polo internationally, having a household staff, and baptizing one of his children with the contents of an 1858 bottle of Madeira wine, Cram and his family resisted the characterization that Cram did not work for a living. For years Cram raised about 500 head of cattle at Foot Point, said his son Peter, and only gained a substantial inheritance after the death of his mother, Edith, who was a noted peace activist. Yet compared to most local families, Cram was exempt from regular hardships. "Harry always lived differently from most of his Bluffton neighbors," said one essay about him. "When the natives were planting cotton and working in sawmills to make a living, Harry was playing polo and shooting birds. He never worried about money."

Not that many people seemed to resent Cram for his good fortune and distinguished lineage, which included the inventor of the first American steam locomotive as well as a mayor of New York City. Lowcountry residents were charmed to be in his company, or to receive an invitation to his home. For his part, Cram took the misrepresentations in stride and sometimes used rumor to his advantage. "I hear these wild stories and sometimes I don't discredit them unless the story is just too fantastic," said Cram, who was known by locals as "Mister Harry," though he said he preferred being called "Harry the Bastard." Cram admitted, nonetheless, to indulging in a fair amount of tomfoolery. Indeed, when he was asked to associate a word with his name, he offered, enthusiastically, "Booze!"

His first marriage was to New Yorker Edith Drexel in 1931, who died just three years later at age twenty-three, leaving her husband and a young son, Jackie, as survivors. Then, in 1936, Cram became engaged to socialite and equestrian Ruth Vaux of Philadelphia. They planned a wedding but then impulsively got married before dawn one morning in October after Ruth came to visit Harry at Foot Point. It was after midnight when they knocked on a judge's door in the small South Carolina town of Ridgeland. Because the couple was alone, the judge pulled his wife from bed to have a witness to the ceremony. Afterward the newlyweds were somehow involved in an accident that overturned their car in Bluffton. They survived and continued on to the DeSoto hotel in Savannah for their wedding night, the management apparently having forgiven Cram for the horse incident.

Just a few years after Vaux settled into life at Foot Point, World War II began, with the United States entering the conflict in December 1941. Harry Cram soon joined the U.S. Coast Guard as an officer and was deployed as a commander aboard a ship guarding the Panama Canal. He apparently saw no combat. "I only fired two shots in anger," Cram recalled after the war. "One was at an admiral and the other was at the Corps of Engineers." His wife Ruth, meanwhile, joined the U.S. Navy, which in 1942 created its WAVES program (Women Accepted for Voluntary Emergency Service) and enlisted tens of thousands of female reservists. It was about this time that Ruth Vaux Cram met Buster Murdaugh at a luncheon.

Buster was home for the war, exempt from the draft on account of his position as solicitor. Though he was far from the front lines, Buster still sought to aid the troops, a group that included his younger brother, Johnny, who had joined the army. Buster became chairman of Hampton County's chapter of the Red Cross just ten days after the bombing of Pearl Harbor and immediately began to raise money—the first of several fundraising drives he orchestrated that contributed thousands of dollars to war relief.

During their conversation over lunch, Ruth told Buster she longed for a discharge from the navy and to be back home at Foot Point, overseeing the cattle plantation's operations. Foot Point, she told him, was the place where she could be of the most use to the war effort. In response Buster offered to help, volunteering to use his position with the Red Cross to help her leave the navy. He promised to write an official letter requesting her return, and subsequently made numerous trips, including two visits with US senators, to secure Ruth's release from the navy in September 1944. She came home to an empty Foot Point, as husband Harry was still guarding the Panama Canal. Buster, about to turn thirty years old, soon took Harry's place.

On November 1, 1945, Ruth gave birth to a boy, Roberts, in the rural Colleton County town of Smoaks, far from Foot Point. He was not the son of her husband Harry Cram, but rather Buster Murdaugh, according to many friends and associates of Buster and Roberts. One friend said the men looked the same, were shaped the same, and walked the same. "You'd have to be an idiot not to see it," he said.

Buster occasionally confirmed his paternity, usually when drunk. One confidante remembers driving Buster home from a meeting they attended together, sipping alcohol as they drove down the highway. At some point Buster blurted out a confession in the form of a question: "You know Roberts Vaux is my son?" Apart from these brief moments of alcohol-induced candor, said another friend of the Murdaughs, the matter "wasn't discussed and wasn't denied." Though Buster did not publicly acknowledge his son Roberts, the boy, and later man, would forever be in and out of his life.

The secret was not kept from Buster's wife for long. Buster told at least two people that one day Ruth Vaux Cram, either while pregnant or having just given birth, paid a visit to Buster's wife, Gladys. The ladies sat together on the Murdaugh's front porch, in view of the goings-on of downtown Varnville and the railroad and highway. It might have seemed from afar like two friends were enjoying lemonade. But really Ruth Vaux was confessing her affair with Buster.

Buster had earlier learned of Ruth's impending visit and bombshell confession, perhaps warned by Ruth herself. He reacted poorly—plain flipped out—and skipped town, his mind racing to discover a way to prevent disclosure and disaster. He fretted over Gladys's reaction. He knew the revelation of such a secret could cause the collapse of his marriage and his budding political career. Buster knew he could be ruined.

As the storm descended he left town with a bottle of liquor in tow. He drove south into Jasper County, a part of South Carolina where the forests are particularly thick and wild, like a dense jungle, until the road terminated at the Savannah River. Stokes Bluff was the end of the line. Across the water lay the state of Georgia. Buster sat and watched the river flow slowly around a bend on its serpentine path to the ocean. The liquor poured down the panicked man's throat made a similar journey, navigating the turns of his guts as he attempted to dull his nerves and formulate an escape. "The drunker I got, the braver I got," Buster later recalled to his friend in the car as they drove down the highway with a drink in hand.

Ultimately, perhaps when the liquor bottle went dry, Buster left Stokes Bluff and returned home to confront Gladys's fury head-on. Whatever the fallout, the Murdaughs' marriage remained intact. In the wake of the disclosure of Buster's affair, he and Gladys traveled to New York City with their friends Oswald and Louise Lightsey, and hosted other couples at their home on Edisto Island for weekend getaways. Gladys, bound by tradition, might have felt she had no choice but to suffer the humiliation of Buster's romance with Ruth Vaux Cram, who soon divorced her husband.

Supposedly, the Murdaugh family's housekeeper overheard the conversation between Ruth and Gladys on the porch and relayed this information to the Murdaughs' friends, S. F. and Betty Crews of Hampton. In the housekeeper's telling, Ruth expressed hope to Gladys that her child would have a relationship with his six-year-old half brother, Randy III, according to the Crews's son, Sam, who grew up close to the Murdaugh family and visited Buster on his deathbed. Gladys supposedly replied that she was aware of the situation. It was not to be discussed further.

There are many things Cam Mixson lost the night of March 9, 2007. He lost his little red car, a Honda Civic, when it crashed into a semitruck stopped perpendicularly across a country road in darkness. He lost most of his frontal lobe when his skull smashed into a steel beam and his brains turned to what he called "silly putty." He lost his lower field of vision and became legally blind, unable to see his shoelaces, the sidewalk, or his plate of food at the dinner table without looking directly downward. He lost the ease with which he used to navigate life, changing from a top-notch high school student and athlete to a teenager struggling with depression, attention-deficit/hyperactivity disorder, and memory lapses. He also lost his fifteen-year-old buddy, Stevie McAlhaney, who was riding beside him in the front seat.

The last thing Cam remembers from that night is leaving the McAlhaney family's driveway. It was Friday night and the two soccer players from Wade Hampton High School were off to join some teammates. Just before 8:00 P.M., ninety minutes after sunset, Cam drove his friend Stevie south on Rock Springs Road, a rural, two-lane highway lined with pine trees, which more or less describes every road in Hampton County. Up ahead, in the darkness, a pickup truck was pulled off on the left side of the road, pointed toward them. The high beams of the truck's headlights burned bright, directly into the eyes of sixteen-year-old Cam, the oncoming driver.

Down the road Jerome Manigo sat in the cab of his semitruck. He had been hired to haul away the seventy-six-foot-long mobile home that sat atop his semitruck's trailer, which stretched behind him. He wasn't transporting the mobile home until the next day, but tonight he and a few men were putting the trailer into position so it would be ready to be hauled in the morning. To do so Manigo had to reverse his semitruck down a narrow driveway on a wooded lot in the dark. As he waited for the mobile home's owner to shine a light behind him so he could avoid hitting trees, the front of the semitruck stuck out of the driveway, into and across the road entirely, blocking both lanes of traffic and even nosing over and onto the opposite shoulder. Manigo had a small, weak yellow light flashing atop his cab, but no lights or reflectors along the trailer or mobile home to otherwise warn motorists of the blocked road. There were no streetlights this far outside of town. His semitruck was essentially a steel wall parked across a country highway, invisible in the darkness.

Neighbor Mark McAlhaney had seen men preparing to move the semitruck loaded with the mobile home and decided he should try and warn approaching motorists of the truck maneuvering across the street in the dark. After speaking with the men, the Good Samaritan pulled his pickup truck onto the grassy shoulder of Rock Spring Road, pointed north, with his high-beam headlights turned on and his flashing hazard lights activated. Soon enough, a car approached but alarmingly rolled past McAlhaney and his truck without slowing. It was traveling at least thirty miles per hour and headed straight for the looming semitruck. "I saw a vehicle coming and tried to wave them down," McAlhaney told police. "They did not stop then I heard the crash."

Moments after the accident, Richard and Karen Sullivan were driving south on Rock Spring Road, traveling the same path Mixson's red Honda had just traveled. They saw a truck parked on the shoulder on the opposite side of the road, pointed toward them with its headlights shining bright, blinding them and distracting their attention to the side of the road. As Richard Sullivan later recounted in a written statement to police: "I waz runing speed of 50 to 55 MPH and thir waz a man on high beam I could not see nonthing."

As the Sullivans unknowingly approached the accident scene, seemingly destined to join the crash and begin a pileup, Richard Sullivan rolled down his window two inches so he could exhale after puffing on a cigarette. This was the rare instance of smoking prolonging one's life.

As he drove past the truck shining its headlights, the truck's driver, Mark McAlhaney, yelled from the side of the road, "Hey, STOP!" Sullivan heard the warning loud and clear, just as he saw the vehicle wreck suddenly materialize in the darkness ahead. He braked hard and pulled to the southbound side of the road. Sullivan credits McAlhaney for saving them from a pileup, writing, "If it were not for him me and my wife would be thir to." Added Richard's wife, Karen Sullivan, in her own statement: "The Honda Civic was halfway underneath the front end of the trailer. We did not even see what had happened until the man driving the vehicle on the side of the road hollered at us to stop."

Richard Sullivan activated the car's blinking hazard lights and exited their car. They questioned the truck driver, Manigo, who was uninjured and kept saying, "Oh my God! Oh my God!" again and again while another man helping to move the mobile home called 911 to report the crash.

Meanwhile another vehicle moving south on Rock Spring Road approached the scene, again threatening a pileup. But driver Linda Stanley saw the bright headlights on McAlhaney's truck as well as the flashing hazard lights on the Sullivans' vehicle, spurring her to pull to the side of the road, behind the Sullivans' car. Her husband Richard exited his car and asked McAlhaney to turn off his headlights, telling him, "We can't see anything."

His wife, Linda, inspected the wrecked vehicles. The red Honda Civic was wedged beneath the mobile home and the trailer, its front end destroyed and its windshield smashed. "I approached the car under the mobile home on the driver's side and the driver was bleeding from the face and alert," Linda Stanley wrote in a statement to police. "I asked about the passenger and no one even knew there was a passenger. I walked around and was unable to see anything other than his arm. The trailer was against his face." This was poor Stevie McAlhaney, who happened to be the nephew of Mark McAlhaney, the neighbor who tried to warn cars with his headlights.

Emergency personnel arrived more than five minutes later and used tools to extricate the teenagers from the wreck. Cam Mixson was taken to the Hampton hospital and then flown to a larger hospital in Columbia. Stevie McAlhaney was airlifted to a hospital in Augusta, Georgia, where he died about five hours later. Stevie was remembered as a kind and gentle teen who enjoyed playing soccer, being outdoors, and spending time with his family.

His high school soccer coach called him "one of the finest young men I've had the pleasure to coach" and his English teacher praised him for a recent speech he gave about the dangers of underage drinking, saying, "He was relaxed and was speaking from his heart. Students like him didn't come along every day. He was a Christian and everybody knew it and he didn't mind that everybody knew it."

Cam survived, barely. He suffered a traumatic brain injury and spent months learning how to walk and talk again, a process his mother Rose Ann Mixson described as a total rewiring of his brain. Cam could only eat pureed food in the immediate aftermath of the crash, which caused his weight to drop to ninety-five pounds. To help him breathe, doctors inserted a tracheostomy tube through a hole they made in his neck and windpipe. When the tube was removed and his neck was left to heal, new skin grew over the wound but also across the inside of his windpipe, gradually restricting his airflow and almost killing him, again.

After all this, he endured reconstructive surgery "to lift my face out and align it properly." He made sure to schedule the realignment of his jaw and lower face after his graduation. As Cam described the surgery in 2009: "It will be sort of like taking your car to the auto body shop. They will cut the titanium plates, lift it up, weld some bars to it to hold it in place and I will be good to go. The best part of all of this is I will be able to get rid of these braces. Later I will need dental implants but I am not going to worry about that now."

In time Cam regained his health and independence. But even as his body generally healed from being crushed, there remained the vision problems, depression, ADHD, and an overall struggle to restore his full self. He tried to stay upbeat about his recovery, but sometimes that positive attitude disguised the challenges he endured. "I certainly do not mean to sound like it has been easy," he wrote two years after the accident. "Even now, every day is still a tremendous struggle, but I will never give up."

After an investigation, the South Carolina Highway Patrol concluded a few factors contributed to the crash. First, Manigo had "illegally stopped" his semitruck with a mobile home across both lanes of the road. He deployed no flares, flagmen, or signals to warn motorists of the obstruction ahead. His trailer and the mobile home lacked reflectors and lights.

Second, the highway patrol found that the well-intentioned efforts by McAlhaney to warn oncoming motorists with his truck headlights "might have created a vision problem for the driver of the Honda." Lastly, the report noted that Cam possessed "limited driving experience," and that, because of his young age and restricted driver's license, he should not have been driving beyond 6:00 P.M., unless for a school event.

In the wake of the crash, Manigo was charged with involuntary manslaughter. Investigators claimed he lacked vehicle insurance, failed to obtain a permit to move the mobile home, and was illegally transporting a mobile home at night. His criminal record included charges for fraudulent checks and breach of trust, said Assistant Solicitor Tameaka Legette, and in the last ten years he was charged with more than thirty traffic violations, mostly for speeding, failure to pay tickets, and for lapses in his insurance. Following the accident, state transport police charged him with a dozen violations for his semitruck, mostly for broken lights and turn signals. Manigo responded by telling a judge, "Ten to fourteen years ago, I was younger and I did speed and got tickets, but I never got a ticket in that commercial truck." Assistant Solicitor Tameaka Legette asked the judge for a high bond and to curb Manigo's driving privileges, stating, "We believe Manigo is a severe danger to the community because he is still allowed to drive on the streets and he can still drive a truck." Comparatively, Cam Mixson had been driving for sixteen months and had a clean driving record. The highway patrol report noted both he and Stevie McAlhaney were wearing seatbelts, the car was not believed to be speeding, and no alcohol or drugs were involved.

After the accident the McAlhaney family retained Alex Murdaugh as their lawyer. In June 2008, fifteen months after the accident, he filed a pair of lawsuits on behalf of Stevie's mother, Linda McAlhaney, who was serving as the personal representative of her son's estate. One lawsuit sought compensation for Stevie's wrongful death and the consequences faced by his family. The other was a survival action, which sought compensation for Stevie's suffering and injuries during the five or so hours he lived following the accident. Alex did not file the lawsuits against the semitruck driver, Manigo, whose business owned the semitruck that was stopped across the road in darkness and lacked safety equipment. He did not sue the owner of the mobile home who had hired Manigo, either, or the Good Samaritan who inadvertently blinded several motorists. Instead, on behalf of his client, Murdaugh sued the father of Cam Mixson, alleging that Richard Mixson negligently allowed his son to drive a family car "when he knew Cameron Mixson was not authorized to drive and that his driving at night posed a threat to others." The lawsuits claimed young Cam did not keep a "proper lookout" and was driving too fast. He failed to stop, slow, or turn to avoid danger, and failed "to act as a reasonably prudent person would under the same or similar circumstances."

Alex's legal strategy was transparent: Forget who might be most liable and focus instead on who can pay the most. In this case it was likely Mixson's insurer, Encompass Insurance. The Good Samaritan's auto insurance policy was comparatively paltry, and the semitruck driven by Manigo was not insured at all. This spurred Alex to target Richard Mixson alone with his lawsuit, especially since his policy allowed for additional financial recovery from uninsured motorists as well as umbrella coverage, which amplifies the typical insurance reimbursements. By targeting Mixson only, Alex did not risk diluting or complicating a reward by requiring a jury to assign blame among multiple parties, including parties unable to pay. It was advantageous, financially speaking, to place all the blame on Mixson alone in the lawsuit. Indeed, one plaintiff's lawyer familiar with this case said it would have been malpractice for Alex to have passed up the chance to sue a party to the accident that was well insured. His duty, the lawyer said, was to his client alone. Typically, plaintiff's lawyers like Alex received 33 to 45 percent of a client's settlement or award at trial, meaning in some cases they earned almost as much as the people they represented.

Alex crafted and directed his legal maneuvers from the big brick headquarters of Peters, Murdaugh, Parker, Eltzroth & Detrick on Mulberry Street in downtown Hampton. In the seven years he had worked at the old family law firm he developed a strong reputation with clients. Alex was "very good at reading people, very good at understanding people, and very good at making people believe he cared about them and building a rapport and trust with them," said one of his law partners, Ronnie Crosby. "And he was very good at strategizing against insurance companies and opposing lawyers . . . (T)he lawyers in the firm would be really amazed at what a good job he was able to do."

Yet Alex could pose challenges in the workplace, too. He kept irregular hours, most often arriving at the office by late morning or early afternoon. Other times he showed up at 5:00 P.M., just when his colleagues and administrative staff were preparing to head home. His entrances were reliably chaotic and disruptive. Colleagues called him the "Tasmanian Devil," because when he arrived things started spinning and getting crazy.

Alex was "always loud, always busy, always in a rush," said the law firm's chief financial officer, Jeanne Seckinger. He was inconsistent as a boss, sometimes yelling when he was irritated. He was forgetful and careless. He talked nonstop on his cell phone and would regularly cut short face-to-face conversations to pick up a phone call, especially a call from his family. Sometimes Alex would even take calls in the middle of legal depositions or meetings. "It'd aggravate the hell out of me," said his law partner Mark Ball. "He was an obnoxious user of a cell phone."

One Hampton man knew a number of young lawyers at the law firm, some of whom regularly worked weekends. Alex was the exception to this industrious crew. "I never thought Alex worked too hard," said the man. He observed that Alex had to be the center of attention at all times, that he was always the loudest person at restaurants and parties, maxing out in every way. Alex "had a volume of 10, all the time," said the man. "100 miles per hour."

One lawyer in the Lowcountry who repeatedly witnessed Alex's loud, overbearing behavior said he judged Alex to be either "not self-aware, or he didn't care, probably the latter." In contrast to other lawyers at the firm, including his brother Randy, Alex had a swagger and acted the alpha male. He'd regularly seat himself in the center of a room, his hulking frame, red hair, and booming voice making him impossible to ignore. Alex always seemed full of himself, said the lawyer.

A longtime acquaintance of Alex shared similar impressions. Alex was a narcissist, he said, who loved to talk about himself but who just stared blankly as someone responded, waiting for his chance to talk again. "He never listened to anyone that wasn't important," said the longtime acquaintance. He considered Alex an "underhanded piece of shit" who acted "a bully all of his teenage and adult life."

Another acquaintance from Hampton County deemed Alex arrogant, though he conceded not everyone was turned off by him. "He had friends, but they were plastic people," said this man. "When it gets hot, plastic melts." Alex was lazy, said this man, and would disappear whenever someone needed help with physical work. If someone had a flat tire, he said, Alex would drive right by them.

Alex did not engage in much self-reflection, and apologies were rarely uttered. One acquaintance remembers a time when Alex slept late and fouled up their plans to go fishing early in the morning. The man complained to Alex about him oversleeping, especially since Alex insisted they get an early start. Alex shrugged it off, a response the man found typical of Alex and his family: "They're sorry you got your feelings hurt, but they're not sorry."

In legal negotiations, Alex was not subtle in his approach, blatantly touting his hometown advantage. "Bo', you know what it's like in Hampton

County," he'd say during negotiations with opposing counsel, just before outlining his proposal for settlement, according to one Lowcountry lawyer. Few other attorneys were so bold, said the lawyer, but "(Alex) said the quiet parts out loud."

Two months after Murdaugh filed suit against Richard Mixson for the auto accident, Rose Ann Mixson, Cam's mother and Richard's wife, filed a small flurry of lawsuits on behalf of her severely injured son. Unlike the lawsuit drafted and filed by Alex Murdaugh, these lawsuits targeted the other parties involved in the collision, namely the semitruck driver Manigo; the owner of the mobile home; the Good Samaritan Mark McAlhaney, and lastly her family's insurance company, Encompass.

From this legal crossfire came cooperation—the McAlhaneys and Mixsons agreed to the creation of a joint settlement fund in which settlement money would be pooled and then split between the families. Soon Alex Murdaugh and the Mixson family's attorneys negotiated approximately $2 million in settlements from the mobile home owner's insurer as well as the Mixson family's insurer. Alex made sure to include a provision in a settlement order signed by Judge Carmen Mullen in December 2008 that made sure he was paid first when some of the money was released to the settlement fund.

In 2007, the criminal case against Manigo for involuntary manslaughter was transferred from the solicitor's office to the South Carolina Attorney General's Office because of a conflict of interest involving the office's volunteer assistant solicitor. As 14th Circuit Solicitor Duffie Stone, successor to Alex's father, wrote to the attorney general's office four months after the accident, "Alex Murdaugh has a pre-existing relationship with the victims in this case. Mr. Murdaugh along with his law firm will be representing the victim's family in a civil matter related to this crime. A few of the members of the Murdaugh firm work for my office. To avoid any appearance of impropriety, I am asking you to take over the Reckless Homicide case."

The criminal case lingered for more than three years, delaying any potential conviction that would have squarely placed criminal responsibility on the semitruck driver Manigo. Meanwhile the civil actions initiated by Alex settled, relying on payments from insurers for the other parties involved in the crash. Finally, in August 2011, after consultation with a deputy Lowcountry prosecutor, a highway patrol officer, and an unnamed plaintiff's attorney associated with the accident, the case against Manigo was dismissed by a prosecutor in the state attorney general's office. "There appears to be a consensus that this is the unfortunate but necessary outcome of this charge based on the applicable legal standards and the totality of facts in this case," wrote Assistant Deputy Attorney General David Stumbo in an email. As Stumbo told the McAlhaney and Mixson families in separate meetings in the Lowcountry, the initial charge made by the Highway Patrol was too severe, a mistake Stumbo said would be fatal to the case. The families were disappointed, but at least took solace that the semitruck driver would be cited for safety violations by the Highway Patrol, according to a memo from the attorney general's office.

Three months later, however, Rose Anne Mixson called the attorney general's office to say she was baffled as to why the case could not be prosecuted; she wanted the semitruck driver tried for manslaughter, not merely ticketed. Behind the scenes, Assistant Deputy Attorney General Stumbo was hardly sympathetic to the plight of the traumatized mother or her son, who suffered severe brain injury and lost a friend in the crash. "These people are just hard headed," Stumbo wrote in a message to a colleague after being told of Rose Ann Mixson's displeasure. "It is as if that 2 hour meeting that we had with them a couple of months ago in Hampton did not even happen."

More than sixteen years after the accident, Cam Mixson has remained disappointed. He resented the fact that he was singled out for causing the accident, accused in the lawsuit filed by Alex Murdaugh of speeding and reckless driving despite the fact that a semitruck lay stretched across the highway in darkness while a pickup truck pointed its headlights' bright beams up the road and into the eyes of approaching motorists. For Cam, this was insult upon injury. To him, Alex Murdaugh caused an already terrible moment to become "worse than it needed to be."

"Why do I feel like I'm the criminal in this case?" said Cam. "There was never any justice."

———

Even if she had sought a divorce, Gladys would have had trouble finding a lawyer to take her case. The first divorce case in Hampton County was not filed until 1949, four years after Buster and Ruth's affair. By that time Gladys was having another of Buster's babies—daughter Brenda. And in any case, the lawyer boldly filing these early divorce lawsuits was none other than her husband. Of the first thirteen filings for divorce in Hampton County, Buster was legal counsel for twelve of them.

Already Buster had gained experience handling at least one divorce case in neighboring Beaufort County: the legal split in 1945 between Ruth Vaux and her husband Harry Cram. After the episode with the navy, this was the second time Buster helped rescue Ruth Vaux from an unpleasant union. According to Ruth, Buster insisted that he handle the divorce case pro bono; he had helped rupture the marriage, after all. Ruth apparently balked and insisted that she pay Buster, though the two never seemed to settle on an exact fee after contemplating assorted arrangements. Despite the lack of clarity Buster filed for Ruth's divorce from Cram. The complaint focused on alleged physical abuse by her husband and not any adultery she perpetrated. In splitting their assets, Ruth took claim to twenty-one cows, all of which now needed a new home. She placed them on Buster's farm in Varnville, supposedly at his invitation.

After Ruth left Foot Point, Harry Cram remained on the plantation and soon married for the third time, about the summer of 1945. One day soon afterward he and his new bride, Eloise, were visiting Savannah when they bumped into Ruth Vaux. In conversation with his former wife Cram mentioned that he had just sent off a $25,000 check to finalize the divorce. Ruth reacted with confusion. Her attorney, Buster Murdaugh, had told her the settlement with Cram was for $15,000. Where was the extra $10,000?

Buster, it turns out, had pocketed this money. When confronted by Ruth he offered a scattered, shifting, and ever-evolving story of why this was justified and how he would repay at least a portion of the difference, though he soon reneged on this promise. Ruth soon became exasperated by Buster's slippery tactics and embarked on a prolonged journey to find a local lawyer with the gumption to sue the solicitor. Finally she hired Hampton attorney Hugh O. Hanna, who proceeded to write Murdaugh what he described as a "fair, polite but firm letter requesting payment." When Murdaugh stalled and made no meaningful response, Hanna delivered an ultimatum: pay by February 6, 1948, or get sued. Backed into a corner, Buster decided to beat Hanna to the punch. Just as the deadline approached Buster filed his own lawsuit against Ruth Vaux in early February 1948, accusing her of misrepresenting their fee agreement and owing him money for the care of her abandoned cows, who languished on Buster's farm during all the years of discord and eventually perished. Vaux responded with her own lawsuit a few weeks later, complaining that since Buster kept the cows he should pay her for the animals.

For as much animosity that existed between Buster and Ruth, the dispute did not immediately explode into public view. That was no accident. At the request of Buster's lawyer Thomas M. Boulware, the case was transferred from Hampton County to Calhoun County in the center of the state after two local judges recused themselves from handling the matter. The law-suits lay undiscovered in the Calhoun County Courthouse for a year until newspaper reporter Frank K. Myers of the Charleston *News and Courier* excitedly learned their details. In a report he described the legal filings as "interesting if somewhat complicated reading . . . Involved are a maze of complaints, charges, cross-complaints and countercharges. Among the verbiage is some wordage that would smoke up asbestos paper."

When it came to money, Buster claimed Ruth had approved all his fees. Moreover, Buster said he advised Ruth on a number of business matters and in turn made her a lot of money. Ruth disputed Buster's claims about his fee. And when it came to her investments, she said Buster only tried to seize control of them, not earn her money. As her lawsuit claimed: "He made a studied effort to find out what investments that this defendant had and (a) studied effort to get his hands on this defendant's investments and securities." Ruth was not the only one to get the impression that Buster had rapacious instincts. One Lowcountry lawyer marveled at the damage wrought by Buster at Foot Point. When Harry Cram came back home from war, quipped the lawyer, "The cows were gone, the trees were cut, the plantation had a mortgage and he had a(nother) son."

When it came to the cows, Ruth complained Buster owed her $2,000 to replace the dead animals. Buster refused, claiming the cows were dumped on his farm without permission, that the animals were diseased, and that many of the cows were "wild and unruly," rampaging through fencing and damaging crops on neighboring farms. Disease spread to his own herd of cows, claimed Buster, and he paid a small fortune to repair the fences, reimburse the neighbors, and pay a veterinarian to treat the ailing cows.

Just as the case came up for a public hearing in Calhoun County, lawyers announced a settlement had been reached, that somehow the conflicts over cash and cows had been privately resolved. Negotiations had been bitter. Ruth's lawyer, Hanna, provided a statement to the Hampton newspaper that lamented he could not share details of the settlement. Said Hanna: "Mr. Boulware, Murdaugh's attorney, asked and stated that he would like to avoid any publicity and avoid making the settlement and its terms a part of the public record in the case."

Buster refused to be humiliated by Hanna without a fierce response. He penned his own letter to the *Hampton County Guardian*, disparaging his opponent by stating "reputable lawyers make it a practice not to try cases in the newspaper." He nevertheless proceeded to challenge Hanna's assertions and minimize the rancor on display between him and Ruth Vaux, who he described, deliberately and unflatteringly, as "a very wealthy Northern woman." He mocked Ruth for having difficulty finding legal counsel, suggesting this meant her legal complaints were trifling. Most notably, in trademark fashion, Buster sought to slyly establish a favorable narrative, to characterize facts in the most beneficial light. Buster's affable yet authoritative take on the matter allowed for no other interpretation of events. "I might say in passing that there was nothing unusual about the matter at all, except a difference between Mrs. Cram and myself as to the amount of the fee," he wrote to the newspaper. "My position was substantiated by many reputable citizens, including two circuit judges, who would have testified had the case proceeded to trial.

"Frankly, an attempt is being made to make much ado about nothing," continued Buster, "and, of course, being in politics my political enemies are attempting to lower themselves and hurt me by spreading malicious rumors and by requesting that statements of this case be printed."

But Ruth Vaux—and unnamed, phantom political adversaries—were not the only people accusing Buster of not paying what he owed. In 1946 Buster and a business partner bought the Hampton Furniture Manufacturing Company, where a staff of twenty-five people made wooden chests, beds, radio cabinets, and more. Three years later the business stopped making its loan payments, leading the sheriff to seize the furniture factory in March of 1949, just a month after Buster paid an unknown amount of money in his settlement with Ruth Vaux, who had been demanding $11,000 from the solicitor.

Despite the sheriff taking hold of the building, Murdaugh would not admit to being broke, or to any problem. He told the newspaper he shut the business down temporarily as he negotiated the sale of the furniture plant, and that a buyer sat waiting in the wings. Three months later, however, no sale had occurred and the business was still in debt. In July of 1949, a judge ordered the furniture business to be taken over by a receiver and sold to the highest bidder. A week later, its furniture merchandise, drum sanders, saws, and stacks of plywood were all being liquidated to settle outstanding loans.

While the bank accused Buster of being delinquent, others believed him to be a deadbeat and outright crook. Beyond Ruth Vaux, Buster was sued for $50,000 in 1949 by another client who accused him of withholding, or stealing, money through a fraudulent breach of trust. Hampton resident J. V. McMillan claimed he entrusted Buster with at least $4,200 and asked him to pay off two small mortgages and hospital bills before obtaining him a new loan. Buster did not pay off the two mortgages as requested, alleged McMillan, but rather kept the bulk of the money for his own use and made minimal mortgage payments to keep the bank satisfied.

Buster responded to the latest accusations much the same way he did before: he denied wrongdoing, downplayed the gravity of the charges, tried to rewrite the script, and complained the financial dispute was really a political attack. "I will welcome a full, complete, and impartial hearing, for I have no fear of a full disclosure of the truth," said Buster. "I know that I have committed no legal or moral wrong in the transaction. I am at a loss to understand fully why these charges have been made." Then Buster countersued McMillan for $825 for financial advances Buster allegedly made on his client's behalf.

This latest complaint from McMillan, as well as other unspecified allegations, prompted an outcry from many Lowcountry lawyers, who urged the South Carolina Bar to convene an investigation of Buster Murdaugh's personal and professional conduct. The bar complied, appointing Murdaugh's new antagonist, fellow Hampton attorney Hanna, as one of two chief investigators. Over the next two months the bar convened closed-door meetings in Columbia and Hampton, listening to testimony from more

than seventy witnesses. At one session in Columbia, the testimony lasted
for two days at the Wade Hampton Hotel, where all witnesses, including
a number of state politicians and a pair of bankers, were sworn to secrecy.
Yet the extensive investigation apparently failed to yield anything damning.
In October 1949, the bar's grievance committee dismissed all complaints
against Buster Murdaugh. The solicitor celebrated his vindication, stating,
"I welcomed a full and complete investigation of my dealings with my
clients and am happy that every possible complaint was heard fully and
was completely dismissed."

Despite having his name dragged through the mud, Buster emerged
from assorted scandals with his reputation intact. Far from being a pariah,
politicians around the state embraced Buster and were proud to share a stage
with him. A few months after Buster was cleared of misconduct, he hosted
South Carolina governor Strom Thurmond at a large barbecue to celebrate
the grand opening of new stockyards in the town of Yemassee. More than
1,500 people stood under a sunny summer sky to chew on pork hash,
gobble up rice, and listen to State Senator George Warren of Hampton
praise Thurmond while also railing against racial integration and the work
of the National Association for the Advancement of Colored People. Three
months later, Buster hunted doves outside of Hampton with Thurmond. A
few years after that Buster hosted US senator Olin D. Johnston for a hunt
at his buddy Oswald Lightsey's sprawling Laurel Spring plantation. It was
hard to turn Buster down.

Beyond making political inroads, Buster earned the respect of local
police. Typical of admirers was Sidney DuPree, who met Buster in 1953
when he was a state trooper. Buster became a longtime friend to DuPree, in
part because Buster was so loyal to the men and women wearing a badge
in the Lowcountry. DuPree described Buster as a "law enforcement solicitor.
He defended and protected the law enforcement officers in his district. He
went to bat for them. He did for me, I know." Judges, too, continued to
appreciate Buster's performance as solicitor. Under Buster's watch, case

backlogs were minimal or nonexistent and conviction rates were high. On May 21, 1951, Judge J. Frank Eatmon wrote Buster a letter of praise that was later published as part of a political advertisement. "My reaction to your work in the Court leads me to say that you have no superior in the office of Solicitor in this state," wrote the judge. "Your work had been most outstanding and you have an unusual sense of fairness and justice . . . Such conduct on your part will certainly have the effect of keeping the public confidence in our judicial system." With this kind of backing, Buster once again cruised to reelection in 1952, easily fending off another attempt by Walterboro lawyer "Stumpy" McLeod to take his place in the solicitor's office.

Between prosecuting criminals, operating his private law practice, and defending himself against assorted accusations, it might seem like Buster Murdaugh eternally occupied Lowcountry courtrooms. He mostly did, though he also made time to enjoy the outdoors and the company of his friends and family. Despite his financial troubles Buster took up flying in the late 1940s and bought an airplane. He took day trips to Georgia and Florida, often in the company of Clyde Eltzroth, his friend and fellow amateur pilot. Eltzroth worked as the county's tax collector by day and studied law books in Buster's office at night, with the goal of becoming a lawyer.

Buster's wife and young children also kept him busy. Gladys was regarded as a true lady—always refined, polite, and elegantly dressed. She and Buster appeared together often at social events and regularly entertained friends. The couple's young daughter, Brenda, particularly enjoyed accompanying her father to Columbia when she was a tot, so she could ride the elevators at the State House. And their boy Randolph Murdaugh III, nicknamed Randy, was a natural athlete, much like his parents. Though he worshipped and emulated his father, Randy's personality was judged to be more like his mother's, meaning he was kinder, less devious, and less greedy. Buster once laughed as he recalled when Randolph first bared his bleeding heart. "I remember a time when I took that there boy fishing," said Buster, pointing at his son as he started spinning a yarn. "He couldn't have been more than six or seven. We were sitting on the bank of the river when the sheriff came down and got us . . ."

The sheriff told Buster that he had recovered a body and detained a suspect, a man who said he would only speak with the solicitor. Buster left the fishing hole and met with the murder suspect, letting young Randy tag along so he could be a witness to a possible confession. The man, who was a brother to the murder victim, indeed confessed, telling a story of hard luck and the extenuating circumstances that led to his sibling's death. Unfortunately for the suspect, he gained the sympathy of the wrong Murdaugh, the one who would not become solicitor himself for another forty years. Little Randy told his father he refused to testify against the suspect and certify the details of his confession. Buster found it all amusing. "I told him he could just sit in court then and hold his subpoena," said the solicitor.

———

Not much changes in Hampton, at least not quickly. Its population—20,000 people in the county, including 3,000 within the town limits—has been static for decades. There is little intrusion from modernity or any other outside influence. One of the few indications of the passage of time is the prevalence of peeling paint.

Bits of folksiness brightened an otherwise rundown community. A giant watermelon slice with a bite taken out of it is painted on the water tower in town, and some of the municipal fire hydrants are painted as watermelons—nods to the famous Hampton County Watermelon Festival held each June, which for a long time was the sole reason outsiders knew about Hampton.

The Chit Chat Show broadcasts on Big Dog Radio every weekday morning from Allendale, just up the road from Hampton, where father-and-son hosts take calls from listeners, sometimes helping facilitate the sale of reclining chairs and aluminum boats, sometimes hearing gripes from feuding public officials, and sometimes listening to the elderly detail their medical challenges. Every day the hosts hold a popular call-in drawing, giving away free lunches from fish camps and other restaurants. They also endlessly plug the Lowcountry businesses they count as sponsors, advertising a rare coin buyer one moment and a purveyor of fresh quail eggs the next.

Forestry products and lumber companies have always been active in Hampton, and their legacy is felt in downtown Hampton, where most developed lots have been cleared almost entirely of trees. Nearby communities, namely Beaufort and Ridgeland, have downtown neighborhoods enchantingly shaded by plentiful live oak and magnolia trees. Those trees are long gone in Hampton, where there is little refuge from the summer sun. Even in Hampton's Exchange Park, a small square where the few crepe myrtles planted on its perimeter have not been pruned as much as lopped. Tree lovers refer to this single, artless, horizontal cut as "crepe murder."

Across the street from the park is the Hampton County Courthouse, a place that handles the resolution of other types of murder. The brick building features a cornerstone. On one exposed face it reads HAMPTON C.H. 1878. On the other is engraved REMODLED 1925, the stone mason making a misspelling that has survived the ages, one of many things to go uncorrected in Hampton County.

Solicitor Randolph "Randy" Murdaugh III walked past that cornerstone each time he reported to the courthouse to prosecute wrongdoing at terms of criminal court. Lowcountry voters first elected him to the solicitor's office in 1988, two years after the governor appointed Randy to the office to replace his legendary father, who retired as solicitor, at least on paper, after almost half a century of service. Not once did Randy face opposition in his five campaigns for public office, a testament to the voters' faith in his legal ability and sense of fairness as well as the hold his family had on the region.

While Buster often instilled fear in others to get what he wanted, Randy instead almost always projected benevolence from the perch of the prosecutor's office. He was not punitive and vindictive like his father, but notably friendly and helpful, said many of his admirers. He was loquacious and charming, especially in comparison to Buster, who engaged in much more clipped and direct conversation as he got older. If Buster ruled by fear and favor, Randy operated through favor alone and was missing the "intimidation factor," said one Lowcountry lawyer. Unlike Buster, he was not quick to anger. No one whispered that Randy dumped people in the swamp. "He helped people," said Jared Newman, another Lowcountry lawyer who was once hired to work as an assistant solicitor for Randy. "That's how people would be beholden to Randolph."

The night and day difference between father and son's temperaments was made apparent to Travis Medlock after his election as South Carolina's attorney general in 1982. Medlock said he was making a speech in Columbia soon after his victory when Buster suddenly stood up in the crowd, waved his arms, balled his fists, and started screaming profanities. He had supported another candidate for attorney general, and he wanted Medlock to know that while other solicitors may cooperate with the incoming attorney general, he would provide no support. Four years later, when Buster retired, Medlock found a much different Murdaugh at the helm of South Carolina's 14th Judicial Circuit. Medlock discovered Randy had a personality very different than his father's. Randy was "genteel" and "friendly," said Medlock. "I got along with him beautifully."

Oftentimes a small effort by the solicitor could resolve a large legal headache for the person seeking his help. Bill Humphries of Bamberg recalled Randy once helped him reinstate his driver's license. There was no fee. "You just thanked them and shut up," said a grateful Humphries.

Former Jasper County sheriff Randy Blackmon worked alongside both father and son. He recalled Buster and Randolph extending loans to poor people, with little hope of being repaid. "They didn't advertise it," said Blackmon. "They were good people and would do anything for you."

Darrell Thomas "Tom" Johnson recalled Randy as "fun-loving," "pleasant," and an "all-around good guy." Randy was always happy to extend a favor, said the lawyer, and the solicitor once asked rhetorically, "What's the use of having the job if you can't help your friends?"

Johnson's wife was once in a small jam and had her hands full, trying unsuccessfully to get the attention of a judge at the courthouse while also holding a small baby on her hip. Randy acted the gentleman and came to her aid. After this introduction they'd occasionally cross paths, sometimes when Randy had his boys Randy IV and Alex in tow. The boys were always polite and greeted him and his wife, remembering their names. "My wife, who is a harsh judge of character, just adored (Randy)," said Johnson, who practiced in Jasper County. "I never doubted he was trying to do the right thing."

Just because they were friends didn't mean this lawyer always got his way. At times he was disappointed with outcomes in criminal cases, said Johnson, but he never believed Randy did anything wrong. Rather, it was just a difference of opinion between him, the defense lawyer, and Randy, the solicitor. "He was somebody you could reason with and persuade," said Johnson.

It made sense to him that Randy would be a nice guy and granted favors when he could. Like every politician, he wanted as many people as possible to like him. As Randy once remarked to Johnson at a cookout: "I've figured out what kind of people I like. I like the people that like me."

And the more favors Randy performed, the more popular he became. One person who sought his help in the early 1990s was Kim Brant, who owned a Hampton carpet cleaning business with her husband. When her daughter was a teenager, Brant became flustered by the constant attention paid to the high school student by a man who was nineteen or twenty years old. Brant was afraid her daughter might start dating the man; he was a few years older and didn't seem to have much ambition. She called Randy at the solicitor's office in desperation and said, "We've got to do something about this!"

"What do you want me to do?" asked Randy.

"I want a restraining order against him," said Brant.

"Okay, I'll do it," said the solicitor.

Randy actually went a step further. In December of 1994, the twenty-year-old man was arrested for contributing to the delinquency of a minor. Seven months later the twenty-year-old had moved on, the charges were dropped, and Randy had banked a favor. "I was on the hook, then," said Brant.

But Randy wasn't the sort to always collect. He was no frills, easygoing, happy-go-lucky, and "more full of shit" than his father, to hear his friends describe him. Newman called him the "accidental solicitor." He played golf with old, dirty clubs and drank beer on the tailgate of a pickup truck after games of men's league softball. His idea of a good time was cold beer, hot meat, a pack of cigarettes, and a lot of friends to consume it all with. He hosted cookouts every month at his father's old farm in Almeda, where he and his wife Libby started living after relocating the almost century-old Murdaugh family home there from downtown Varnville in 2000, an effort that required the removal of mailboxes along two miles of country highway to accommodate the wide load.

The old home was not big or fancy, but it was charming and looked good set off the road next to a pecan grove. The farm in Almeda was typical of the Murdaughs' wealth in that it was nothing extravagant but was more than most enjoyed. One local lawyer admired the home's wraparound porch but said no one would confuse it with Tara, the grand, columned plantation house depicted in the classic Southern novel *Gone with the Wind*. Behind the home was a shed and the cookhouse, which featured a kitchen and a room with a television and couch.

One perk at the house in Almeda was the employment of Barbara Ann Mixson, who started cleaning and cooking for the couple in 2001. Murdaugh family friend Dayle Blackmon praised Mixson's culinary talents, particularly her dish of egg salad with tomatoes and Ritz crackers. "The best thing I've ever eaten," said Dayle, the sheriff's wife.

The Blackmons enjoyed a close relationship with Randy Murdaugh that was evident in their teasing of each other. When Randy the solicitor became a grandfather, he asked for his grandchildren to refer to him as Handsome—a descriptor he said he always coveted. In that spirit Randy then coined a new nickname for the sheriff—Ugly.

While Sheriff Randy Blackmon made arrests and cases in Jasper County for the solicitor's office, his wife Dayle worked as an administrator within the solicitor's office for six years, managing indictments, drug seizures, and capital cases. Dayle was sweet until someone made her sour. One day an attorney told the solicitor she was a bitch. Randy Murdaugh did not necessarily disagree, but told the man Dayle was a keeper. "There's two types of bitches," Randy explained. "There are good bitches and evil bitches. She's a good bitch. She will tell you the way it is. The evil bitches will hurt you."

Randolph applauded South Carolina's debut of its pretrial intervention program, which is intended to reduce incarceration rates and offer alternative forms of rehabilitation. He instituted his own "solicitor's probation" program, too, and was delighted when a defendant made the most of a second chance, such as the man who thanked Randy each Christmas for a previous act of mercy. "To be a good solicitor," said Randy, "you have to develop the insight and be able to recognize when you can help a person and keep him a productive person in society."

Randy sought capital punishment in a handful of cases during his two decades as solicitor, most of them involving shootings that cost the lives of police officers. This hardly made him an aggressive prosecutor by South Carolina standards. His friend and contemporary, Donnie Myers, convicted twenty-eight men on capital charges in his forty-year career as a solicitor overseeing four counties in the central part of South Carolina.

At his best, Solicitor Randy Murdaugh projected a homey, friendly demeanor during criminal trials that inspired kinship between him and the jurors. The theater he performed in the courtroom was more subtle than his father's histrionics. He did not reenact executions on the courtroom floor, like his dad. But he did have a couple of favorite bits, including having one expert witness—a doctor who regularly performed autopsies of homicide victims—use a red marker to draw bullet wounds on his white dress shirt when she was called to the witness stand. Taking off his suit jacket and handing the doctor the marker, Randolph would ask her to detail where the victim had been shot. Inevitably this doctor would make a cute remark, like, "I know your wife is gonna be mad that I ruined your shirt," but Randy insisted she proceed to draw on the immaculate garment stretched across his torso. The staining of the white dress shirt was hard to ignore, and the conspicuous crimson blots remained on Randy's ruined button-down for the rest of the day, long after the witness had left the stand.

Year in and year out Randy deployed the same tactics that had long served him and his father so well. He hosted cookouts to have fun and curry favor and influence. He trotted out the pathologist to mark up his shirt with a marker. He waved victims' bloody clothing in his hands as he strutted around the courtroom. He echoed his father's regular courtroom argument that implied juries were tolerant of crime if they accepted the word of the defendant and voted to acquit a suspect. "If y'all believe that, y'all turn her loose, find her not guilty," he told jurors in the trial of Sarah Nickel, the Lowcountry teenager accused of robbing and murdering her mother, Nell Davis, with two other teens at her marshside home in the Okatie area of Beaufort County in 1999. During his closing argument for Nickel's trial two years later, Randy pleaded fatigue in a bid for sympathy. As he said in court: "Madam foreman and ladies and gentlemen of the jury, I feel like I need to get my walker to come up here and talk to y'all, I'm so much older than that other lawyer over there. And I am old and I'm tired and I'm worn out and I know y'all are. And I promise you I'll be brief."

He then used an analogy mentioning kitchen implements, aware its meaning might be lost on jurors who were one or two generations younger than him:

None of y'all are old enough to remember an old flour sifter. You used to have to put the flour in this sifter and go through it because that left some of the chaff in it and all that. You had to get right down to the flour. Well, that's what y'all have got to do. Y'all have to take the evidence from that witness stand and these physical items and you've got to sift through them and get to the truth.

The jury convicted Nickel of armed robbery but acquitted her of murder. At least one Beaufort County lawyer observed that Randy's grip seemed to be slipping in cases like these, commenting that younger residents, as well as many of the people moving into fast-growing Beaufort County, were not impressed by his aw-shucks personality and country bumpkin act. If so, this was significant; toward the end of Randy's tenure, half the 14th Judicial Circuit's caseload was in Beaufort County alone. On the other hand, Randy did convict each of Nickel's accomplices of murder and armed robbery, though some grumbled the plea deals he struck were too lenient. It was perhaps impossible for any prosecutor to please all parties affected by the murders.

In 2004, Libby Murdaugh retired after teaching for thirty-one years, though she soon campaigned successfully for election to the county school board. Her husband was not far behind her, retiring at the end of 2005, though he remained on the solicitor's office staff as an assistant prosecutor, winding down his career slowly. It was the end of an era, with no other Murdaugh seeking to take his place. Randy's oldest son, sometimes known as Little Randy or Randy IV, was judged by many to be too nice to become a hard-nosed prosecutor, no matter his reputation as a top-notch litigator at the old family law firm. Even Randy III once admitted, "You have to have a little sonofabitch in you to be a prosecutor."

That left Alex, who many said had inherited his grandfather's gift for gab and natural ability to politick. Many people saw him as more friendly and outgoing than his siblings; his law partner Mark Ball said Alex "could talk to a fence post." He had what Dayle Blackmon described as a "likable, boisterous personality." As a young lawyer in Hampton, Alex was "always very respectable," said Dayle's husband, Randy, who would have guessed Alex the likeliest Murdaugh to assume public office. Ball said that at one time Alex said he hoped to succeed his father in the prosecutor's office.

Technically Alex was already a member of the prosecutor's office. Alex's father had made him a volunteer assistant solicitor in 1998, making the appointment official by giving him an assistant solicitor's badge, which Alex normally kept displayed in plain sight atop his car's dashboard or in a cup holder beside the front seat. Alex also obtained a second badge, the one that belonged to his grandfather, Buster, when he was hired by Randy as an assistant solicitor shortly after his retirement from the head of the office in 1987. Alex never took an oath when his father appointed him a prosecutor. "It was a very informal process when I became volunteer assistant solicitor for my Dad," said Alex. "Really the purpose of me being assistant solicitor was to get to spend time with him, do things with him."

But to become the solicitor full-time meant lots more work and lots less money. His public salary would be less than $100,000 a year—a pittance compared to his annual law firm earnings, which sometimes exceeded a million dollars. But beyond this, even, there was the basic incongruence of Alex's character and the integrity the job of solicitor was supposed to demand. Even Alex seemed to appreciate the awkwardness of a man about to embark on an unprecedented criminal spree also angling to uphold the law.

"I wanted to be a solicitor for a long time, but . . . at the time when my dad retired I was already struggling with pills and I knew I couldn't do it."

He never campaigned to become solicitor, letting the Murdaugh's nearly century-long streak in the solicitor's office come to a close in 2006 when his father retired.

—

In the spring of 1939, a few Hampton County men decided their section of the state would benefit from a campaign promoting local watermelon. They threw a three-day celebration in honor of the mythical King Melon that included baseball games, political speeches, gatherings at the Varnville pool, and a parade led by the Parris Island Marine Band, the semi-local military musical ensemble that would become a mainstay of the annual festival.

Hampton had no unique claim to watermelon, which is grown worldwide. The fruit was first harvested in Africa thousands of years ago, while Hampton County shipped its first melons to market in 1894. But watermelons grow well in Hampton County soil—whether Charleston Greys, Congoes, Fairfaxes, or Garrisons—and little more reason was needed for local boosters to organize a midsummer melon-themed bash. After all, it was a common sight to see farmhands in the fields of Hampton County, hauling one oblong melon after another into the beds of trucks. The melon pickers sometimes sang as they schlepped:

> *Possum is good, tater is good.*
> *Ice cream and cake is mighty fine.*
> *But gimmie, Oh gimmie, I really wish you would,*
> *Dat watermillon smilin' on de vine.*

Despite almost dying on the vine its first year due to an episode of mass food poisoning, the Watermelon Festival returned each subsequent summer, save for a few years during World War II, and soon grew to be the main event of the Hampton County social calendar. Other towns across the Lowcountry and Midlands regions of South Carolina came to support similar events, inspired in part by the success of Hampton County's annual shindig, which grew to be a weeklong extravaganza. Summerville started the Flowertown Festival. Walterboro created the Rice Festival. In Pelion the people host an annual Peanut Party. And Irmo has the Okra Strut, which is not to be confused with the Chitlin Strut, which takes place in Salley, where townspeople declare, "It takes a ton of guts to make Salley strut." None of these down-home soirees are older than the Hampton County Watermelon Festival, which is not to be confused with the plain ole Water Festival, which takes place in Beaufort about a month later.

Alan Young grew up in Hampton in the 1950s, the son of the town jeweler, and attended many a Watermelon Festival. He remembers politicians droning on while children ran wild, doing anything but listening. He remembers attending the street dance on Friday night of the festival, when crowds surrounded the fine town clock on Lee Avenue, which had four faces and stood atop a narrow tower twenty feet tall. A rock band would typically play on one end of the main street, near the courthouse, he said, while a country band performed three blocks away at the other end, near the train tracks. Boy Scouts sold barbecue. When Alan was about nine years old, he and a friend got hold of a discarded wedge of watermelon. They packed its soft red flesh with a firecracker and lit the fuse. When the firecracker exploded, fragments of melon splattered across the baby blue dress of a nearby girl, ruining her garment. Alan and his buddy ran like hell.

Slices of chilled melon were passed out to the crowd at no charge. On Saturday night, a beauty pageant was held to crown Miss Coastal Empire. In the early days of the festival, the contestants paraded up and down the center aisle of an elementary school auditorium. Martha Bee Anderson, the ever-chipper, longtime columnist of the *Hampton County Guardian* was particularly enlivened by the annual blowout, writing countless articles about the "frolicsome fun" to be had by festivalgoers "when the door of Hampton swung open to them at Melontime."

"Beautiful girls and beautiful watermelons are traditionally plentiful," wrote Anderson, an earnest, civic-minded woman who, for almost fifty years, used her "Around the Clock" newspaper column to advocate for safer roads, the sprucing up of the town, and the planting of more trees. She also faithfully recounted the history of the Watermelon Festival, from its first-year "flop," when "hundreds of persons became ill after eating chicken pilau that was spoiled by heat" to later years when special guests included future Miss America Marian McKnight, who competed to be Miss Coastal Empire, and former United States vice president Alben Barkley, popularly known as "Veep." Anderson was such a melon maniac that once when it snowed in Hampton, rather than make a snow*man* she made a snow*slice* of watermelon in her backyard, using food dye to stain the sculpted snow red and green. Martha Bee, as she was known, was one of Hampton's biggest boosters, and felt that at no other time of year did her town shine so bright. "For memories in technicolor," she wrote, "it's a Lowcountry custom to count on the Hampton County Watermelon Festival."

Beyond the beauty pageant and street dance, another festival staple was artist Carew Rice, who cut hundreds of silhouettes during his annual visits to the Watermelon Festival over the course of twenty-five years. Rice would set up a table on the courthouse square and cut the silhouettes of festivalgoers who paid him a visit. He used self-sharpened manicure scissors bought at a dime store to cut silhouettes from black gummed paper, which he then mounted on white stock.

He did not cut his first silhouette until he was thirty-three years old. After that he made up for lost time, traveling a circuit of Southern arts festivals and state fairs, cutting individual profiles in as little as two minutes. Rice sometimes depicted more elaborate landscape scenes, such as ducks landing among palmetto trees in a marsh, or a pair of boys hauling delicately striped melons as they ambled beneath a live oak with their dog. On a trip to England, he decided to cut silhouettes of all the major London landmarks as well as the profile of a bobby standing guard outside 10 Downing Street, the home and office of the prime minister of the United Kingdom. "I have the gift of creation," said Rice. "I must use it."

Rice wore a beret and sang tunes of his own invention as he snipped silhouettes, many of them ballads hearkening back to old times or invoking the natural splendor of the Lowcountry. He lived away from civilization on a river, in a place called Green Pond. This was in the heart of the ACE

Basin, the vast estuary between Beaufort and Charleston where three Lowcountry rivers—the Ashepoo, the Combahee, and the Edisto—empty into the Atlantic Ocean. The Combahee River is formed near Yemassee by the joining of the Salkehatchie and Little Salkehatchie rivers as they finish their journey through the swamp that lines one side of Hampton County. The tea-colored waters of these tributaries become increasingly blue and brackish as they flow into the tidal Combahee, where the river is lined by vast, old rice plantations, including Laurel Spring.

Neighbors are few and far between as you head inland through the Salkehatchie Swamp, up through the submerged cypress forests that supplied Hampton County's early timber economy. Though the Salkehatchie swamp had been logged heavily before the Depression, with the largest cypresses toppled and whisked out of the watery woods to the sawmill, the untrained eye would be oblivious to the absence of these titans. As the naturalist Winthrop Packard noted, the swamp is so dense it's almost impossible to discern what might have been removed.

The cypress swamps surrounding Hampton are a good place to get lost. People have disappeared there for centuries, whether intentionally or not. When it comes to the Salkehatchie, the term river is a bit of an overstatement; better to describe it as a wide but barely moving stream. When it rains the river does not rush forward as much as it spreads wide, making a puddle that swamps the forestland to the point where it can be difficult to determine where the water came from and where the water is going, if anywhere. The blackwater is indeed going somewhere—the ocean—just not very quickly or directly.

In 1928, three men from Varnville attempted to become the first people to navigate the Salkehatchie River by motorboat. This journey proved more challenging than imagined. The trio launched their homemade motorboat one Saturday morning in the fall at Tobys Bluff, on the Colleton County side of the swamp, and started puttering south. They told friends and family to expect them a few hours later, at 2:00 P.M. in Yemassee. The men did not show up that afternoon, nor that night, causing their families to panic and search parties to deploy. But the three men did arrive safely Sunday morning, completing their journey one day late. They explained that a recent storm had littered the river with fallen tree trunks and branches, making for a clogged, obstructed waterway and a prolonged passage. For dinner, the men cooked emergency provisions above a fire they started atop exposed tree roots. They tied their boat to a tree before going to sleep in the bottom of the hull. Alligators and snakes, they said, were their constant companions on the cruise.

After news of their uncomfortable ordeal spread, it's possible the three men were not only the first to navigate the Salkehatchie River by motorboat, but also the last, at least until memories faded. The swamp promised a slog, no way around it. Others stumbling through South Carolina's cypress swamps encountered just as much difficulty. Almost seventy-five years after the overnight motorboat excursion, a South Carolina nature guide described the state's cypress swamps as a place where people are destined to struggle: "Too shallow and obstructed for most boats, and too muddy for easy walking, this environment of dark shadow and dappled sunlight seems inhospitable to most humans, but a great variety of plants and animals find it ideal."

Few people linger in the swamps. To overstay is to be molested, probably by mosquitoes, perhaps by something else. The swamp is a place of concealment. Pools of swamp water, tinted black by the tannins leached from sunken leaves and peat, cloak what lies beneath. The accelerated decay of the swamp overwhelms the life on display. But plentiful creatures lay in the shadows and the shallows, just out of sight. As onetime Allendale County resident Harry Lightsey Jr. wrote, "Some people think of the swamps as dead places. All they see are dead limbs and mud and still water. The swamps have always seemed very alive to me, with the smallest of flowers and the quietest of birds."

When he was a young man, Lightsey and his wife operated Belfast, a sizable family plantation in Allendale County, before leaving country life behind to pursue a legal career and become a leader of the state's law school as well as the College of Charleston. Lightsey excelled in South Carolina's academic, legal, and political circles, but he never forgot the unique Lowcountry habitats that he abandoned to pursue his career, including the swampland. As he wrote in a wistful tribute: "Within it all, there is a brooding, waiting, yet living nature. When I was often in the swamps, I used to have the feeling that they were watching me, as they watched everything."

For Lightsey, a visit to the swamp seemed a psychological escape, a needed change of scenery. For others, the swamp promised physical escape, freedom from bondage. Enslaved people in South Carolina sometimes ran away from plantations and disappeared into the wilderness, braving the forbidding swampland to eke out a life of their own design. Known as maroons, these intrepid and desperate people found high ground and hunted local game. Little evidence of maroons' existence in the cypress swamps survives, for maroons were few in numbers, had few belongings, and did not build permanent settlements. For many escaped slaves, life as a maroon was a semi-temporary existence until they had the means to find true freedom and comfort elsewhere.

Once slavery was abolished in the United States fewer people felt the urge to live in the Lowcountry swamps. Human interlopers were generally day-trippers, whether loggers, hunters, or hikers. Outlaws also used the solitude of the swamps to their advantage. Fugitives in the Lowcountry inevitably intersected with swamps if they ran far enough. The swamp was a place to hide and catch one's breath, at least until police released the hounds.

In the twentieth century the cypress swamps became ground zero for local bootlegging, specifically the making of illegal whiskey, otherwise known as moonshine. South Carolina created a restrictive state dispensary system for alcohol in 1893 and then prohibited alcohol sales entirely in 1916, four years before Prohibition took effect across the entire country. Even after national Prohibition ended in 1933, South Carolina did not relax its stance on alcohol for two more years, and even then the state decided spirits would be heavily taxed. These restrictive policies spurred people to take to the swamps and make their own liquor in illegal stills, at first to sidestep the state and federal prohibitions, and later to avoid taxes.

Beyond isolation, the swamps provided plenty of water, which was mixed with some combination of grains and yeast and sugar or fruit to make a mash. The mash was then left to naturally ferment in large tanks for weeks before being transferred to a series of other tanks, where the mash was heated and distilled into moonshine. Police regularly found and eliminated illegal stills in the Lowcountry, dumping the mash and destroying the pipes and boilers and barrels. In 1955, federal agents reported smashing 24,000 stills, almost all of them in the South, where the warm weather allowed for mash to ferment outdoors without a heat source for much of the year.

Arrests occurred only on occasion; most moonshiners did not loiter at their stills and worked at least semi-secretly. About 1954, though, the bootlegging and the associated proliferation of unlicensed honky-tonk bars serving homemade, high-octane spirits—which locals knew as swamp-hole juice or alligator oil—became too flagrant to ignore in parts of the Lowcountry. One day, Solicitor Buster Murdaugh was traveling through Colleton County in a car with Riddick Herndon, a sheriff's deputy, and B. Cecil Hamilton Jr., a furniture store owner in Walterboro who was also the foreman of the county's grand jury. Hamilton confronted Buster about "getting something done" about illegal whiskey making and honky-tonks. Local police weren't bothering to enforce the law, he complained.

Once Buster heard this, the car was steered to the home of Sheriff G. Haskell Thompson, where Hamilton urged the sheriff to conduct more raids of illegal stills. Thompson's reply was surprising: he didn't really want to do that, and anyway his deputies were already overworked, but he'd be glad to raid stills later, said the sheriff. When the men departed, Buster gave Hamilton a ride home. The solicitor seemed stunned by the sheriff's lack of resolve. "You see what I'm up against in this county," he fumed to Hamilton.

Despite the sheriff's initial apathy, Hamilton's complaint got results. Haskell's deputies made a number of raids in Colleton County, including one in a barn and another in which deputies destroyed a still in front of a Charleston newspaper photographer while he clicked away with his camera. The county grand jury, led by Hamilton, then indicted George W. McPeake for operating an illicit still in the barn, making some progress in the dismantling of the local bootlegging scene.

Or so it was supposed to seem. In reality the raids were all staged and designed to deceive the grand jury, according to Deputy Herndon. After Hamilton complained about lax policing, Buster circled back and told Herndon to initiate "friendly raids" of local bootleggers. "For God's sake make the raids even if you have to warn them in advance, catch them, and set up fines," Buster said to Herndon. "I'll take care of them."

One of the first men rounded up, McPeake, was told to bring $500 to the courthouse in order to secure a light punishment. Deputy Herndon collected the money before court commenced, keeping $100 for himself and giving the rest to Sheriff Thompson. When Thompson saw Buster at the courthouse he peeled two $100 bills away from the wad of cash. "I wish I could get one like that every day," he exclaimed to the solicitor, passing him the money. Buster was incensed, said Herndon, and later "raised hell" with Thompson for distributing the bribe so indiscreetly. At court that day McPeake pleaded guilty to making illegal whiskey and was fined $200 by a judge. But he received no time in prison.

Before becoming a deputy, Herndon served twenty years in the U.S. Marines, retiring as a master sergeant. He returned home to Colleton County in 1949, became fishing buddies with the sheriff, and three years later was invited by Thompson to help raid a still. Afterward, the sheriff gave Herndon his "share"—two cases of illegal whiskey. After this, Herndon was hired as a sheriff's deputy. He earned no official salary but instead made money by acting as the sheriff's collector of protection money. Each month Herndon collected payoffs from area bootleggers, which was supposed to shield them from legal consequences. He took a 20 percent cut and passed the rest of the cash along to the sheriff.

Herndon also invested with bootleggers, buying a share of a still and its profits. When the solicitor ordered him to make friendly raids, he invited a Charleston photographer to witness the demolition of his own moonshining equipment. As Herndon later stated, "The *News and Courier* ran a picture of me on May 28, 1954, showing me wrecking my own still."

Herndon's disclosures, shared with federal agents, contributed to a federal grand jury issuing several indictments in 1956 that charged twenty-nine men with conspiring to operate an illegal whiskey ring in Colleton County that in five years manufactured 90,000 gallons of moonshine. Among the first indicted were Sheriff Haskell Thompson and a number of his deputies. Months later, the federal government also charged Solicitor Buster Murdaugh as a conspirator, accusing him of advising a bootlegger to move his still across county lines.

Buster hotly denied the charges. "An injustice has been done!" he thundered, promising to seek a speedy trial. He surrendered to authorities and was freed after posting a $10,000 bond. A few weeks later, he pleaded innocent during his arraignment at the Charleston Federal Courthouse. He attempted to evade the media—arriving at a rear entrance by limousine—but a photographer captured a scowling Buster entering court with one of his lawyers.

The charges sullied Buster's good reputation back home. He was running for reelection again, and, on account of his popularity, was once again without opposition. He was recently the leader of Wade Hampton High School's Parent Teacher Association and had just been elected an officer of the Hampton Lion's Club. And lately Buster had become, by his own estimation, a "champion of youth," as he mentored his teenage son Randy and his friends. "Some of the boys sort of look to me as a housemother, a term I use advisedly," said Buster. "There are times when some of them come to me for advice and even loans of money to get out of temporary jams." Buster also helped form the first PONY (Protect Our Nation's Youth) Baseball league for teenagers in Hampton. Coach Buster claimed such activities reduced juvenile delinquency, stating, "Giving the youth plenty to do keeps them out of trouble."

But it wasn't the boys who were in trouble, Buster was. A federal grand jury indicted the solicitor again in September 1956, just before trial, adding allegations of obstructing the county grand jury, taking bribes, procuring protected sites for stills, and other crimes. Buster was depicted by prosecutors as a ringleader of the whiskey conspiracy, its chief enabler. This was the second time in two years federal authorities had accused Buster of wrongdoing. In 1955, Buster was accused and exonerated of federal tax fraud charges. Judge Clarence Opper of the U.S. Tax Court decided that the Internal Revenue Service failed to prove Buster committed a crime. "However much his method of keeping records and assembling information for his tax returns left much to be desired, carelessness is not synonymous with fraud," wrote Opper, who nonetheless ordered Buster to pay $6,000 in back taxes.

The whiskey conspiracy charges, however, potentially promised more serious consequences for the solicitor. Newspaper editors began calling for his resignation, including an old adversary of Buster's from college days, Howard Cooper, who owned, published, and edited the *Beaufort Gazette*. Cooper called for Buster's resignation within a week of his indictment, writing, "A law enforcement officer under indictment should immediately relinquish his office until such time as he is acquitted."

Cooper got his wish. A week before trial, Buster wrote to the governor to resign his elected position, explaining he must concentrate fully on defending himself in court. The charges threatened his personal integrity and freedom, wrote Buster, and impugned the thirty-six years he and his father served as solicitor, not to mention ruined his wife and children's honor and happiness. "I wish to reiterate to you my innocence and I welcome an early opportunity to clear my name of the outrageous charges brought against me," wrote Buster. "With the help of Almighty God the falsity of the charges will be bared and I will return to the office of solicitor."

After a judge in South Carolina recused himself, the high-profile case was given to visiting federal judge Walter Hoffman of Virginia. When he arrived in Charleston, lawyers told him to brace for a long trial. He ignored them and ordered that the court operate nights and also on Saturdays to hasten the proceedings. "These lawyers down here told me it will take one or two months for this case," said Hoffman. "I'm setting my sights on two weeks and I'm promising everybody some work." Hoffman considered the conspiracy trial to be a tax case; while it was not illegal to make whiskey, he explained, the law did require distilleries be registered and all applicable taxes paid.

When South Carolina's whiskey ring trial started September 17, 1956, Buster Murdaugh stood in court dressed in a blue suit and blue tie. Gladys stood by his side, clad in a brown dress and a feathered hat. Sixteen-year-old Randy accompanied his parents, sporting fashionable penny loafer shoes. Buster was seen to chew on his lip nervously as the morning session unfolded, perhaps because the government's very first witness, the wife of a bootlegger, accused Buster of mistreating her, trying to eliminate evidence, stealing the couple's money, and failing to prosecute a federal agent who shot her husband in a raid. Another witness claimed Buster received $100 payments from bootleggers seeking light punishments. Deputy Herndon testified that when he went to Buster to confess being a bagman for the corrupt sheriff, the solicitor was unfazed by all the bootlegging admissions and told him to hush up. "For God's sake keep quiet about this," Buster told Herndon. "If you need money or get in trouble, come to me. I'll help you."

Testimony revealed the government's investigation featured an undercover federal agent working as one of Sheriff Haskell's deputies, an informant posing as a bootlegger, and a secret recording of an incriminating conversation in a car made by a man hiding in the trunk. The high point of the trial arrived when Buster took the stand in his own defense. He was questioned about his former friendship with Robert Clifton, a bootlegger who Buster, while a South Carolina solicitor, once defended against federal bootlegging charges.

"I've known Clifton a long time," answered Buster, before assassinating the opposition witness's character. "He supported me politically on several occasions. We've been on deer hunts and dove shoots together but we were never close. We're not in the same social class at all. I've never visited him at his home or he in mine. I recall planning a suit against him once for wife beating."

Federal prosecutor Irvine Belser Jr. expressed confusion as to why a prosecutor would be representing an alleged criminal, a man caught with forty-six gallons of untaxed whiskey. "And yet, you defended him in federal court," said Belser. "Why didn't you prosecute him in your state court?" The back and forth between Buster and Belser became barbed. At one point the judge stopped the questioning and admonished both men for their poor conduct. "Now you two lawyers quit arguing," said Hoffman. "Next week, if you like, I'll arrange for boxing gloves and you can have it out. Right now, let's get on with the case."

In two weeks, 141 witnesses were called to testify. Among them were several witnesses favorable to Buster, including Judge J. Henry Johnson, who testified Buster never asked him to extend leniency for bootleggers, and the sheriff of Allendale County, who spoke of Buster's dedication to the job. "I call the solicitor and he comes, day or night," said the sheriff. These character witnesses were offset by at least four government witnesses who spoke disparagingly of the solicitor, including the sheriffs of Hampton and Richland counties.

Buster suffered much more insult during closing arguments. US Attorney N. Welch Morrisette Jr., who led the local federal prosecutor's office, characterized Colleton County as a "cesspool of lawlessness" and the whiskey conspiracy a "sordid, sorry, sinful mess." Murdaugh was no better than an outlaw from the Old West, he claimed. "Jesse James rode a horse, but this man Murdaugh rides a Cadillac with a low license number," said Morisette, referencing the license plates issued to state leaders.

Belser took a turn and delivered his own withering attack that branded the solicitor as a backwoods puppeteer, "the top control, the man with the brains, the man who ran the show . . . There's no defense for what he and others have done and for the disgraceful situation they allowed and helped to develop in Colleton County." Among the defendants on trial, said the federal prosecutor, Buster was most crucial for the success of the whiskey ring. "He is a cut above some of these other defendants in intelligence. He wasn't caught at a still. He's too smart to get his fingers caught in the mash barrel . . ." said Belser. "The conspiracy couldn't have existed and gained the scope it did without the knowledge and participation of the solicitor."

The prosecutor dismissed criticism that some of the government's witnesses were unreliable by virtue of being confessed criminals. His contempt for the solicitor and law enforcement officers on trial was obvious. "I'd rather have a self-admitted, penitent bootlegger, thief, or perjurer testify than to see this bunch of hypocritical liars, thieves, and perjurers come into this court and hide behind a battery of talented lawyers," sneered Belser.

Finally, as a finishing touch, Belser used Buster's trademark tactic for closing arguments: he told the jury that if they dare acquit this defendant they can thank themselves for anarchy and endemic corruption:

> *This man Murdaugh used to be called "Righteous Randolph" but now it's "Bootlegging Buster." If you want a solicitor who takes bribes, counsels bootleggers, and takes part in deceiving the grand jury, if you want a sheriff and deputies who participate with him and if you want bootleggers running rampant in your community, then bring in an acquittal. You should know, however, that a conspiracy of this sort is a vicious thing. It is a web, sending its tentacles out into the entire community.*

In their own closing arguments, defense lawyers countered that the government's witnesses were not to be trusted. "This is really 'old grudge week' and these bootleggers finally got a chance to get even with these fine Colleton County people who have been giving them so much trouble," said James P. Harrelson, who defended a sheriff's deputy alleged to have collected payoffs from moonshiners. Buster employed no less than four lawyers to plead his case. They had waited two weeks to unload arguments saturated with grievance, scare tactics, and near-slander, offering a hodgepodge of reasons Buster Murdaugh was not guilty.

Richard A. Palmer belittled government witnesses' credibility: "Do you believe Clifton, Padgett, and Phillips weren't promised anything? If you do, you'll believe in Santa Claus. (Federal) agents have never said a word against Mr. Murdaugh."

Claude N. Sapp Jr. said the government was promising liberty in exchange for lies: "I'm sure that there isn't a soul in this case who couldn't have gotten out if he had agreed to swear against Murdaugh and (Sheriff) Thompson."

W. Brantley Harvey blamed politics: "Each government witness who tried to belittle Mr. Murdaugh had a very personal or political reason for doing so. There has not been one stigma placed against him by anyone of good character."

And Henry H. Edens complained the government was trying to prove guilt through association. He spoke apocalyptically of the government's abuse of conspiracy law and that people would soon be charged with conspiracy for asking their spouse how they're feeling.

"Are you going to let it come to that? The government has used all its facilities for five years to gather slop to throw on Mr. Murdaugh and they haven't done so good a job. There aren't many men who could keep going for six years while they were being spied on, tracked, and plotted against by people who wanted to get him."

Members of the jury deliberated for a day before reaching verdicts for Murdaugh and the nineteen remaining defendants. They presented their decisions to Judge Hoffman late at night on October 1, 1956. A hush lingered over the courtroom as the judge proceeded to read each man's fate in alphabetical order. *Guilty . . . Guilty . . . Guilty . . .* intoned Hoffman, again and again, reading the list of names. Buster once again chewed his lip as he and the other defendants stood before the judge, waiting for their names to be called. Gladys waited nervously downstairs in the lobby.

Halfway through, as Hoffman read the name of Ben Magwood, he then said, "Not guilty" for the first time. There was a glimmer of hope for Buster, who began breathing heavily as the judge read his name and then said, "Not guilty." Buster nervously dragged his hand along his mouth in rapid motions and appeared to be on the verge of sobbing he was so relieved. A man sprinted downstairs to tell Gladys, who immediately burst into tears and lost her composure for the first time at the trial. When the judge finished, Buster immediately thanked his allies for their support, stating, "I appreciate from the bottom of my heart and will be ever grateful for the loyalty displayed by my many friends who have openly stood by me and my family during this ordeal."

The jury convicted seventeen members of the smuggling ring, including Sheriff Thompson, and acquitted just two men beyond Buster. Judge Hoffman convened court again the next day to sentence the convicted men. Although Buster was no longer in the courtroom, he remained at the forefront of Judge Walter Hoffman's mind. Never mind the seventeen defendants deemed guilty, Hoffman dwelled on the one that got away. In open court he condemned the acquitted man and opined that Buster, whose name would be on the ballot again in a month, should stay out of public office:

> *I can't get involved in Colleton County politics but I notice by the newspapers that Mr. Murdaugh plans to go back into office as solicitor. He is an acquitted man and that's his prerogative and his business. However, his completely unethical conduct was so grossly unethical by his own admission in this court—that I couldn't go*

back and face my people if I were he. But that's his business and it's
also the business of the people there.

Though Hoffman was from tidewater Virginia, another low country, he was naive in his understanding of this region's inhabitants. Any student of the American Civil War could tell you South Carolinians don't like being told what to do. What's more, the pricklier people of the Palmetto State aren't afraid to start a fight, including a war of words.

Buster's friends soon helped restore his honor. Within a month, two grand juries lauded the former solicitor and celebrated his acquittal. "We are delighted that you were exonerated of all charges against you in federal court," said a report from the Allendale grand jury. The grand jurors of Hampton County felt similar emotions. "We commend Randolph Murdaugh for the splendid manner in which he has handled the affairs of the office of the solicitor. We deplore the outrageous charges brought against him and rejoice in his vindication."

When the Charleston *News and Courier* suggested Buster remove his name from the ballot, a prominent ally dashed off a response that deemed the editorial "as unwarranted and uncalled for as were Judge Hoffman's remarks." The fiery letter to the editor was penned by M. T. Laffitte, president of the Exchange Bank in the Hampton County town of Estill, who said locals resented the newspaper's criticism of Buster. "It might serve a better purpose if you devote your talents to cleaning and keeping Charleston clean rather than butting in where not asked or wanted," wrote Laffitte. "It does appear that when a man has been tried in court and acquitted, the case should end."

But the case would not end. Almost immediately after the whiskey trial, Buster's cousin, traveling salesman Alex G. Murdaugh of Orangeburg, was indicted for tampering with a federal juror. The government had discovered that a few days before Buster's trial, Cousin Alex met with an old acquaintance he learned would be serving on the jury for the whiskey case. Cousin

Alex hadn't spoken but twice to the man in thirty years but nonetheless called him to meet for a steak dinner just before the trial. He warned his old acquaintance the federal government was crooked, claiming, "They are attempting to prosecute Randolph Murdaugh solely for political reasons."

This juror, who became the jury's foreman, said the steak dinner conversation had no bearing on his verdict. Just before he began deliberating, though, the foreman received a phone call telling him that his father was dying. Judge Hoffman offered to excuse him and replace him with an alternate, but the foreman declined and began deliberations with his fellow jurors that ultimately resulted in Murdaugh's acquittal and the conviction of most other defendants.

Federal prosecutors later complained in a government newsletter about the foreman's "odd" behavior as well as the practices of opposing lawyers. "The defense resorted to some highly questionable tactics, all apparently designed to bring about an acquittal or mistrial as to Solicitor Murdaugh even at the risk of sacrificing the remaining defendants," said an item in the United States Attorneys Bulletin of Nov. 9, 1956.

One of these alleged tactics was witness tampering. The bulletin alleged that defendants and their lawyers attempted to influence witnesses by both making threats and promising rewards. When trial began, "strange incidents occurred . . . which sorely taxed the patience of the prosecutor," such as one of the government's main witnesses suddenly waffling in the middle of the trial, claiming to have lied on the stand. Also strange were the handful of defense witnesses who related outlandish tales. This included railway agent L. O. Browning, who claimed he heard a government witness say at a remote Hampton County freight depot that he was going to "get even with Murdaugh if it's the last thing I do." When the government witness Browning referenced was recalled to the stand, he looked Browning over and claimed to have never seen Browning in his life. Similarly, defense witness Graham E. Easterling of Colleton County testified that a government witness, the sheriff's bagman Herndon, divulged to him in a vulnerable moment, "I'm not doing so well. These revenue fellows have got me so cracked up I don't know what's up or down. I've been lying all through this court, Graham. I've lied on Mr. Murdaugh and everybody else." This testimony was challenged, and Judge Hoffman ordered it stricken from the record. Nonetheless federal prosecutors finished the case, concluding that some of the Lowcountry was an irredeemable backwater that accommodated corrupt lawyers just as well as bootleggers. When it came to Buster, the newsletter said, prosecutors could at least take solace in the fact he was "publicly castigated for his unethical practices" by Judge Hoffman.

But a scolding from a federal judge in Virginia mattered not a lick to Lowcountry voters. On Election Day in November 1956 Buster once again scored an easy victory, defeating a last-minute opponent's half-hearted write-in campaign with six times the number of votes. This was the fifth time voters across five counties elected Buster as solicitor—the same number of times they elected his father. Though the solicitor's term officially started the next year, the governor appointed Buster to his old public office a month ahead of time. The early start was useful, for Buster was itching to settle some scores.

———

The hunting retreat was cut from swampland and forest, an 1,800-acre sportsman's paradise crawling with wild game. The Murdaughs called the place Moselle, which conjures images of the classic Southern plantation, of which there are scores in the South Carolina Lowcountry. Hidden behind many humble roadside gates along country roads are expansive tracts of woods and wetlands with impressive manor homes. These plantations are worlds unto themselves, semi-tamed wildernesses and wonderlands with grand-sounding names like Bonny Hall, Buckfield, Nemours, Tomotley, Turkey Hill, and so on. Many of these historic plantations once fueled fortunes with enslaved, imported African people and their descendants planting and harvesting cash crops, especially the indigo, rice, and cotton that made the landowners exceedingly rich. But after slavery's end, as economic ruin shattered the South, many of these plantations were bought by wealthy Northerners and repurposed as vast hunting retreats. Wealthy New Yorkers could hop an overnight train south and be dropped off close to their South Carolina estates, picked up by the side of the tracks by a servant.

So conspicuous was this influx of Yankees and their gobs of money that writer Chalmers S. Murray of Edisto Island described the movement as "the second invasion." These Northerners' new homes may have been secluded and tucked deep into huge estates in out-of-the-way areas, but that didn't mean the newcomers' arrival went unnoticed. Like his contemporary Chlotilde Martin of Beaufort, Murray wrote articles in the Charleston *News and Courier* in the 1930s about Lowcountry plantations and their out-of-town owners.

For Murray, an initial fascination with the moneyed crowd soon turned into resentment. Murray admitted he "watched the [N]orthern millionaires in action so long that I have perhaps grown a little bitter." It was hard for any local to live vicariously for too long, to constantly observe the carefree existences of the Lowcountry's imported aristocracy, to constantly live in normal routine while others seemed to be forever on holiday with endless amounts of money at their disposal. Murray objected to the lack of seriousness:

> *They came riding in private planes, mahogany decked yachts, and chartered pullman [sic] coaches, bringing with them white servants who turned up their noses at everything they saw around the countryside . . . (in addition to) polo ponies, snooty foxhounds . . . imported whiskeys, antique furniture and sporting clothes fashioned in London that never seemed to fit the wearers. Then came camp followers—baseball stars, titled Europeans, fat United States senators and their flashy wives, and friends and relatives who hunted in the morning, slept in the afternoon, and spent the night drinking.*

Alex's swampy spread did not have this type of pedigree. There was no old manor house, no slave cabins, and no abandoned rice fields. One of the previous owners of Moselle was no heir to a Gilded Age fortune but instead a commercial fisherman and drug smuggler who suspiciously kept an airstrip maintained on the property. Alex bought the property in 2013 as a rural playground for him and his family, a place outside of town to roll across the land in pickup trucks and tractors and blast away at animals any time of year. Or at least it was a playground for most of the family. To Maggie, the hunting retreat was isolated and overrun with yellow flies and wild hogs. She'd much rather be at the beach. As her sister, Marian Proctor, described Moselle: "Not Maggie's favorite place to be but the boys loved it."

Moselle was not the formal or historic name of the property but rather the name of an area within the rural community of Islandton. The Murdaugh family had a habit of referring to family properties by their geographic location, which could be confusing, implying the region and their property were one and the same. Alex would tell people he's going to Moselle for the weekend, or visiting his parents at Almeda, or that he'd be hosting friends at Chechessee, the riverside retreat his grandfather established in Beaufort County on Chechessee Creek, and which also was called Buster's Island. When it came to Alex, little was straightforward, not even his own name. He introduced himself as what sounded like *Ellick*, to the point that people often wrote his name as *Alec*. His last name was tricky, too, with a preferred pronunciation somewhere between *Murdick* and *Murdock*.

Similarly unclear were the murky waters of the Salkehatchie River, which trickled along more than two miles of swampy riverbank that was part of Moselle. The hunting retreat sat on the eastern side of the river, placing it just within Colleton County, across from Hampton County on the opposite bank. Much of Moselle sat between the river and Moselle Road, which ran parallel to the Salkehatchie, but some of the property sat on the other side of the asphalt.

Waterfowl and fishponds dotted the property. There was a rifle range, a twenty-acre dove field, and thinly forested sections of young pine trees planted neatly in rows, all connected by three miles of dirt roads.

A brick gate stood at the main entrance and behind it a tree-lined drive that led to a large, white cottage with a big front porch. This was the big house where the Murdaughs lived when they came out to the country—Maggie's one true refuge on the property. The four-bedroom home was built in 2011 and featured traditional, and expensive, Lowcountry materials and finishes, such as a metal roof, heart pine flooring, and cypress paneling in the gun room, where the family kept a pool table and a few dozen unsecured firearms that stood upright in racks.

The decor emphasized that Moselle was a hunting retreat. Deer skulls and antlers as well as impressive steer horns hung on walls. Light emanated from at least seven tortoiseshell lamps. The family's colorful majolica dinnerware featured scenes of scampering game and slain quarry.

The furniture, such as a burgundy leather couch and armchair, was large and overstuffed, and held huge throw pillows adorned with Maggie's monogram. Inside the 5,000-square-foot house, too, was a framed poem titled "The Man in the Glass." The poem, whose author is unknown, eerily warned against the danger of deception and fakery. It ended on an ominous note:

> *You may fool the whole world down the pathway of years*
> *And get pats on the back as you pass*
> *But your final reward will be heartache and tears*
> *If you've cheated the man in the glass.*

Further from Hampton, another quarter-mile east on Moselle Road, was a second and less impressive entrance to the hunting retreat, this one not anything more than a break in the trees. At the road here was a small, green caretaker's cottage and an old, abandoned wooden shed. Then, behind the trees, hardly visible from the road, was the hub of Moselle's opera-tions, where almost all the property's outbuildings and equipment were located. The largest of the farm structures was an airplane hangar used as an oversized shed, filled with tools but no airplane. Nearby was a quail house, a tractor shed, and a skinning shed where wild game was butchered, the animal's blood spilling to the floor before flowing out through a central drain in the floor. Against a stand of pine trees, dog kennels stood in a row. Each kennel was enclosed with wire fencing, with a long roof overhead and a concrete pad underneath. A small feed room stood at the end of the line of kennels.

Alex acquired Moselle from the wife of his friend Barrett Boulware, to whom Barrett had transferred the property four years earlier. Barrett Boul-ware was a colorful but mysterious character. He had a few run-ins with the law as a young man, including his arrest in 1983 at age twenty-seven in connection with the seizure of 34,000 pounds, packaged in 854 bales, of marijuana from the shrimp boat *Jeannine Anne*. Those smuggling-related charges soon were dropped after a crucial government witness was struck and killed by a car in Florida. A few years after that, in a separate case in the late 1980s, Boulware was convicted in Georgia of trafficking cocaine and possessing marijuana. A handful of his acquaintances swore he also smuggled Cuban citizens into the United States over the years.

Two decades later, Barrett and Alex had become friends and invested in real estate together. Among their purchases were several islands in Beaufort County—something else that raised eyebrows given Boulware's rap sheet and the region's rich legacy of marijuana smuggling. A few decades earlier in the early 1980s, when the late Buster Murdaugh was wrapping up his long tenure in public office, a number of local boys were running wild across the Lowcountry, piloting one pot-laden boat after another to remote docks, where they unloaded their illicit cargo under moonlight.

Alex and Barrett were close, just as their grandfathers had been close. Thomas Boulware, who would become a judge, represented Buster

Murdaugh when he was countersued by his suspected former lover Ruth Vaux back in the late 1940s over allegations of stealing her money when she hired him to obtain a divorce. These days it was a Murdaugh serving a Boulware's legal needs. At one point, Barrett granted Alex power of attorney, allowing Alex to independently make legal decisions for him. "Alex had a POA for Barrett, that's how much he trusted him," said Alex's law partner Ronnie Crosby, who was also a friend to Boulware.

Moselle proved the perfect place for Alex to continue fostering his sons' love of the outdoors. They could launch boats in the swamp, sight and fire their rifles at the shooting range, use farm equipment to plant crops, and bait the fields and duck ponds. Crosby, who lived beside Alex in Hampton for years, was also a neighbor to the Murdaughs in Colleton County, where he also owned property. Crosby invited the Murdaugh boys to hunt on his land and remembered how Paul became "obsessed" with hunting wild hogs. Paul kept "hog dogs" for a time, said Crosby, which flushed feral hogs from their cover and allowed Paul to shoot the beasts.

There are no limits to the number of hogs one can kill in South Carolina, and the animals can even be legally hunted at night with a thermal scope. The animals are regarded as a destructive nuisance, particularly for farmers, because of their rooting behavior in which they dig for food below ground. Wild hogs uproot crops and vegetation and generally make a mess of the landscape. A state wildlife department bulletin spoke of the "rude awakening" experienced by South Carolina residents when they are introduced to feral hogs. "Most people are completely unaware of these non-native animals until they walk out of their front doors in the morning to find that their yards were 'roto-tilled' by wandering wild hogs during the night," said the bulletin.

The wild hog population has increased significantly in the South in recent decades, making them even more of a hated pest. Hogs—mature, full-grown pigs—were brought to North America in the sixteenth century by European explorers and settlers. For centuries in South Carolina, small populations of escaped wild hogs lived mostly within forested floodplains surrounding the state's largest rivers and could be found in about half the counties in the state. By 2011 wild hogs lived in every county of the Palmetto State, and they were particularly prevalent and problematic in the swampy areas of the Lowcountry. Crosby said he's dispatched hundreds of the animals, considering himself "pretty much an expert about killing hogs." He is on constant lookout for the feral, foraging swine. "We have a rule," said Crosby, "that you don't ride (my) property without a rifle because you want to try to eliminate as many hogs as you can."

Alex and Crosby's law partner Mark Ball also owned land in the Lowcountry and told of killing scores of wild hogs, calling their presence a "scourge." Whereas Crosby's kill count was in the hundreds, Ball waged a wild hog holocaust, claiming to have killed thousands of the animals. No matter how many of the critters were sent to hog heaven, there were always more. Crosby welcomed Paul Murdaugh to his property any time the youngster felt the urgings of sport and bloodlust. At first Paul and his friends used a rifle to slaughter hogs, said "Uncle Ronnie," as Paul called Crosby. But then, said Crosby, "they got where they were catching them and killing them with knives."

While visiting Crosby's land, Paul also killed some of his first deer—a memorable moment for any young hunter. Nearly two centuries earlier the wealthy planter William Elliott wrote of a companion killing his first deer at his Chee-Ha plantation, located between the Ashepoo and Combahee rivers, also in Colleton County. In between the rivers, the Harvard-educated planter wrote in his hunting and fishing memoir *Carolina Sports by Land and Water*, "there remains a wide expanse of barrens, traversed by deep swamps, always difficult and sometimes impassable, in which the deer find a secure retreat." In February of one year in the early nineteenth century, Elliott gathered at a cabin on his plantation with three friends, some servants, and a dozen dogs. Two of the hunters were veteran sportsmen, wrote Elliott, while two others "had not yet fleshed their maiden swords" and were hoping to make their first kill.

The hunting party soon cornered a deer, and two hunters, Mr. Loveleap and Mr. Tickle, fired rounds to bring down the animal, the latter scoring the kill shot. "We all rode to the spot," wrote Elliott, "to congratulate our novice on his first exploit of sylvan warfare—when, as he stooped to examine the direction of his shot, our friend Loveleap slipped his knife into the throat of the deer, and before his purpose could be guessed at, bathed (Tickle's) face with the blood of his victim."

This bloody "ablution," wrote Elliott, was "hunter's law." The custom of the country demanded this upon the first conquest by a sportsman. "Maussssa Tickle, if you wash off dat blood dis day—you neber hav luck again so long as you hunt," said a man named Robin, who was likely enslaved given Elliott's decision to depict his speech in dialect.

The other hunters agreed the bloody mask must remain on his face until day's end. "Wash it off . . . who ever heard of such a folly?" said the hunters, in accord, according to Elliott. "He can be no true sportsman, who is ashamed of such a livery." Elliott reported proudly that Tickle returned home to his wife that evening, "his face still adorned with the stains of victory."

Two centuries later, nimrods continued to stalk deer every fall in South Carolina, followed by ducks in the winter, turkey in the spring, and hogs anytime at all. Little matched the thrill of the chase. In his book *Mind of the South*, published in 1941, Wilbur J. Cash, a native of South Carolina, sought to answer the question of why the Southerner loved to hunt:

> *For the same reason that, in his youth and often into late man-hood, he ran spontaneous and unpremeditated foot-races, wrestled, drank Gargantuan quantities of raw whiskey, let off wild yells, and hunted the possum;—because the thing was already in his mores when he emerged from the backwoods, because on the frontier it was the obvious thing to do, because he was a hot, stout fellow, full of blood and reared to outdoor activity, because of a primitive zest for the pursuit at hand.*

Indeed, the Lowcountry abounded with so much game that the obvious thing for any predator to do was to capture or kill it. A South Carolina travel guide published by the Works Progress Administration the same year as Cash's book described the cornucopia of quarry available along the eastern section of Hampton County, within and along the Salkehatchie and Little Salkehatchie rivers: "The bream, flat fish, sturgeon, and perch of these streams have lured fishermen for decades. In the swamps are wild deer and turkey, and the hedges hide dove and quail. Wildcats, 'coons, alligators, and an occasional black bear leave their tracks on the fresh earth that smells of ancient vegetable mold. Thick vegetation has preserved the animals from extermination."

During colonial times and during the early days of US history, a variety of naturalists and artists visited the South Carolina Lowcountry to document and illustrate the abundant and exotic wildlife of the South, including Mark Catesby, William Bartram, and John James Audubon, who spent winters in Charleston for much of the 1830s and 1840s. When Northern sportsmen made the same forays into the interior a half-century or more later, some did so on their own private plantations, but others did so on the grounds of exclusive Lowcountry hunt clubs, such as Palachucola Club, Okeetee Club, Cherokee Plantation, and Pineland Club, a few of which continue in operation today, with Okeetee Club offering more than 50,000 acres of hunting property for its members to enjoy.

Despite owning almost 2,000 acres of his own hunting land, Alex Murdaugh belonged to Green Swamp Club, which owned 7,000 acres of swampy land along nine miles of the Savannah River. Alex was one of about forty members of the club, where shares are valued at about $250,000. Both of Alex's brothers, too, owned hunting property, and his parents lived on their farmland in Almeda, just outside of Varnville and Hampton. Between the club membership, holdings of family, friends, law partners, and also public lands, Alex and his boys had a plethora of places to spill blood.

CHAPTER FOUR
BUSTER'S LAW

S ome lawyers specialize in mediation and arbitration. Randolph "Buster" Murdaugh Jr. was an expert at retaliation. Like a rattlesnake dumped from a burlap bag, Buster bristled and flexed after his acquittal. He hissed and seethed and struck back at the people who tried to cage him. It was "old grudge" time again in the Lowcountry, and Buster was taking scalps.

Restored to his throne by voters, the solicitor soon targeted three men, admitted bootleggers, who all served as witnesses for the federal government during the whiskey ring trial. Despite Buster's recent protests regarding his own prosecution, and a previous habit of being soft on alcohol violations, he did not refrain from pursuing related state charges against the men to compound their troubles. Meanwhile, Buster subpoenaed three of his friends who were convicted as part of the whiskey ring—Sheriff G. Haskell Thompson as well as a former sheriff's deputy and a magistrate—so they could be on hand to testify at these and other criminal trials, if needed. This required them to be jailed locally, meaning they would start serving their federal prison sentences close to home, in county facilities the corrupt law enforcement officers used to manage, and delay their departure to a federal penitentiary.

Buster reserved some venom, too, for Judge Walter Hoffman of Virginia, who had insulted him immediately after his acquittal on a conspiracy charge. Buster, no longer under threat of legal consequence, responded in slick, acid fashion, characterizing the judge's comments as "unwarranted and entirely uncalled for in every respect." Buster then invoked the issue of state's rights, that eternal hot topic for South Carolinians that once spurred them to civil war, complaining, "When the federal government sends a Republican judge into this state to tell South Carolinians how to handle their politics it's a perfect example of the further encroachment by the government on the rights of the state."

These days it was no longer slavery that some South Carolinians were trying to preserve, but instead the similarly reductive system that succeeded it: segregation. In Hampton County in the 1950s and 1960s, there was much sentiment to preserve the status quo and keep Blacks and Whites separated. There existed a feeling among many Whites that each race fared best within their own sphere. Life seemed just fine in the Lowcountry, in other words, before the civil rights movement and the suggestions, and then federal court mandates, to integrate nearly every aspect of life. Why come together, many wondered, instead of maintaining a separate but equal coexistence?

One prominent White man in the Lowcountry who took exception to the insistence on segregation was federal Judge J. Waties Waring of Charleston. In 1952 he was a member of a three-judge panel that decided *Briggs v. Elliott*, a case in which Black families in the town of Summerton sought access to public schools used by Whites. Waring's two colleagues decided to deny the Black plaintiff's claims under the basis they already enjoyed separate but equal school resources and facilities. Waring disagreed with the majority. In a dissenting opinion he called for drastic change and warned of the danger of sowing prejudicial attitudes in the young minds of future generations. "Segregation in education can never produce equality and that it is an evil that must be eradicated . . ." wrote Waring. "(A)ll of the legal guideposts, expert testimony, common sense and reason point unerringly to the conclusion that the system of segregation in education adopted and practiced in the State of South Carolina must go and must go now."

Though Waring was on the losing end, the sentiments he expressed were enshrined into law two years later in 1954 when the United States Supreme

Court ruled, momentously, in *Brown v. Board of Education*, that public schools could no longer be segregated by race, beginning the slow process of desegregation. Yet the people of South Carolina hardly recognized Waring as precocious; in fact, many harassed and ostracized the judge. Concrete was thrown through the Waring home and his wife was spat on. Waring, an eighth-generation Charlestonian, responded by moving to New York with his wife after retiring from the bench in 1952. He returned to Charleston upon his death and was buried in the city's Magnolia Cemetery.

Similarly bitter reactions to the threat of desegregation erupted in the Hampton area, where a split society was in full effect. Public facilities typically contained three bathrooms, labeled MEN, WOMEN, and COLORED. At the Palmetto Theatre on Lee Avenue in Hampton, Whites sat downstairs and Blacks were steered to seats in the balcony at the rear of the cinema house. One local doctor's office had a waiting room with a wall down the middle to separate Black and White patients. White and Black beauty queens competed in separate pageants. And the cooling, blue waters within the big swimming pool in Varnville—the center of summer fun for many Hampton County youths—did not ever wash over the skin of Blacks, who were excluded from the private pool.

In one county under Buster's control, Black men were kept from serving on juries entirely. Lawyer and civil rights activist John Bolt Culbertson of Greenville caused the cancellation of court for a year in Jasper County after objecting in 1953 to the county's inability to field a representative jury at consecutive terms of court. Solicitor Buster Murdaugh could more or less only observe from his seat at the prosecutor's table as Culbertson's protested to a judge the actions of Jasper County's clerk of court and its jury commissioners. Culbertson compelled these county officials to confess on the witness stand the racist tactics they employed to keep Jasper County juries purely White in composition.

"You don't believe that Negroes should serve on juries, do you?" Culbertson asked R. L. Sensenbach, Jasper County's top court administrator.

"I believe in 100 percent segregation," replied Sensenbach, the clerk of court. "Does that answer your question?"

A Jasper County jury commissioner, John Foster Smith, made no apology, either, for preventing the selection of Black jurors. "God made me White and made them Black," Smith said to Culbertson. "If they would stay in their place I would stay in my place."

Over in Hampton, the *Guardian* reprinted a letter in 1957 from a state Masonic publication entitled "Konfesses to Konfusion." The writer claimed to be a farmer perplexed by recent court rulings. The farmer wondered if he could plant black peas and white peas in separate crop rows, or "if I will have to mix them and plant them broadcast." It was the same dilemma with his hogs, he said: "I have always been careful to keep them separated in order to preserve and protect the strain. Must I now mix these hogs? Or may I continue to keep them in separate but equal pens? And when I go to sell them can I just sell white hogs or must I sell an equal number of black ones at the same time?"

A few years later, the *Guardian* published an editorial that labeled integration as "a trap," reasoning that the regular mixing of Blacks and Whites would lead to "clashes that might erupt anytime into a racial war." To prevent such violence, the newspaper advised people of all races to voluntarily segregate. "For his own protection, no white man should attend functions where the races mingle freely and where full police protection cannot be provided," said the *Guardian*. "The wise Negro, too, will abstain, whatever he may think his right is, from subjecting himself to situations which might result in his injury or in harmful psychological damage to his ego."

The wife of R. A. Kinard of Allendale County was more compromising. She wrote to the paper to say she would tolerate Blacks and Whites shopping alongside one another, but schooling should be separate, and interracial love and procreation forbidden. "People are forgetting all reason. Even the birds of different kinds and different kinds of snakes don't mix," wrote Kinard. "It does not matter to me about mixing in business, barber shops, eating places . . . It does matter that my children and their children can have the right to live with their own race and go to school with their own race, and that the Negro have that same right and freedom."

Even Martha Bee Anderson, normally sweet and sunny in her "Around the Clock" newspaper column, struck a very rigid tone when it came to the idea of desegregation, lamenting so many people had conceded the issue and were beginning to demolish racial barriers. "I never want to see colored people treated unfairly or denied their rights anywhere," said Anderson. "Like most born Southerners, I challenge only the feared mixing of the two races in schools, churches, eating places, and clubs."

Buster Murdaugh, too, was in no rush for unity, especially not if it was politically unpopular. In 1950, at a Democratic convention at the Hampton County Courthouse, Buster and two hundred people listened to a keynote speech by State Senator George Warren with the theme of "No Integration." In the crowd stood three men wearing bright red shirts meant to evoke the violent Red Shirts paramilitary group who once terrorized Blacks and so fervently supported the town of Hampton's namesake, Wade Hampton III, the former governor and Confederate lieutenant general. These men caught Buster's eye and, when it was his turn at the podium, he saluted the Red Shirt impersonators as he delivered his remarks.

The salute could be interpreted as mere posturing. Buster was hardly ideological, more concerned with currying favor. He was also more likely to become righteous and indignant over criminal justice matters than social issues. While Buster would never be confused for a civil rights activist, he typically refrained from racial rhetoric, especially compared to political contemporaries like South Carolina Governor Strom Thurmond, who in 1948 left the traditional Democratic Party to run for president as a Dixiecrat, or member of the States' Rights Democratic Party, which opposed desegregation. During a campaign speech that year in Virginia, Thurmond famously boasted, "There's not enough troops in the Army to force the Southern people to break down segregation and admit the nigra race into

our theaters, into our swimming pools, into our homes, into our churches."
While the governor failed to become president, South Carolinians elected
Thurmond to the United States Senate in 1954 via write-in votes. He would
serve in the Senate for the next forty-nine years, retiring only after his
100th birthday, when infirmity confined him to a wheelchair.

After the senator's death in 2003, it was revealed that in 1925, at the age
of twenty-two, Thurmond fathered a daughter with Carrie Butler, a fifteen-
year-old Black housemaid employed by his family. He never acknowledged
to others the existence of Essie Mae Washington-Williams, but he did
maintain a limited relationship with his daughter, providing some amount
of money, sending birthday cards, and meeting in person about once a
year. A mutual respect existed between them, said his daughter, as well
as an understanding that the truth should remain concealed. "It wasn't to
my advantage to talk about anything that (he) had done," Washington-
Williams said after her father's death, when she publicly introduced herself
as Thurmond's daughter. "It certainly wasn't to the advantage of either one
of us. He of course, didn't want it to be known. Neither did I. We didn't
have any agreement about not talking about it, we just didn't talk about it."

The reason for Strom's silence regarding his daughter Essie Mae was
obvious—his political career would collapse in an instant. Forget sharing
swimming pool water and church pews with people of assorted skin tones,
that type of intimacy was nothing compared to interracial sexual relationships. Thurmond's supporters would be appalled to learn of his scandalous
behavior. People such as Kinard, the woman in Allendale who pointed out
birds and snakes stick to their own species, and who also wrote that "God
never would have put different races of people on his green earth if he
had intended them to mix." Kinard's letter to the *Guardian* newspaper
included several anecdotes of interracial relationships she had observed,
all of which ended depressingly, suggesting any love between Black and
White people results in misery. Her note reflected the discomfort and even
revulsion some people felt over the blending of races.

Such was the social context in the Lowcountry when in 1959 two nearly identical racially tinged crimes occurred within a month of each other in downtown Beaufort. Both were cases of alleged rape, and each of the cases was the racial inverse of the other, meaning that in one case a White man allegedly raped a Black woman, and in the other a Black man allegedly tried to rape a White woman. Buster brought both cases to trial on consecutive days in June 1959. The proceedings promised to stir strong feelings, especially since news cameras would be allowed in the courtroom for one of the first times in South Carolina, meaning the trials would receive maximum media exposure. Already there was enough tension without amplification from the press. As J. E. McTeer, Beaufort's longtime sheriff, once wrote: "An interracial rape case is the most upsetting crime a community can experience and racial relations in the entire county can be disrupted long afterwards."

The first incident occurred April 7, 1959, when Fred G. Davis, a twenty-four-year-old private in the marines, allegedly grabbed a fifty-five-year-old Black woman off a Beaufort sidewalk and raped her in the bushes beside tennis courts and across from the Beaufort National Cemetery, threatening to kill her if she resisted. Two high schoolers chanced upon the woman after hearing her moaning after the attack. They noticed Davis's clothing was disheveled and chased after him, ultimately helping the police subdue him. Davis admitted to Sheriff McTeer he had twice raped the Black woman, and that he also attacked White women in Georgia and Florida. Beyond these claims, nine months earlier Davis had been arrested in Beaufort County for allegedly molesting and attempting to rape a thirteen-year-old girl. He confessed to police of having an "overpowering sex urge" and that he "got pleasure out of using force on women." Given such desire, he said, he was going to have sex with a woman, whether White, Black, or whatever color.

Then, late at night on May 5, 1959, another attack occurred a few blocks away in the Point, a historic neighborhood of oak-shaded streets, charming wood-frame cottages, and fine mansions overlooking the Beaufort River.

Here a twenty-one-year-old mother of three was sweeping her kitchen and preparing baby formula to feed her newborn when she was jumped by nineteen-year-old Israel Sharpe just before midnight. Her home was locked tight, but Sharpe, wearing a white handkerchief across his face, waited until she unlocked a back door to discard some waste and forced his way inside. He grabbed her throat, fondled her body, and began tearing off the woman's clothes as he also started choking her. The woman screamed when her throat wasn't being squeezed and at one point bashed her assailant's head with a bottle she grabbed off an ironing board. Police arrived to find Sharpe and the woman struggling on the kitchen floor, her clothes torn to pieces. Sharpe bolted from the scene, hopping fences and hedges as he dashed through backyards, only briefly delaying his capture.

Sharpe's mother soon visited him in jail. He had a knot on the side of his head and bloody scratches across his body. She was convinced of his guilt, telling him "Israel, as many colored women as it is in this town why in the world did you go and get messed up with a white woman . . . You will just have to pay your penalty."

When Davis was arrested, McTeer sent him to Columbia to be evaluated for mental health issues at the state hospital. When Sharpe was arrested, McTeer sent him to Columbia to be housed in the state penitentiary, so he wouldn't be yanked from the Beaufort jail and lynched. Though they were alleged to have committed, or at least attempted, the same wrongs, only the Black man was threatened with vigilante justice. Buster Murdaugh, for his part, would not extend preferential treatment. The solicitor smoothly sidestepped any racial controversy by charging both suspects with sexual assault charges and, as was permitted by state law at the time, insisting on the death penalty for each of them.

Fred Davis's trial was called first, on June 29, 1959, at the Beaufort County Courthouse. A jury of twelve White men listened to testimony from the alleged victim as well as from Sheriff McTeer and the young men who stumbled upon the victim. All indicated Davis was responsible for the rape. Davis declined to take the stand himself or call any witnesses. His attorney argued the sexual encounter was consensual and that he never confessed to raping anyone. When the solicitor made his closing argument, he pleaded for the jury to withhold mercy and sentence Davis to die, saying the suspect "must be removed from society just as you would a mad dog." Then, employing his trademark line, Buster advised that if the jury failed to convict Davis, he'd just free the other alleged rapist since justice wasn't valued in Beaufort County. "I have one or more similar cases to the one being tried, to be brought up later in this court," said Buster, "and if you turn this defendant loose, you might as well be turning these other defendants loose also, because if you turn this man loose I'm going to turn the others loose." Buster's performance was impressive; the jury took just seventy minutes to decide upon Davis's guilt and recommend his execution.

The next day, June 30, Buster tried Israel Sharpe on a charge of assault with intent to ravish. In this case, too, Buster established definitively to a jury of six Black men and six White men that Sharpe had attempted to rape the woman while she was home alone with her children and her husband was away at work. What's worse was the fact that Sharpe was trying to target the previous tenant of the house, a woman who testified against him months earlier for Peeping Tom charges. Sharpe, fresh off the chain gang and eager for revenge, admitted to police that he realized the mistaken identity when he broke into the house but decided to try and rape the stranger anyway.

The evidence of Sharpe's guilt was overwhelming. Nonetheless, during closing arguments, the solicitor asked the jury to do more than consider the facts. Directing himself to the Black members of the jury, Buster appealed for decency, stating, "We White people are going to stop our people from messing with your women and I know that you want to stop your people from messing with our people." He referenced yesterday's heavily publicized conviction of Davis, a White man, for the rape of a Black woman. He said it was only fair for this jury to extend the same consideration to this case. "We treated you the same way we want you to treat us," said Buster. "We stood by you all, now you stand by us." The jury complied, convicting Sharpe and withholding mercy, meaning he would be sentenced to death, too.

Following the verdicts, the judge of both trials, J. Henry Johnson, praised South Carolina's legal system. The two convictions represent equality, he said, and these verdicts would "forever set it clear whether a man could get a fair trial in South Carolina regardless of race, religion, or color." Johnson was one of South Carolina's longest-serving judges, on the bench for thirty-six years. He was something of a prodigy, graduating from the Citadel military college in Charleston before the age of eighteen and becoming a lawyer at age twenty, an accomplishment that required a special act of the state legislature to admit the youngster to the bar. He often spoke his mind in court, sharing his thoughts on current events, including racial matters. During court in Colleton County in 1938, Johnson mentioned his objection to a Black man leading a prayer at the previous Democratic Convention and said there were two things he cared most about—white supremacy and state's rights. There was enough room in the country, he said, for Blacks and Whites to stay out of each others' way.

Twenty years later Johnson was more subdued in his hostility toward Blacks, but still was of the opinion that it's better for Blacks and Whites to coexist rather than commingle. A few days after the convictions of Davis and Sharpe he sentenced both men to death, per the jury's binding recommendations. Johnson, an outspoken critic of lynching, was not bothered by state-sanctioned killings. In fact, he considered the death sentences of the rapists auspicious and an argument for maintaining the status quo. "The two verdicts rendered in Beaufort this week prove the excellent relationship between the races here," said Johnson, ever the segregationist, who noted the Davis case was likely the first time a White man in the United States was sentenced to death for the rape of a Black woman.

—

Buster Murdaugh was obsessed with payback. His grandson was purely interested in pay.

By the time he was forty-five, Alex Murdaugh had earned a small fortune as a personal injury lawyer at the Lowcountry law firm that bore his family name. In 2012, he made more than $2 million. The next year, he collected an income of more than $5 million—two banner years of earnings that validated his decision to skip the solicitor's race seven years earlier. Alex was one of the "big dogs" at the Hampton law firm, with a "big reputation," said his friend and fellow lawyer Chris Wilson. Alex, he said, "didn't ever seem to have problems."

Chris Wilson knew Alex since playing baseball in his high school days. The men went to law school together, lived with each other for a bit, and stayed close friends as their legal careers flourished and they got married and started families. Wilson practiced thirty miles from Hampton in the town of Bamberg and he saw and spoke with Alex often, sometimes meeting at sports games at the University of South Carolina. The men's wives had been sorority sisters, and their children were close, too.

Wilson held Alex in high personal regard, impressed by the big-dollar settlements and awards he achieved for his clients. Alex had a knack for finding good cases and then maximizing their return. Such was the method of the entire Peters, Murdaugh, Parker, Eltzroth & Detrick law firm. The firm was regularly involved with more than half the civil cases on the docket in Hampton County, which inspired resentment among other local lawyers. One lawyer at the firm was said to have attended a funeral wake for a victim of electrocution and persuaded the family to change their legal representation for the accidental death on the spot, producing paperwork that the family then signed atop their loved one's casket. "They took business out of our pockets," said one Lowcountry lawyer.

For a number of years, lawyers at the old Murdaugh firm were exempt from being appointed to represent defendants who could not afford to hire a lawyer. These court appointments for criminal cases were generally undesirable, as they paid little, if any money, from a state reserve and could sometimes become protracted. Yet such service is considered a lawyer's duty, allowing for all people charged with a crime to have the benefit of legal counsel. According to this lawyer, the Hampton firm claimed a conflict of interest owing to the firm's long-standing relationship with the solicitor's office, an argument that worked for a number of years before there were calls for change, which by this lawyer's recollection happened in the late 1990s.

The law firm suffered another setback in 2005 when a change in state law, as well as a state supreme court ruling, reduced the ease of forum shopping, limiting the ability of plaintiff's lawyers to try cases in counties of the state with tenuous connections to a legal case. The new law was the result of corporate lobbying efforts that followed in the wake of bad press about the law firm and Hampton County. Beginning in 2002, the American Tort Reform Association mentioned Hampton County for five straight years in its annual "Judicial Hellholes" report, which highlights legal jurisdictions across the United States that return favorable verdicts for plaintiffs and big awards. As the trade association's report in 2004 claimed, "Conversations with local attorneys and residents indicate that something is amuck in Hampton County . . ."

Also in 2002, *Forbes* published its "Home Court Advantage" article about the law firm and its longtime partner Johnny Parker. The magazine profile did something near impossible—made the reader feel sympathy for some of America's largest corporations, all of whom complained of being fleeced by the small firm of country lawyers. The railroad holding company CSX was noted to be a favorite target of the law firm, paying more than $18 million in settlements and award fees over the last decade after being sued by the firm forty-eight times.

The railroad's freight operations in Hampton County exposed it to considerable legal liability, opening the door to cases involving accidents around the state, or even out of state, being routed to Hampton County because it's a place where CSX transacts business. At the time of the article's printing, seventeen cases against CSX were pending on the county docket, but only two of them involved incidents within Hampton County. Coming into town from Augusta, Georgia, near the West End of Hampton, the company's tracks ran beside the former Westinghouse plant where Micarta laminates were made. On the other side of the rails was Rigdon's Fried Chicken, a place where patrons waited in line and broiled themselves in summer atop an unshaded asphalt parking lot while waiting to step up to the order window.

Rigdon's had a motto: "Chicken Good Enough to Stop a Train." Not only was it catchy, it was true. CSX workers would stop their train at Rigdon's, hop off the engine and grab a lunch, said Amon Rigdon, who opened his namesake restaurant in 1981. The CSX employees came in so often that he got to know them as well as the locals, even though they may have lived up in Georgia or down on the coast near Charleston. Rigdon fondly remembered those friendships decades later. "We got to know all the train people and they got to know us as well," he said.

The trains used to stop for ten minutes or so while the crew picked up a bag lunch of Rigdon's famous fried chicken and some french fries. Sometimes the crew switched out train cars on a spur line nearby, prolonging their stay. But one day the train didn't stop at Rigdon's Fried Chicken, or anyplace else in Hampton County. And it stayed that way each day that followed, too. A train conductor later told Rigdon that the train crew was now forbidden from stopping in the county unless absolutely necessary. Rigdon's chicken might have been good enough to stop a train at one time, but it was no match for Hampton's legendary law firm.

At the turn of the century, a number of corporations, including CSX, Alcoa, Chevron Phillips, and Duke Power decided they'd tolerated the status quo in Hampton County for long enough. They began lobbying for changes to South Carolina's venue law, and, after a few years, found enough enthusiasm among the Republican-dominated legislature to clip litigators' wings and amend the venue rules. Yet even with these tweaks to the Palmetto State's legal code, there remained plenty of other ways for talented lawyers at the Hampton firm to find pay dirt, and they did.

Harder to regulate was the law firm's influence in the five counties of the 14th Judicial Circuit. The persuasion campaign mounted regularly by the law firm was judged by some other lawyers to be insidious and unfair. Attorneys at the old Murdaugh firm were said to spend county bar funds to wine and dine visiting judges but failed to invite the full membership to these gatherings. Eyebrows were raised when the firm bought a building and law practice in Walterboro belonging to Perry M. Buckner after the attorney was elected by lawmakers to become a state judge in 2000. Two years later, the law firm hired Gerald C. Smoak Sr. after he had served for a decade as a judge and presided over some of Parker's cases.

For decades, the law firm was said to hold a special sway with jurors, especially when Buster Murdaugh operated as both a solicitor and a plaintiff's trial lawyer. But even after Buster's era, there existed suspicions that jurors were often under the spell of the lawyers at Peters, Murdaugh, Parker, Eltzroth & Detrick. During the opening of each seasonal term of court at the Hampton County Courthouse, when county residents reported for jury duty, one lawyer said nearly every member of the law firm would come and sit in the courtroom and make an appearance before the potential jurors, reminding them of friendships and favors. One Lowcountry lawyer faulted the Murdaughs in particular for generations of inappropriate behavior. "I think they were worse than the mafia," said the lawyer. "It was sickening to watch them in action."

Tom Johnson considered the allegations of improper influence by the Hampton law firm to be overblown. "Home field advantage" was a fact of life in every rural county in South Carolina, said Johnson. In nearby Barnwell County, he cited, by way of example, outside lawyers were traditionally wary of the influence of the law firm of Solomon Blatt Sr., a longtime speaker of the South Carolina House of Representatives. In Bamberg County next door, lawyers were trepidatious of the law firm of

Julius J. "Bubba" Ness. Ness became a judge and then chief justice of the South Carolina Supreme Court before retiring and joining the Barnwell law firm Ness, Motley, Loadholt, Richardson & Poole, which represented fifty-two state governments and territories in their landmark legal settlement with four tobacco companies in 1998 that paid out more than $200 billion for public health care costs attributable to smoking-related illnesses.

In other words, there existed other top-shelf legal talent in small-town South Carolina. If the Murdaugh firm happened to be the locally dominant firm, so what, said the lawyer—someone had to be on top. "Other than being somewhat ruthless in getting business, getting cases, everything I know about them is fine," said Johnson, who practiced law in the city of Hardeeville.

Yet Johnson understood others' suspicions and gripes about a perceived good ol' boy system. They acknowledged that a slew of people in the justice system, including public officials, police, judges, jurors, and witnesses seemed to defer to members of the law firm, especially when Buster was alive and in full effect. But Johnson isn't sure how the lawyers at the Hampton firm could act differently to appease their critics. "What are you supposed to do? Pick the (jurors) who don't like you, just to level the playing field?" he said, emphasizing that a lawyer is obligated to act in the best interest of their client. "Would it even be right to squander the advantages you have?" Johnson asked.

Regardless of the reasons for the law firm's success, what was undisputed was that Peters, Murdaugh, Parker, Eltzroth & Detrick was not to be taken lightly. Even after reform to the state's venue law, the conventional wisdom among the South Carolina legal community remained the same: "You don't want to try a case in Hampton County."

Alex Murdaugh reaped the benefits of his firm's fierce reputation, negotiating a string of lucrative settlements, mostly for auto accident cases he handled. His results attracted attention, and in 2015 Alex was chosen to lead the South Carolina Trial Lawyers Association. The members of this group, later renamed the South Carolina Association for Justice, met each

August at a resort hotel on Hilton Head Island for their annual meeting. By day, the lawyers golfed and swam and attended continuing legal education seminars. At night, they mingled at political fundraisers, cocktail receptions, and fancy dinners. Many of the Palmetto State's highest-performing and wealthiest lawyers attended each year. These men—they were mostly men—wore expensive dark suits, enjoyed fine wine, and cruised the highways of the Palmetto State in sleek black Mercedes sedans. But even those standards of luxury were basic to some; one successful young lawyer who doubles as a state representative drives a Rolls-Royce sport utility vehicle to county courthouses and the State House. The car's vanity license plate reads SETTLD.

Alex didn't drive a black Mercedes, but he did eventually buy one for his wife to replace her Range Rover. He was much less refined than some of his peers in the legal world, staying true to his country roots, and, like his forebears, never developing champagne tastes. That's not to say he was humble. Alex spent money on extravagances like private school tuition, household staff, property maintenance, a swimming pool, private plane travel, far-flung vacations, three homes, investment properties, firearms, sporting and fishing trips and equipment, golf outings, and more.

To pay for all this, Alex had to regularly win big in the courtroom or around the negotiating table. He hit his stride just a few years into his employment at his family's old firm in Hampton, capitalizing on a handful of tragedies that resulted in serious injury or death. One case involved members of the Plyler family, two of whom died in a car crash on July 16, 2005, on Interstate 95 in Hampton County. Angela Lynn Plyler was driving her Ford Explorer north on the interstate on her way to Columbia. Her fourteen-year-old son Justin was sleeping in the passenger seat to her right, and her daughters Alania, twelve, and Hannah, eight, sat in the back.

Alania remembers hearing a pop. This was a tire failing. She heard her mother scream as she lost control of their vehicle, which careened right, off the highway, down an embankment, and into a forest. The car crashed through a few trees before squarely hitting one trunk and coming to an abrupt halt. It was very quiet, said Alania. There was the smell of "pine and blood."

Alania's sister was moving. Her mother and brother were not. Their heads were bloodied. Alania was trapped in the wreckage, beneath her dead brother and the front passenger seat, which had collapsed. When Alania moved her arm it became twisted. She told Hannah to climb out the back of the car, run up the hill and signal for help. Eventually rescue crews responded to the accident, employing the Jaws of Life to free all the bodies from the mangled vehicle. While rescuers labored to extricate young Alania she helplessly viewed an unmerciful horror show. "I watched them load my fourteen-year-old brother and my mom into the body bags," she recalled. Alania was taken by helicopter to a hospital in Savannah, Georgia, where she was treated for a crushed shoulder, torn knee ligaments, a shredded leg muscle, a twice-broken femur, and more.

Following a chance meeting, Alania's father brought the accident to the attention of a Columbia-area lawyer. This attorney soon involved, or associated, the case with Alex Murdaugh and two of his partners at the Hampton law firm, Johnny Parker and Ronnie Crosby. Lawsuits were filed on behalf of the Plyler family against multiple defendants, including Ford Motor Company and tire manufacturer Bridgestone Corporation. Alania remembers interfacing with Alex. "Alex was the talker," she said, "the one that informed you what's going on."

In 2009 the case settled for a multimillion dollar payout. Alania was sixteen years old, still a minor. She said she was not told exactly how much money she would receive in two years, when she became an adult, but that it was substantial enough that she would never have to work a day in her life. Alania, who was living in a challenging, impoverished situation while attending high school and waiting for the lawsuit to resolve, began to dream of the money waiting for her, picturing it as a "bottomless pit" that would enable her to buy a car and a beautiful home. "It was never going to run out," fantasized the teenager. Until she and her sister became adults, she was told, her money would be safeguarded by a court-appointed conservator, in this case Hampton banker Russell Laffitte. To enable the appointment of Laffitte, his longtime friend, Alex allegedly misrepresented in court paperwork that the Plyler girls lived in Hampton County.

As the Plyler family lawsuits settled, Alex began work on another case involving alleged tire failure causing an accident on Interstate 95. In this incident on August 22, 2009, Pamela Pinckney suffered a tire blowout that caused her car to roll into the highway median. Her sixteen-year-old niece Natarsha Thomas was injured in the face, and her nineteen-year-old son, Hakeem, hit his head as he was tossed from the car, becoming paralyzed from the neck down. Alex was hired to represent the two teens. The lawyer then persuaded Pamela Pinckney to personally hire Cory Fleming, his college buddy and godfather to his son Paul.

Two years later, in 2011, Alex negotiated substantial but undisclosed settlements for his clients. Again Alex arranged for Laffitte, vice president at his family's Palmetto State Bank, to become a conservator for those injured in the accident. This meant Laffitte was entrusted, and compensated for, safeguarding money paid to the severely injured Hakeem Pinckney. Hakeem, a hearing-impaired man who played football at the South Carolina School for the Deaf and Blind, relied on a ventilator to breathe since the car accident and required full-time medical care. Laffitte also was appointed conservator for Natarsha Thomas, even though the settlement was finalized just days away from her eighteenth birthday, when she would become an adult. Court paperwork signed by Laffitte stated Thomas was years younger and, as a supposed minor, therefore in need of a conservator.

And then, as the Pinckney/Thomas case wrapped up for Alex, he accepted another accident case involving the Badger family. In 2011, while Arthur Badger was driving in Allendale County, a UPS truck collided with his vehicle, killing Arthur's wife Donna. Arthur hired Alex to represent him, and Alex negotiated a settlement with UPS that paid Arthur

Badger and his six children millions. Arthur Badger said he liked working with Alex: "I looked up to him because he helped me out." Among the papers Alex asked Badger to sign without explanation was a form that switched control of his late wife's estate to the banker Russell Laffitte.

Most lawyers would have been ecstatic to negotiate these settlements and win so much money for their injured clients. But these windfalls were hardly enough for Buster's disciple. Alex turned to stealing, taking as much money as he made. He pilfered from the most pitiful people around: kids who lost their parent, kids who were injured themselves in car crashes, and a paralyzed man on a ventilator. The more vulnerable and desperate the client, the more of their money Alex was inclined to grab for himself.

Alex said he cannot recall the first time he stole, one of his few believable claims given the sheer magnitude of his fraud and theft. Possibly Alex was always taking from others in some way or another, going back at least to the sham raffle during his college days. Since then the stakes of his trickery grew much larger. His later victims would lose much more than a few bucks on a bogus prize ticket.

Alex's thefts were as brazen as they were simple. He looted his clients by taking advantage of the trust they placed in him as their lawyer. Instead of helping these clients in the wake of tragedy, as he pledged to do, Alex robbed them blind. His scheme mirrored the old tactics of his grandfather, suggesting his criminal instincts were inherited and/or learned at Buster's knee. Alex used his position as a lawyer to manipulate legal settlements and intercept and redirect money intended for his clients. In many cases Alex stole most of the money owed a client, and in at least one case he stole all of it. Few people were wise to his crimes, taking his wealth at face value given his family name and his position as a partner at the law firm. The thought that Alex was horribly crooked never crossed most people's minds. Why would anyone so successful need to steal?

In many cases, Alex stole by simply never revealing the true amount owed to a client. He typically would negotiate for some money to be paid to his client in cash, and use other money to fund annuities for the client, which would give them regular income payments over a long period. But Alex also withheld and disguised other money, and then, with the help of Laffitte, routed it through Palmetto State Bank to be distributed for Alex's own use.

In the case of Natarsha Thomas, Alex directed the law firm to send $350,000 of her money to Palmetto State Bank through two checks made payable to the bank with the following description in the memo line: "Settlement Proceeds—Natasha Thomas." Laffitte said he didn't read the memo line and the misspelled name of the woman whose money he was supposed to be protecting. He deposited this check in the bank's account and then, per Alex's instructions, redistributed the money to Alex, members of his family, and others. None of it went to Thomas. Similarly, Alex had his firm send $310,000 of Hakeem Pinckney's settlement money to the bank, where Laffitte received the check and again redistributed the proceeds at Alex's direction. No money went to Pinckney.

While some of the money taken from Thomas and Pinckney went to Alex and his family, other money was used to pay off some of the fourteen secretive loans Laffitte extended, without collateral, to Alex from money held in trust for the underage Plyler girls. Laffitte loaned himself at least $225,000 from Hannah Plyler, too, using the borrowed money to pay off loans and to pay a swimming pool company. Hannah was never informed of this arrangement, that her settlement money, on which Laffitte was making tens of thousands of dollars to manage and safeguard, was being loaned to her conservator and lawyer.

As Hannah's eighteenth birthday approached, Alex and Laffitte scrambled to replenish her account. This was accomplished in part by borrowing money from trust accounts belonging to Alex's other clients, and also by Alex stealing even more money, this time from the Badger family. Just like before, his firm wrote checks to the bank and Laffitte redistributed the money, claiming to have overlooked the Badger name written in the corner of the check. About $1.3 million of the Badger money was given to Murdaugh, his family, and others who had extended him loans, while Arthur Badger separately received about $370,000 in cash and was never told of the additional money.

Though Alex was stealing hundreds of thousands of dollars outright and had easy access to loans from his underage clients' trust funds, he could not get ahead financially. His bank accounts were regularly negative and in overdraft. Each time he stole or borrowed money, it more or less disappeared in a flash, used to satisfy some other loan or restore his balance at Palmetto State Bank. He borrowed large amounts from friends, family, and a law partner, too, but these transactions only bought him time until the next financial emergency. He spiraled further and further into debt, desperate for a way out.

So Murdaugh devised a new scheme to steal money from clients—he would divert their money to an account he controlled that mimicked a legitimate financial services company used by him and his law partners. In the process he'd betray a friend he had known for years named Michael Gunn, a principal of Forge Consulting, which provided financial services for the recipients of legal settlements. He saw him each year at the legal conference in Hilton Head, where they'd normally squeeze in a round of golf and a meal. Gunn was formerly a lobbyist for the South Carolina Trial Lawyers Association and more recently ran Atlanta-based Forge Consulting's office in Columbia. The men were close enough friends for Alex and Maggie to be invited to his wedding in New York City, which they attended despite a snowstorm.

Alex and his law partners typically worked with Gunn to establish annuities for legal clients receiving a settlement. The money funding these investments was paid directly by the defendant or their insurer, and never from money held by the client or their lawyer. While Gunn would work with a plaintiff's lawyer like Alex to devise the best type of settlement plan and annuity for a client, he would never expect for them to hand him a check.

In 2015 Alex quietly established a bank account in the name of "Richard A. Murdaugh, Sole Proprietor, Doing Business As 'Forge'." He then directed his law firm, as well as a client, to write checks from clients' funds payable to Forge, exploiting the similar names. "I want it to be Forge," Alex told his paralegal Annette Griswold, telling her she should think of Forge Consulting as the big company and Forge as a smaller part. She accepted the explanation. At first glance, a client's funds were simply being placed into an annuity.

Griswold would pass her boss's request along to the law firm's accounting department, which would sometimes nonetheless issue a check to the more familiar "Forge Consulting." Griswold would then send the check back and tell them to print it again. Alex insisted on handling these checks personally. One time he told Griswold he was meeting his friend Gunn from Forge Consulting for dinner halfway between their homes and would deliver the check himself. Another time Alex said Gunn was coming to hunt at Moselle, and he'd pass the check along then. Knowing Alex's habit of misplacing things, Griswold thought this a bad idea. "I was so worried he was going to lose these checks," she said.

Alex did not lose the checks; he made sure to deposit them in his own Forge account. Gunn never received a hand-delivered check from Alex, never met him halfway for dinner, and never hunted at Moselle. These were some of Alex's many, many lies, yet unexposed. His brazen theft went undetected, too. Alex followed the playbook of his grandfather Buster, and never told his clients the true amount they should expect in the settlements he negotiated on their behalf. As he siphoned away their money, he made sure to at least toss a few scraps to his clients, who were often grateful to receive anything to ease their hardship.

But not all his attempts to collect other people's money went undetected. One year the law firm attempted to repay Alex's brother Randy Murdaugh $125,000 for money he loaned to the law firm for operating expenses. The firm wrote a check intended for Randy but it was mistakenly issued to Alex.

Instead of drawing attention to the error because he knew he had not loaned any money to the firm, Alex held the check and then supposedly lost it. Alex then asked the law firm's accounting department to recut for him the check he was not owed. Once they did so he deposited this money. Six months later, Alex supposedly rediscovered the original check and deposited that one, too, collecting a grand sum of $250,000 that did not belong to him. When eventually confronted by a law partner Alex pledged it was all an honest mistake and he paid the money back with interest. His partners gave Alex the benefit of the doubt, knowing him to be sloppy with his personal finances, much like his grandfather.

This kind of behavior had come to be expected from Alex, who had to be policed like an incorrigible child when it came to spending the firm's money. He inappropriately charged the law firm for assorted expenses, even school tuition, but always paid back the money when confronted. These mistakes were forgiven, chalked up to carelessness, tolerated as goofy behavior from a lawyer who brought in big cases. Said his law partner Mark Ball: "He just wasn't a very good rule follower at all."

———

Baked into the rebellious, defiant attitudes toward federal desegregation orders was the sting of South Carolina's humiliation during the Civil War and the South's slow recovery under federal policies of Reconstruction. South Carolina paid dearly in the war, forfeiting much blood, money, and pride. The state's undoing began as Union general William Tecumseh Sherman and his troops left Savannah, Georgia, to begin a march of terror through South Carolina's Lowcountry that would take them to the state capital, Columbia. David Conyngham, the war correspondent for the *New York Herald* who traveled with Sherman and his men, said a rage stirred inside the Union soldiers as soon as they entered the state where the Civil War began:

The feeling among the troops was one of extreme bitterness toward the people of the State of South Carolina. It was freely expressed as the column hurried over the bridge at Sister's Ferry, eager to commence the punishment of "original secessionists." Threatening words were heard from soldiers who prided themselves on "conservatism in house-burning" while in Georgia, and officers openly confessed their fears that the coming campaign would be a wicked one. Just or unjust as this feeling was toward the country people of South Carolina, it was universal.

The torches came out early and often. The soldiers burned hundreds of bales of cotton as well as whole towns. The Union Army burned Gillisonville and Lawtonville and McPhersonville down in the Lowcountry, more or less wiping those communities out for good. Then the Northern troops torched Barnwell, Lexington, and Orangeburg as they approached Columbia, which was also extensively burned. Conyngham observed assorted infernos across the South Carolina Lowcountry, writing:

In Georgia few houses were burned; here, few escaped; and the country was converted into one vast bonfire. The pine forests were fired, the resin factories were fired, the public buildings and private dwellings were fired. The middle of the finest day looked black and gloomy, for a dense smoke arose on all sides, clouding the very heavens. At night the tall pine trees seemed so many huge pillars of fire. The flames hissed and screeched, as they fed on the fat resin and dry branches, imparting to the forests a most fearful appearance.

Soldiers and civilians looted homes and stores. Many stray dogs were shot and killed. Railroad tracks were destroyed, made into "Sherman's neckties" by burning piles of railroad ties atop tracks and then twisting and warping the rails when they turned red-hot. Sherman himself even participated in the burning of most combustible things in South Carolina when he stayed at a formerly fine plantation home outside Beaufort, where the branches of live oaks lining the driveway had been hacked off by troops to use as firewood. Apparently Sherman's underlings forgot to supply their general with a bundle. As he wrote in a memoir: "I slept on the floor of the house, but the night was so bitter cold that I got up by the fire several times, and when it burned low I rekindled it with an old mantel-clock and the wreck of a bedstead which stood in a corner of the room—the only act of vandalism that I recall done by myself personally during the war."

Like the mantel-clock, South Carolina soon was in ashes. Sections of the formerly proud and prosperous state lay devastated if not outright destroyed. But Conyngham had little sympathy for the "Spartan State . . . that had hatched treason," believing South Carolina deserving of the hardships it courted through its secession. As Conyngham summed up the scene in South Carolina after Sherman swept through half the state: "Her cities are in ruins; her plantations are devastated; her domineering aristocrats are houseless, homeless outcasts, scattered over the world, while a wail of anguish goes forth from her widows and orphans."

So broken and tattered was South Carolina after the Civil War that the past seemed better by default. Over time the romanticism of the past created a Southern mythology promoting the rebel spirit, the celebration of state's rights, and of not standing for being told what to do. The Southerner became someone who drew his identity through defiance, or outright rebellion. This attitude was encapsulated by a symbol that in the mid–twentieth century became ubiquitous in the South—the Confederate battle flag, popularly known as the rebel flag or Confederate flag.

In Hampton, the rebel flag was proudly flown at the Loan and Exchange Bank that fronted, fittingly enough, Lee Avenue. The bank's owner Ralph O. Bowden, whose father was said to be a veteran Confederate soldier, hung oversize rebel flags from an awning and across the front door during the

Watermelon Festival and on holidays, including Confederate Memorial Day and Jefferson Davis's birthday. After a photograph of the bank's flag-draped facade was published by the Associated Press in 1949 it created a small tempest. Bowden began receiving lots of mail about his rebel flags, both letters of condemnation and letters of praise. He kept the rebel banners flying and complained about the fact that his largest Confederate flag was made by a Yankee manufacturer. When it came to the Confederate flag Bowden was a lifelong devotee; the symbol topped the cake on his seventy-sixth birthday.

Bowden founded the Loan and Exchange Bank in Hampton in 1907 with two partners, back in the days when he brought over the oak bucket of lemonade to the share with the boys each afternoon—old Hampton's version of a happy hour. The Loan and Exchange Bank was one of the few financial institutions in the area to survive the Depression. The only time the bank closed its doors, it was said, was when Bowden went fishing. Bowden considered his enterprise a "briar patch bank" and, as the rebel flags fluttering outside the bank indicated, he was resistant to new federal rules, including ones for community bankers who had been in business for decades. The *Guardian* labeled Bowden as Hampton's "unreconstructed banker," and one of his successors later marveled at the loans Bowden would extend, such as putting mortgages on mules and moonshine stills. "The mortgage listed so many feet of copper pipe and so many pounds of mash," said Charles Laffitte Jr., whose father took over the bank. "The bank examiners had a fit, but Mr. Bowden didn't care."

Beyond decorating his bank with the Confederate flag, Bowden spiffed up Hampton by striking a deal with the town to split the cost of a town clock, provided it be placed in front of the bank on Lee Avenue. In 1948 laborers installed a large and handsome bronze-encased clock atop a tall, metal tower in the middle of Hampton's main street. Made by O. B. McClintock Co. of Minneapolis, it featured four thirty-inch clock faces and sounded off every quarter hour by playing the melody of

Westminster Quarters, also known as the Cambridge Chimes. Young journalist Martha Bee Anderson was so ecstatic over the new installation she named her "Around the Clock" newspaper column after the time-telling tower. "Meet me around the clock" was a popular catchphrase for locals, with the clock serving as a rendezvous point for teens and as an axis for lines of dancing Hampton residents to snake around after homecoming games and school pep rallies.

The clock was not wound on its face but operated by controls housed inside the bank and connected by underground wire. Bowden's bargain with the town stipulated the bank would be responsible for the clock's upkeep, an easy concession for Bowden to make since he would only own the bank for a few more years. In 1955 an elderly Bowden, who had outlived both his original partners, sold the Loan and Exchange Bank to Charles A. Laffitte, the president of a bank in Allendale. Laffitte was the son of Moses Tucker Laffitte, the banker and mayor in the town of Estill who came to Buster's defense in the pages of the Charleston newspaper. Upon the Laffitte family's purchase of the Hampton's Loan and Exchange Bank, the families became even closer, with friendships, and financial relationships, to continue for generations.

When Charles Laffitte bought the bank he also acquired responsibility for the clock, an obligation that was part civic duty, part thankless headache and continual expense. But the new owner agreed to make sure the town clock kept ticking and chiming, just as he agreed to keep other bank traditions alive. "I want to wish Mr. Bowden happiness in his retirement and say that the new board of directors on last Thursday resolved to fly the bank's Confederate flag every Watermelon Festival day in memorial to Mr. Bowden," said Laffitte upon taking ownership.

One thing that would change, however, was the bank's ugly, spartan interior, which featured two bare light bulbs hanging from the ceiling and three adding machines plugged directly into the lights. The decor would be modernized, said Laffitte, with liberal use of Micarta, a plastic laminate made right down the street in a giant factory owned by Westinghouse Electric Corporation that began operation in 1951. Micarta was all the rage in Hampton in the 1950s, used in almost every new or renovated building in town. The hospital coated the surfaces of its operating room and nursery in Micarta, the power company upgraded the counters in its Hampton offices, and the Hampton Country Club renovated its bar with the local laminate, choosing a teak-like paneling for the walls and a speckled "Beige Constellation" design for its bar tops. A formaldehyde factory covered its reception room in Micarta laminate, a full-circle, meta-type situation given that formaldehyde is an ingredient in Micarta. When it came time to replace the basketball hoops in the school gym in Varnville, down came the old plywood and up went white backboards made of, what else, Hampton-made Micarta.

Micarta was exceedingly popular outside of Hampton, too, used across the world, deep under the sea, and up at the edge of space. Micarta was used to make radiation shielding for nuclear submarines, missile components, the interiors of jetliners, electrical and textile equipment, decorative screens, countertops, the inside surface of refrigerators, body armor, water skis, and lots more. To meet overseas demand, Westinghouse produced the versatile, durable material in Belgium, too, and marketed it as Panolux.

To make Micarta, workers in Hampton bathed fabric in liquid plastic resins before pressing and curing the combined material into thin sheets. By changing assorted variables—such as the type of fabric or resins or the production process—innumerable types of Micarta could be made by the thousand employees who came to work at the growing plant, which took over a plywood and laminate factory operated for the last decade by the Plywoods-Plastics Corporation. The jobs provided by these two corporations came as sweet relief to a local economy flattened by the closure of Hampton County sawmills. The Big Salkehatchie Cypress Company succumbed to the financial difficulty of the Depression and its Varnville sawmill shuttered in 1933 and then burned down a year later. Up in Miley within the Salkehatchie Swamp, the Lightsey Brothers Lumber Company's sawmill operated for twenty more years before it, too, closed in 1954 due to lack of profitability. As Judge Johnson once remarked from the bench, "Our Lowcountry has no money and little industry but it is a most delightful place in which to live."

Almost overnight Westinghouse supercharged Hampton County. Not only did the Micarta plant provide three shifts a day of steady jobs, the factory became a point of pride for locals: Micarta was incredibly useful and in high demand, and one of the few places it was made in the world was Hampton. The Micarta plant provided another opportunity, too. Some employees earned promotions that sent them to postings at Westinghouse headquarters in Pittsburgh or to Europe. For a community out in the sticks of South Carolina, these pathways were the modern-day equivalent of the old railroad, providing connections to the wider world. "Micarta had been like the Midas touch to Hampton," wrote the *Guardian*'s Anderson, whose husband worked at the Westinghouse Micarta plant.

The Micarta factory's payroll helped many families obtain a middle-class existence that previously eluded them in the heavily agrarian community. New homes were built for the workers who moved to town to make plywood and laminates, creating a West End of Hampton. A sense of small-town vibrancy pervaded the community. People, if not rich, at least had the pocket money to buy a cold treat at the soda shop beside the movie theater, summer passes for the kids at the Varnville Pavilion and Pool, and clothing and housewares at places like the Parker Bros. shoe and department store. During this upswing, Morris Young moved from Beaufort to Hampton to open his own store, Morray Jewelers, on Lee Avenue. He and his family were the only Jewish people in town, said Morris's son Alan, not that anyone cared. "I think the numbers were so small nobody worried about us," said Alan, the boy who once made a watermelon explode across a girl's dress.

To keep up with the times Buster Murdaugh moved his law office into a new, one-story building on First Street in 1954, along Lawyer's Row, where a line of law offices sat just across the street from the courthouse and a block off Lee Avenue. On the outside Buster's boxy, semi-modern-looking new building was made of concrete block and brick, with large windows and a massive door. Inside it featured some building materials made in Hampton, such as walls lined with plywood paneling, both in natural tones and in striated, eye-rest green. Fluorescent lights hung from above and the rooms were filled with chrome and leather furniture set upon floors covered in asphalt tiles. The building featured automatic air conditioning and heating, a luxury for the time.

Buster shared the new law office with Clyde Eltzroth, who had the distinction of being the rare lawyer who passed the South Carolina bar without attending law school. Eltzroth moved to Varnville as an infant from the bayous of Louisiana, his mother accompanying her brothers to work for the Big Salkehatchie Cypress Company, trading one cypress swamp for another. He served in the navy during World War II and returned home to work as Hampton County's tax collector. At night he studied law in Buster's law office and in 1952 began practicing law alongside him. Four years later they were joined by lawyer J. Robert "Bob" Peters Jr.

The law firm of Murdaugh, Eltzroth and Peters won a number of vehicle accident cases in the late 1950s and collected large awards for their clients. One accident brought an award of $42,000 after the firm sued the surviving driver of an accident that killed a passenger. Another delivered $140,000 to the family of a mother of eight who was killed in a collision with a car trailer in Hampton—one of the largest civil lawsuit awards in state history. And in another case a jury decided the Seaboard Air Line Railroad should pay $110,000 for its role in a crash between a train and a car that killed three people in Garnett in Hampton County.

While the high-dollar verdicts pleased the clients of Murdaugh, Eltzroth, and Peters, for others they were emblematic of a legal trend poisoning the entire country—too many lawsuits that paid out too much money. As Buster and his partners won a string of big cases, a piece in

Harper's Magazine in January 1959 argued that the personal injury lawsuit had become a "national pastime . . . Cherished traditions of honesty and fair play are being eroded away for an accidental injury is now all too often viewed as a golden opportunity to harvest a windfall." Martha Bee made similar observations back in 1954, pleading with her "Around the Clock" readers to shake off apathy and resist the legal squeeze being implemented by plaintiff's lawyers. "As long as we condone outrageous lawsuits against individuals and companies and sit on juries and join the crowd to vote 'like they vote,' we're stealing our own rights and privileges and threatening our own peaceable lives."

When lawyers for the Seaboard railroad complained a jury's award was inflated, a judge agreed with the argument and reduced the amount to $60,000, which Buster's client accepted instead of retrying the case. After the verdict, the opposing lawyers also noted that Solicitor Murdaugh attended the coroner's inquest of the accident in his official capacity and then turned around and filed a civil lawsuit, which they claimed was a violation of state law. The judge ducked the issue, ruling the defense lawyer's protest came too late. This complaint, that Buster leveraged his prosecutorial powers to influence civil cases, was one that was often grumbled about in South Carolina's legal community.

When it came to consuming alcohol, Paul Murdaugh was a determined young man. He began drinking as a young teen, his intoxication captured often on camera, with photos of his mouth pressed tight against assorted containers of alcohol. His face appeared flush and expressive in these photos. In one he clung to a friend in order to stand up. Family habits and history made Paul's early relationship with alcohol unavoidable. Booze had been a mainstay in Murdaugh households for generations. With every illicit gulp, Paul was keeping family tradition alive.

The underage teen counted on the help of his family to access alcohol. He purchased booze with his mom's credit card and his older brother's ID. Paul didn't seem to mind that he hardly looked like Buster and was also considerably smaller than his big brother. Paul used Buster's ID so often that Buster called home from college to complain and demand its return.

Fake IDs didn't always work. Once a bartender at a bowling alley confiscated Paul's bogus ID, prompting Paul to call his father to complain. Another time Paul enlisted the help of his mother in his quest for alcohol, persuading her to call and badger the manager of a grocery store after Paul was denied the chance to purchase beer. Other times Mom and Dad provided the alcohol, or at least let it be consumed in their presence when they joined the party. During summertime, Alex would knock back drinks on the boat with the boys and their friends, and was once photographed swallowing a plastic syringe of alcohol plunged into his mouth by Paul's teenage, bikini-clad girlfriend. Back home at Moselle a case of cold beers reliably chilled in the deer cooler within the skinning shed—free for the taking for the boys' visiting friends.

Alex and Maggie seemed unconcerned with the legal consequences of such permissiveness and took few, if any, steps to prevent their sons and their friends from drinking as teenagers, even when Paul regularly became intoxicated to the point he could not speak clearly or walk without stumbling. Even as a high schooler Paul Murdaugh had the reputation of a first-rate drunk. To hear friends tell it, Paul developed a split personality when he became severely inebriated. These friends gave a name to Paul's evil alter ego: "Timmy." Nobody liked Timmy. Timmy was trouble. "It started one night at Moselle—Mr. Alex's house in Moselle . . . I don't remember who came up with the name, but it's just a different name because he turns into a completely, totally different person," said Anthony Cook, one of Paul's friends from Hampton. "So somebody will say—when they can tell he's drunk, somebody will say, 'All right. Here comes Timmy. We got to go.'"

When Timmy came out, Paul crashed his Ford truck. This happened at least twice, and Paul once enlisted his parents and grandfather, Randolph Murdaugh, to help clear one of the accident scenes of beer cans and guns, said his high school girlfriend, Morgan Doughty. When Timmy came out, Paul abused Morgan, also more than once. And when Timmy came out, said Anthony, "(Paul) loved to tear stuff up."

Beyond smashing automobiles and mistreating his girlfriend, one telltale sign that Timmy had arrived was Paul's display of strange, seemingly involuntary mannerisms. "When he goes to point, he can't point with one finger. His hands are doing this the whole time," says Anthony, mimicking Paul's open-handed jabbing motion. "They are stuck wide open and his eyes (are) as big (and) round as half dollars and he don't blink. It's crazy."

Paul's reckless behavior attracted unwanted attention, especially when he was out on the water. Paul was cited at least once for underage possession of alcohol by the South Carolina Department of Natural Resources (DNR), whose law enforcement division has authority over recreational boating. It wasn't Paul's only run-in with the marine patrol. Connor Cook, also an experienced boater and a cousin to Anthony, says Paul "always had problems with DNR . . . like showing out (off) and getting pulled over in the boat and stuff," says Connor. "He told me DNR doesn't like him."

No matter where Paul went, alcohol was within easy reach. One friend to his parents remembers seeing Paul on Edisto Beach, when he was about fifteen years old, walking around with a beer in hand, unabashed. Buster and Paul impressed some people as polite and friendly young men. Yet others considered the boys cruel bullies and spoiled brats who never faced consequences for their misbehavior. Alex was said to be amused by their antics, even when schoolteachers and principals were not. "He never disciplined them. He always laughed about it and thought it was funny," said one acquaintance of Alex and his family.

Like his father, Paul found it a challenge to follow rules. He changed schools a few times, leaving public school, where his grandmother Libby

Murdaugh served on the local school board, for private school, finishing at Thomas Heyward Academy in Jasper County, one of the state's legacy segregation academies, which were private schools that formed across South Carolina in the wake of school desegregation orders during the civil rights era. Paul was hardly much better behaved there, where he was remembered for making obnoxious comments and bragging to school employees how he escaped trouble when stopped in his vehicle by the police. As he neared graduation, Paul was among a small group of students sent to the library toward the end of school each day in an attempt to keep him contained and under control until the dismissal bell rang. One man associated with Thomas Heyward Academy remembers Paul regularly acting obnoxiously. To him Paul's eyes appeared dead. "If Paul wasn't a sociopath," said the man, "he was at least close."

While Paul finished high school Buster was enrolled at Wofford College, a small private institution in Spartanburg, in the Upstate area of South Carolina, a corner of the state far from the coast and within the foothills of North Carolina's Blue Ridge Mountains. Buster joined the same fraternity, Kappa Alpha Order, as his father and grandfather, and set his sights on attending law school after graduation. During the fall semester of his junior year in 2016, a series of blog posts attributed to Buster Murdaugh were published on a website associated with a digital photography class at Wofford College. The posts contained critiques of assorted photographs, but also provided a glimpse of the author's thoughts and life. The author of these blog posts discussed family vacations alongside photos of Bermuda, Kentucky, and Jackson Hole, Wyoming. He commented on wildlife images, including a blue marlin leaping from the ocean, writing:

> *I picked this picture because I really enjoy to go offshore fishing. I have a beach house and a boat and we usually go most of summer weekends. I also chose this because I think that the marlin is the prettiest fish in the ocean. Catching a marlin are one of the more*

rare things in life for not many people are able to experience it. I on the other hand have been very fortunate to have been able to catch one of these fish.

In another post he wrote about the wood duck, a handsome and colorful inhabitant of South Carolina's wetlands:

They are very indigenous to the low country of South Carolina, which is where I am from. I chose this picture because I believe that they are one of the more beautiful creatures on this earth . . . The second reason I chose this picture is because I am an avid hunter so I spend many cold wet mornings perusing these ducks. I have had many of them mounted because of their sheer beauty. The lines of the ducks feathers is what I find so amusing. How the white almost acts as a border toward the alignment of other colors.

One post discussed *Lunch Atop a Skyscraper*, the famous photograph of ironworkers eating on a steel beam of the unfinished RCA Building in New York City in 1932. "One thing that I like about this picture is the composition," he wrote. "You can clearly tell this picture was taken a long time ago. Another thing that appeals to me is that the people are perpendicular to the beam they are sitting on." He also critiqued World War II combat photographer Joe Rosenthal's iconic 1945 image of United States Marines raising the American flag on the Japanese island of Iwo Jima, writing, ". . . you can tell that the picture is very old. The flag is one of my favorite parts of this picture. You can see how the flag is blowing in the wind also, to me the flag seems to be brighter than anything else in the picture which is very cool."

One of Buster's short blog posts, too, contained an image of the Hampton County Courthouse, which had both aesthetic and sentimental value to the college student.

I chose this picture one, because Hampton is a really small town with a small population of 2,837 so the courthouse is quite the iconic building. I also chose this picture because the courthouse plays an important role within my family. My entire family is in the law business so I have spent a fair amount of time within this building. Its also very important because one day I wish to be a lawyer and a good portion of my career will take place within the building. I also think that the character of this building presents good lines and a lot of photographic potential.

During the same semester Buster published these photographic critiques, his parents and brother moved from the family's home in town to their hunting retreat at Moselle. The fierce gusts of Hurricane Matthew knocked pine trees onto the Hampton house in the fall of 2016, prompting the Murdaughs to vacate the home while it underwent repair. One summer in college Buster moved to Moselle, too. He didn't live in the main house but instead camped out in the roadside cabin with two buddies, Rogan Gibson and Nolen Tuten. Gibson had lived next door to the Murdaughs in Hampton when he was a boy and considered them a second family, calling everyone by nicknames. He knew Miss Maggie and her parents, Papa T and Grandmar. He knew Alex, otherwise known as Big Red, and Alex's mom and dad, Em and Handsome. He knew Buster as Bus and Paul as Rooster.

Gibson joined the Murdaughs at their house on Edisto Beach, where Alex, Maggie, and the boys went almost every weekend during the summer. He spent a lot of time at Moselle, too, hunting and fishing and helping maintain the feed lots to attract wild game. Come nighttime Gibson would take his turn laying waste to hogs, using a high-powered rifle with a thermal imaging scope to see the swine in the dark. There was always the question of what to do with the carrion. Sometimes the boys skinned the animal, other times they gave it away or left it to rot in the woods.

The best way to kill hogs was with Buster and Paul's expensive semiautomatic rifles, which were identical save that Buster's rifle was black and Paul's rifle was tan. These AR-style rifles were configured to fire .300 Blackout ammunition, which enabled them to spew big, heavy, slow-moving rounds that are especially effective at short distances. According to one former police officer, .300 Blackout rounds "pack a punch" and "penetrate like a bitch."

Buster and Paul received the twin rifles as Christmas gifts in 2016, when Buster was twenty years old and Paul was seventeen. The high-end rifles had been purchased from a second cousin of Alex who worked as a state wildlife officer and moonlighted as a gunsmith. The boys' aunt, Marian Proctor, recalled her surprise when her sister Maggie told her about the gifts. "She seemed to be fine with those," said Proctor. "I remember when she wanted to give them those for Christmas and I, just, just growing up with girls and not in the hunting world . . . I said, 'Maggie, why would you give those boys those guns?'"

"They love to shoot hogs," Maggie replied.

Proctor accepted this justification, although with some reservation. "I understood that the hogs were tearing up their property, but it just scared me that they would, that the boys would have such a dangerous weapon," Proctor later reflected. "But I know nothing about guns."

She and Maggie were close and their families celebrated holidays and family milestones together, often with the sisters' parents. Though they were both raising families in the Lowcountry, their lives had major differences. Something—everything—changes with the crossing of the swamp. Maggie and Alex were raising two boys out in the country in one of the state's poorest counties. Proctor and her husband were raising three girls in ritzy downtown Charleston, their multimillion-dollar home surrounded by some of the city's finest and largest mansions. Though Charleston and Hampton are separated by a mere seventy miles as the crow flies, they seem worlds and generations apart.

When Alex bought rifles for Buster and Paul he also purchased expensive accessories, such as thermal scopes and suppressors, the latter of which, better known as silencers, muffle the crack of the rifles. Yet Alex never completed the government paperwork required to obtain the suppressors, causing Alex's gunsmith cousin to withhold the devices, even though Alex had paid in full. The whole Murdaugh family was similarly casual and careless with their weaponry. Dozens of rifles and shotguns sat unsecured in their gun room at Moselle, and ammunition was spread across assorted shelves and other surfaces. Other guns were left out in the open in the shed and were stashed in the cabs of the black and white trucks parked around the property—pickups that had names like *White Boy* and *Dolly*. The keys to these vehicles were typically left in the ignition or center consoles, the Murdaughs being utterly unconcerned about theft.

The Murdaughs were messy elsewhere, too. "They'd leave a gun, they'd leave a coat, they'd leave a flashlight—maybe all three—and it was just sort of a running joke that . . . you had to kind of go around and gather up their stuff after they left," said Mark Ball, a law partner who often hosted Alex and his boys at his farm. Another time when Alex and Buster visited the home of law partner Ronnie Crosby, Alex brought along a small bag containing a pistol. "Of course, in classic, Alex, Buster, and Paul style, [Alex] ended up leaving the bag there when he left," said Crosby. Yet out of all of them, Paul in particular was notorious for not collecting his belongings. His uncle John Marvin Murdaugh remembers Paul once coming over to hunt on his property. A week later John Marvin was hunting again on the land when he stumbled upon a bunch of gear that had been left behind in a blind. "I had to smile when I saw it," said John Marvin. "That's Paul."

Eventually the carelessness caught up with Paul. Less than a year after receiving his new rifle, Paul's weapon was purportedly stolen from his unlocked truck while he attended a Halloween party in 2017. He didn't realize it was missing until days later. This kind of behavior informed a common opinion of Paul as entitled and arrogant, as a person who wasn't expected to follow rules, or clean up his messes, or ever learn from his many mistakes. In the case of the missing gun, Paul's parents bought him a replacement six months later, which Maggie picked up and paid for with a check.

But in the hearts and minds of those people closest to Paul, he was a loyal and thoughtful teenager whose occasional bad behavior did not overshadow his positive traits. Crosby praised Paul's patience with his young son, whom Paul took hunting and served as a mentor. Paul was kind and inquisitive, said Crosby, and was not defined by his misadventures with alcohol and his struggles in school. Crosby didn't approve of all of Paul's choices, but that's to be expected of any adolescent. "I don't know what a perfect kid is," he said.

Ball also watched Paul grow up. He credited Paul for being a polite person as well as a talented gardener and outdoorsman. "I could have picked up the phone and called Paul and said, 'Hey, I need some help over here on my farm,'—that kid would have come in a heartbeat. He was just a good kid," said Ball.

Except for the times he was not so good. "Did he do some devilish things? Absolutely," said Ball.

Ball didn't elaborate, but others filled in the blanks with rumors of animal cruelty, race-related BB gun shootings and the uploading of pornography to school computers to name a few alleged misdeeds; all of which are difficult to prove or disprove. More consistent are tales of Paul's loutish, drunken behavior, which was once so out of line that it prompted a physical confrontation with his father. Other times Paul abused his girlfriend after drinking too much, or endangered her by driving drunk.

Once Paul himself allegedly hinted he had committed an evil act. He began chuckling to himself in school at Thomas Heyward Academy one day, seemingly apropos of nothing, and then continued laughing to the point where his mirth was impossible to ignore, said a Lowcountry resident associated with the school. When he collected himself he finally explained to a teacher what was so funny: "People are saying I hit Stephen Smith with a baseball bat, but I would never do anything like that," Paul allegedly said before succumbing to another fit of involuntary giggles.

Paul was referencing the death of Hampton County teen Stephen Nicholas Smith who was found dead in the middle of a rural county road early in the morning of July 8, 2015. There were pine trees on one side of this section of Sandy Run Road and a cornfield on the other. Nineteen-year-old Stephen lay along the center line of the road, his head resting in a large pool of blood. "He was laid out in the road like a snow angel," said his mother, Sandy. "His head was crushed."

A man was driving to work in his tow truck about 4:00 A.M. that morning when he drove past Stephen's body. He thought his body was roadkill at first, then realized that the mass illuminated by his headlights was a person. He called 911 and spoke to a dispatcher. "I was going down Crocketville Road and I see somebody laying out," the driver said. "He in the roadway . . . Somebody gonna hit him."

When police arrived on the scene they saw Stephen was clothed in a black T-shirt, khaki shorts, and a pair of sneakers. It was apparent he suffered blunt force trauma to his head. Police immediately dismissed the idea this was some kind of hit-and-run incident. Instead, they believed the seven-inch wound on his head was the result of a gunshot, and that his body was possibly dumped on the road. The suspicion of foul play spurred South Carolina Highway Patrol investigators to relinquish the crime scene to local police and agents with the South Carolina State Law Enforcement Division (SLED). Stephen's body was soon taken to Charleston for an autopsy.

Stephen's small, yellow Chevrolet Aveo automobile was found parked on the side of rural US Highway 601 about three miles away. The car's gas cap was unscrewed and hanging outside the car. Since Stephen's body was found between his home and the location of his car, police speculated he may have been walking home after running out of gas. Or perhaps Stephen had mechanical trouble, as police were unable to start the car after retrieving a key from his pocket and unlocking the doors. These early theories were imperfect. If Stephen had run out of gas, would he have felt compelled to peer into the gas tank in the dark before setting off toward home or a gas station? Why would Stephen walk down the middle of the road in the dark instead of along the shoulder, where cars would not threaten him?

An autopsy was performed hours later, when Stephen's body was still warm, at the Medical University of South Carolina in Charleston. His head wound was not caused by a gunshot, said a doctor, but rather was the result of a vehicle collision. Stephen's shoulder was dislocated, too. The highway patrol was stunned, as this conclusion conflicted with the findings of every law enforcement officer who responded to the scene of Stephen's death. As Lance Corporal D. B. Rowell wrote in a report: "I saw no vehicle debris, skid marks, or injuries consistent with someone being struck by a vehicle. The victim's shoes were loosely tied and both were still on." Nonetheless, the autopsy findings caused the state highway patrol to once again be placed in charge of investigating Stephen's death even after they had yielded the supposed crime scene to SLED.

Two weeks later, Lance Corporal Todd Proctor visited the medical university to again discuss the doctor's autopsy findings. Proctor described previous discussions about Stephen between the highway patrol and the doctor as "heated," and complained there was no basis for the doctor to state Stephen died from a vehicle collision. The next round of conversation was no more cordial, Proctor reported the doctor in Charleston greeted him with a "negative tone" and "basically called me a liar." Despite the hostility he asked questions about Stephen's injuries, as he documented in a report:

> I asked her if someone with a baseball bat could do that and she stated "no". When I probed further saying what about someone in a moving car, with a bat she stated "well I guess it's possible". She then asked if we found a bat as evidence. I could see that this conversation was not going to yield any positive results. As I was leaving she

stated that the report was preliminary and it was my job to figure
out what it was struck him not hers.

No matter what the doctor determined, Proctor did not believe Stephen Smith was the victim of a hit-and-run incident. "It looked like it was more staged," said the fifteen-year veteran of the state highway patrol. "Like possibly the body had been placed in the roadway."

Stephen's shirt, shorts, and shoes were taken to a police lab and analyzed. Metallic blue paint flecks were discovered on this clothing, and an automotive paint database indicated this type of paint was used to coat a broad array of products, including industrial tools, garbage dumpsters, signposts, and 1980s Toyota vehicles. Investigators would need to narrow down the possibilities before drawing any conclusions.

The police pursued other leads, interviewing two of Stephen's romantic partners. The gay teenager's current boyfriend told investigators he had talked to Stephen hours before his death and that he believed foul play to be involved. The police also spoke with Stephen's siblings and parents. His twin sister, Stephanie, told police Stephen had been secretive in the weeks before he died. His mother, Sandy, said the same, and that oddly Stephen had been skipping school and skimping on his studying lately.

The police fielded a variety of tips and rumors. One name came up repeatedly—Buster Murdaugh. In a recorded interview with highway patrol investigator Proctor, one source summed up the basic narrative that was mentioned in conversations and text threads between assorted Lowcountry youths. As the young man told investigator Proctor:

I heard that these two maybe three young men were in a vehicle,
um, they were riding down 601, saw the car on the side of the road,
I guess saw the boy walking, um, they turned back around, I guess
they were attempting to . . . mess around with him . . . and stuck
something out the window and it you know hit him . . . in the head

or the back . . . That's pretty much all I heard. I did hear names, or heard a name, that name was—he goes by Buster Murdaugh.

This person told Proctor he was a lifelong acquaintance of Buster, and he thought such an action would be "out of character" for the college student, unless, as rumored, he committed these actions while intoxicated. Buster's younger brother Paul was more likely to be a "troublemaker," said the source, and was someone who used the vaunted family name to escape responsibility. Paul projected an attitude that this source characterized as, "My last name's Murdaugh, I can do whatever." The source said the Murdaugh boys threw parties almost weekly at Moselle, and he had visited once. "Big parties, kids from Wade Hampton and kids from Barnwell, Bamberg, anywhere you can think of, and that was where the party spot was in Hampton," said the source. "A lot of fights, alcohol, drugs kinda, thrown in there all at the same time."

Proctor told this source that he was not the first to disclose Buster's name and that the family is aware of the highway patrol's interest. "He's on our radar, he has been on our radar, they know that he's on our radar," said the investigator. What's more, Proctor said allies of the family were attempting to gag potential witnesses, claiming, "People associated with this name have been going around, kinda, kinda threatening or putting the heat on people, saying, you know, 'Keep your mouth closed if you've heard something,' whatever.

"Matter of fact," said Proctor, "I talked to one of their guys yesterday and told him, you know, 'I'm gonna talk to Buster here soon,' and he said, 'Hey, okay that's fine.' So they're aware of it."

Proctor shared that Buster and his friends were alleged to be coming home from a softball game. The source said, in contrast, that he had heard the men had left Moselle for Hampton when Stephen was encountered. The source also emphasized all the information he was relaying was "strictly hearsay," to which Proctor replied, "At this point you know, we'll take whatever we can get."

As the conversation continued, Proctor became chatty. "I don't know how much you know about law enforcement, things like that, but typically you don't see the highway patrol working a murder, and that's what this is," said Proctor. "There's no doubt. We're not classifying this as anything other than a murder."

The highway patrolman told the source that local police couldn't be trusted. "There's a reason why Hampton County Sheriff's Department is not handling this and I'll leave it at that. You go back to . . . the Murdaugh name and, you know, their ties in their community . . ." said Proctor. "What we've done is we've taken the investigation out of that . . . reach."

Proctor called and emailed Buster, but there's no indication from reports that police ever spoke with him. Years later Buster denied the rumors concerning him and Smith, stating on television, "I never had anything to do with his murder and I never had anything to do with him on a physical level of any regard." Though recordings of Proctor's interviews with assorted people indicate a strong interest in Buster and his whereabouts that night, there are hardly any notes about these suspicions in a master report about Stephen's death. There is limited information, too, about a tip called in by a man who said a friend of his stepson allegedly killed Stephen while drunk driving. The man said Randy Murdaugh encouraged him to call, not specifying whether he meant Randolph Murdaugh III or Randolph Murdaugh IV, who went by the same nickname. This man then failed to respond to investigators' calls.

As these leads were pursued, police received a new tip that said young Buster Murdaugh and two Black males were responsible for Stephen's death. One of Buster's alleged companions denied culpability in an interview with police. He said he did not even know Buster, though an investigator later noted he and Buster had previously befriended each other on social media. Police learned that text messages and gossip passed between Lowcountry teens suggested a possible romantic relationship between Buster and Stephen, but this too was not substantiated. None of the rumors, it seemed, could be proven by the highway patrol. "I'm not saying that the Murdaugh boy did it because I don't know he did," Proctor said at one point.

Six months or so after Stephen's death, the trail went cold. No one was arrested for killing Stephen. Proctor complained to a source that an investigation that "started out strong" was now beginning to become "watered down." He became frustrated by locals' locked lips and his inability to pierce the veil. Proctor sought to convey to skittish sources that he was an earnest investigator seeking justice. "I know the Murdaughs are highfalutin around Hampton and you know some people say have a lot of power or whatever, but that name doesn't mean anything to me . . ." Proctor told another source. "You don't have to agree with Stephen's lifestyle but that don't mean he gets to be killed and no one gets to find out what happened."

Like many people, Proctor got the feeling the Murdaugh family didn't play fair down in the swamps, that family members and their cronies constantly muddied the water. "They're going to go on living their lives . . . So they can play that card of, 'Oh, we care about everybody else,'" Proctor said to a source. "No, they don't. They care about protecting themselves."

———

Their relationship almost seemed scripted by a screenwriter the way it clung to cliché. He was a four-letter varsity athlete, captain of the Wade Hampton High School football team, and class president. She was head cheerleader, part of the basketball squad, and a thespian. Their senior year they were each voted "Most Athletic" by their sixty classmates. They posed for a photo together one day outside the school in Varnville. Libby Alexander wore a light dress and carried an oversize megaphone with RED DEVILS printed in large letters down its side. Randolph Murdaugh III stood beside Libby, a head taller, gripping a basketball between his hands, wearing his varsity jacket. Big smiles beamed across both their faces.

Libby was an earnest student in high school. At age sixteen she won a civics-themed public speaking contest, and then won a blue ribbon from a garden club for holiday decorations in her family home, her ribbon-winning scene featuring a porcelain lamp and perfume bottle beside an open Bible. As cheer captain her senior year, she demanded top effort from the team, whose members, as the weather cooled, wore uniforms of sweaters, long skirts, and bobby socks. Libby organized practice in early August despite brutal summer heat and pesky gnats. "We're determined to have a new and better school spirit this year," she declared in a report about the team. "So we're all going to have to help and participate. Let's show these other schools that we're for our team, one hundred percent."

Randy Murdaugh was an amiable, likable teenager whose popularity was enhanced by his exploits on the gridiron. Randy, fond of his varsity jacket and cuffing his jeans, played football all four years of high school and also excelled in baseball, basketball, and track and field. Randy was flame-haired like his fair mother, Gladys, but worshipped his father and wanted to be just like him. Buster groomed Randy to become a lawyer ever since he first brought him to the Hampton County Courthouse as a boy and let him draw juror names from a box, much like his father once brought him to work at the courthouse. Randy imagined no other future. "I would like to follow in my father's footsteps and work toward a law degree," he said in 1957 at the end of his senior year in high school.

This gravitational pull to the law did not exist for every Murdaugh. Buster's brother Johnny Glenn, in fact, was better at breaking the law than practicing or upholding it. He moved back to Hampton and Varnville a few years after World War II and in 1953 married VerLee DeLoach, a beautician with three young children. At some point he began farming under the direction of Buster on land his brother owned out in Almeda, living in an old wooden two-story home on the farmland that once belonged to one of Hampton's early doctors, T. H. Tuten.

While Buster had a general reputation, even if undeserved, of being an upstanding person and prosecutor, locals felt very differently about his brother Johnny. He was always drunk, always crazy, said one acquaintance. Another local called him "crazy as hell," and yet two other people described him as having a "few marbles loose" and "a screw loose." Johnny seemed to agree with the assessment of his peers: He put a sign outside his house that said, DON'T WORRY ABOUT THE DOG, BEWARE THE OWNER.

It was no wonder Johnny was erratic—he was a battered man, traumatized since the moment he drew his first breath. His birth was difficult and prolonged, and his mother died just days after his delivery, say longtime Hampton residents. Every decade since that rotten beginning Johnny suffered additional injury, his head absorbing assorted blows. There was the car accident at age twelve, when he flew out of an automobile driven by his school principal and cut open his head. Then he suffered multiple injuries as a soldier in World War II, including head wounds while in combat in France in 1944. Johnny returned home from the war with an unspecified disability, decorated with two Purple Hearts. Acquaintances said it's likely he was shell-shocked—suffering from post-traumatic stress disorder.

Johnny was short like Buster, but beefier. He was ornery, ready to fight in an instant. His physique reminded some people of Popeye, the muscular cartoon sailor. But instead of emptying cans of spinach to energize, Johnny downed cans of beer and bottles of liquor. Johnny had been a boxer, said one acquaintance, another activity in which his head was pummeled. His nose had been broken and knocked sideways and made crooked.

Johnny lost his driver's license from drunkenness, say locals, so he drove a tractor around town. He chugged up the highway shirtless from Almeda, sometimes weaving all across the road. One time, in a fit of rage against Buster, Johnny was said to have parked the tractor right across the door to his brother's law firm and walked away with the ignition key, blocking the entrance until he got what he wanted, which was supposedly money.

Johnny called everyone "Pard"—short for "Partner." In warm weather he was a frequent patron of the Varnville Pavilion and Pool, just up the street from his home in Almeda. The two-story pavilion beside the swimming pool featured dances, concerts, and skating upstairs, with concessions and duckpin bowling on the ground level. For many years it was owned by Sidney Varn, who clerked for the South Carolina House of Representatives for forty-nine years. Once the legislature adjourned, he hurried home from the capital city to open the swimming pool the day after school ended. He'd surveil the pool as children and adults swam, making sure no one was in danger or misbehaving. If a child did break the rules they risked the mortification of Mr. Varn calling out their name on the loudspeaker, whether it was a kid running on the wet deck or two teens who couldn't keep their hands and lips off each other. "No scooterbootin'," he scolded patrons who smooched more than they swam.

Sometimes people jumped or dove off the second story into the pool, which was a risky endeavor considering the pavilion was close to the shallow end of the water. Johnny, who favored small swim briefs over swim shorts, was a talented diver. One day, though, very likely while heavily intoxicated, he launched off the pavilion roof and dived straight into water about two feet deep. Almost as soon as Johnny hit the water his face smashed into the bottom of the pool—yet another jolt to the head. When Johnny stood his face was bloodied and the top of his nose scraped clean. His face was scabbed for weeks as he healed, said one man who recalled the mishap.

Such antics, and other behavior, unsettled pool patrons. One woman said when she was a girl her father warned her about three men in Hampton, Johnny Glenn Murdaugh being one of them. Her father was friends with Buster, and he saw nothing wrong with Buster giving her a peck on the head as a greeting. But the same gesture would not be considered innocent coming from Johnny. The girl's father instructed her to forgo any interaction with Johnny or else she would be forbidden from the pool. "You are not allowed to talk to Mr. Johnny," said the girl's father. "You are not allowed to be flipped by Mr. Johnny into the pool."

One time the man who recalled Johnny's scabbed face gave him a ride home from the Varnville pool. Johnny was usually trying to bring females back to his house but on this day a drinking buddy would do. "C'mon, pard, let's have a drink," said Johnny, inviting the man inside.

The walls inside Johnny's home were covered in pictures of nude women from pornographic magazines. As the guest observed the decor Johnny went into another room and returned with a pile of panties in in his hands. He indicated the pairs of underwear were trophies of his sexual conquests. "The pretty little girls at the pool love to fuck," said Johnny.

Johnny's guest was skeptical of the boast. For all he knew, the panties weren't sexual souvenirs but simply undergarments swiped from the women's changing room at the swimming pool. "Yeah, right," the man thought to himself. "Ain't none of them getting in bed with you."

———

At first Maggie Murdaugh was calm. After dialing 911 she twice stated her address on Moselle Road. It was 9:24 on the morning of February 2, 2018, and the Murdaugh family was reacting to an emergency. "My housekeeper has fallen and her head is bleeding," Maggie said flatly to a dispatcher. "I cannot get her up."

The dispatcher began to ask a stream of questions: She's bleeding from the head? How old is she? Where did she fall from? Is she outside or inside? How many steps are there? Is she on the ground or at the top of the stairs? Is she conscious?

Maggie grew impatient. Her voice sounded flustered as she spoke with the dispatcher about her injured housekeeper, fifty-seven-year-old Gloria Satterfield. Maggie told the dispatcher that her housekeeper was walking up a set of eight brick exterior stairs when she fell, hit her head, and tumbled to the ground. Maggie told the dispatcher Gloria was not really conscious yet also awake.

"Is she just not like responding appropriately but she is awake?" asked the confused dispatcher.

Maggie sighed loudly before stating, "Ma'am she's not, no, she's not responding."

The dispatcher responded in a similarly irritated tone, telling Maggie, "I've already got (an ambulance) on the way, me asking questions does not slow them down, ma'am." As the conversation resumed, Maggie clarified that Gloria was merely mumbling. When Gloria tried to stand and collapsed again Maggie passed the phone to her son Paul, who had been assisting Gloria. The dispatcher asked Paul if he could pose questions to Gloria about her health.

"Ma'am, she can't talk," said Paul, echoing the exasperation of his mother. "She's cracked her head and there's blood on the concrete and she's bleeding out of her left ear . . ."

The dispatcher asked about Gloria's fall. Paul explained he "was holding her up and she told me to turn her loose . . . then she fell back over."

She asked if Paul and Maggie knew Gloria.

"Yeah, she works for us," said Paul.

She asked if Gloria had ever suffered a stroke, irritating Paul. "Ma'am can you stop asking all these questions?" he said.

For the second time the 911 dispatcher curtly explained that it was important for her to learn as much as possible to inform the emergency personnel rushing to the scene. "I already have them on the way," she said. "Me asking questions does not slow them down in any way. These are relevant questions I have to ask for the ambulance."

As the six-minute call came to a close, Paul told the dispatcher a man in a six-wheeled recreational vehicle would be waiting down at the gate to the property to lead emergency medical technicians to Gloria at the main house. He suggested Gloria might have a concussion.

Maggie would later tell investigators that she and Paul were sleeping when Gloria arrived at the house to pick up a check that morning. She heard the family's dogs barking—"as if something bad happened"—and went outside to see Gloria on her back on the steps. Her head was bleeding and pointed toward the bottom of the stairs. Four dogs milled about her body. Beyond calling 911, Maggie called Alex at work to tell him the bad news.

The news got worse. Gloria was battered, with twelve broken ribs and other internal injuries. She was soon transferred by helicopter to Trident Medical Center in North Charleston, where she suffered a stroke and cardiac arrest and died on February 26, 2018. During the three-and-a-half weeks she was in the hospital, Maggie was the only Murdaugh to visit Gloria, a woman who had worked for the family for almost two decades and once served as a nanny for the boys. Her obituary stated she loved Alex, Maggie, and the boys like they were her own family.

But once Gloria died, Alex displayed great interest in the Satterfield family. He encouraged her two sons to file a lawsuit against him to obtain money for funeral expenses, telling Tony Satterfield, "Let me go after my insurance company for this and get your medical bills paid."

Alex referred the brothers to his friend, lawyer Cory Fleming, to handle negotiations and a possible lawsuit. In a bid to secure a large insurance payout he then lied to insurance investigators, falsely claiming that Gloria Satterfield was knocked down the stairs by four of his dogs.

It was not difficult to imagine an older person losing their footing after being mobbed by the family's pets. The Murdaughs had lots of dogs, too many to keep straight. There seemed to be a rotating cast, with some dogs favored as family dogs, others used for hunting, and others kept as temporary boarders as favors to friends. There was Armadillo, Blue, Bourbon, Bubba, Dahlia, Grady, Maggie, Sassy, and Tappy Toes, to name a few. The dogs were not kept in the house at Moselle because of allergy concerns, but they instead slept near the shed in covered, open-air kennels equipped with lights and fans.

Bubba, a yellow Labrador Retriever, was perhaps the most loved, especially by Maggie, who allowed him the privilege of sometimes accompanying her on visits to the family's house at Edisto Beach. Part of Bubba's appeal was his irrepressibly rebellious and rambunctious nature. Bubba, who was both a bird dog and a family dog, would run away when called and refuse to relinquish any game he captured, such as the chickens and guinea hens the Murdaughs kept at Moselle. Maggie liked to walk the dogs some nights before sunset, though the family employed a neighbor to take care of them on a regular basis.

Roger Dale Davis Jr. visited Moselle every day and night to feed the dogs and clean the kennels. He'd grab dog chow from the small, roughly finished plywood-walled feed shed at the end of the line of kennels. Here the Murdaughs stored dog and chicken feed, shock collars, GPS tracking collars, and animal medicine. The few family dogs such as Bubba were fed twice a day, while the hunting hounds were given one meal a day.

Alex was "very particular" about the job, said Davis, wanting the kennels sprayed clean of waste daily, and all feed and water buckets kept free of grime and slime. Alex's high standards didn't bother Davis, who was particular, too. After washing the kennels he made sure to coil the hose very carefully to avoid kinking, making one neat loop after another before hanging it on the kennel wall.

Davis's routine brought him in constant contact with the Murdaugh family and their assorted personalities. Alex could be slightly uptight and preoccupied, observed Davis, and was sometimes hard to reach on account of his busy work schedule. Maggie was more "laid back," he said, and Paul was "a little wild and crazy." Despite the different personalities, life at Moselle seemed happy and harmonious. Alex and Maggie acted very "lovey-dovey," said Davis. He never witnessed any moments of anger between Alex and his wife or son Paul.

But while Maggie was easygoing at home, some locals who encountered her in town still perceived her as stiff and unfriendly even twenty years after she moved to Hampton. But in the beginning she at least tried to embrace small-town life, though on her own terms, which sometimes proved a poor fit. Beginning in 2005, Maggie operated a boutique in downtown Hampton named Branches, partnering with her mother-in-law, Libby, and some other Hampton County women. The wares were nice enough but the prices in her boutique were "to the moon," said one Hampton woman. Maggie was sweet and patient when she encountered her, said this woman, but Maggie could also seem out of touch. When Maggie ran errands she conspicuously wore fur coats and lots of expensive jewelry, including diamond rings, earrings, and bracelets. "She'd wear that to the post office in Hampton," said the woman.

Kim Brant, who operated a carpet cleaning business in Hampton, initially considered investing in the boutique, but decided against the idea, fearing she would have little control. Maggie, she said, could be two-faced, smiling at somebody before talking behind their back. Maggie was a "catty" and "unhappy" person, said Brant. "She didn't fit into Hampton because she didn't want to." Like her husband and son Paul, Maggie was always on her cell phone. This was the case when she drove about town, said Brant, a habit that seemed to affirm Maggie's perceived disinterest in Hampton, of wanting to be anywhere else with other people. "Who does she even talk to so much?" Brant wondered.

A Lowcountry lawyer who knew the Murdaugh family well agreed Maggie seemed unhappy. Alex, on the other hand, was "grinning his ass off all the time." Alex thrived in his hometown and kept up friendships across the Lowcountry. Some of these relationships were to be expected—boyhood buddies and classmates from high school, college, and law school—while others raised eyebrows.

Alex interacted frequently with Curtis Edward "Eddie" Smith, a Colleton County man who said he regarded Alex like a brother. Alex and his father once worked together to represent Smith in a personal injury lawsuit. Smith had fallen in a ditch while on a logging job in 2007, injuring his spine. The lawsuit settled for unknown terms in 2012, and Alex represented Smith again for a speeding offense a year later. He stayed in touch with Smith afterward, allegedly using him to obtain opioid pills and launder money.

Both Alex and Smith had at one time legitimately used opioids, highly addictive painkillers that are legally obtainable only with a prescription from a doctor. Smith was prescribed pain pills following surgery to replace three discs in his injured spine with artificial components. Alex, meanwhile, was introduced to opioids during his recovery from a knee surgery about 2004, when he was prescribed hydrocodone. He became addicted, he said, and within a few years had switched to abusing oxycodone pills, which are even more potent. This led to a full-blown addiction to opioids that began to cost Alex tens of thousands of dollars a week, at least by his estimation. Police allege Alex obtained the bulk of these opioids from Smith. From 2013 to 2021, Alex wrote Smith 437 checks totaling $2.4 million, according to South Carolina authorities. Opioids became indispensable to his life, said Alex, who claimed the pills provided him energy. "Whatever I was doing it made it more interesting," he said. "At the beginning, it made everything better."

Some people scoffed at Alex's supposed levels of consumption, wondering if it's even possible to sustain an addiction of such proportions without appearing conspicuously intoxicated, falling asleep, or dying from an overdose. Yet Alex claimed to have developed a secret opioid habit so strong that each time he quit he experienced severe symptoms of withdrawal. When Alex stopped gobbling pills he said he experienced a miserable withdrawal that unfolded in stages. At first came agitation, which was then accompanied by sickness that mimicked the flu. Alex said his joints would begin to hurt and he would start sweating profusely, as if he was "running a marathon." After twelve hours he developed "jumpy legs." This restlessness lasted for about a day, then gave way to severe intestinal problems. "You literally can't control yourself," said Alex. "You have diarrhea like you have food poisoning."

Alex estimated he tried to kick his opioid habit dozens of times. Most of the time he attempted to quit at home, but at least three times he visited a substance abuse treatment facility in Atlanta that offered a weeklong detox program. But it never took too long for Alex to relapse and return to bad habits, sometimes consuming as many as sixty opioid pills a day. "If you saw me, I had pills on me," he said.

Despite indulging this gargantuan illicit drug habit and stealing millions from his clients, Alex chose to remain a volunteer assistant solicitor and occasionally enforce South Carolina's laws by prosecuting a case, almost always with his father. And no matter his volunteer status and limited role in the office, Alex had police blue lights installed in his personal vehicle, which was issued to him by the law firm, claiming to have received the permission of a few local sheriffs. Like the three generations of Murdaugh men that came before him, Alex maintained all sorts of friendships with law enforcement and local government officials.

Among his closest cop buddies was Greg Alexander, the chief of police of the small Hampton County town of Yemassee. Yemassee is a tiny place with a little more than a thousand residents, but is chock-full of wonders, oddities, and intrigue. The town is pressed tight against wetlands and is otherwise surrounded by huge, picturesque plantations, many with pre-served rice fields where enslaved people once labored. Yemassee's name honored a local Native American tribe, sometimes spelled Yamassee, that inhabited the Lowcountry until an unsuccessful war against English colonists in 1715 resulted in the Yemassee's retreat south to Georgia two years later.

Like almost anywhere of significance in Hampton County, Yemassee began its existence as a rail town. Timber moved up and down these rails at first, but in 1915 the Yemassee train station witnessed large volumes of young men arriving regularly for transfer to Marine Corps Recruit Depot Parris Island, thirty miles away. Yemassee, not much more than a clearing in the pines, was the last bit of civilization these young men would taste before enduring weeks of hellish boot camp. So many recruits passed through the Yemassee train depot that the Marine Corps leased a nearby building from the railroad after World War II, operating their own receiving station staffed by Marines and military police for twenty years.

The town and its train station were the focus of a seven-page photo essay by Alfred Eisenstaedt in *Life* magazine in 1942 that described Yemassee as "a railroad junction not too big to be confusing, not too small to be trivial." The description mimicked lawyer and statesman James L. Petigru's famous observation of South Carolina as a place "too small for a republic but too large for an insane asylum." Petigru, an outspoken Unionist in Charleston, made that remark late in life, after South Carolina's leaders decided to secede from the Union in 1860. Petigru had once served as attorney general of South Carolina, and before that as solicitor of Beaufort District, the same Lowcountry prosecutor's post that came to be occupied by three generations of the Murdaugh family.

Yemassee had other claims to fame besides being a Marine Corps way station. After the recruits stopped coming by rail, a different kind of primate arrived en masse to Yemassee—monkeys. Beginning in the 1970s, the Lowcountry became home to several facilities that raised monkeys for use in research laboratories. Two of these monkey farms operated in the Yemassee area, and another close by in Beaufort County on an island known officially as Morgan Island and unofficially as Monkey Island. Every so often a monkey escaped, whether by slipping out of their cages in Yemassee or swimming off the island. The animals dashed off into nearby wilderness, with designs to live as the maroons did.

Exotic animals could be found, too, at Auldbrass Plantation, a low-slung residential complex designed by famed American architect Frank Lloyd Wright that began construction in 1939 and was built piecemeal over decades. The home sits just off the Combahee River a few miles outside of town, and is unique for the fact that the walls of its assorted buildings, clad in cypress, slope inward at an 80° angle, with supposedly not a single right angle in sight. Auldbrass was purchased in 1986 by a movie producer who painstakingly restored the property and also established a menagerie with zebras, longhorn cattle, and a pygmy hippo. Perhaps inspired by the daring monkeys, the pygmy hippo made its own escape one day in 2004. Its freedom was sadly short-lived, as a car struck and killed the 500-pound animal as it roamed the rural roads around Yemassee.

Once the Marine Corps left downtown Yemassee, nothing took the place of the military. Yemassee stayed a quiet town, apart from weekend nights at Harold's Country Club when people from all walks of life, from blue-collar workers to the plantation-owning gentry, and the occasional Hollywood star, shared the dance floor and the karaoke microphone. No membership is required for a good time at Harold's, which is not so much a club as a bar and restaurant that has operated inside an old gas station and garage since the late 1970s, serving steak dinners every Saturday. Though Harold's can be booming, much of Yemassee appears depressed—a stark contrast to the immaculately maintained plantations just down the road, where it is almost required to employ a planation manager to keep Mother Nature in check. Most of the motorists zooming by on nearby Interstate 95 don't bother to stop in downtown Yemassee, two miles off the highway, and don't stay too long if they do. Decades after the departure of the Marine Corps, most buildings beside Yemassee's railroad tracks became abandoned.

On one of these vacant properties along Wall Street lived Shemuel Yisrael, a squatter who waged war with the town constantly, accusing them of false arrests, police brutality, and attempting to seize the cluttered property, which he claimed as his own, named Plantation Yisrael. He was arrested so often, mostly for trespassing, that he began keeping canisters of homemade cop repellent on hand in a bid to thwart contact with police. When Yisrael encountered lawmen he would douse himself in a repulsive concoction of paint, chemicals, urine, and other liquids, all in an attempt to thwart his arrest and prevent manhandling. Yisrael often taunted local officials with the display of handmade signs along Wall Street. He called

Yemassee's mayor the Devil once, and another time painted a message for Solicitor Randolph "Randy" Murdaugh III that read, "Murdaugh passed the bar exam by drinking more than anyone else the night before." The solicitor was one of many public officials and local governments sued and lambasted by Yisrael, as was his son Alex's friend, Yemassee police chief Greg Alexander.

The chief was a decade younger than Alex and a veteran of the navy. He left the military when he was about thirty years old and then began a career in law enforcement, working for assorted police departments in Hampton and Colleton counties. Alexander was a police captain in Yemassee in 2012 when he was charged for allegedly stealing $11,000 that was seized during two traffic stops. He had previously denied the charges and submitted to a lie detector in a bid to prove his innocence. But Alexander failed, with the polygraph examiner finding that "deception was indicated" when Alexander answered questions about the money that went missing from a safe in his office. No matter what the polygraph results were, Alexander, one of two people with access to the safe, said he didn't do it. According to a report by the State Law Enforcement Division:

> *During the post test interview, Alexander continued to deny taking any of the drug seizure money. He stated that there were times he and other employees took money from the office petit [sic] cash fund that was keep [sic] in the safe. He also stated he had intended to "borrow" one hundred dollars ($100) from the seizure money but when he looked in the safe the money was gone.*

Despite Alexander's denials, he was indicted by a state grand jury on three public corruption charges for allegedly stealing the seized money. Alexander's boss, Police Chief Jack Hagy, did not support the state grand jury's conclusion about his right-hand man. "We have full faith and confidence in Captain Alexander and that these matters will be resolved," said a statement he issued from the town in the wake of Alexander's arrest.

The town's confidence was well placed. In November 2012, Alexander was acquitted by a Hampton County jury of two charges, which prompted the state attorney general's office to then drop the third. Alexander's defense received a boost from Alex Murdaugh and his father, Randy, who not only attended Alexander's trial, but sat with him during the proceedings. Alex said he and his father were so outraged by the criminal charges and SLED's investigation of their friend that they decided to publicly support Alexander as he was tried in Hampton County by prosecutors from the state attorney general's office. "The charges against Greg Alexander were so . . . wrong that my dad and I made a conscious decision, even though (my dad) was a career prosecutor, made a decision to go to the courthouse and sit with Greg Alexander while his trial went on," said Alex. "It was terrible what they did to Greg Alexander . . . My dad and I truly thought the evidence was manufactured."

It's not often that working prosecutors sit with a defendant being tried in their jurisdiction. But these were the Murdaughs, and per usual, they fashioned themselves a murky role in the Lowcountry's legal system. Randy was no longer the solicitor, but he was an assistant solicitor earning $2,500 a month on a contract basis to work on cases in Hampton County. Alex, meanwhile, had his badge and credentials as a volunteer assistant solicitor renewed in 2013, just months after Alexander's acquittal. As a card signed and certified by Randy's successor, Solicitor Isaac M. "Duffie" Stone III stated, Alex Murdaugh is a deputy solicitor across five counties, "authorized to enforce the laws in the Fourteenth Judicial Circuit of South Carolina." It was a privilege granted to no other practicing attorney, just Alex Murdaugh and Alex Murdaugh alone.

CHAPTER FIVE
PREDATOR AND PREY

His coat was stuffed with so many indictments, Buster Murdaugh had become a walking filing cabinet. Before every term of criminal court the solicitor's jacket pockets bulged this way, crammed full of paperwork enumerating alleged crimes across one of the five counties he ruled as solicitor. Buster liked to keep this information handy, close to the vest, whenever a week of court approached, which was every two or three weeks or so for the solicitor. This way he was well-versed in each and every case in his jurisdiction. This way he was always ready to talk shop and make a deal.

When negotiating with Buster, seasoned lawyers of the Lowcountry knew to observe from which part of his coat or suit jacket Buster drew their client's indictment. One pocket, say on his right side, contained all the cases Buster was ready to try immediately, the ones he felt most bullish on winning. His left outside coat pocket, meanwhile, contained a separate group of indictments that he planned to continue, or save for another term, for one reason or another. And then in a third, perhaps his breast pocket, were a bunch of indictments that would soon go away, to be dismissed or "nol-prossed" by Buster, to use the abbreviated Latin legal parlance that he did. Former Hilton Head Island lawyer Walter Czura coined his own term for Buster's improvised, one-of-a-kind system: "sport coat justice." Added Jasper County lawyer Tom Johnson: "You'd get a feel for where you stood based on what pocket he pulled from."

Czura enjoyed a chummy relationship with Buster. Once he asked the solicitor if he would dismiss charges against a client who was accused of fighting at a nightclub, explaining the suspect and his rival had made amends. Buster pulled out the relevant indictment from his coat and held the sheaf of paper between them. As he and Walter studied the charges, dark, tobacco-stained spittle fell from Buster's mouth, plopping onto the indictment's white pages and conspicuously staining the paper. Czura forgave the escaped swill of saliva and chewing tobacco for he got the action he wanted—Buster agreed to cut his client loose. When Buster replaced the indictment in his coat, it was placed in a different spot. "Justice was served in the nol-pros pocket," Czura said of the dismissed charges. "It was over in ten minutes. It went from ten years to zero."

If the criminal catalog Buster kept tucked in his coat was conspicuous, so, too, was his tobacco habit, as underscored by the episode with Czura and many others. Buster was fond of Red Man chewing tobacco and cheap cigars, and one or the other was almost always in his mouth. Lawyer Lewis Pitts remembers Buster removing rubber bands from printouts of criminal indictments and using the elastic to floss flecks of tobacco leaves out of his teeth. It was "just his way of life," said Pitts.

Buster always kept a spittoon nearby. Oftentimes this was just a wastebasket, and it functioned like an inverted bell, ringing across the courtroom every time Buster spattered its sides with a spurt of his saliva. Inevitably Buster sometimes missed the target, and tobacco juice ejected from his mouth would dribble down the outside of the trashcan. Buster's legacy for many years included a dark ring on the carpet of the Jasper County Courthouse.

Buster's tobacco sludge coated many other things across the Lowcountry. Dried and caked torrents of tobacco-infused spit ran down the side of the solicitor's car. The slick it formed on the car door could grow to something substantial, said Randy Blackmon, a former sheriff of Jasper County. "It was more than a few stains," said Blackmon. "He spit like a goose with diarrhea."

Like an animal, Buster did not bother to clean up his tobacco messes, not in the courtroom, not in his own car, and not in other people's automobiles, either. One woman recalled how she once cleaned her husband's car a day or so after he had given a ride to Buster. She opened all the doors and started cleaning as her two-year-old son played nearby. At some point, said the woman, her son found a cup of tobacco spit that Buster had left on the passenger side floorboard. The boy found the cup, raised it to his lips, and started gulping. When the woman looked up from her cleaning, she was horrified to see her toddler chugging from the cup, tobacco juice running down both sides of his mouth, under his armpits and down the sides of his body into his diaper. The woman later fumed to her husband and suggested what he could tell Buster the next time he saw him. The husband laughed it off and looked on the bright side. "He won't have no worms," he said of his son.

Local lore has it that a new judge once tried to stop Buster from smoking in the courtroom. Buster gave him an earful and no cigar was ever extinguished. A similarly semi-specific and oft-repeated story involves Buster's experience at the first Heritage Classic, an annual golf tournament on Hilton Head Island that debuted in 1969. Officials tried to curtail some type of behavior by Buster—whether him using a golf cart, carrying a brown bag of liquor, or trying to picnic with his wife along the 18th hole, etc.—prompting him to fly into a rage and threaten to shut down the tournament for all sorts of alleged violations and illegalities. Realizing their mistake, the tournament officials quickly yielded; Buster could do whatever he wanted.

As the golf officials deduced, to cross Buster was to guarantee misery. Buster had few enemies in his fiefdom, mostly because few people were foolish enough to challenge him. "You got along with him, that's about it," said Duane Swygert, a former federal agent who also worked as a South Carolina highway patrolman and police chief in the Lowcountry.

The woman whose father warned her of Johnny Murdaugh also heard dark whispers about his brother, the solicitor. "You don't want to cross

Mr. Buster, you could end up in the swamp," people would tell her. Sometimes this warning mentioned not any swamp, but Whippy Swamp specifically, the wetlands near the Lightsey Brothers sawmill that drained into the Salkehatchie, full of gators and snakes. Whippy Swamp was spanned by what was known as the Miley Bridge, and this roadway over the swamp was referenced specifically, too, in warnings. Don't mess with the Murdaughs, another Hampton County resident was told, or "you might end up over the bridge like the rest of them."

Some view such comments as far-fetched. Buster didn't need to resort to violence because he had plenty of other ways to hurt an enemy. As solicitor he controlled the criminal docket across five counties, deciding which cases to call and when to call them, if ever. If he chose not to try a case, at least immediately, a defendant either skated by until a possible trial or rotted in jail indefinitely, depending on whether or not they could afford bail. "If Buster wanted you to burn, you got burnt," said Swygert. "If he wanted you to walk, you walked."

For lawyers Buster liked, he'd give them advance notice when their clients' cases would be called. He might even grant a lawyer more time to prepare a case and agree to a continuance, allowing an indictment to move from one coat pocket to another, at least temporarily. But for lawyers Buster didn't like, such courtesies were lacking. He would give no advance notice and cut no deals. One such lawyer was Bob Warren of Allendale, who practiced law as some combination of a hippie, reformer, environmentalist, and crusader. He did not mesh with the South Carolina establishment in any way, which was quite intentional on his part. He and his partner, Pitts, who witnessed Buster clean his teeth with elastic bands, were known as the "no necktie" lawyers for their refusal to wear ties with their coats, which especially infuriated an older class of lawyers and judges. Neckties, said Warren, were worn by society's rule makers, and he was one of the people, not the elite.

Warren engaged in many a Quixotic fight on behalf of the common man. His battles, against racism, against corporate America, against the government, against the local political boss and prosecutor, were all uphill, and sometimes hopeless. Many of his clients could not pay him, or at least not very much. Power company employees sometimes shut off his electricity because of overdue bills. If the victories were sometimes few and far between, they at least tasted sweet. Warren said he felt an obligation to use his smarts to aid his neighbors in one of the poorest parts of South Carolina, where racism stubbornly lingered in the face of the Civil Rights Movement. "Listening constantly to desperate situations didn't give me much choice but to try and help them," he said of his life as a lawyer in Allendale.

One time, said no-necktie Pitts, Buster offered a deal on a case but Warren refused it. This irritated Buster, and in retaliation the solicitor began calling case after case in which Warren was counsel, tying him up in court, unexpectedly, for days on end. Buster may have thought he was punishing Warren, said Pitts, but it was Warren's poor clients who truly suffered the most when Buster hastily called their cases, deeming such a tactic a "nightmare of injustice."

Warren wasn't stupid, but rather stubborn and unwilling to compromise. He, along with a few other hapless souls and martyrs, found out the hard way that the Lowcountry was Buster's domain and that he fiercely fought anyone who challenged the throne. One lawyer recalls how a colleague once grew so frustrated with Buster's behavior in court that he filed a complaint with the bar. The complaint went nowhere, of course, and when Buster learned who had filed the grievance, he blackballed the man and no longer referred him clients, crippling his small-town law practice.

In another instance of Buster's hot temper, witnessed by a class of elementary school students, a lawyer complained to a judge in court that Buster was only prosecuting his client because his client owed Buster money. Buster flew into a fit of rage, throwing files on the floor and screaming names at the opposing lawyer as he balled up his fists and readied for a fight. In another case, Buster admitted to using the law to exact revenge, telling a real estate developer he convicted of escrow account violations that he pushed for higher fines because he despised his lawyer. "I just want you to know I could have saved you a bunch of money if you didn't hire this son of a bitch," Buster said to the defendant, according to Buster's longtime friend, lawyer Charles "Mike" Macloskie of Beaufort. "Buster sometimes would play with people," said Macloskie. "If he likes you, he's gonna do everything he could to help you. If he didn't like you, he'd think about ways to hurt you . . . He was just as loyal to his enemies as he was to his friends."

Turf was everything to the swamp king, and Buster guarded against all intrusions. He constantly played political boss and gatekeeper in the Lowcountry, influencing the selection of judges, game wardens, police officers, law school students, and more, placing friends as chess pieces across local and state government. "If you wanted to be the county dog catcher you went and saw Mr. Buster," said one friend and client, Bill Humphries of Bamberg, only semi-facetiously. Buster made more friends by agreeing to prepare countless letters of recommendation for friends and acquaintances, though, according to Sam Crews III, some went straight into a file folder and never even left the office. But don't worry, Buster told Crews when he was a young man, "I'll mail yours."

When Sidi Limehouse of Charleston County decided to run for Congress in 1972, he soon learned Buster was "the man to see" south of Charleston. He made a trip to Hampton to meet the solicitor, but Buster, a die-hard Democrat, didn't have the time, perhaps because Limehouse was a Republican candidate. In any case Limehouse shrugged it off and campaigned around town. He didn't have to travel far to appreciate Buster's influence. "I remember entering one store located right next to Murdaugh's law office," recalled Limehouse. "I walked in, introduced myself to the woman behind the counter and asked for her vote. I'll never forget her reply: 'I'm sorry but we have to vote for who Mr. Murdaugh tells us to.'"

Buster was not unaware of the spell he cast over the Lowcountry. In 1970, he crossed paths in the courtroom with Pat Conroy, a young man protesting his firing as a schoolteacher on Daufuskie Island in Beaufort County. Conroy, accused of nontraditional teaching methods, gave a spirited defense of his efforts, which amused Buster, who observed, but did not participate, in the proceedings. Afterward the solicitor, smoking a cigar, introduced himself to Conroy, claiming to be "the cock of the walk in this part of South Carolina.

"Boy, you really know how to put on a show. You scared the living hell out of those bastards. But you're going to lose your ass," said Buster, predicting, correctly as it turned out, that Conroy would lose his bid to teach again.

Conroy, who would soon become a bestselling novelist, recognized a character. He said to Buster, "What if I'd had you as a lawyer?"

The answer was obvious to the solicitor. "You'd be teaching in that little school of yours tomorrow morning. But you ain't going to be teaching ever again," said Buster, blowing a puff of smoke in Conroy's direction. On the spot he offered Conroy, an out-of-work teacher, a legal education and a job. "Let me send you to law school; then you come back and work for me. I'll make you the goddamnedest lawyer you've ever seen."

The boat puttered away from the dock just before seven o'clock. Six friends were aboard, all giddy as they sipped drinks and snapped pictures of the setting sun. The young adults were in God's country and they knew it, floating within a vast coastal paradise of low-slung islands and saltwater rivers and creeks. It was late February, long past the marsh's summer splendor, yet the scenery remained stunning. Cordgrass, formerly electric green, had turned golden, and the water, which months earlier shimmered a bright blue, now displayed a much cooler, silvery cast.

The six friends soaked it all in, savoring the winter sunset, even if they'd seen it a thousand times.

It was date night, and the three couples on board were cruising to an oyster roast upriver, at a place called Paukie Island, in a rural area north of Beaufort. Most guests were coming to the oyster roast by car, driving across a small causeway to reach the island. Paul Murdaugh, however, insisted he and his friends travel by water on the night of February 23, 2019. Police checkpoints were expected on nearby roads that evening, and Paul wished to avoid the risk of an encounter with law enforcement given he was underage and intent on becoming intoxicated. So Paul obtained use of a family boat, as well as his family's weekend house off Chechessee Creek on Buster's Island, as an alternative to driving to and from the oyster roast from the tiny town of Hampton, about forty miles inland, where he lived with his parents. This way he could drink to his heart's content without risk of consequence.

The three men and women, all nineteen or twenty years of age, had known each other for years growing up in Hampton. The other two men on the boat—Anthony Cook and Connor Cook—were first cousins. The three women—Miley Altman, Mallory Beach, and Morgan Doughty—were close friends who worked together at a clothing boutique. Morgan had dated Paul on and off for years, and Miley and Connor were also a long-term item, dating since middle school. Mallory had gone off to college at Clemson University for a year but was now back home in Hampton, often found in the company of her girlfriends and Anthony. All the girls were beautiful, their big smiles and pretty faces framed by long blond hair. The boys were handsome, too, though not nearly as uniform in appearance. Connor had a shaggy head of dirty-blond hair while his cousin had closely cut brown hair and a bit of stubble along his chin. Paul was recognizable as the curly-haired redhead of the bunch, and, at 5'7", was shorter than his buddies.

The sunset cruise to the oyster roast was no quick and easy excursion, but a twenty-mile journey along dark waterways. Even in the fairest weather, South Carolina's coastal rivers and creeks can prove confounding to navigate. Serpentine in form, they split and turn continually through expanses of cordgrass, a maze of ever-narrowing capillaries, many of which ultimately peter out into dead ends. There are few distinct landmarks to observe on the horizon, and it's amazing how quickly everything can start to look the same, a blur of water and cordgrass and pluff mud and trees and islands. Oyster banks and sandbars are ever-present, too, hidden at high tide but laid bare at low.

Simply put, boating in the Lowcountry can be perilous. It's even harder to boat safely at night, and near impossible if one is also drunk. Paul was not yet drunk, but he was working on it. He had met Connor and Miley a few hours earlier, about mid-afternoon, at a convenience store and gas station close to his family's river house. The couple, sitting inside Miley's car in the gas station parking lot, watched as Paul entered the store and then exited minutes later, packages of beer and alcoholic seltzer drinks raised triumphantly above his head. Climbing into the boat he had trailered behind his truck from Hampton, Paul packed a cooler with the beer and hard seltzer, which was for his girlfriend, Morgan. Already there was a half-empty bottle of Crown Royal liquor on the boat—leftovers from a previous outing.

Most of Paul's friends on the boat also had fake IDs. Mallory and Anthony each brought their own personal supplies of alcohol when they arrived to the Murdaugh river house. Miley, meanwhile, bought beer and a six-pack of mango-flavored hard seltzer for her and Connor from the same convenience store as Paul. The result was each teen possessed a substantial stash of alcohol for the night. As soon as they reached the river house they started digging in.

The Murdaughs were hardly the only people from Hampton who kept second homes around Beaufort, where there was plentiful access to salt water and a bustling summer boating scene with daytime parties on exposed sandbars. The family of Connor's girlfriend, Miley, owned a home on Boyd Creek, a few miles up the Broad River from the Murdaugh home. And then just past the Altman house, on the north side of the Broad River and up the Whale Branch, Connor's grandparents kept a river house on Paukie Island, as did the Wood family, which was hosting the night's oyster roast.

Islands are everywhere in this part of South Carolina, some large enough to contain whole towns, others so tiny they're lucky to boast a single palmetto tree. Paukie Island is on the smaller side, containing twenty or so closely packed homes, about half of them with docks extending into the water. The views across the nearby Coosaw River and an adjoining creek are to die for, though an honest real estate agent would disclose one drawback to living on Paukie Island: the regular roar of fighter jets taking off and landing from Marine Corps Air Station Beaufort, which sits just south of the island. As a sign outside the military base advises: THE 'NOISE' YOU HEAR IS THE SOUND OF FREEDOM.

Out on the river that evening, Paul and his friends were listening to their own sound of freedom—the whine of an outboard motor as they glided across the water with a drink in their hands. The Murdaugh speedboat, about seventeen feet long with a white fiberglass hull, was close to capacity with six adults on board. Morgan and Miley sat up front, alternating between a bow seat and the beer cooler, which doubled as a small bench seat. Behind the cooler was the boat's center console, which contained the steering wheel, throttle, and controls. Paul stood here at the helm with Connor beside him, leaning against a captain's bench. Behind the two boys stood Anthony and Mallory, in front of the outboard engine.

As Paul steered Connor pointed a handheld flashlight ahead of the boat, though the beam hardly pierced the dark. More helpful was a GPS device attached to the center console, whose screen displayed a route to Paukie Island that would keep the boat in deep water and clear of sandbars and oyster beds. Connor kept his eyes glued to the screen, watching to make sure the boat was staying on course and generally keeping to the center of the waterways, the low tide giving the boaters less margin for error. Though the navigation required Connor's close attention, the mood was otherwise light and carefree on the boat. Everyone was bundled up warm, as temperatures were dropping toward the 40s and felt even colder on the water, zooming along in an open speedboat.

After leaving the Murdaugh dock, Paul had steered his family boat out of the Chechessee River, across the Broad River, and then into narrow Archers Creek. This was a shortcut, jogging through marshland beside Parris Island, the infamous East Coast training facility of the U.S. Marine Corps. More than 20,000 men and women graduate from Marine Corps Recruit Depot, Parris Island each year, enduring thirteen grueling weeks of boot camp to become Marines. Sometimes at night the voices of these recruits carry, their individual whoops, howls, and shrieks combining into an intimidating warriors' song reverberating across the water, evoking thoughts of wild, unseen savages among the civilians living on the opposite shore. About halfway through Archers Creek there is a small bridge passing overhead, the first of three bridges the six friends would pass beneath on their way to the oyster roast tonight. Part of the only road leading on and off Parris Island, the R. C. Berkeley Bridge is a simple concrete span in the middle of a long causeway across a wide marsh. The bridge is supported on its underside by dozens of steel-and-concrete pilings projecting out of the creek. A narrow channel cuts between some of these pilings, enabling passage of small boats.

The tight channel demands a boater's attention. Beyond the bridge pilings, there were also the pairs of dolphin structures at each entrance to the passage, imposing clusters of timber rising out of the water. A dolphin's three timbers are bound together above the surface by loops of steel cable but are spread apart underwater, making for a firm and rigid semi-submerged tripod. Dolphins serve as both navigational markers and hazards, telling a boater to stay between the immovable obstacles. Should the current prove too swift through Archers Creek, or the helmsman prove too sloppy, there was ample opportunity for collision.

For now, Paul's hand was steady. He steered the boat safely between the first pair of dolphin structures, under the bridge, through the narrow passage, and then out between the other pair of dolphins on the opposite side. He and his friends then continued north, out of the creek, and into the much wider Beaufort River, which is part of the Intracoastal Waterway. Straight ahead was the Sands, a small beach and boat landing in the town of Port Royal. Paul bore right and motored upriver, toward the town of Beaufort, about five miles ahead. As Paul steered Connor kept an eye on the GPS, making sure they didn't inadvertently run aground as it turned dark.

Nearing Beaufort they cruised past another military facility, Naval Hospital Beaufort, and then crossed under the J. E. McTeer Bridge, named for the "High Sheriff of the Lowcountry" who once worked with Paul's forebear, Randolph Murdaugh Sr., as the longtime sheriff of Beaufort County. When McTeer policed Beaufort County during Prohibition, one of his biggest challenges was stopping rum-running, as Beaufort's myriad waterways were near-perfect avenues for smuggling liquor by the boatload. There was simply too much ground, or in this case soft and sticky pluff mud, for law enforcement to cover. As Randolph's great-great-grandson was still proving nearly a century later, if you don't want to get caught with booze in Beaufort County, it's wise to go by water.

Sheriff McTeer's century-old connection to the Murdaugh family was likely unappreciated by Paul's friends on the boat, preoccupied as they were with each other and their drinks. As the boat traveled north of the McTeer Bridge, the lights of downtown Beaufort glowed ahead, about two miles upriver. Dead ahead was the Bluff, a rare bit of elevated, waterfront terrain that afforded a tremendous view of a dramatic bend in the Beaufort River, where the water curls around postcard-perfect downtown Beaufort, one of South Carolina's oldest cities. Elegant historic mansions line Bay Street, which runs along the top of the Bluff, as it gently descends into downtown Beaufort. The closer one gets to town, the finer the homes on Bay Street become, places with names like Tabby Manse, the Cuthbert House, and the Anchorage. At the foot of Bay Street sits the core of Beaufort's historic district, where a number of bars and restaurants line a waterfront park and a swing bridge spans the river. The six boaters didn't know it, but they'd be docking downtown later that night, when Paul became desperate for a nightcap.

But first they had the oyster roast. Still motoring toward downtown Beaufort, Paul and Connor made sure the boat steered clear of a large, exposed sandbar in the middle of the river—a place of frequent parties in the summertime, when the daytime temperature was about 50° warmer than the temperature this night. To the left, on the riverbank, stood the Beaufort Memorial Hospital, its dock projecting into the river—one more obstacle for the boys to avoid. The boat glided past the hospital, up the river, through the dark, past the lights of downtown Beaufort, and under the swing bridge. The six boaters didn't know it, but four of them would be returning to the hospital later that night, brought not by boat, but by ambulances.

———

For all the bravado and admitted cockiness, Buster earned his reputation as one of South Carolina's top lawyers. He practiced law with a natural ease that inspired envy. His boldness was unrivaled, for no other lawyer would dare try some of his stunts. Beaufort County lawyer Jared Newman recalled working as a detective and investigating an alleged rape on Hilton Head Island. Buster brought a case against two suspects, said Newman, and began to question the alleged victim on the witness stand. She began to lie, said Newman, and her testimony was unconvincing. Finally Buster turned to the judge and said in exasperation, "Your honor, the state is nol-prossing this case. This girl up here ain't nothing but a lying whore."

Buster himself once recalled a day in court when he was preparing to try two men for armed robbery. Right before he called the case he spoke up loudly in the courtroom, his voice booming: "Would the two defendants who committed the armed robbery please stand up?" Lo and behold, two men immediately rose to their feet.

Buster also liked to exhibit his flair for the dramatic, particularly in murder cases. He often playacted executions before the jury, sometimes in the role of the victim, lying still on the ground with a shotgun pressed against his skull, and other times he impersonated the killer. During one trial in the Jasper County Courthouse, he used the court reporter as a prop, pointing a gun at the back of the man's head as he pulled the trigger of the empty murder weapon. Each time the gun clicked, said former sheriff Randy Blackmon, the court reporter jumped in his seat. During another trial, recalled the lawyer Jack Swerling, Buster used his finger to outline a rectangle in front of the jury and said, "This is where Johnny is laying in his grave right now." When the jury returned to the courtroom to announce a guilty verdict, said Swerling, "they all avoided stepping on that imaginary box Buster had drawn."

Buster acted audaciously so often that it became hard to discern what, if any, behavior remained truly out of bounds. He was not only shameless but also fearless, having survived so many investigations into alleged misconduct. It became normal for Buster to do exactly as he pleased. He practiced little, if any, self-examination. Empathy, too, was in short supply. Alan Young, whose father owned Hampton's jewelry store, said Buster would "slap you on the back, shake your hand, and, after the handshake, put a summons in your pocket. He was that kind of guy."

Buster would often attend and host cookouts—cooks, for short—with a guest list that was heavy on law enforcement, judges, and lawyers, but also included people from other walks of life. Sometimes, said Blackmon, criminal defendants might be in the crowd, eating Buster's food, before facing him in court a day or two later. No matter the neighborly feelings, said the former Jasper County sheriff, a sense of professionalism always prevailed with Buster. "It ain't personal," he imagined Buster telling a guest under indictment, "but first thing tomorrow I'm gonna try you and send you to prison."

One Hampton County man said Buster was the Lowcountry's Robin Hood as well as its mafia Godfather. His influence was vast but also undefined, which kept people guessing at the limits of his power. Buster used this ambiguity to his advantage. Most people erred on the side of caution and tried to stay in his good graces—that was just plain common sense. "If he ever needed something, you never say no," said this same Hampton County man. "You never say no to Buster Murdaugh."

Many of Buster's most loyal friends were, like him, members of the local law enforcement community, including cops, sheriffs, judges, game wardens, fellow solicitors, etc.—what Tom Johnson deemed "a cult following of Buster." It only made sense, for Buster delivered results. "They viewed him as the Bear Bryant of their team," said the lawyer, referencing a champion college football coach. "They obviously wanted convictions." The Hampton County grand jury expressed the general sentiment felt about Buster Murdaugh in a statement in 1960, just before Buster was reelected for a sixth four-year term, "We feel Mr. Murdaugh is one of the finest solicitors in the state, and we are for him 100 percent."

The idolization of Buster extended to the state capital and among agents of South Carolina's state police force. When Buster visited SLED headquarters in Columbia, Chief J. P. Strom would always be there to greet him, according to a man who once interned for the state police force. "You would have thought that King Charles was coming," he said of Buster's arrival. Many of the state's fifteen other solicitors, said the intern, were usually greeted by one of the chief's deputies instead of the chief.

Buster traveled to the state capital often, including for meetings of the South Carolina State Democratic Party, of which he was the longtime Hampton County representative on the party's executive committee. One night, said a companion who traveled with Buster to Columbia, the meeting was progressing slowly, Buster watched the clock, worried that liquor stores would close before the meeting adjourned. The meeting dragged on, so at the last minute he dispatched the second-in-command officer at SLED, who was attending the meeting, off to buy him a bottle.

When the meeting finally ended, Buster and his companion started their two-hour journey home to the Lowcountry. Buster drove the car while his companion was "playing bartender" and pouring drinks for them both. At some point, the passenger asked Buster if he wanted to trade places and let him take over the wheel. "Nah, I got this," Buster told his passenger. "If we get stopped, I might know a few more people than you."

SLED agents down in the Lowcountry, too, were known to do Buster's bidding. Before a weekend cook he'd call one favorite agent and bark out a short shopping list, mainly liquor, shrimp, and ice. The SLED agent would bounce around town, procuring the goods at assorted businesses but not paying for a thing, instead cashing in on Buster's reputation and using the currency of favors, said Jared Newman, the Beaufort County lawyer who's worn almost every hat in law enforcement, working stints as a sheriff's deputy, detective, and assistant solicitor.

In the Lowcountry, there was no shortage of policemen hoping to gain favor with Buster. Newman recalled another encounter between the solicitor and a policeman in Allendale County, when the solicitor was gathering information to prepare for an upcoming trial. The question-and-answer session was anything but straightforward.

"What color car was the defendant driving?" Buster asked at one point.

"What color you need it to be?" asked the cop.

The courtesy extended both ways. Unlike his father, who prosecuted a number of policemen for misconduct and unlawful shootings, Buster's exceptionally long tenure in the solicitor's office featured remarkably few, if any, prosecutions of police officers. Intriguingly, the sheriffs and police officers said to be the most corrupt in the Lowcountry were some of Buster's closest friends.

One tactic that endeared Buster to law enforcement officers, ironically enough, was indicting policemen for unlawfully shooting a suspect. With an indictment in hand, pulled straight from his coat pocket, Buster would go so far as to have a jury empaneled, or a witness called, before dismissing the case. The idea, said Johnson, who witnessed Buster do this twice, was that the officer could not be charged again. "He went far enough that it was legally double jeopardy" to try the policeman again, he said, noting that Buster's ploy was never challenged and "may have been just pure gamesmanship."

Newman saw Buster execute the same legal maneuver when the solicitor briefly tried a sheriff's deputy for a charge of vehicular manslaughter. Once the first witness was sworn in, Buster announced he was dismissing the case. These machinations could seem unnecessary and excessive, but for Buster they paid dividends. These types of efforts burnished his reputation among police, displaying cunning and loyalty. Jim McClary recalled his first day on the narcotics squad within SLED, when his supervisor tasked him with transporting a troublesome, mentally ill patient. The supervisor warned him, semiseriously: "Careful, you might want to shoot him." Then he offered some advice, also semiserious: "Just get to Buster's circuit before you stop shooting."

If anyone questioned Buster about his aggressive, arguably premature, and overcautious tactics, he explained: "I don't want the officer looking over their shoulder, because one day I might not be solicitor." That scenario was unlikely. Nobody could dislodge him from the solicitor's office. After 1952, nobody even bothered to put their name on the ballot against Buster Murdaugh again. With every term, his power became more entrenched, the list of debts accrued much longer. As Johnson said a local expression went, "Governors come and go, but Buster stays forever."

Buster ended up getting more than free shrimp and liquor for his association with the police. He hired a police investigator exclusively for the solicitor's office and, beyond having him fulfill law enforcement duties, used him as a chauffeur. This investigator, too, would run errands and perform chores for Buster, such as thawing out the water pipes at the homes of assorted friends and family, building a porch, or organizing hunts for local law enforcement, judges, and politicians. Supposedly the investigator even built Buster a causeway to his small private island that was known as Buster's Island, or Chechessee.

Buster burdened other people, too, with his requests. One Hampton County resident summed Buster up this way: "If you could benefit him, you were his best buddy." Another, a policeman, explained that if you grew up in Hampton and became a cop, sooner or later, he said, "you're gonna get a call" from the solicitor. And yet another Hampton man recalled his mother once delivering a stern warning about the family: "It's alright to know them, it's alright to like them, but don't ever owe them anything, 'cause one day they will call it in."

"And she was friends with them!" said the son.

Buster extended favors as a matter of habit, to all sorts of people. Most of the time it cost him little, usually just some degree of restraint when it came to punishing lawbreaking, or a little bit of legal work that he completed free of charge. This system of favors was integral to his existence, its benefits spilling over into every aspect of his life, whether his job as solicitor, his job as a lawyer in private practice, or his roles as a friend, a family man, a politico, and so on. Buster developed a defining reputation as a fixer, someone who could help you out of a scrape. "If you ever got in trouble and were a decent person, you just had to go talk to him and (he'd) take care of it," said one Hampton County man, describing Buster as "lenient—to a degree."

Some people recognized Buster's deviousness but forgave him for it. His friend from Bamberg, Bill Humphries, said Buster may have been a crook but he was at least a "benevolent crook." Humphries was once sued for crashing his car into the back of another vehicle. Buster quashed the lawsuit with a single phone call, threatening that the plaintiff, a paralegal, would never find work in South Carolina again if he didn't drop the matter. "He reamed that guy a new one," said Humphries, who sat in Buster's office and listened to one side of the conversation. Hanging up the phone, Buster looked back to his friend and said "Alright, Humphries, what else you need?"

At some point, Buster's reputation, or notoriety, began to precede him. As a young lawyer Tom Johnson remembers meeting Buster for the first time, prepared to dislike him. Johnson had worked briefly for Buster's sometimes nemesis Bob Warren, who regularly disparaged the solicitor and accused him of abusing his power. But working independently, Johnson came to form his own distinct opinion of Buster. He came to like the short, stocky, and intimidating prosecutor, though he didn't entirely trust him. Buster, he knew, might have a different agenda than he advertised. Yet Buster never asked him to do anything wrong and Johnson never witnessed any corruption. He formed a cordial relationship with Buster, and found it was best to find Buster at the office early, which wasn't hard to do since the solicitor rose before dawn, about 4:30 A.M. every morning. "I want to be the first person to talk to you before anyone else pissed you off," Johnson would tell Buster when he popped in to review upcoming criminal cases. Buster always gave him his full attention and the time necessary to plead his clients' cases.

Mike Macloskie first heard of Buster Murdaugh in law school, before he even moved to the Lowcountry to become a lawyer in 1967. "It wasn't good. He had a reputation for being . . . powerful, kind of ruthless," said Macloskie, who acted cautiously when first meeting Buster. "But I found out while he was a very aggressive lawyer, he always treated me fairly." Macloskie, too, said he was never asked by Buster to do anything wrong. He and the solicitor became fond of one another, growing so close that Buster would issue greetings like, "Good morning, you old sonofabitch." To this Macloskie would reply, "Good morning, you old bastard. How are you?"

"I think Buster genuinely loved me," said Macloskie. "I know I genuinely loved him."

Buster was similarly affectionate of Dayle Blackmon, though he called her "Junior" instead of assorted profanities. She came to adore Buster and credited him and the Murdaugh family for many unheralded charitable contributions. It was clear to her which way the stream of favors flowed—away from the Murdaughs and to the people of the Lowcountry. It's no wonder, she said, that the solicitor attained a particular prominence. "You're damn right everybody looked out for Mr. Buster," said Blackmon, who is married to the former Jasper County sheriff. "They may need him one day. It's not that he needed them—they needed him."

One secret of Buster's political success was his oscillation between ruling through fear and favor. Another Lowcountry lawyer noted that while Buster could count a remarkable number of friends, none were unaware of his unpleasant edge. "All my life down in Hampton," said the lawyer, "people were intimidated by Buster." At the end of the day, said this lawyer, "Politics came first with Buster." He wanted to act like he was helping you, said the lawyer, "but he sure didn't want you to look too good."

Just like a federal judge once noted about Buster's personal finances, Buster's favor system had no precise accounting. The system's operations were murky. Rarely was an outright quid pro quo established. Instead, the preferential treatment ebbed and flowed like the local tides, sometimes flooding in, sometimes rushing out. Casual as it all seemed, "there was an acute awareness" of favors owed, said Johnson. For some things, Buster had a long memory. This included debts owed, but also slights and insults.

———

Don't bring a knife to a gunfight, but do bring a knife to an oyster roast. Sure, there's normally a community pile of oyster knives about somewhere, but they disappear fast, and half are grimy or rusted or scabbed with bits of dried oyster juice and cocktail sauce anyway. Better to bring your own, locals know, and an extra glove, too, because slipping on a cold, soggy, used oyster glove is just about as gross as reusing a discarded knife.

Oyster roasts are to be enjoyed on cold days, and it's even better if the weather is rotten, when it's not only frigid but also damp and misty or foggy. In these unpleasant conditions, one is truly appreciative of the heat radiating from both the bonfire and piles of piping hot oysters. The best oyster roasts are held right beside a creek or river, have a bluegrass band working away off to the side, in the shadows, and a practiced hand tending to the fire, one who won't remove the oysters too early, before the shells have cracked open sufficiently, or keep them on the fire too long, causing the oyster meat to dry out and shrivel. The basic setup is simple: start a fire beneath a metal grate or sheet. Throw a few clusters of local oysters on top. Cover the oysters with a damp towel. As the towel steams, watch for the oyster shells to crack apart. Once they do, dump the pile of hot steaming oysters on a slatted wood table and let the guests dig in. Then start roasting the next batch of oysters.

Early in the night the oyster tables are always crowded, with guests lined up shoulder to shoulder around both sides of the table. Some people like to eat their oysters with hot sauce and a squeeze of lemon, others scrape them from the shell and drop them on top of a cracker, maybe slathering it all in butter. Those most serious about their oysters often forgo any competing flavors, preferring to taste the salty, squishy, and slimy oyster meat alone. In any case, one starts by grabbing a small cluster of oysters with their gloved hand, so as to avoid slicing their bare fingers on the craggy shells, and then jams the knife edge between two shell halves and pries the oyster open. Inside lies the prize.

People have been eating oysters in the Lowcountry for ages, as evidenced by the assorted shell mounds scattered up and down the coast—huge, man-made accumulations of shucked oysters. While the oyster consumption of previous eras was necessary for survival, modern-day oyster roasts are better appreciated for their nourishment of the soul, for their unique ability to bring friends, neighbors, and strangers around a common table. Novelist Pat Conroy achieved bliss at these outdoor feasts, writing, "The camaraderie and the gossip and the sheer goodwill of the crowd set the oyster roast apart for me as something particularly Southern and indigenous."

Not everyone in Conroy's family was so fond of the shellfish. "I wouldn't eat one of these balls of mucus in a famine," his mother, Peg, once exclaimed with a wrinkle of her nose. Locals don't take offense at such distaste; that just means more oysters for everyone else. And for those inclined to gorge, the opportunity grows greater as the night unfolds, as stomachs start to fill and the crowd around the table migrates piecemeal toward the fire. Soon only a handful of gluttons remain with the oysters, their piggishness justified by the fact that this opportunity will not repeat itself immediately, and perhaps not for at least half a year, when it starts to get cold again. Pat Conroy was among those who pushed his gastric limits. "I never have left an oyster roast without thinking that I should not have eaten the last seven oysters I forced down," he wrote. "But how do you turn your back on something so enchanting and delicious?"

Just as Conroy gobbled down oysters, the young adults from Hampton gulped alcohol. The remainder of their journey, in which they snaked around downtown Beaufort and then traveled north through Brickyard Creek alongside the 7,000-acre Marine Corps air station, had been uneventful, save the worsening of the weather. As they motored upriver Anthony and Paul passed time by shotgunning, or guzzling, beers while the gals sipped less aggressively on their own stock of alcohol. After turning into the Coosaw River, Paul soon spied Paukie Island and steered the boat to a dock close to the oyster roast, where the friends tied the boat off and stepped ashore. It was 8:00 P.M. and a fog was descending.

The Saturday night roast was hosted by a couple from Hampton whose daughter was close friends with Mallory, Miley, and Morgan. The crowd was a mix of young and old, with lots of familiar faces. Miley's parents were in attendance, unaware she was arriving at the oyster roast by boat until the moment they observed her pulling up to the dock. Paul's aunt and uncle were there, too, as well as about a dozen other friends and acquaintances from Hampton. Considering all the adults, Paul and his friends elected to leave all their alcohol on the boat, where they could secretly refresh their drinks in privacy. Miley and Morgan spent the night sipping on cans of hard seltzer while Mallory and the boys drank beer. At some point Anthony discovered the Crown Royal. Still, the discretion was minimal, with the young adults drinking openly from their beer bottles and cans as they snacked on oysters and crab, shot hoops, and tossed beanbags while playing games of cornhole.

Morgan took pictures to post on Snapchat. One image shows Mallory with a Corona beer, eating cauliflower. Another oddly shows Miley sucking potato off of Morgan's hand, an oyster roast incident never mentioned in the pages of Conroy.

The party broke up close to midnight, four hours after the friends had pulled up to the dock and soon after one last basketball competition—a game of H-O-R-S-E—in which Morgan made "a beautiful shot," said the oyster roast's host, Kristy Wood, a local school principal. Wood, along with other adults, was concerned about the friends' return voyage. She and other guests urged the youngsters to accept a ride, call an Uber, or just stay on Paukie Island for the night. "(You'll) freeze your butts off" on the river, Wood told the six friends, hugging them goodbye as they prepared to depart. Beyond the temperature being cold, it was dark and foggy—romantic conditions for an oyster roast, but horrible weather for boating. Anthony agreed with the adults: they should call an Uber. When the rest of the gang stubbornly refused that idea, he resigned himself to tagging along.

Not among Wood's concerns for the boaters was drunkenness. She had served no alcohol at her family's oyster roast and said she did not observe any underage drinking save for Miley sipping on a single alcoholic seltzer drink that she soon discarded upon her arrival to Paukie Island. Out of sight, however, the friends managed to imbibe plenty of beer, hard seltzer, and, in the case of Anthony, whiskey. By the time the party ended and the friends headed to the dock, signs of intoxication were apparent, especially in Paul. As he waved farewell, Morgan noticed her boyfriend's hands were making a "very weird" but telltale motion, with his fingers extended and spread apart. Uh-oh. Timmy was showing up.

The friends stepped off the dock and into the boat. Paul took the helm, started the engine, and pulled the boat away from the dock. He steered out of the Coosaw River and south into Brickyard Creek, heading toward downtown Beaufort, a reversal of the route he had taken to the oyster roast. Connor stood to Paul's right-hand side, helping to navigate by watching the GPS device and occasionally shining the small flashlight. The boat's running lights, which announce a boat's presence in the dark and are required by law, were not functioning, but Paul had tied a small camping headlamp to a rear cleat on the boat as a substitute.

It was cold on the water, and nearly everyone in the boat was tired and chilled and eager to get home. The exception was Paul, who was "riled up," "really drunk," and "wanted to still party," said Morgan. While Morgan had stopped drinking alcohol for the night, Paul kept going, opening more beers as he drove his family's boat back toward the family river house. Approaching downtown Beaufort, he steered the boat under the Richard V. Woods Memorial Bridge. The swing bridge, whose central section rotates 90° to allow the passage of sailboats and small ships, was named for a state highway patrolman shot dead in the line of duty in 1969. Here, too, was another historical connection to the Murdaugh family, as Paul's great-grandfather, Randolph "Buster" Murdaugh Jr., convicted the three men accused of murdering Corporal Woods, though he failed to send them to the electric chair. But Paul wasn't thinking about great-grandpa at that moment; he was thirsty. He needed a drink.

Conveniently for Paul, the boat was now idling along downtown Beaufort's waterfront, where a half-dozen bars stood within sight. Connor liked Paul's idea of a nightcap, but the four others in the boat urged the boys to forget it and motor home. Paul, however, was insistent, arguing with his friends as he pulled the boat alongside Beaufort's public dock, making his friends more annoyed by the minute. This was lunacy, Morgan and

Miley yelled to their boyfriends. Anthony agreed with the girls, and told Paul to take them home, nearly coming to blows with him as they argued. In the face of Morgan and Miley and Anthony's fury, Connor backed down and urged Paul to leave. Paul reluctantly conceded, it seemed, as he motored back out into the river, toward his family's river house on the Chechessee. A minute or two later, however, he changed his mind. He turned the boat around abruptly and again pulled beside the dock in downtown Beaufort, ignoring the jeers from his friends. He was getting another drink, he said, no matter what they thought.

Since Paul could not be dissuaded from drinking further, the friends adjusted their plans. Connor decided to accompany Paul to a bar while Anthony and the three girls decided to pass the time on the boat and in Beaufort's waterfront park, where they sat on some of the parks' swinging benches. From here they gazed at the dark and foggy river, and watched the Woods bridge swing open to allow a small ship to pass through. Paul and Connor, meanwhile, crossed the park and approached the rear entrance of Luther's Rare & Well Done restaurant and bar. A bouncer on the porch checked their IDs, deemed them legitimate, and stamped the boys' hands with an Rx symbol, a nod to the pharmacy that once operated in the building. Inside Luther's, Paul spied an acquaintance behind the bar, a woman a few years his senior with whom he attended high school. Paul said hello and asked if she could get his friends inside. Not if they're under twenty-one, replied the bartender matter-of-factly.

Denied additional drinking buddies, Paul ordered himself and Connor a pair of Jäger bombs, paying for the drinks with his mom's Discover card. Down the liquor went in one big gulp. Within moments Connor witnessed a transformation, as if the Jäger bomb was the same potion used by Dr. Jekyll to conjure Mr. Hyde. Paul's eyes began to bulge and widen. His arms straightened and his hands jabbed the air, his fingers fully extended and spaced wide apart. Paul started being mean, or "Just being Timmy," says Connor, who recognized, even in the midst of his own inebriation, his friend's telltale signs of extreme drunkenness. Still, the boys wanted more. Five minutes after their first drinks, Connor paid for a pair of lemon drop vodka shots. These went down the hatch, too. A moment later, having had enough, Connor and Paul walked out the door.

About this time Miley and Morgan walked to the back entrance of the bar, eager to retrieve their boyfriends and get back on the boat. As everyone left Luther's, Paul immediately caused trouble, knocking over a porch chair and causing a scene. "What did that chair ever do to you?" asked a nearby patron in jest. The teasing enraged Paul. "What did he say to me?" Paul asked incredulously of Connor as he turned to confront the man, daring the stranger to get physical.

Connor firmly grabbed hold of his buddy and pulled Paul away toward the dock, insisting they leave to rendezvous with Anthony and Mallory.

Back in the boat, all six friends assumed their former positions. Miley and Morgan sat on a small bench seat toward the bow, with the boat's center console at their backs. Behind the center console stood Paul and Connor, the former driving while the latter watched the navigation display. Toward the stern were Anthony and Mallory, sitting on a bench seat looking backward. It was cold on the water this early in the morning, and very foggy, with visibility limited to ten feet in the thickest patches. Morgan and Miley huddled under a camouflage-patterned blanket to combat the chill. Anthony and Mallory stayed close to each other, too, with Mallory soon climbing onto Anthony's lap for the boat ride home. Should everything go smoothly, the friends could expect to be warm in their beds in a half hour.

Things did not go smoothly. Pulling away from downtown Beaufort, Paul immediately headed the wrong way, back upriver, and nearly drove into the Woods Bridge. Only when Connor intervened and turned the wheel at the last minute did the friends avert disaster. Both Connor and Paul were visibly intoxicated, so much so that they started "horseplaying" at the helm, said Anthony. Also conspicuous were Paul's mannerisms; he stretched his arms and spread his fingers out as wide as he could. Morgan noticed it and so did Anthony, who told himself this behavior only meant one thing: "Timmy is out."

Unwilling to step away from the helm, Paul steered the boat back downriver, toward his family's river house. Though he boated this stretch of river often in his young life, the fog and his drunkenness were making him quite disoriented. He sped up and slowed down the boat repeatedly, without reason, and then began driving in circles at a low, idling speed, unable to find the way forward. His friends laughed off his confusion at first. The hour was indeed late, they'd all enjoyed a few drinks, and it was especially hard to see through the fog and darkness. But after Paul nearly drove into a sailboat moored in the river, and then again began circling aimlessly at idle speed, his friends began to complain and called for Paul to step aside. Anthony volunteered to drive, and Miley insisted that Connor take the wheel given his own boating experience. Paul refused their pleas and grew defensive. "You all think you know this river better than me?" Paul replied. "This is my boat I'll be damned if anyone else drives."

Slowly the six friends motored downriver. The progress was painstaking, as every few minutes Paul would become lost and begin circling slowly as he attempted to regain his bearings. His friends, all cold and tired, had now lost confidence in Paul. They continued to complain about the delay, but to no avail—Paul would not budge from the helm. Miley fretted about having to go to work in a few hours, and told Paul he was acting like a fool and should let someone else drive. "Shut the fuck up and sit the fuck down," Paul shouted back. "Nobody is driving my boat."

The friends passed by Beaufort Memorial Hospital about 1:30 A.M. and then cruised under the large McTeer Bridge, toward the town of Port Royal. The five passengers increasingly worried about Paul's driving, leading Anthony to suggest they find a dock, disembark, and get the boat in the morning. When that plan didn't take hold, Anthony asked that he and Mallory at least be dropped off at the nearest dock, that they'd find their way home from there. Paul told them all to shut up again, provoking a tense exchange of words between him and Anthony, which then led to a quarrel with Morgan, whom Paul accused of being disloyal and taking Anthony's side. In the end Paul prevailed, assuring his friends that everything was under control. "(It will) be all right," said Paul. "We're fixing to make it home."

On and on it went, with Paul repeatedly losing his way on the river and reacting angrily to any dissent. He stepped away from the helm a handful of times while the boat was in motion, mostly to walk a few steps to the bow and argue with his girlfriend, Morgan, but at other times to remove pieces of clothing. First his jacket came off, which was a bewildering action considering the coldness of the night. But as Morgan said of Paul: "He's a crazy drunk. He does weird things." Whenever Paul would engage in one of these rage-filled, clothes-shedding walkabouts, Connor would seamlessly take the helm—like "a switch," as Morgan described it—grabbing hold of the wheel and making sure the boat, mostly going in circles, would not crash into anything.

By the time the boat finally neared the entrance to Archers Creek everyone was exasperated with Paul's stubborn and drunken behavior. First Paul had insisted on stopping at downtown Beaufort for extra drinks. Then he nearly started a fight as he exited the bar. Finally, Paul was driving recklessly through the darkness and fog, unable to find the way home, and yet he wouldn't relinquish the wheel. His response to criticism, says Connor, was always the same: "No one could operate his boat like him and no one is driving his fucking boat!"

Just before the boat entered Archers Creek, Paul abandoned the helm again, this time to remove his shirt. He walked forward and sat down across from Morgan. The couple's protracted fight, which started an hour earlier in downtown Beaufort, was about to reach a violent climax. Paul, bare-chested and belligerent, began screaming in Morgan's face, berating her, insulting her father, and spewing profanities so vile that Morgan could only describe Paul's tirade as "horrible" and "degrading." Repulsed, Morgan pushed Paul away. In turn he shoved her off the cooler and onto the floor of the boat. Morgan braced for further assault, shouting, "What? Are you going to hit me like you have all those times before?"

The answer was yes. Paul slapped Morgan on the right side of her face as she sat on the floor, and spit on her, too, leaving his girlfriend in tears. Miley consoled her friend, who buried her head under their shared blanket after striking back at her boyfriend. Paul returned to the helm, unashamed, while Miley shouted at him. Paul responded with more ugly words, which hung awkwardly in the air as Connor remained silent. This spurred Anthony to remark that Connor shouldn't stand for his girlfriend being treated that way. Mallory then joined the fray, telling Paul he was acting stupidly and that it was time to stop fighting and head home.

Mallory's scolding infuriated Paul; no one was in his corner. He stared daggers at Mallory, raised his arm and pointed toward her in a menacing manner. He appeared ready to unleash his rage again, to cuss out his friend, but Anthony stopped him short, advising Paul not to "make that mistake." Paul then shifted his gaze to Anthony, glaring at him for a second before turning back to the wheel.

Date night had devolved into disaster. The six friends had traveled this last leg of the journey at a snail's pace. Paul had alienated and assaulted, either verbally or physically, almost everybody on board, the exception being Connor, who loyally stood in for Paul at the wheel whenever his friend wandered to yell or remove his clothing. Miley and Morgan, who hours earlier sat in the bow with ear-to-ear smiles as they posed for photos, now clung to each other tightly as they huddled under a blanket and shivered. Morgan was sobbing. In the back of the boat, between a bench and the outboard motor, stood Anthony and Mallory, both of them eager to get to sleep. And in between, at the helm as usual, stood Paul, with Connor just to his right. The boat idled forward gently. Ahead was Archers Creek.

Suddenly the outboard motor roared and the boat surged forward. The boat's bow shot up in the air due to the quick acceleration, knocking

Anthony and Mallory to the floor. They stayed there as the boat kept plowing forward and picking up speed, its raised bow cutting through the fog. Anthony wrapped his girlfriend in his arms, squeezing her close. Things were getting hairy.

After such a plodding voyage down the relatively wide Beaufort River, it was surprising for the helmsman to speed so quickly down narrow Archers Creek. The tide was high, which made the waterway wider, and more forgiving of sloppy navigation, but still the creek's turns demanded caution, especially given the limited visibility. The boat nonetheless tore along the water, snaking quickly through the marsh. To the south was Parris Island, with hundreds of Marines and recruits sleeping quietly in their beds. And ahead, not too far past Archers Creek, was the Broad River and, on the other side, the Murdaugh family river house on Buster's Island.

The friends were indeed "fixing to make it home" as Paul previously said, and soon, given the boat's breakneck speed of nearly thirty miles per hour. Anthony and Mallory were still lying on the floor of the stern together. Up front Morgan and Miley were pressed together, too, beneath the blanket. Miley kept her head up, peering ahead through the fog, while Morgan kept her face pressed into folds of the camouflaged fabric. It was Miley, sitting forward of everyone else, who saw the bridge first. First there was fog ahead, and patches of night sky, and then, in an instant, the empty air was crowded with wooden and steel pilings. It was the Berkeley Bridge, leading to Parris Island. Miley braced herself and screamed out her boyfriend's name—"CONNOR! CONNOR!"—but it was too late.

The boat first slammed into a dolphin structure, the cluster of tethered wooden posts driven deep into the creek bed. The light, fiberglass boat bounced violently off the barrier like a pinball, careening right back across the channel to the other side, where it crashed into a concrete piling before making a rough beached landing on rocks under the bridge. The night air was quiet for a brief moment, then filled with shrieks and screams. Morgan's hand was cut and bleeding and she was becoming hysterical from her injuries and the trauma of the crash. Connor was in bad shape aboard the boat, too, his face having slammed against the boat during the collision, breaking his jaw. Miley, who had escaped serious injury, tended to each of her friends' injuries while also trying to tackle a bigger problem: Where were the rest of her friends? Where were Anthony, Mallory, and Paul?

———

Brent Cooper was getting ready to waterski with his friends. He and a group of teenage buddies were enjoying a summer day on Battery Creek in Beaufort on July 31, 1961, using his family's two small motorboats. While Brent was driving one of the boats, his fifteen-year-old friend George Rodgers jumped into the creek and started swimming toward the motorboat. His foot struck the propellor, causing a cut. George was taken for medical treatment and received more than twenty stitches for four lacerations on his foot and was hospitalized for five weeks.

Randolph "Buster" Murdaugh Jr. soon filed a lawsuit on behalf of George's mother, Margaret T. Rodgers, against Brent's father, Howard Cooper. The Cooper family could not help but suspect the suit was personal and coming as much from Buster as from the Rodgers family. Howard Cooper and Buster had been students in college together, and, four years earlier, when Buster was indicted as part of the whiskey ring, Howard had aggressively called for the solicitor's resignation in editorials he wrote in the *Beaufort Gazette*. After Buster's acquittal Cooper weighed in further on the matter, praising federal Judge Walter Hoffman of Virginia for his criticism of the solicitor and other aspects of South Carolina's legal system. "The pity of it is that there was cause for such remarks," wrote Cooper in the newspaper. "We cannot hide our responsibility for a situation by getting mad at the person who reminds us of our shortcomings."

The lawsuit asked for $100,000 in damages, an eye-popping amount at the time for nonfatal injury. Even worse for Cooper, one side of the lawsuit was stacked with court insiders, as the solicitor was trying the case for his client, Margaret Rodgers, Beaufort County's deputy clerk of court, who was married to T. Legare Rodgers, the clerk of court for Beaufort County. No settlement was reached between the plaintiffs and Cooper's insurance company, and the ensuing trial in March 1963 featured much conflicting testimony. Some witnesses testified the victim showed no signs of long-term injury after cutting his foot, others said he limped and suffered psychological damage that led to moodiness and a decision for him to leave home and live with a family friend. His mother, Margaret Rodgers, the plaintiff, said both her son's feet shrank after the accident by more than a shoe size. At another point in trial, Buster explained that the victim was under the influence of pain-killing drugs when he made statements absolving his friend Brent, the defendant, of blame.

During closing arguments, Buster said he personally would not even accept $100,000 for the pain endured by the boy, a statement the judge asked the jury to disregard, as the jury needed to make their own determination of the value of his suffering. During deliberation, jurors agreed Cooper was liable but differed on what constituted a reasonable award. Eventually the jurors each wrote their own suggested amount on a sheet of paper and then took the average of these numbers, arriving at an award of almost $26,000, which impressed the local bar as atypically large. A few months later the trial judge reduced the verdict to less than $13,000, calling the original amount "larger than is justified."

The trial cost Cooper and his family more than money. In personal notes taken at the time he detailed how stress from the lawsuit caused "severe emotional and mental strain upon son, Brent, resulting in personality change, and upon wife, Elsie, aggravating ulcer conditions and necessitating hospitalization." Howard Cooper was irritated that his lawyers and insurance company did not settle the case, a feeling that was amplified when he heard comments like those of acquaintance A. R. Nicholson, who told Cooper, "You were stupid to let yourself be tried in a county where Buster and Legare were in such a position to control things." The newspaper publisher and editor ended up selling the *Gazette* the same year he lost the lawsuit. He took solace in his belief that he had at least won the battle of public opinion. As he recorded in his notes: "Community reaction terrific: rigged jury, Murdaugh known crook, absurd testimony, Legare has lost my vote, etc."

———

Anthony was swimming. Upon the boat's collision with the bridge Anthony had gone airborne, tumbling through the air, near the pilings, before skipping across the surface of the water and finally splashing down into the creek. The cold water shocked him—"It was literally like waking up," he said—and as he regained his bearings he realized he was awash in a swift current, being swept under the bridge and away from the beached boat. He grabbed onto a piling to avoid being carried away, and removed one of the two jackets he was wearing, the extra garment doing nothing but weighing him down in the water. Unable to swim directly to the shore against the current, Anthony opted for a less straightforward journey, swimming from one piling to another, angling his approach such that he purposefully overshot his target, knowing the current would counteract his approach and sweep him back into the next piling. After a few minutes he reached the shore. It was dark and he couldn't see anything. Anthony started hollering, convinced his friends were all in the water, too.

As he walked the shore, Anthony heard yelling and screaming. It was his friends, but they were on the other side of the creek. So Anthony jumped back in the water and made his way toward them—a grueling, twenty-minute swim made from piling to piling, against the current, in waterlogged winter clothing. When Anthony finally emerged on the other side he found Paul laying down on dirt under the bridge, alive. Morgan was wailing in the background. Miley spotted Anthony emerging from the creek and ran toward him.

"Where's Mallory?" asked Anthony.

"What do you mean where's Mallory?" answered Miley.

"She's not up here?" he said.

"No!" said Miley.

Now nearly everyone was screaming, this time for Mallory. Anthony jumped back in the water to search for her, but was soon overwhelmed by the creek's current. His body was now cold and tired, and his shoulder, which had become dislocated in the crash, was aching badly. A feeling of futility came over Anthony as he began to fear the worst, that he would not find his girlfriend. He climbed out of the water and continued searching along the water's edge.

"MALLORY!" Anthony screamed in anguish. "MALLORY!"

There was no reply. Anthony kept screaming Mallory's name. All the shouting annoyed Paul, who interrupted Anthony's search to hush his friend. "Shut up," Paul said. "Stop talking . . . everything is going to be okay." Paul's indifference enraged Anthony. He shoved and struck Paul and accused him of "killing his girlfriend." As Paul walked away Anthony resumed his search.

"MALLORY!" he wailed. "MALLORY!"

While Anthony searched the shore, Connor dialed 911 on Miley's cell phone, walking away from the scene in an attempt to escape all the shouting and fighting. Connor was exceedingly drunk and his jaw was broken, but nonetheless he spoke relatively clearly to the dispatcher. Still, she suffered great confusion.

"Nine-one-one, where's your emergency?" said the dispatcher at 2:26 A.M. "Police, fire, EMS. Hello!"

"We're in a boat crash on Archers Creek," said Connor after a slight pause.

"Whereabouts on Archer Street?" said the dispatcher.

"In Archers Creek," said Connor. "The only bridge on Archers Creek."

"Archers Street?" asked the dispatcher.

"Archers Creek," repeated Connor, adding that he was near Parris Island.

The conversation continued for a few moments, with the dispatcher next asking for the details of Connor's emergency. Again she became confused.

"What, what's going on?" said the dispatcher.

"We're in a boat crash," said Connor.

"You're in a—What kind of boat?" asked the dispatcher.

"A boat crash," said Connor.

"A boat—Did you say a boat crash?" the dispatcher asked.

"A boat crash," said Connor, yet again.

"So are you at the dock?" asked the dispatcher. "Hello, are you, are you at the dock?"

"No. We just crashed in a boat . . ." said Connor. "We have someone missing."

As Connor hung up and began waiting for police and paramedics to arrive, Paul took hold of Miley's phone. Miley overheard Paul call his grandfather, Randolph "Randy" Murdaugh III. If anyone knew how to handle a mess like this, it was Handsome.

Law enforcement officers and paramedics began nearing the accident scene about twenty minutes later. The fog was thick around the bridge, preventing the first responders from finding the injured boaters immediately. Anthony had walked atop the bridge by this time, watching as the blue lights neared and police arrived along the causeway that connected to the Berkeley Bridge. Eventually he was approached by Beaufort County sheriff's deputy Stephen Domino. Anthony was in shock, observed Domino, and fixated on finding his girlfriend. He persuaded Anthony to sit in the back of his patrol car and relate the night's events, promising he was not in any trouble.

"Sit right here, we got everybody coming out here . . ." Domino told Anthony, leaving the patrol car's rear door open. "You're, you're my concern, okay."

"I'm fucked," said Anthony, slurring his words.

"No, you're not," countered Domino quickly. "Listen, listen, (Anthony), I'm here for you, alright. Me and you, we're, we're chilling. I understand you're upset, I ain't about to sit here and tell you to calm down, okay. But I'm gonna get you a cigarette."

Anthony sat in the rear seat of the warm patrol car while other police and paramedics spoke to his friends nearby. Soon Anthony asked if he could call his mother. Domino helped him make the call.

"Mom, y'all need to come to Beaufort *quick*," said Anthony, his voice emotional. "We hit a bridge in the boat. Connor is fucked up. Connor's messed up bad, we can't find Mallory. Morgan's messed up bad. We can't find Mallory, Mom."

Moments passed as Anthony's mom absorbed the stunning news. Anthony continued to impress upon her the severity of the accident. "Mom, there's fifty cops here, Coast Guard, everything. We can't find Mallory. It's been thirty minutes, Mom. You probably need to call Miss Renee or Mr. Philip," Anthony said, breaking into sobs as he suggested calling Mallory's parents.

Connor, Miley, and Paul, meanwhile, were speaking to other law enforcement and paramedics nearby. Paul was hard to miss, given that he had now also removed his pants and was standing around in the cold wearing nothing but boxers and socks, all of which were dripping wet. Someone soon handed him a towel to wrap around himself. Paul was also hard to miss because he was acting so obnoxiously, uttering profanities to first responders and refusing to cooperate. Soon enough his presence caught Anthony's attention.

"Get that motherfucker right there away from me!" shouted Anthony, his breathing becoming heavy and labored.

"You talking about that one with no shirt on," asked Domino, referring to Paul. "Hey, do not, I don't want you getting into any trouble, you hear me? Listen to me. Don't get in no trouble. Did you hear what I said? Your mom's on the way . . . I'm hanging with you until your mom gets here, okay. You're not in trouble . . ."

Officer Domino told Anthony to stay seated in the patrol car, but these cautions did little to stem Anthony's rage. He cursed Paul and Connor for not letting him drive, then exclaimed that Paul "needs to rot in fucking prison," but fretted that "he ain't gonna get in no fucking trouble."

"Oh yes, trust me," Domino replied, promising justice.

At this point a smirk came over Paul's face, further incensing Anthony. As Domino instructed him again and again to remain seated, Anthony let loose his fury. "Bo', you fucking smiling like it's fucking funny?" Anthony screamed at Paul. "My fucking girlfriend's gone, bo'! And you think it's fucking funny! I hope you rot in fucking hell!"

Domino distracted Anthony with more cigarettes. "I ain't got a lot, now, don't waste 'em," said Domino as other police and paramedics led Paul away from Anthony. So tense was the atmosphere that a supervisor from Parris Island's fire department warned colleagues responding by boat to expect chaos as they neared the bridge. The boat crew, however, was already facing trouble, hampered by heavy fog that limited visibility to less than ten feet and required the use of spotlights and electronic navigation devices to proceed along the waterways. So bad was the fog that the state police and U.S. Coast Guard were unable to safely launch helicopters to aid in the search. The Coast Guard sent a boat instead, and volunteers with a local rescue squad also searched the creek by boat. Along the bridge, local, state, and military law enforcement officers secured the scene and began identifying and interviewing the survivors. Among their initial questions: Who was driving the boat?

Paramedics began treating the injured boaters and prepared them for transport to Beaufort Memorial Hospital. First to leave for the hospital was Morgan, still suffering from a cut hand. Another ambulance contained Connor, Miley, and Paul, though Paul repeatedly tried to exit the vehicle in search of Morgan. He was told by police and paramedics to sit down again and again. These commands only provoked further foolishness as Paul yelled, cussed, and insulted those trying to help him. Paul became so rude and unruly that paramedics requested a police officer accompany Paul in the back of the ambulance as he was transported to the hospital with Connor and Miley. Paramedics strapped Paul tight to a gurney, but left Connor and Miley unrestrained. While four of the boaters left the accident scene in ambulances, Anthony stayed behind by the bridge, not willing to abandon Mallory. His shoulder, he decided, could be treated later.

Buster had gone too far. That was twice the opinion of the South Carolina Supreme Court on November 14, 1961, when the court ordered new trials for the two Beaufort men Buster convicted for rape and had sentenced to death two years earlier. In the conviction of Fred Davis, a White man, the court took issue with Buster's promise in court not to try the other high-publicity, racially tinged rape case if the jury failed to convict. "It would be hard to conceive of a statement more likely to excite the emotions of the jury and to coerce a conviction," said the court's opinion. Similarly, they felt Israel Sharpe, a Black man, received a trial in an atmosphere improperly charged by Buster's comments to a jury panel as well as a judge's decision to allow news cameras in the courtroom.

Following these orders, Sharpe agreed to a plea deal that spared him the death penalty. A judge sentenced him to forty years in prison for his attempt to rape the young mother. Davis, meanwhile, maintained his innocence and claimed the sexual encounter with the alleged victim was consensual. In June 1962, he was again tried for raping a Black woman in the bushes of downtown Beaufort. This time, though, Buster Murdaugh was not present at the blockbuster trial, having recently suffered heart problems that required him to withdraw from court. In his place the case was tried by another solicitor and prosecutors from the South Carolina Attorney

General's office. Travis Medlock, a young deputy attorney general, remembers he felt bullish about the trial that featured confessions from the defendant and testimony from numerous eyewitnesses.

Yet Medlock's confidence was misplaced; a jury of twelve White men acquitted the rape suspect. Medlock recalls that he and his colleagues were shocked and appalled to the point they were speechless. The veteran lawyer, who later served twelve years as South Carolina's attorney general, said the Davis acquittal remains "the most vivid memory I have of any trial in which I was involved during my career.

"It was the most blatant travesty of justice I have ever seen in sixty-three years of practicing law," wrote Medlock in correspondence about the case. "We were so stunned and saddened by the verdict, (my fellow prosecutor and I) rode back to Columbia together and neither of us can remember a word being said during the trip."

Medlock said the outrage in the courtroom was palpable. When the jury foreman asked Judge William Rhodes for permission to make a statement, Medlock remembers the judge replying, "I don't want to hear it." The foreman spoke anyway, saying, in effect, "This jury is proud to have done our patriotic duty to our country, and we are available to do it again at any time." Such insolence inflamed the judge, a well-regarded jurist from Hampton who later served on the state supreme court. "The face of Judge Rhodes suddenly flashed red and he quickly wheeled his chair around turning his back on the jury and its foreman," recalled Medlock. "His anger was infectious. Everyone in the court room felt it."

Buster did not comment on the acquittal at retrial, as it was not his style to agonize, second-guess, or wail about injustice. Besides, there were other things occupying his mind in the 1960s, including more charges of misconduct. Buster stood accused again of pocketing a portion of proceeds owed to his client—in this case $15,000 made from the sale of the client's sawmill in 1964. A judge dismissed the charges against Buster after a three-hour hearing, persuaded that Buster had otherwise not been paid.

Dogging Buster, too, was his embroilment in an interstate adoption ring scandal operated in part by his friend and college classmate, Delmar N. "Tiny" Rivers, a former state representative and lawyer from Jasper County. In 1963 Rivers confessed to forging the signatures of a judge, solicitor Buster Murdaugh, and parents on assorted legal forms for more than a dozen adoption cases he had handled in the last four years. Rivers was the last stop in a baby supply chain that ran up and down the East Coast. It typically worked like this: a couple wanting a child hired a particular Miami lawyer. The Miami lawyer found and paid pregnant women to give up their soon-to-be-born children and arranged for the mothers to give birth in Georgia, which has looser adoption rules, and then give the babies to the adoptive parents in Florida at the Jacksonville airport, just south of the Georgia border. While the new family and the birth mother headed back to their homes, the Miami lawyer coordinated with Rivers to register the adoption in South Carolina, where the state's lax laws essentially permitted out-of-state couples to adopt out-of-state babies in a single day, with minimal oversight. Nothing Rivers did in relation to the adoptions was apparently illegal, except that he forged signatures instead of submitting paperwork to a judge and the solicitor. Bewilderingly, Rivers supposedly forged Buster's signature on some forms, but Buster signed others himself after meeting with prospective adoptive couples. "I signed some of them but I frankly don't remember how many," said Buster.

The network operated by Rivers and the Miami lawyer was hardly the only baby business in South Carolina. Years later, a judge in Charleston County celebrated the many Jewish couples who were able to sidestep restrictive laws and waitlists at home by adopting children in the Palmetto State. "I didn't know there were so many New York Jewish CPAs till [Charleston lawyer] Tom Lowndes started parading 'em in here, but I'll tell you one thing, I don't see anything wrong with letting them have these little unwanted babies. These babies will never want for a single thing," said Judge Mendel Rivers Jr., the son and namesake of a longtime Lowcountry congressman, and no known relation to Tiny Rivers.

The judge was supportive of loose regulation for adoption, keeping government oversight at a minimum. In more bureaucratic states, he said, "Babies stay on foster care instead of going directly into a family . . . they spend weeks counseling the birth mother instead of doing what's best for the child, when they know and everybody knows, the last thing these women need or want is a baby." Judge Rivers favored streamlined adoptions that placed babies in new homes as soon as possible. He and some other South Carolina judges shared the sentiment that if a couple was willing to pay thousands of dollars for a child, it was a good sign they would make fine parents. Certainly, said Judge Rivers, they'd make better parents than the adopted child's biological mother and father, whom he disparaged in general terms:

> *Their mothers are the scum of the earth, the dregs of society, and if they kept the children, they'd raise them over in the Franklin Trailer Park on welfare and give them no father figure, or only a fleeting father figure with all their boyfriends in and out . . . Those little babies would have no stability in their lives, getting dumped on their welfare mama's welfare mama or welfare grandmama, and sooner or later we'd see them here in family court with cigarette burns where their ears used to be and marks where's she's beat them with an electric cord . . . One good thing about adoption is letting people who deserve to have children have children.*

Tiny Rivers was arrested for forgery but a Jasper County grand jury declined to indict him. After that the attorney general's office filed a civil action to sort out the adoption mess and to legitimatize the improper adoptions. When called to the stand to testify about his role in the scheme, Rivers asserted his Fifth Amendment right 120 times, refusing to answer any question posed to him.

Despite avoiding criminal consequence for the adoption scandal, Rivers was disbarred from practicing law in South Carolina in 1965. The scandal ended there, though some mystery remained about how Rivers became involved in the network. One report on the adoptions speculated that Rivers met the Miami lawyer through legal work he performed for the owners of a Lowcountry brothel called the Green 'Gator. Buster Murdaugh's exact role, too, was less than defined. He was a close friend and hunting buddy to Rivers, and Rivers once represented Buster as legal counsel when the solicitor was investigated for allegedly stealing money from clients in 1949. One lifelong Hampton resident said they were always told, "Buster could get a baby for you." And Alan Young remembers his father, Hampton jeweler Morris Young, once mentioning the existence of a "whorehouse" just short of the Georgia border, near the town of Hardeeville. When prostitutes got pregnant, the jeweler told his son, their babies were given to Buster so he could sell the newborns.

Buster was not the only Murdaugh alleged to have an interest in young children. His brother Johnny Glenn Murdaugh, who boasted of bedding the "pretty little girls at the pool," allegedly preyed upon youngsters, too, though in an even more depraved manner. The children Johnny exploited weren't so lucky to be sold away to another family. These children lived with him. They were his stepchildren.

Sheryl Polk McKinney was four years old when her mother, VerLee, married Johnny Glenn Murdaugh about 1951. Within a few years the family moved into the old Dr. Tuten house on farmland owned by Buster in Almeda, just a few minutes' drive south of Varnville. Johnny farmed for a living while VerLee operated a beauty parlor, first in Hampton, then in a drug store in Varnville, and after that at home. Sheryl's little brother lived with her at the old doctor's house, and the siblings had a sister who resided with relatives.

Like everyone else, Sheryl thought Johnny "crazy." For a decade he inflicted severe sexual, emotional, and physical abuse on her and her family, she claimed. Sheryl became so petrified of Johnny she sobbed uncontrollably when she was in his presence, provoking additional fits of anger and violence in him. She did not escape his grip until she ran away at age sixteen to live with friends. "He was a psycho," said Sheryl.

Like his brother, Buster, Johnny brought his family to the Methodist church in Varnville every Sunday. Johnny made sure she paid attention to the sermon, said Sheryl. He wanted people to believe he cared for his family. At home Johnny was strict, too, and, in echoes of his military service, wore his uniform and enforced many rules and regulations. The punishments he doled out for alleged transgressions varied, said Sheryl, but all were intended to cause suffering. Sometimes Johnny shut off electricity in the house. Other times he sprinkled minced bits of hot pepper in a bowl of peas and made the children eat it. Johnny placed snakes and lizards in Sheryl's bed. When Johnny wasn't in uniform, he was usually walking around the house naked. When he disciplined the kids he made them strip naked, too, and stand in line at attention and watch each other be beaten. He refused to return the children's underwear after he beat them, telling them they "didn't deserve underwear." Johnny would scream at the children with such fury they would often lose control of their bladders on the spot, said Sheryl. When her brother wet his pants, Johnny shamed him by making him wear a dress and walk to town.

Like Buster, too, Johnny took his kids fishing, though in Johnny's version of angling with the family, he did the fishing while the kids cleaned the fish. Johnny sometimes drugged his wife, VerLee, says Sheryl, and during one incident laughed when VerLee stumbled on the beach and fell into the waves. Other times he did not find VerLee amusing. Johnny once knocked his wife's teeth out when he slammed a cooking pot into her mouth as she cleaned the refrigerator. Sometimes he was arrested for abuse, says Sheryl, but there was never ultimately any consequence for the brother of the solicitor. "He'd beat us home from the jail, they'd let him out so quick," she said. "Before we could get packed up, he was back."

Sometimes Johnny would come home drunk at night and round up the family and put them in his truck. He'd drive them to a cornfield, says Sheryl, and tell her and her brother and mother to run while he fired guns at them as they disappeared among the cornstalks. Sheryl usually ran to the end of a nearby road and sat down. When the shots died down she headed home. By then Johnny would be passed out.

Sometimes when Johnny came home Sheryl hid from him in the stair hall, other times upstairs in her brother's room, in an old closet with sliding doors and a built-in table. Given that the house previously belonged to a country doctor, her family surmised the closet with the table had been a morgue. Now it was occupied by two living children, terrified youngsters who might have *wished* they were dead and free of their tormentor. The closet's possible use as a morgue did not spook the children; no ghosts could be more horrifying than Johnny.

Sometimes instead of hiding when Johnny came home, Sheryl's brother grabbed her and they fled the house. Wherever brother and sister escaped they would play church. "We'd pray and we'd talk and ask why is this happening," said Sheryl. "We'd ask for God to protect us from Johnny."

Those prayers were not answered. The children could not always escape Johnny. They were caged with a predator and unable to hide in the morgue forever. Johnny first molested Sheryl at age four, she said. His breath was distinctive. More than seventy-two years later she can still remember its smell from that first forced kiss. When thirty-three-year-old Johnny pressed his lips to Sheryl's small face he nearly swallowed the young girl, his mouth consuming her mouth, nose, and chin all in one gobble.

Sheryl soon told her mother what Johnny was doing to her. When her mother confronted Johnny, said Sheryl, "He beat the hell out of her and then he beat the hell out of me." After that, said Sheryl, she didn't tell her mom anything.

Johnny was not deterred by his wife's protest. He forced himself on young Sheryl again and again, raising the sexual stakes. Sheryl was soon

performing oral sex on Johnny, she said, "giving blow jobs" at the age of six
or seven. In Johnny's mind, though, this was hardly the limit. He promised
Sheryl he would teach her so many new things. He was relentless, exploiting
every opportunity to obtain pleasure. Sometimes he would take a bath when
his wife VerLee worked in the beauty parlor at the front of the house. He'd
call Sheryl into the bathroom to scrub his back. She wouldn't leave until
Johnny ejaculated.

———

It was only five miles to the hospital. The ambulance pulled forward and
proceeded down the causeway connecting Parris Island to Port Royal,
rolling across the marsh. After passing the main guard gate and leaving
the military base, the ambulance turned right onto US Highway 21 and
almost immediately traveled over the Russell Bell Bridge, which spanned
another creek.

Just like the Woods swing bridge in downtown Beaufort, the Bell
Bridge is named in honor of a fallen law enforcement officer. And just like
highway patrolman Woods's case, this fallen officer's killer was convicted
by a Randolph Murdaugh, specifically Randolph "Randy" Murdaugh III,
whom Paul had just called.

Randy, after being phoned by his grandson Paul, was now rushing to
Beaufort Memorial Hospital, the same place where Sheriff's Deputy Bell
died nearly three decades earlier after being shot in the stomach and chest
by a mentally ill man. The veteran lawyer and former prosecutor knew the
earlier he could intervene on behalf of his grandson, the better. Hurrying
to the hospital, too, was Paul's dad, Alex.

Morgan arrived first to Beaufort Memorial Hospital's emergency center,
close to 3:00 A.M., and was promptly admitted and taken to a private
room for treatment of her left hand. Minutes later the other ambulance
arrived, delivering its three patients to the hospital. Miley walked into

the emergency center beside Connor, who was wheeled in on a gurney. The couple insisted on being seen by a doctor together, and Miley soon declined to be examined at all so she could stay by Connor's side. Behind Connor and Miley came Paul, also on a gurney. But unlike Connor, who suffered his broken jaw quietly as he was being wheeled through the emergency center to his own private room, Paul yelled rudely as he entered the hospital, causing alarm and hijacking the staff's attention as he rolled along corridors. In the blink of an eye, said emergency center technician Laura Kent, the hospital had been transformed into a "weird, corny, teen drama movie." The cast of characters would soon be expanding.

Upon being wheeled into his own room, Paul's behavior did not mellow. Despite instructions to stay still, Paul rose repeatedly to leave, yelling at medical staff as he ripped off leads to a cardiac monitor and sought to walk away, though he nearly fell over each time he attempted to stand. The drunken teenager's arrogance astonished the medical staff. Nurse Karen Taylor became frustrated by Paul's refusal to answer basic questions about his actions and injuries. "Y'all should be doing your jobs and looking for my friend," Paul responded to Taylor again and again, his entitled attitude remarkable to the nurse. On the rare occasion Paul did provide an answer, he forgot what he said by the time Taylor asked a follow-up question. Other times Paul exaggerated, confusing his caregivers.

Were you drinking? asked the medical staff.

"Yes, all kinds of alcohol," said Paul.

And were you doing drugs?

"Yes, all kinds of drugs," said Paul.

So slurred was Paul's speech, and so unruly his behavior, that the medical staff was inclined to believe the half-naked man lying before them, wearing nothing more than soggy boxer shorts and socks, had indeed truly consumed all kinds of alcohol and all kinds of drugs. A doctor ordered Paul's blood drawn and analyzed as a precaution, worried that Paul, who suffered a number of abrasions in the crash, was perhaps so intoxicated that he might fail to recognize and disclose the true extent of his injuries. The sample eventually revealed Paul's blood-alcohol content was .286, more than three times the legal limit to operate a motor vehicle in South Carolina. Also ordered was a urine sample. When technician Kent handed Paul the collection container he smiled at her and asked if she was going to hold his penis for him. Then, moments later, Paul pointed at Kent's backside and exclaimed, "Oh, wow, that's nice!"

About 4:00 A.M. Paul received a new visitor to his hospital room—law enforcement. Officer Austin Pritcher of the South Carolina Department of Natural Resources had followed the accident victims to the hospital from the crash scene on Archers Creek. Starting in Paul's room, he inquired about the night's events. There was one essential question Pritcher and his colleagues needed to answer: Who was driving the boat? Paul, his eyes noticeably bloodshot and his speech unclear, did not provide Pritcher with an answer.

"Why do you need to know who was driving? That isn't going to help find Mallory," said Paul. "What if it was me who was driving the boat?"

"Was it you who was driving?" said Pritcher.

"I definitely was not driving," said Paul. "These are all my best friends."

Making little progress, Pritcher walked to a nearby room holding Connor and Miley. Connor was soon due for a CT scan, which would help diagnose the traumatic injuries to his jaw. Minutes earlier a nurse had tended to him, asking Connor questions about the night and his medical history. The questions upset Connor and he became defensive, replying only vaguely. He asked the nurse why it was important to learn so many details. Similarly, Connor shared little information with Pritcher when the officer came to his room. In brief, slurred statements, Connor said he couldn't remember who was driving the boat at the time of the accident, or who was driving the boat before the accident, either. "We were heading down Archers Creek, heading toward (the) Broad River," said Connor. "I remember seeing the bridge and that was about it." Miley said she didn't know who was driving, either.

Pritcher walked back to Paul's room and stepped inside. He asked Paul if he was able to make a formal statement about the night's events, and Paul said yes. Pritcher began to gather the appropriate paperwork only to be interrupted moments later by the arrival of Paul's father and grandfather. Immediately Randy and Alex advised Paul that he did not need to make a statement to law enforcement. This prompted Pritcher to inform the Murdaugh men that he, alone, was speaking with Paul. The Murdaughs ignored Pritcher. "Well, I am his lawyer, starting now, and he isn't giving any statements," said Randy, bringing an end to the matter.

Now ensconced within Room 10 of the Beaufort Memorial Hospital's emergency center, Alex and Randy immediately began their own triage, of the legal variety. Former solicitor Randy kept watch over Paul, advising him to keep his mouth shut. Despite this counsel, Paul's profane outbursts continued, causing Randy to marvel at the depth of his grandson's intoxication. "He is drunk as Cooter Brown," Randy said to a security guard the hospital posted outside of Paul's room. But in conversation with his grandson, Randy was unamused, ultimately telling him to "Shut the fuck up!"

Paul was not the only Murdaugh causing a scene. While Grandpa Randy, or Handsome, as he was known, tried to keep Paul quiet and still, Paul's dad, Alex, roamed the hallways looking for the other boat accident survivors, one of his law enforcement badges conspicuously hanging from a pants pocket. In the hallway he encountered Connor, who was being pushed in a wheelchair, en route to a CT scan. Alex stopped the staff member from wheeling Connor any further and took the young man aside. "We will figure this out. It will all be okay," Alex told Connor, echoing the assurances his son made creekside that morning, minutes after the boat crash, when Mallory was discovered missing. A nurse soon approached the men and ended Alex and Connor's conversation, insisting Connor continue his journey to the CT machine. Connor remembers one overarching message from his encounter with Alex: "That everything was going to be all right. I just needed to keep my mouth shut and tell them I didn't know who was driving and that he's got me."

Alex attempted to deliver similar messages to the other survivors. "I'm responsible for all these kids," he told the charge nurse who intervened after he stopped Connor. Hospital staff observed Alex peering obviously at a tracking board that listed admitted patients and their room assignments. Alex tried to enter Morgan's room as she recovered from surgery on her hand, but Morgan turned him away. "I am responsible for her," Alex protested to a nurse. "I have to tell her what to say."

Morgan's mother soon arrived at the hospital, as well as Connor and Miley's parents. Alex chatted with them all, sometimes suspiciously ceasing conversation when medical staff walked within earshot. Hospital staff saw Connor's dad in conversation with Alex in the hospital hallway, and then, minutes later, Connor's father entered Connor's room and motioned for his son to cease an interview with law enforcement, drawing his hand across his throat to emphasize the point. After witnessing this exchange, Nurse Taylor was left with the impression that "the concern was staying out of trouble rather than (telling) what occurred." Medical staff also observed Alex speaking on his cell phone as he roamed the hallways and purchased a drink from a vending machine. The medical staff that overheard him grimaced at the casual comments he made on the phone. "She's gone, don't worry about her," a security guard and a nurse overheard Alex say in reference to Mallory.

By this point, Alex's behavior was becoming more disruptive than Paul's. One nurse claimed to smell alcohol on Alex, and the security staff assigned to watch the youngest Murdaugh was asked to keep an eye on Alex, too, and not allow him to wander the halls. Before being discharged from the hospital, Paul declined to take a field sobriety test offered by the South Carolina Department of Natural Resources. Connor, who was due to be transported to a larger hospital in Charleston for jaw surgery, also declined the field sobriety test. In the hours ahead, authorities kept asking Connor for clarification about the night's events, but he was unable or unwilling to provide it. As he told one member of the Beaufort Water Search and Rescue squad who called him for help at 4:54 that morning in the ongoing search for Mallory, "I was not driving the fucking boat and I do not know who was driving the fucking boat. You need to talk to my mother. I am in the hospital."

As dawn loomed and Connor waited to undergo surgery, Paul left the Beaufort hospital with his grandfather. He was dressed in paper scrubs, walking out of the emergency center, when he suddenly reversed course, abandoned his grandfather, and reentered the hospital. Striding back into the restricted area, Paul soon cornered Morgan and forced her into an awkward "side-hug," according to registered nurse Elizabeth McAlhaney. "It was obvious," said McAlhaney, "that the female did not want to have a conversation with the male." Paul left the hospital for the second time after being retrieved by his father.

Upon her own discharge, Morgan returned to Archers Creek to stand vigil for her missing friend. Boats were in the creek and nearby rivers, filled with crews looking for Mallory. Other rescue teams searched by land. As the fog lifted at daybreak a Coast Guard chopper searched from the air. Divers took to the water, using sonar devices to look for a body beneath the surface.

The Murdaugh boat rested on rocks beneath the bridge. There was blood on the boat's floor and on the bow seat. A six-foot-long gash had been ripped along the top of the fiberglass hull. The boat's floor was muddy and littered with empty cans of alcohol.

Law enforcement personnel came and went from the accident scene, including First Sergeant Adam Henderson of the South Carolina Department of Natural Resources. He soon spotted Anthony, who had still not left the scene, sitting on the ground with a blanket wrapped around his shoulders, seemingly lost in thought. Henderson introduced himself and listened as Anthony related details of the boat ride home. "Me and Paul have been friends for a long time, but no more," said Anthony. "I can't forgive him for this."

About 7:00 A.M. Mallory's parents arrived at the accident scene. They were told to stay near their car and discouraged from approaching the creek. Henderson observed they were "obviously upset and wanted information."

An hour or so after that, investigators from the South Carolina Department of Natural Resources returned to the accident scene from the hospital, having finished their interviews. They told a colleague it was unclear to them whether Paul or Connor was driving the boat, and that Paul was from a powerful family of lawyers in Hampton County. Then, as if to prove the family's legal prowess, the investigators related how Paul's father and grandfather showed up at the hospital and cut short their interview with Paul within about an hour of the crash. The Murdaughs, the officers added, were requiring the law enforcement agency to obtain a warrant before searching the boat.

These officers weren't the only ones wary of an absence of justice. Earlier that morning, as Anthony sat in the police cruiser with sheriff's deputy Domino, he became emotional imagining worst-case scenarios, specifically that Mallory was dead, and that Paul would face no consequences for his role in her death.

"Can you feel that heat in there?" Domino asked Anthony as he sat in the rear seat, the twenty-year-old still damp from his swim in the creek.

"Dude, I'm not cold," said Anthony.

"I know," said Domino. "Well you are, but your adrenaline is up, you can't feel it. Smoke a cigarette."

"I haven't smoked a cigarette in three months," said Anthony.

"Well, it's alright," said Domino. "Don't start, but it's okay to have one now."

A few moments passed. Anthony's concern for his girlfriend kept nagging at him.

"Is anybody in the water looking for her?" said Anthony, his voice cracking with emotion.

"Yes," replied Domino, quickly. "We got MRO . . . fire department's got their boats in the water, Coast Guard's on the way with a chopper, and DNR's en route, alright," said Domino, rattling off a list of assorted rescue personnel.

Anthony feared it was hopeless. "She is at the bottom of the river man, fuck!" he said, his voice betraying devastation.

Domino sought to comfort him: "They're gonna have a dive team, we got a dive team, we got a bunch of resources. Okay? Regardless, like I told you, regardless of outcome, we will find her, alright? You just have to keep faith that she's somewhere on the bank, or, see what I'm saying?"

More time passed. Anthony and Officer Domino chatted above the creek as the lights of emergency vehicles flashed intensely before them, giving the night air a red glow. All of a sudden, Anthony piped up with a question. He could not stop thinking of Paul and his family.

"Y'all know Alex Murdaugh?" he asked the police officer.

"Oh yeah, I know that name," grunted Domino.

"That's his son," said Anthony. "Good luck."

———

For more than thirty years she never had a single day off, never took a vacation. She spent these decades in jail, though not behind bars. For fifteen years Mamie Heape Woods was married to the Hampton County jailer—a position that allowed him no time off and required him and his family to live in a first-floor apartment inside the jail, beneath the second-story cells. When William Lee Woods died in 1952 she was appointed his replacement, beginning a twenty-year term of her own as jailer that ended with her retirement in 1972, at the age of seventy-eight.

For many years Mamie Woods was the only female jailer in the state, and among the state's oldest jailers, too. Yet in thirty-five years she had few prisoners abuse her trust, despite the jail being regularly occupied by about a dozen vandals, roughnecks, rapists, killers, and so on. Woods came to expect weekends to be particularly busy. "I don't know why it is, but these men work all week and get drunk and have to be locked up on Friday nights," she said. "By Sunday they are sober enough to go back to work."

Woods wore no uniform and carried no weapon. Just one inmate escaped the jail during her thirty-five-year tenure. She kept order through kindness, and recognized she was meeting many people at their lowest point. She counseled many of the inmates, especially wayward boys, and was particularly heartbroken when a fifteen-year-old was jailed for killing his parents. Woods said her job as jailer allowed her to serve mankind and she sometimes gave money to those behind bars. Prisoners loved her cornbread, and she strived, with the help of a maid, to provide vegetables, meat, rice, and a dessert to inmates at each meal.

Woods raised three children in the jail, including one daughter who remained in residence with her mother into adulthood. Her children regularly visited the inmates upstairs, and Woods said their home at the jail, where she kept chickens in the yard and grew flowers and vegetables, was just as peaceful as a private home. "Sometimes a drunk raises a fuss, but he eventually goes to sleep," she said.

Beyond watching the inmates, Mamie was the "trouble hub" of Hampton County, the central dispatcher coordinating telephone and radio communications between townspeople and law enforcement. This responsibility added to the difficulty of getting away from the job, though she did go to church on Sundays and occasionally visited the doctor. When she went shopping in Hampton she cut to the front of the line and was served first, everyone else understanding the importance of keeping the cells supervised.

While William and Mamie Woods administered the jail, another married couple similarly managed another important local institution, the *Hampton County Guardian* newspaper, published weekly since 1879. Writing, printing, and delivering a newspaper on time and with minimal mistakes was a regular, Herculean task endured and accomplished by every newspaper editor, but Tom and Martha O'Connor had additional challenges. Beyond the *Guardian*, the O'Connors published the *Allendale County Citizen* each week. Tom also persevered against a disability, as a bout of a childhood polio had crippled his legs and made him reliant on crutches his whole life. He took his medical challenges in stride, as O'Connor once remarked that crutches were so much more than walking aids, as they had proved "handy in fights, in keeping out of fights, as an excuse for not climbing the courthouse steps . . . for moving presses, prying open doors, and maintaining a reputation for doing the impossible."

O'Connor, who dreamed of writing a novel, became editor of the *Guardian* and *Citizen* in 1947 after stints as a newsman in New York City, Miami, and Augusta, Georgia. The native Bostonian felt right at home in the Lowcountry, residing in Allendale, fifteen miles northwest of Hampton. After putting all the news and ads and legal notices and photos and comics and so on into place each week he finally turned his attention to his editorial column, "The Time Has Come," and reliably struggled to fill it with words. The owner, publisher, and editor of two newspapers was overwhelmed. To compensate he wrote columns about his recurring inability to write anything of consequence in the face of a deadline, and how one way to fill empty column inches in the newspaper was to write about the challenges of filling empty column inches in the newspaper, and that, gee whiz, writer's block sure is something, and what else is there to say, anyway, and just a few more sentences should do it, and next week's column will be better . . . a habit that certainly grated on the nerves of at least one reader.

Yet other columns were stirring. Among his best, and most wrenching, were those written from the perspective of a heartbroken father. O'Connor's only child, U.S. Marine sergeant Tommy D. O'Connor, was killed in action on January 3, 1968. "My son came home from Vietnam early this year . . ." was how the grieving editor's column began a few weeks later. O'Connor wrote of his ambitions to build a record cabinet before his son finished his deployment, and to refurbish a darkroom to encourage his son's new interest in photography. But then came the news that Tommy was dead, and he wouldn't be spinning vinyl or clicking his camera anymore.

During his son's funeral, O'Connor hobbled after a Marine Corps honor guard processioning up the aisle of his family's small country church. He wrote:

> *There was somewhere in me, on that bitter day, a block of ice that contained and constrained all of me that could be called me. I was not cold in the sleet and rain and wind that blew across a dark day, when the skies wept and I could not. Just as the rifles barked sharply in a last salute and from a distance the bugle began its mournful declaration of farewell, the rain brushed coldly, softly against my cheek. For a moment I raised my eyes and remembered that he liked, on days such as this, to go booted and wrapped off across the fields into our woods.*

O'Connor died in 1969, nearly two years after burying his son, and the newspaper was then operated by his wife for five more years. He never published the novel he contemplated, which is perhaps no surprise given the difficulty he had finishing a mere column each week. But O'Connor at least thought hard about that novel, which was to be titled *County Seat*. He poked fun of his procrastination in a "The Time Has Come" column in 1967, when he said, "Through the years of not writing I have accumulated a lot of what a novelist would term research material." The difficulty, said O'Connor, was deciding what of this material to actually use, balancing the value of its disclosure against the damage such revelations might cause, even in semi-fictionalized form. How true a depiction of small-town actors should the author construct, he wondered. "Now the troubles with such a book is that you have to work like a surgeon, cutting deep in the proper places," wrote O'Connor in his column. "A surgeon, however, has the excuse that he is mending an ill. The author seems to need a certain streak of vindictiveness which has no regard to the health of the patient or the healing of much of anything."

For a newspaper journalist, O'Connor was strangely averse to telling the truth in his proposed book. "When you consider the petty vanities, the degrees of snobbery, the political deals, the polite chicaneries, the gentler throat-cutting, that goes on in a small town, you get a little discouraged," he wrote. But more than good manners, it was a sense of duty that appealed to O'Connor. He fretted that an honest portrayal of a community and its stalwarts might only result in disillusionment: "The highbinder, the rounder, the cheater, the sneak, finds somewhere someone to love him, to overlook his faults, to see in him the epitome of manhood," wrote O'Connor. "His outer orb of respectibility [*sic*] is all they see. To uncover the dark slime of his real nature might be to do a great harm, not to him, who is not blameless, but to those who so love him and so live for him."

Rather than consign a community to the abyss, to expose its people as rotten or foolish, to ruthlessly document its shortcomings, O'Connor capped his pen and never completed *County Seat*. "Can one write about human beings without dumping out the garbage cans and retailing their contents?" he asked. "Somewhere in the human relation there ought to be some sort of line drawn beyond which authors do not go."

O'Connor did not disclose who exactly inspired the "highbinder" of *County Seat*, the crooked politician and member of what O'Connor called "The Establishment," who inspired so much love and support. To condemn him would be to condemn an entire county and beyond. So he kept his "research material" under lock and key and gave up on the idea of whacking the proverbial hornet's nest by publishing a thinly veiled novel. He decided to let someone else collect the "few bucks, the movie rights, the emoluments which accrue to the successful author." When explaining his rationale for keeping mum, he was self-righteous: "I would much rather pretend to a kind of blindness, than to turn a pitiless light on the real nature of those involved," wrote O'Connor. "In high place or low they are to be pitied as their nakedness is revealed, their hungers told, their greeds uncovered."

But without a "pitiless light," evil festered. Sunlight—the best of disinfectants—was often shut out of parts of the Lowcountry, whether by the tree canopy above the cypress swamp, by the skittish and squeamish newspaper publisher, or by corrupt officials, racist jurors, and those who stayed mute in the face of the serial molestation of a child. Buster Murdaugh, more than anyone else, drew a thick curtain around the Lowcountry, shielding five counties from scrutiny. The result was a near-total blackout.

One place of darkness, one corner many judged better left unexplored, was the farm in Almeda, where Johnny Glenn Murdaugh kept his home. Here young Sheryl Polk was perpetually molested by her stepfather for years, with no intervention. Much like his transparent invitations for Sheryl to wash his back in the tub, Johnny would demand Sheryl lie down beside him on the couch. Typically she would start to cry, she said, which would lead to a beating. Then at some point he'd be "slobbering" all over her.

By age eleven Sheryl was worried about getting pregnant. Johnny was worried, too. Not worried to the point he refrained from raping her any longer, but concerned enough to give Sheryl books and magazines about teen pregnancy so she could possibly attempt some precautions.

Once Sheryl and her mother both went to the hospital to be treated for vaginal inflammation. The doctors and nurses grew suspicious during their examinations, said Sheryl, wondering why both a mother and her young daughter had vaginitis and if perhaps they were sharing a sexual partner. The hospital staff briefly kept Sheryl in a room away from Johnny and her mother, but their inquiry fizzled once Johnny called his brother, Buster.

Johnny never called his stepdaughter *sweetie* or *darling*. Instead he referred to Sheryl as a "bitch" or "slut" or "whore." He told Sheryl she was "used material" and "tainted goods." He told her no one would ever want or love her, and that she would have to stay with him the rest of her life. When

Sheryl was a sophomore in high school a boy came to the house to ask her on a date to the movies. Johnny did more than dash the teen's hopes. "He threatened him, told him he'd kill him if he came back around," said Sheryl.

Johnny was almost never kind, and if he was, it was motivated by self-interest, said Sheryl. Her childhood was bleak, because of one man. "I don't remember happy times as much as I can the trauma," said Sheryl. "I can't say we had happy times."

Johnny was a sadist, inflicting pain on nearly every living thing within his domain. He beat his wife. He beat his stepchildren with a belt. He beat Buster's hunting dogs with that same belt when they barked. Johnny hated anything that seemed weak, said Sheryl. Once when Johnny returned inside from beating the dogs, young Sheryl asked him if he beat Jack, a dog who was missing a leg and was blind in one eye. "Hell, yeah," said Johnny. "I beat him more than I beat you!"

Three-legged, one-eyed Jack got off easy compared to some of the other farm animals and family pets. In one two-week span, said Sheryl, Johnny punished her by engaging in a spiteful, pet-killing spree. She recalled Johnny calling to her one day, asking her to come close, that he had something to show her. "Look what I found," he said when Sheryl stepped near. Johnny had a hammer in one hand and was holding one of her cats by the tail in the other. A moment later he grabbed the cat by its scruff, and slammed it against the ground, holding the animal in place as he brought the hammer down on its skull, splattering the animal's brains. Sheryl ran away, screaming.

Days later Johnny used a hammer to smash the skull of another of Sheryl's cats, a mother who had just delivered kittens. Johnny had killed the kittens the day before, piling them in a muslin flour sack and sinking them in a pond. Johnny also killed two of Sheryl's dogs—Blackie and Susie—by driving vehicles over them, including one who was asleep in the yard.

Johnny threatened similar violence on Sheryl's mother. He would leave with VerLee and threaten to return alone, telling Sheryl she would never see her mother again. Sheryl would then keep a tearful vigil at a window, waiting for her mom to return home and prove Johnny's threat hollow.

It wasn't just the rapes, the whippings, the brained cats, and the beatings of a crippled dog that made Sheryl fear Johnny, nor that the traumatized military veteran stalked the farm with a .45 caliber pistol tucked into the small of his back. Johnny frequently boasted of killing people, and told Sheryl he had placed five bodies in the pecan grove at the Almeda farm, using a tiller to cut the corpses apart and plow the remains into the soil. "He said nobody would ever find them and no one would ever know," said Sheryl. "I believed him."

Part of that belief was informed by the disappearance of George, a Black farmhand in his thirties. Johnny hated George, said Sheryl, especially after Buster told George to assume a truck and several farm responsibilities from Johnny due to Johnny's laziness. Soon thereafter, Johnny told his family he and George were going for a ride. Before the men left, said Sheryl, Johnny announced cryptically: "If you all want to see George, better come now, because, when I come back, he won't be with me."

"And he wasn't," said Sheryl.

She thinks he might be in the pecan grove.

CHAPTER SIX

FIXED OUTCOMES

When Hampton County's fall term of the Court of General Sessions began on October 8, 1973, a very important person was in attendance, or at least a very important kid. Standing in the Hampton County Courthouse that Monday morning was five-year-old Alex Murdaugh, or "Alec" as he was listed in the *Hampton County Guardian* two days later. As Alex dipped his hand into the jury box and plucked out the names of county residents to serve on juries for criminal trials, his grandfather, Buster, and father, Randy, looked on with feelings of pride, but also curiosity. Solicitor Randolph "Buster" Murdaugh Jr. and his assistant solicitor, Randolph "Randy" Murdaugh III, would soon be attempting to convince the people listed on those scraps of paper to convict alleged criminals, such as the twenty-three-year-old man from Ridgeland about to go on trial that morning for charges of attempted rape and housebreaking. How many of those names did father and son know?

Picking the jury was a family tradition. When Randolph "Randy" Murdaugh III was a boy in the 1940s, he, too, visited the Hampton County Courthouse to pick names out of the jury box while his father watched approvingly. Now it was young Alex's turn to play a judicial Fate, drawing juries for consequential criminal legal proceedings, such as the trial of the alleged Ridgeland rapist, who was convicted and sentenced to thirty-five years in prison. The case was unremarkable except it underscored the fact that the local criminal justice system, if not the entire legal system in the

Lowcountry, had become a Murdaugh family affair. In the case of the trial
of the rapist, one Murdaugh picked the jurors and two other Murdaughs
persuaded these men and women to convict the suspect of his alleged
crimes. This was not an isolated event. As *Guardian* columnist Martha Bee
Anderson wrote, all of Randy's four children got a chance to pick names,
"each taking a turn at drawing juries until they passed the age limit of
nine or ten."

At least a few people grew uncomfortable with such familiarity in
the local legal system, though their specific objection was not with the
Murdaugh children picking juries, but rather that the kids' father was
hired by their grandfather. After a unanimous vote, the Beaufort County
Council sent letters of protest in August 1975 to the governor, legislators,
and other state and local officials, denouncing Buster's employment of
his son as an assistant solicitor for six years. Neither Murdaugh sympa-
thized with this complaint. Randy said he was qualified for the job and
earned every bit of the $10,000 salary plus expenses. His father replied
that he'd gladly jettison Randy if he could find another lawyer to do
work for such low pay.

Beyond the small salary, any prosecutor in Hampton County had to
suffer the indignity of working in one of the state's worst courthouses.
The last renovation was in 1950, and people were still grousing more than
twenty years later about all the changes and the lack of general care for
the county hub. The grounds of the Courthouse Square, where the trees
were depleted one by one over the course of a century, remained similarly
disappointing. Sections of wrought iron fence lay collapsed in the grass,
no one bothering to right and repair the metalwork. Part of the square had
been made into a parking lot, further marring the parklike setting. New
outbuildings cropped up around the courthouse, crowding the lawn, and
there was discussion of building more, which infuriated town watchdog
Martha Bee Anderson, who couldn't believe the county would pave a
parking lot in the square instead of planting more flowers and trees. "We

must not permit continuing abuse of the Square and we certainly can ill afford to give up one more inch of it to any purpose," she wrote in a call to arms in her "Around the Clock" column that same year.

No one heeded the call. So six months later she again decried the dismal state of the courthouse and its square. "Sadly, the 'blushing pink' exterior with its ironwork stains streaking the exterior advertise to all coming and going the state of disrepair of this valued structure," wrote a fiery Martha Bee, who lived three blocks away, at the end of Lee Avenue, almost with a direct line of sight to the courthouse. "A chewed up, chopped up parking area permitted within the falling wrought iron fencing also speaks in continuing disrespect for the square."

Still the newspaper columnist was ignored. Six months later, in September 1974, Martha Bee vented her rage again, unwilling to surrender this fight. "Look at those sections of valuable antique iron fencing left lying where they fell. Not much sense of pride or preservation in evidence here," she wrote with a tinge of uncharacteristic bitterness. She implored residents to take action, asking, "Doesn't anybody really care?"

Working alongside Martha Bee at the *Hampton County Guardian* during her crusade to clean up the Courthouse Square was the paper's new editor, Patrick Tyler, who had just graduated college. He became enchanted with the columnist, finding Martha Bee to be an earnest and compassionate Southern newswoman who produced an upbeat, practical form of community journalism in place of muckraking, preferring to extol praise rather than wag a finger. "She had a strong bent toward good character," said Tyler. "She had a serious agenda and admired good people."

For as many times as Martha Bee was published over decades in the *Guardian*, she always had more to say. Unlike her late editor Tom O'Connor, who never could get around to finishing his novel about small-town intrigue, or even most of his weekly editorials, words poured forth from Martha Bee at a torrent much swifter than the nearby Salkehatchie. Her voice usually seemed to arrive before the rest of her did, and "she was talking from the moment the door opened without knowing who was in the room," said Tyler.

Martha Bee's fashion sense was frozen in the 1950s, when she had been a young woman. Tyler remembers her wearing ensembles of sweaters and scarves and flowing, gabardine skirts with half a dozen bags slung over her shoulder. "She reminded you of an era that was over but she was holding onto it," said Tyler. Martha Bee was a constant presence in the *Guardian* office, said Tyler, especially since the scent of her perfume lingered in the newsroom long after she had left.

In her campaign against the degradation of the courthouse and its surrounding square, Martha Bee sought to add another voice to the fray. She requested a guest newspaper column from Will Cox, a Hampton resident who worked for a local building contractor, and he responded with a frank appraisal of the county centerpiece:

> *It is no great contribution of colonial architecture. It was not designed by a master architect such as Robert Mills. It has not been maintained as well as could be over the years. The additions and renovations over the years have not been completely in keeping with "that which is good," and its arrangement and mode of function brought about by its very design does not serve us today as would a new and modern building . . . To be honest, there was a time when it was more beautiful than now—when it had circular stairs on the front and when no front and rear wings existed.*

Yet Cox noted the building had also proved resilient and facilitated the operation of government, especially the local court system. The guest writer turned sentimental, praising the valuable role the building has served:

> *It is a building with a heritage. No man can walk in that courtroom without—for a split second—a lump coming in his throat from*

acknowledgement that he is in a place of meaning—of the "real" real thing. From such rooms our very nation was birthed, and this very courtroom is, in its own way, as significant as any landmark in our nation. If this is difficult for you to believe, walk in that courtroom around dusk while it is yet sort of "reddened" with sunset and sit quietly for five minutes. Those old, thick brick walls are bulging with heritage.

The courthouse may have been full of heritage, but it was devoid of comfort. For ninety years the courthouse lacked air conditioning, and by the early 1970s judges and members of the grand jury began to consistently complain about this deficiency. During a term of court in June of 1971, Judge William Rhodes thanked jurors for working in oppressively hot and humid conditions, and, in an attempt to provide some perspective, mentioned the sacrifices American soldiers were making while fighting a war in the jungles of Vietnam. The absence of air conditioning, the judge said, "is a small price to pay for citizenship, small indeed in comparison to the price being paid by men serving our country."

Hampton County leaders agreed later that year to install air conditioning in the courthouse. But then there was Allendale County, an even more rural county just up the road with a reputation of perhaps being even more behind the times than Hampton. In 1974, to the chagrin of Judge Rhodes, the Allendale County courthouse still lacked air conditioning. Rhodes was scheduled to preside over a contentious, racially motivated murder trial in Allendale in July, when warm, if not scorching, weather was almost guaranteed. He knew the courthouse was sure to be a sweatbox. As the judge told Solicitor Buster Murdaugh and other lawyers involved in the case a few weeks before trial, "It will tax the patience of all involved to be working in this type (of) facility. So gentlemen, come dressed in your work clothes and cancel your vacations."

The rare summer term of court in Allendale was being called for the trial of five White men charged with murdering a Black teen in an act of racial retaliation. Four years earlier, during the early morning hours of May 16, 1970, eighteen-year-old Wallace Youmans was walking past a store in the Allendale County town of Fairfax when he was shot dead with a shotgun. The tiny town, located just ten miles from Hampton, had previously experienced days of racial unrest that featured the shooting of a White man at a small grocery store and the arrests of twenty-five Black people who were protesting police actions. The turmoil culminated with the shooting of Youmans.

For years the killing went unsolved by local police, state police, and the FBI. But then other organizations and individuals began their own, interrelated investigations of Youmans's death and started to unearth information. This included the National Association for the Advancement of Colored People, reporters from the *Charlotte Observer* and other newspapers, as well as Beekman "Beek" Winthrop, a scion of one of America's oldest and wealthiest families. Winthrop lived three months of the year with his wife and infant son in a contemporary home in Allendale County that he built on his family's 25,000-acre Groton Plantation, which was one of South Carolina's largest estates. The Winthrops had forever been among the elite in America. One of Winthrop's forefathers was an early colonist and governor of the Massachusetts Bay Colony. Other ancestors made fortunes in banking, which enabled the purchase of lands to form Groton in 1906 as a vast hunting retreat along the Savannah River. Beekman Winthrop was a polymath, studying literature at Columbia University as an undergraduate before earning a graduate degree at the same university in urban planning. After that he became a divinity student at Harvard University before going to work for an antipoverty organization in Washington, DC, that he also financially supported. When Winthrop wasn't living at Groton Plantation he lived in Washington's posh Georgetown neighborhood.

One day Winthrop was visiting Groton with his young family when he learned of the unsolved death of Wallace Youmans. Immediately Winthrop was compelled to discover the truth. "I was appalled that such a thing could still happen in the United States in the 1970s," he said. For more than a year he interviewed dozens of people, chased leads, and spent thousands of dollars in order to ultimately construct a narrative of the killing. Much of the information came from a man who confessed to NAACP officials, shortly before dying, to planning the murder with four other men, including his own brother, a town magistrate. The confessor said he and his coconspirators sought revenge for the Black community's perceived unruliness in Fairfax. He claimed the men planned an ambush outside the grocery store, planning to shoot the first Black person that walked by after midnight. It happened to be Wallace Youmans, who for some reason stopped outside the store and briefly picked up a crate of glass bottles before setting it down roughly, causing some bottles to shatter. His girlfriend and two friends were walking behind him, at a distance. They heard the bottles break and then someone whistle in the dark before a shotgun blasted twice. They saw Youmans's head jerk to the side when the first shot hit him, and then his body spun to the ground when he absorbed the second blast. The high school student died eight hours later in a hospital in Charleston. The victim's mother, Fannie Youmans, remembered her son Wallace as "a good boy who didn't give nobody any trouble."

Winthrop shared this information, including a list of suspects, with a former governor from Allendale and officers at SLED. When those efforts yielded no results he submitted a 110-page report to the United States Department of Justice titled "Fatal Shooting of Wallace Youmans, May 16, 1970." The experience was emotional and cathartic for the young husband and father, who was looking for purpose within a life of privilege. "The Youmans case was my opportunity to step in and make a difference," he said.

The report spurred state and federal investigators to restart investigations and redouble their efforts. Winthrop was soon being cheered in the national press, lionized by *People* magazine and covered in the *New York Times* and *Charlotte Observer*. The reporting done by these publications dwelled on South Carolina officials' inability to solve the crime and convict a murderer. These officials included Solicitor Buster Murdaugh, who otherwise seemed to have absolute control of the Lowcountry when it came to matters of law and order. Buster said that despite the best efforts of law enforcement, a convincing case could not be made against the suspects, stating, "We think we know who did it, but we can't get the evidence." The solicitor also complained of a double standard, wondering why the White man injured by a gunshot during the racial strife in Fairfax was not receiving as much attention in the press. "It seems right strange to me—and color doesn't mean anything to me—but a White man was shot at about the same time this thing happened, and I've never seen one word printed about that."

Public outrage began to mount, even locally, where Buster had otherwise long been untouchable and beyond reproach. It helped that Winthrop had befriended a number of journalists. This included Tyler, the new editor of both the *Hampton County Guardian* and the *Allendale County Citizen*. The young newspaperman made a point to cover the Youmans trial closely in each community publication, both on the news and opinion pages. In an editorial entitled "Four Years is Too Long," the *Guardian* criticized SLED and the solicitor's office for the lack of arrests, accusing them of being "corrupt or paralyzed or emotionally involved." The editorial, which asked for federal prosecutors to take over the case, read in part:

> *Perhaps the most difficult thing to understand about the case is how, in a town of 2,000 population, a murder could take place, out in the open, with witnesses, and with nearly four years of "active investigation" without anyone being arrested. It is no wonder that community blacks and fair-minded whites are skeptical and cynical over SLED's investigative integrity—as well as that of the FBI. But further, that cynicism should also be cast at those who make the indicting decisions.*

A month later, an Allendale County grand jury indicted five White men for murder. The solicitor denied that public pressure had anything to do with the charges, but Winthrop couldn't help but wonder at the timing. "I'm not saying that my involvement brought about the indictments," said Winthrop, "but for years there weren't any, and suddenly now there are." Even though there were now indictments, some activists doubted Buster would vigorously prosecute the case. The solicitor didn't seem bothered by the doubters, responding:

> I hadn't heard anyone was trying to get me off this case, but if you see anyone that does, you tell them all they've got to do is come to me and ask, and I'll gladly get off, but I'll tell you one thing, if they want a conviction in this case, they stand a better chance of getting one with me on it, than if someone from the outside comes in because I know the people here, I know how they think.

Buster knew, too, that Winthrop was fighting a hopeless battle. While Winthrop's efforts made him friends in the Black community, many Whites shunned or castigated him. This hostility, as well as the loneliness of his mission, caused Winthrop fits of despair and moments of self-doubt. It didn't help that his uncles turned on him, or that he perhaps turned on them and threatened their traditional existence. Winthrop once detailed the family strife:

> [My uncles] think it's very inappropriate for me to have become involved. They feel this is a part of the world that hasn't been disturbed and that it is great to have it as old-fashioned and out of the 20th century as it is. They and my father are in a position to enjoy this part of the world on their own terms. That means coming down and shooting birds and vacationing and having people feed them and set their fires—a very quaint, old-fashioned life.

Publicity over the unsolved racial killing embarrassed Allendale County and a slew of South Carolina law enforcement officials, which made for hard feelings. At a pretrial hearing in the Allendale County Courthouse a few weeks before the murder trial, a SLED official took the stand to rebut the suggestion that the agency was not motivated to solve the case. He said that the case was slow to develop because witnesses were distrustful of the police. The eventual suspects also lied to investigators about their whereabouts the night of the murder. Furthermore, said Assistant Chief J. Leon Gasque Jr., it wasn't helpful to have Winthrop and other "kangaroo people" conducting their disruptive parallel inquiries. "It's no wonder it takes (the police) four years," he said. "I resent the fact that we were not able to do our job." Outside of court Gasque threatened Winthrop with a lawsuit if he impugned SLED's reputation and derided him as a "professional do-gooder."

When Winthrop testified at that same pretrial hearing, he was berated by a pair of defense attorneys. In one tense exchange, attorney W. E. Myrick said in a belligerent tone, "The point is Mr. Winthrop, as a result of much influence, and I don't know what, on your part, we have five men charged with the despicable crime of murder with their life and liberty at stake . . ." Next came attorney George Harold "Rip" Kearse who accused Winthrop of bias in his version of events. "We resent one side of the picture being told . . ." said Kearse. "Why don't you go to some other community?"

Winthrop did not waver in the face of such adversity, but in the end it really did not matter. The murder case, which took so long to solidify, began to fall apart as the trial neared. Buster Murdaugh dropped murder charges against three of the defendants due to lack of evidence, having no witnesses that could place those men at the scene of the crime. It seemed the grand jury had overreached, though the men were still charged with conspiracy and accessory to murder.

That left two men, Albert Cook and Preston Polk, to stand trial for murder. During a four-day trial each man took the stand to testify in his own defense. Cook and Polk each admitted to being at the grocery store, which Cook owned, around midnight to stand vigil and protect the property. They had guns in their hands. Cook lurked behind an old bus while Polk hid inside a dog pen outside the store. But while Cook said the pair went home before seeing Youmans or his friends, Polk said they witnessed Youmans break the bottles and then heard a gunshot from an unknown weapon. Polk testified that he and Cook then walked to town along the railroad tracks, supposedly leaving the place they had come to protect at the very moment trouble unfolded.

The men's defense counsel, "Rip" Kearse, insisted in his closing argument that his clients were innocent and being made scapegoats to compensate for the failure of law enforcement to find the true killers. Buster countered that this was nonsense. "They talk about sacrificial lambs but it looks like the only one is Wallace Youmans. I didn't see anyone else in the grave," the solicitor said acidly during his own closing argument.

Then, curiously, Buster sabotaged his own case and sent mixed signals to the jury when he told them he did not support the grand jury's indictment and the charges he was now prosecuting. "Frankly, I don't think it's murder," Murdaugh told the jury, urging them instead to strongly consider convicting Cook and Polk instead on the lesser charge of manslaughter. "I don't think there was any conspiracy. I don't think they went down there to kill anybody."

Buster then delivered another variation of his trademark line for closing arguments, telling jurors that their decision would send a loud and clear message to all the would-be killers of the Lowcountry, that the community's fate as a place of order or lawlessness hinged on the jury's verdict. "I know how you can stop this from happening again," Buster told the jury. "If you'll find these two White men guilty of shooting this Black you won't have any more of this kind of shooting in the county."

After this, a jury of seven Blacks and five Whites deliberated for a little more than an hour before returning verdicts—Cook and Polk were not guilty. A gasp rolled across the courtroom when Judge Rhodes announced the men's acquittal. Solicitor Murdaugh soon dismissed the remaining charges against the other three alleged conspirators, citing a lack of evidence. Despite so many people and organizations investigating the killing of Wallace Youmans over the previous four years, no one would be held responsible for shooting him dead with a shotgun. Tyler, the young newspaper editor, remembers the acquittal as a sobering moment that snapped him back to reality. He later thought to himself: "How did I ever manage to imagine justice would come out of this?"

———

Mallory Beach was still missing. Her parents were getting desperate. They knew only one place to go as they prayed for her safe return, the bridge where she was last seen.

Renee Beach was standing vigil there soon after the early morning accident, hoping for a miracle. There was an old road before her that ran down one side of the causeway, to the base of the bridge, beside Archers Creek. She asked if she could proceed down the road, beyond a police cordon, to see the scene of the accident that had caused Mallory's disappearance and injuries to five of her friends. An officer said no, that it was a crime scene as well as an accident scene. He was under strict orders to let no one pass.

No one, that is, except the Murdaugh family. Soon after the police officer denied Beach access to the place where her daughter was possibly last alive, a car approached the police cordon. Driving the vehicle was former solicitor Randolph "Randy" Murdaugh, and in the passenger seat Maggie Murdaugh—Paul Murdaugh's grandfather and mother. To Beach's shock, the Murdaughs were waved through the police checkpoint and allowed to drive to the bottom of the bridge. The heartsick mother was stunned. "That's when I started to realize the Murdaughs, they were more worried about a cover-up than they were trying to find Mallory," said Renee Beach. The special treatment so rankled Beach she called lawyer Mark Tinsley in nearby Allendale, who got involved that very day. Tinsley's hiring would prove consequential. Beach had found the rare lawyer in South Carolina willing to challenge the Murdaugh family and their associated Hampton law firm.

It took eight days, but finally volunteers and rescue crews found Mallory Beach on March 3, 2019. Her body had floated into a section of marsh a few miles from the bridge over Archers Creek. Authorities preliminarily identified the nineteen-year-old from her blond hair and muddy clothing. A coroner confirmed the body was Mallory's and determined she died of blunt force trauma to the head and drowning. At her funeral a few days later Mallory was remembered for her kindness, megawatt smile, and love of animals. "They say the good ones go young, you know?" said her friend Olivia Boyles. "She really was a good one."

Though Mallory was buried, little else associated with the case had been put to rest. Paul and his friend Connor Cook were accusing each other of driving the boat at the time of the crash. There were suspicions regarding a host of relationships that existed between the Murdaugh family and law firm, and some of the law enforcement officers who responded to the scene, especially given possible evidence that Paul was extended favors, such as not being given a field sobriety test and failing to record a statement from passenger Anthony Cook that Paul was driving the boat. A state grand jury would eventually be convened to look into these actions by police—an investigation of an investigation. Yet compared to the fallout ahead, any possible public corruption would only be a mere sideshow.

Much more than a boat hull split apart during the deadly crash that dark winter morning on Archers Creek. The violent collision of boat and bridge broke open an entire Lowcountry Pandora's box, spilling details of long-suppressed wrongdoing by the extended and ancestral Murdaugh family. This was more than a drunken accident, it was the beginning of an overdue reckoning that would be on display to the world.

The early murmurs alone concerning the boat crash quickly "gripped the Lowcountry like little we've ever seen," wrote David Lauderdale, a longtime columnist for Hilton Head's newspaper, *The Island Packet*. The Murdaugh name was a "lightning rod" he wrote, an appellation long intertwined with local law enforcement, not to mention controversy. Given the longtime political influence of the family, Lauderdale suggested perhaps the FBI should investigate in place of local and state authorities. He wondered what consequence might come for those involved in the crash and any attempted coverup. "And so everyone's watching. Can justice be done, under these circumstances?" he wrote. "The question came from many as soon as they heard about the fatal crash and the name attached to the boat. Justice is in the spotlight now, more so than any of the individuals involved . . ."

It was not long before the Murdaugh family was publicly blamed for the boating tragedy. A month after the crash Renee Beach, acting as the personal representative of her daughter's estate, filed a wrongful death lawsuit against a variety of defendants, including the businesses and social hosts that provided alcohol to Paul Murdaugh and his friends, as well as three members of the Murdaugh family—Paul's father Alex, brother Buster, and grandfather Randy. Three weeks later—on what would have been Mallory's twentieth birthday—Paul was indicted on three felony counts of boating under the influence.

The Murdaugh family was in turmoil. Beyond Paul's problems, Buster left law school in the spring of 2019 because of reported low grades and an allegation of plagiarism. This was in addition to him being sued over claims he let his brother use his ID to buy alcohol the night of the boat crash. "It's definitely an uneasy feeling," Buster said later about being sued.

Maggie, meanwhile, felt that the community had turned against her in the wake of the boat crash. "It kinda consumed her," said Buster. "It caused her to distance herself from Hampton." Shunned by her neighbors, Maggie started shopping in Walterboro. She also spent more time at the family's house at Edisto Beach, which was already her favorite spot. Maggie's sister, Marian Proctor, characterized the fallout from the boat crash as a "devastating blow." No matter the extra stress, the family all supported each other, said Buster, especially Paul. Among the family, he said, "none of us thought he was driving the boat."

Two weeks after his indictment, Paul pleaded not guilty to three counts of boating while under the influence. He surrendered his passport and was allowed to walk out of the Beaufort County Courthouse on a $50,000 bond. "He's not leaving the state. He's not leaving the country," said one of Paul's slick, newly hired defense attorneys, State Senator Dick Harpootlian. "So when you waive extradition, it's normal conditions, so we did exactly what's normal. It is being handled in a very normal fashion."

Despite Harpootlian's repetitive claim, Paul was not treated normally. He was not put in handcuffs and brought to jail—in fact, a prosecutor shooed away a guard when he attempted to cuff Paul. Then Paul's mugshot was taken in a courthouse hallway with a cell phone while Paul wore plainclothes. He was not fingerprinted at the jail using modern technology, but instead in the courthouse using an old-fashioned ink wooden fingerprint kit. All of it seemed designed to avoid the spectacle and indignity that typically accompany criminal arrest, as well as the disclosure of more details of his alleged crimes.

Alex's fingers were possibly destined to be pressed in ink, too. His actions at the Beaufort hospital, when he walked the halls with a badge from the solicitor's office hanging out his pocket, telling Paul's injured friends what to say and do, were being investigated as possible obstruction of justice. But criminal charges were a maybe, something he still had hope of evading or minimizing. Much more significant, and already realized, was the financial distress he was facing. Alex had already been deep in debt before he had expensive legal bills to pay for both Paul's criminal defense, as well as the defense of lawsuits against the family.

The possibility of having to fund a large settlement with Renee Beach also loomed, one not completely covered by his insurance policies. After Beach's lawsuit was filed, intermediaries for Alex delivered his insurance information to Tinsley, Beach's lawyer who practiced in Allendale County.

Negotiations between Alex's side and Tinsley began badly. Lawyers affili-
ated with Alex complained to Tinsley's partner and another lawyer who was
a friend, accusing Tinsley of being unreasonable and aggressive, especially
since Tinsley was insistent that any insurance payout must be supplemented
by money from Alex himself. Tinsley said there were complaints he had
crossed a "line in the sand" and "there was a lot of grumbling and sort of
shock that I'm actually going to hold Alex personally responsible."

Tinsley grew up elsewhere in South Carolina and moved to Allendale as
an adult, where he lived on a 1,000-acre property with an old house and a
pecan grove. He did not appreciate the squeeze from the homegrown lawyers in Hampton County. It was insulting that there was no responsibility
taken for the accident, especially given the loss of Mallory. "The Beach
family stood on a causeway for eight days while their daughter's body was
in the water," Tinsley later said of his clients' sorrow. "I don't know that
there's any amount of money that . . . someone would willingly take to go
through what they've gone through."

Alex's side initially offered a $500,000 boat insurance payout that
would be shared among all the boat crash passengers. The potential payout
from Alex's boat insurance policy was minimal because he no longer
had very much insurance coverage, his policies being canceled or down-
graded following one of his insurers' amplified payout of $4.3 million
for wrongful death claims regarding his former housekeeper Gloria
Satterfield. Tinsley and his associates were underwhelmed by the small
offer. Tinsley had thought Alex would settle quickly given the public
sympathy over Mallory's death. He expected much more, and at least
something from Alex personally to recognize the magnitude of the
Beaches' loss. "He was always going to have to pay, and a lot of money,"
said Tinsley. "Alex was going to have to pay out of his own pocket to
settle these cases."

A few months later in August 2019 Tinsley traveled to Hilton Head
Island one weekend to attend the annual trial lawyers' conference at a

seaside resort, where for many the daily mix included continuing legal education classes, rounds of golf, rounds of drinks, time at the pool or beach, and attendance of dinners. One evening he joined a political fundraiser, perhaps for Paul Murdaugh's lawyer State Senator Harpootlian, he recalled. There, in a crowded room, Tinsley was confronted by Alex, who had made a beeline toward him from across the room. "Hey Bo', what's this I'm hearing about what you're saying? I thought we were friends." Tinsley was taken aback but refused to be bullied. "Alex, we are friends," he replied. "(But) if you don't think I can burn your house down, and that . . . I'm not gonna do everything, you're wrong. You need to settle this case."

Alex could not settle the case. He had insufficient insurance coverage. He also had virtually no money himself, though Tinsley believed the opposite, that Alex was flush. He had three homes, after all, and lived large and handled plenty of cases. Of course he had money.

The parties remained at an impasse for months. Then the coronavirus pandemic interrupted life across the world, including the operation of the court system in South Carolina. During this lull Tinsley redoubled his efforts. He arranged for a mock trial of the case to be performed and sent the results to Alex's defense lawyer. Tinsley also shared with Alex's lawyer social media posts that helped bolster his case. Those efforts elicited a half-hearted offer from Alex's side. His lawyers said he was broke but perhaps he could scrape together $1 million. "I didn't believe it," said Tinsley. He asked to see financial statements to ascertain the representations made by Alex's side. He was stonewalled, he said, so he next filed a motion in court to compel this information be provided to him. As he waited for a judge's decision he traveled to Florida at the beginning of 2021. For the next three months he would be receiving cancer treatment, hoping to rid himself of stage IV prostate cancer.

Solicitor Randolph "Buster" Murdaugh stood beside the railroad tracks at the murder scene, close to where Wallace Youmans was shot dead. A news photographer snapped a picture of the prosecutor, who was dressed in a light coat and pants, what onetime *Hampton County Guardian* editor Patrick Tyler characterized as the "classic Southern boss's suit." Buster pointed in the direction of the camera while three other men looked his way, all paying him close attention. This image came to define Buster in Tyler's mind. "He just looked like the boss out there," said Tyler. "That's the way he carried himself."

While Buster's son, Randolph "Randy" Murdaugh III, was engaging and loquacious in a way that reminded Tyler of a stereotypical fraternity brother, Tyler found his father, the solicitor, gruff and circumspect. In conversation Buster seemed interested only in gathering intelligence and not willing to give much of anything in return. He struck Tyler as transactional, "moving like a great white shark through the town." When Tyler moved to Varnville for the newspaper job he soon heard stories about Buster and his reputation for using the solicitor's post for the benefit of his own law firm. "People believed it was kind of a racket," said Tyler, adding that half the county seemed to fear Buster and the other half groveled for his favor. Or, as a Lowcountry lawyer who handled cases frequently with Buster said, "He was in business to make money. He happened to be solicitor, too."

In 1976, South Carolina lawmakers sought to curb the power of the state's sixteen solicitors and prevent this kind of improper influence, which was not exclusive to Buster's Lowcountry fiefdom. They passed a new law to make the solicitor's post a full-time job and forbid any moonlighting in private practice. The Charleston *News and Courier* supported the restrictions wholeheartedly, writing in an editorial:

> *It would be incongruous, to say the least, if the corps of prosecutors continued to function as in the past, when private interest has often taken precedence over public. No doubt some incumbent circuit*

solicitors may opt out, rather than give up their lucrative private practices. That would be their privilege and they won't be missed. The needs of the public and the judicial system outweigh those of individuals.

The change in law meant Buster had to make a decision. He could leave the prosecutor's post and make a small fortune as a partner at the law firm opened by his father sixty-five years ago, or he could remain solicitor and make a much smaller salary disposing of criminal charges across five counties. Buster hemmed and hawed for a bit before deciding to remain solicitor and leave the family law firm where he had worked for forty years and once practiced alongside his father. The decision was more palatable because although Buster was complying with the new law, not much was actually changing.

As always, Buster masterfully blurred the lines, even after a change in the rules. While he officially disassociated himself from the old family law practice, he was keeping his office within the law firm's building, running the solicitor's office from familiar surroundings among old colleagues. He was keeping his legal secretary, too, though now the state would pay her salary, and he was also getting the solicitor's office its own phone line. Though Buster's last name was technically dropped from the firm, it was replaced by his son's, who now was a partner at the law firm while also a part-time prosecutor, an arrangement that was still permitted by state law. Buster eventually hired another lawyer, Paul Detrick, who similarly split duties between a part-time assistant solicitor's position and a job at the Hampton law firm. No matter that the new law intended to curb solicitor's power and separate the criminal and civil dockets, the crossover between the law firm and the solicitor's office remained constant, which was exactly how Buster Murdaugh intended it to be.

These were not the only ways Buster knew how to continue to cast influence. He also supported the election of friends and associates as judges who would then preside regularly over the cases brought before them by the solicitor, his son, and other members of the law firm. In December 1974 Buster attended the swearing-in of Judge Rodney Peeples, who he had watched grow up in Hampton and who had been a law school classmate and friend to his son, Randy. Peeples credited Buster for inspiring him to study the law when he was a mere thirteen years old. "I always thought a great deal of Buster. I'd go over and watch him in court," said the freshly minted judge, who noted he would show the Murdaughs no favor, "deciding each case on the circumstances."

Buster's wife Gladys was in attendance at the South Carolina Supreme Court to celebrate Peeples' ascent to the bench, as was son Randy, and his wife, Libby. Attending, too, was the rest of the Murdaugh family firm, including Buster's longtime partners Clyde Eltzroth and Bob Peters as well as two recent hires, John E. Parker and Jack Eltzroth, Clyde's son.

Nine months later this same crowd attended another swearing-in ceremony, this time for one of their own, Clyde Eltzroth, Buster's longtime friend and law partner who came to Varnville as an infant with his widowed mother, grandmother, and two uncles, who all left jobs in the bayous of Louisiana to cut cypress for the Big Salkehatchie Cypress Company. Eltzroth, who skipped law school in favor of gaining a legal education by reading the books in Buster's law office, inspired some controversy when he became a judge. While some were impressed by the self-taught lawyer, others were dubious of his competency, wondering how a judge could do their job without a law degree. At the ceremony Buster lauded the new judge's impressive worth ethic and determination, noting, "He didn't come up easy." The new judge returned the praise, calling Buster "the brother that I didn't have." Eltzroth previously said he saw no conflict of interest in handling cases involving the solicitor. "It wouldn't bother me a bit, and it wouldn't bother him a bit," he stated. "I have no friends to reward and no enemies to punish."

Eltzroth was a large man with a booming voice said to reverberate like a foghorn. His temper was fierce and easy to trigger, quickly making him one of the most feared judges in the state. In his courtroom he demanded order and got upset and cranky when it wasn't upheld. Oddly enough, the humorless stickler and courtroom autocrat often brought his two black Labrador Retrievers, Smoke and Spook, into courtrooms around the state, letting them rest at his feet behind the bench.

When Eltzroth wasn't wearing a robe he was a more likable fellow. Eltzroth made plenty of friends at the State House in Columbia when he served as a state representative for four years in the 1960s. These friends proved crucial during his bruising battle to join the South Carolina judiciary, as state lawmakers, not the people, elect judges in the Palmetto State. It also helped that Buster Murdaugh was one of Eltzroth's best buddies and law partner, but that only went so far, especially outside the five counties of the 14th Judicial Circuit.

The main obstacle to Eltzroth's judgeship was his conduct during a six-year tenure as chairman of the state's wildlife commission, from which he resigned in 1973 after years of controversy. According to Eltzroth's critics, he fired wildlife department staff for political reasons and initiated cost-cutting while also building a multimillion marine research facility bearing his name. He took his family on vacation to Europe using taxpayer money and claimed it as a work trip. He permitted policies that allowed state legislators to use the wildlife department's airplanes as personal taxis and to buy boats through the department at deep discounts.

In Hampton County the wildlife department operated the historic Belmont Plantation, a natural preserve owned by the state since 1941. During Eltzroth's tenure it became more or less a private hunting club for the legislature, with little public access. Eltzroth explained that legislators visited Belmont to learn about the wildlife department and that the hunting was desperately needed because the grounds of the former 6,000-acre plantation were overstocked with wild game. This claim was hard to defend against the disclosure that the wildlife department purchased 5,000 quail for hunts at Belmont. Nonetheless, Eltzroth said the purchase of the quail was an experiment: "We are seeing how many we can put out and harvest with a gun."

On and on the assorted scandals went, making constant headlines in the state's newspapers. The governor suggested to Eltzroth that he should resign but Eltzroth refused to go unless he was fired. Finally, he left the wildlife commission after it was revealed that he sought to be reimbursed for automobile mileage for travel he had made via state airplane, discrepancies that Eltzroth described as accounting errors and "mistakes of the head, not the heart." Eltzroth reimbursed the state for $169.10 but refused to apologize as he left the commission. "Whether I did things right or wrong with the wildlife commission, everything I did I thought was for the benefit of South Carolina," said an indignant Eltzroth.

With Eltzroth beginning his judgeship and Buster exclusively serving as solicitor, big changes were afoot in the mid-1970s at the law firm of Murdaugh, Eltzroth & Peters. Yet the more things changed the more they remained the same in Hampton County. Buster's shoes were filled by his son, Randy. Judge Eltzroth was replaced by his son, Jack. The law firm didn't need to change their name except for the addition of one more new partner—John E. "Johnny" Parker—a thirty-year-old former teacher who would come to be regarded as the one of the finest plaintiff's attorneys in the state.

Parker was raised in a modest but sophisticated household in Hampton. His mother, Frances, taught piano, and his father, Horace, was an Army-officer-turned-small-businessman with a literary bent, known to quote verse from memory. Horace opened a department store with his brother after returning home from World War II, and later operated The Jabberwock Inn. Parker served up sandwiches, suds, and servings of frozen custard at The Jabberwock, which he advertised as the TEEN-AGE HEADQUARTERS FOR CHOICE CHOW. The eatery's name was a reference to an imaginary creature immortalized by English writer Lewis Carroll in his nonsense poem "Jabberwocky," which he included in his 1871 novel

Through the Looking-Glass, a sequel to *Alice's Adventures in Wonderland*. As one stanza reads:

> *And, as in uffish thought he stood,*
> *The Jabberwock, with eyes of flame,*
> *Came whiffling through the tulgey wood,*
> *And burbled as it came!*

Like the poem "Jabberwocky," Horace Parker was recognized as brilliant but also hard to understand. Many people in Hampton knew Horace as a plucky town drunk. While Johnny Glenn Murdaugh drove around town intoxicated atop a tractor, Horace is vividly remembered by townspeople for riding atop a donkey during his boozy benders.

Lieutenant Colonel James Walker DeLoach was a fellow army officer and lover of literature who befriended Horace C. Parker as a boy. They saw each other occasionally as adults when DeLoach returned to their hometown. The colonel knew Horace as a "captivating but highly volatile person" who "could have made an enviable mark for himself in the military, as a teacher or in any profession he chose." DeLoach was so taken by Horace's intellect and passion that he always wondered what could have been if Horace had broken free of his hometown. In a eulogy published after Horace Parker's death in 1966, DeLoach pondered his friend's decisions:

> *Why then did he choose the seamier side of the motel and restaurant*
> *business? Because he liked people. Why did he repeatedly follow*
> *habits deleterious to his health? (Horace) was bored; yet he had and*
> *was devoted to a lovely wife and family; their musical ability would*
> *have given the ordinary man the emotional outlet needed.*

In DeLoach's telling, Horace made himself a caged bird in Hampton to satisfy family obligation:

*He loved his family and was a good provider. But the provincial
life of a small Carolina coastal town just didn't provide the outlets
needed to calm this exceptional, almost fictional character. (Here
I'm trying to be factual, I love Hampton as did Horace.) And when
boredom reached a given point he'd tear loose because Horace Parker
was a romanticist, and as such he eschewed the ordinary and commonplace Neo-classic approach to life.*

Such was the unfulfilled romantic who raised one of South Carolina's
most respected litigators. Johnny Parker, slight in frame, did not bully
people like his mentor Buster Murdaugh, but rather relied on his shrewd-
ness to succeed. No matter his unassuming manner, people in Hampton
learned not to underestimate the modest country boy. As one woman said,
Parker wasn't "oozing" intelligence, but "you just knew he had it, and he
knew he had it."

Lawyer Travis Medlock recalled once being blindsided by Parker in a
trial in federal court involving the alleged wrongful firing of the principal
of Wade Hampton High School. During cross-examination of Medlock's
client, Parker elicited a surprise confession from the former principal,
prodding him to reveal that he had once defrauded an elderly invalid
woman. Medlock was shocked by the revelation, as was everyone else in
the courtroom, including the jury. Medlock moved almost immediately
to dismiss his client's lawsuit. The episode humbled Medlock, exposing
his preparation for the case as inadequate, at least in comparison to the
work done by Parker. "Johnny taught me a lesson," recalled Medlock, who
became South Carolina's attorney general. "Johnny had a big smile on his
face. He enjoyed it."

Not only was Parker generally regarded as the smartest man in the room,
he was also usually the wealthiest. According to family lore, money was
always important to Johnny, who was said to have once come home from

church as a child with coins from the collection plate jingling in his tiny pants pocket. As an adult he took money—lots of it—through lawsuits against corporations, to the point that lawyers in South Carolina avoided Hampton County like the plague. Parker was said to love to do legal work and not much else, save family and some fishing. He also cared about his surroundings, as evidenced by his old downtown home, which he kept in pristine shape, as well as the law firm, which moved from a cinder block building to a stately new brick headquarters.

Though he enjoyed a few fine things, Parker was otherwise described as miserly. He would loan money to friends, but at rates higher than the bank rate. One of his colleagues once gently warned an attorney from another county about messing with Johnny's cases, explaining "Johnny's a nice guy but he's not that way about money."

Much less interested in money, and much more interested in a good time and catching up with friends, was Parker's gregarious law partner, Randy Murdaugh. Randy made time to fish and hunt and host cooks and play softball and keep up public appearances and fulfill the many civic responsibilities he undertook, such as running the watermelon festival, leading the election commission, and serving as president of the local chamber of commerce. He projected an earnest and wholesome persona, preaching to high schoolers at a sports banquet in 1976, that "No matter what you do, now or in the future, it will take hard work and dedication."

But when Randy loosened his tie and cut loose outside the courthouse, he revealed a less respectable and more fun-loving side. He was fond of telling lewd and racist jokes at social gatherings. Among his favorites was "How can you tell a (Black man) is well hung? When you can't get a finger between the neck and the rope." Another frequent jest was uttered when someone mentioned his wife. "Oh, you know Libby, huh?" Randy would say. "Do you know what Libby and I have in common? Ain't either one of us have ever sucked a dick."

Libby, predictably, did not always find the father of her four children—Lynn, Randy IV, Alex, and John Marvin—very funny. Libby would yell at Randy when he crossed a line, his sense of humor hardly consistent with her churchgoing reputation. As a longtime schoolteacher she was much more prim and proper. She had a reputation for being friendly and earnest, and, unlike others in her extended family, cared about someone's answer when she asked how they were doing. Also unlike others in her family, she did not so flagrantly press the advantage of her last name, yet wasn't one to forfeit privilege entirely. "She used the power of the Murdaugh name, but she didn't abuse it," said one acquaintance.

Some other Hampton and Varnville residents felt differently, claiming Libby could be heavy-handed and even vindictive, frequently meddling in the school system and demanding her way. She could be manic, fast-talking, and tough to please. She was said to act the schoolmarm, even when she was off campus. Other days she was more pleasant, and then sometimes completely aloof, baffling people who greeted her and hardly received a response. Some Lowcountry acquaintances unapologetically described her not just as crazy, but "batshit crazy" and "crazy as a shithouse rat."

In 1977, Libby was one of a number of residents in Varnville urging the demolition of Varnville's original brick schoolhouse, which was deemed unsafe and impractical to repair. Though the historic preservation movement was in vogue at that time, with the nation's bicentennial celebrations drawing attention to the value of old buildings, Libby and other like-minded residents were determined to modernize school facilities and remove an old structure deemed a firetrap. No one raised a fuss about these plans until the demolition began, when native son and retired colonel DeLoach, who eulogized Horace Parker, wrote another guest newspaper column titled "The Requiem" that lamented the loss of the "only public building with character in the countryside." DeLoach recalled his school days when boys got in fistfights, the heating system sometimes failed, and Clyde Eltzroth "couldn't sit still and got in trouble." He wondered why the old schoolhouse couldn't have been converted into a library and wished he had been more vigilant, writing:

> *I felt a twinge of guilt when I viewed the ripping apart of old Var-nville School; surveyed her, stark and naked, divested of her majestic facade; torn brick by brick and timber by timber as if to insult and wreak vengeance upon her. . . . Old School didn't turn out presidents or men of state, just solid citizens who fought our wars, withstood the trials of a major depression, and attended to community affairs.*

DeLoach's words spurred a last-minute effort by a few residents to salvage what remained of the building. This desperate effort to save Old School infuriated Libby Murdaugh, a member of the local Parent-Teacher Organization, who felt the protests came too late and prioritized sentimentality over school safety. Displaying a bit of eccentricity, bitterness, and a flair for the dramatic, the teacher penned a long and fierce response to DeLoach's column about his boyhood school. The essay was titled "Let Her Die!"

In an extended metaphor, Libby compared Old School to an elderly woman on her deathbed forced to suffer an unwanted life-prolonging intervention. Libby complained of the interference, of how the "machines were hooked up to Old Varnville School" by people who had previously ignored the old building's disrepair. "As she was taking her last breaths, some few decided they wanted her to live so they could continue to look at her and live in a state of fond remembrances," wrote Libby. Speaking on behalf of the building's "school family" Libby shooed away the would-be preservationists:

> *We beg you, those who want to build her back, please let her die at the hands of skilled people. People who know what they're doing and can make it easier for her. Don't let her die by giving her false hopes of an eternal physical life. Don't let her deteriorate and rot away.*

Don't let her dying be saddened by the tragic death of a child who wanders too near her. Accept the fact that you stood back too long, busy with other things, and now, at the last minute, want to put her back. It can't be done and shouldn't be done. She wouldn't want it and her family doesn't want it . . .

Libby then struck a positive note, suggesting the whole community rally behind the New School and support its teachers and staff. But by no means, she insisted, should Old School be resuscitated. As Libby wrote, "I think if Old School could speak she might say, 'Thank you for your care, your concern, your money and your time. But most of all I thank you for your children. Grant me one last wish—allow me to be torn down but keep me alive in your memories.'"

Two weeks later, Libby's plea for Old School's peaceful death was answered. Linda Gallagher, a writer for the *Hampton County Guardian*, wrote a column titled "Don't Give Up The Ship! Let Her Live!" that claimed the demolition had become an obsession for a "small but powerful group of zealous parents and school people." She accused the zealots of cowing the opposition and asked why Old School could not simply stand empty alongside the new school until it receives new purpose. "All of a sudden old is useless and new is terrific," said Gallagher, who proceeded to mock Libby's metaphor. "I keep hearing Old School called 'her.' 'Let her Die,'—As if the building were made of flesh and blood like fragile people. Not so. Old School is made of good brick and plenty of heart pine."

Gallagher and DeLoach put up a good fight, but Old School soon came down. Libby had prevailed.

This was not the first time Libby made headlines. A year earlier, readers of *The State*, the largest newspaper in South Carolina, were surprised to read Libby's obituary on November 18, 1976, which disclosed the thirty-seven-year-old teacher and church leader died in her home. Upon seeing this unexpected news, one of Libby's neighbors in Varnville was said to have hurried over to the Murdaugh house so he could offer his condolences to Randy. The neighbor rang the doorbell and received a shock when Libby opened the door.

Libby was alive, but maybe not well. Employees of the telephone company and state police were investigating who might have called in the hoax to the newspaper. Some people wondered if it was Libby herself. The obituary was very detailed, listing her scholastic and professional accomplishments, a multitude of civic contributions, and a long list of survivors and their places of residence. Those who suspected Libby of planting her own fake obituary believed the stunt to be a cry for help, or at least a plea for attention.

Some people thought Libby agonizingly alone, destined to play a supporting role in a loveless marriage. For whatever their initial attraction in high school, Randy and Libby did not seem the perfect match. She aspired to be refined and proper. He liked being raw and rough around the edges. She was reserved and liked to play by the rules. He sometimes flaunted the rules and also selectively enforced them.

People observed that the couple did not appear together often in public, though that could have simply been the result of Libby and Randy each working full-time jobs and raising four children, beyond attending to their other responsibilities and commitments, many of which were listed in the sham obituary. Libby was said to be overwhelmed and to have suffered nervous breakdowns. Part of her stress was attributed to her sometimes failing marriage to Randy, who by many accounts was an unabashed philanderer. One woman remembers attending a legal conference at a hotel in Myrtle Beach and entering one of the rooms rented for attendees from the 14th Judicial Circuit. A number of people were milling about in the corridor, she said, and when she approached she spied Randy inside the room, lying under bed sheets with two women, neither of them his wife. "You ain't seen nothing, get out of here," said Randy upon being spotted.

About the time of the hoax obituary, Randy moved out of the family home in Varnville to live in a condo on Hilton Head Island. The difference between Hilton Head and Hampton County was vast. Hilton Head had become a resort island crammed full of new homes, golf courses, and swimming pools. In the air was a vibe of permanent vacation; life just felt lighter when floating on a sea breeze. On Hilton Head Randy could wade in the ocean and rinse his problems away. On the island he was free from the demands of young children and a nagging wife.

Randy took full advantage of his furlough, "having the time of his life in Hilton Head," said Dayle Blackmon, the Murdaughs' longtime family friend from Jasper County. A lawyer who knew the family well said that Randy embarked on a sex spree, enjoying the company of larger women in particular, while on indefinite leave from his family. "He had a grand time screwing fat girls," said the lawyer. "Fat girls fuck."

Since Randy would not come back to his family, his family came to him. After weeks of separation, Randy's holiday came to a sudden end when Libby showed up on Easter to drop the children off all dressed in their Sunday best, said the lawyer. Blackmon heard the story slightly differently, being told that Libby dropped the kids off on the doorstep along with a suitcase full of their clothing. In any case, the special delivery prompted Randy to come home. After this interlude, Randy told Blackmon, "I became happily married again."

But the lawyer also heard that Randy returned home after Buster came by the condo to lambast his son and order him back to Varnville. Similarly, Dayle was told by Buster's longtime secretary, Janie Murdaugh, that the solicitor called Randy and Libby into his office after the publication of the hoax obituary, in which no official suspect was ever named. Janie Murdaugh, who was of no immediate relation to her boss despite their shared last names, told Blackmon that Buster was livid, and that "he put the fear of God in both of them. He said they needed to get their shit together and this will never happen to them again."

———

One of South Carolina's most prolific criminals, Alex Murdaugh was accused of more than 100 crimes, including the theft of millions from legal clients and the murder of his wife and son. The disgraced former lawyer testified in his own defense at his murder trial in February 2023. *Grace Boehm Alford, Charleston* Post And Courier, *pool photo.*

Alex Murdaugh's mug shot.

The legendary Randolph "Buster" Murdaugh Jr. served as the elected prosecutor of a five-county section of South Carolina for forty-six years. "If Buster wanted you to burn, you got burnt," said one former Lowcountry police chief. "If he wanted you to walk, you walked."

Alex, right, and a Kappa Alpha Order fraternity brother wearing Confederate uniforms at an Old South party held in Savannah, Ga., in 1989.

Paul Murdaugh's mug shot, taken May 6, 2019, in the Beaufort County Courthouse, after Paul was charged with three counts of boating under the influence for his role in a 2019 boat crash that claimed the life of Mallory Beach. Paul is notably wearing civilian clothes for his mug shot, having been spared arrest and normal processing through the county jail.

The first Randolph Murdaugh opened his own law office in Hampton in 1910 and became an elected prosecutor ten years later, serving until his unexpected death on July 19, 1940 when his car collided with a train. *Photo by author.*

CAROLINA·LAWYER

THE UNIVERSITY OF SOUTH CAROLINA SCHOOL OF LAW·VOLUME IX, 1989

"The Murdaughs of Hampton"

Three generations of Murdaugh men graced the cover of the alumni magazine of the University of South Carolina School of Law in 1989. *Courtesy of University of South Carolina School of Law.*

Randolph "Buster" Murdaugh Jr.

Randolph "Randy" Murdaugh III.

Randolph "Randy" Murdaugh IV.

Four generations of Murdaugh lawyers have been minted at the University of South Carolina School of Law. Young Randy IV is pictured here as a law student. *Courtesy of University of South Carolina School of Law.*

Based on a field sketch, "Weaver's Brigade Charging Across the Little Salkahatchie [sic]" (or "At the Salkehatchie") depicts Union troops trudging through Lowcountry swamps in early 1865, three months or so before the surrender of the Confederacy. *The Miriam and Ira D. Wallach Division of Art, Prints and Photographs: Picture Collection, The New York Public Library.*

An undated view of Hampton's main street, Lee Avenue, looking away from the courthouse, toward the railroad tracks. *University of South Carolina Libraries, Digital Collections.*

The Hampton County Courthouse as seen on a vintage postcard. Built in 1878, the courthouse originally featured a portico and pair of exterior curving staircases which delivered visitors directly to the upstairs courtroom, where members of the Murdaugh family have tried cases for more than a century. *University of South Carolina Libraries, Digital Collections.*

Hampton's Loan And Exchange Bank on Lee Avenue in 1914, decades before becoming part of Palmetto State Bank, owned and operated by the Laffitte family. *University of South Carolina Libraries, Digital Collections.*

Hampton's town clock in 2023, seventy-five years after its installation in the middle of Lee Avenue.

Rigdon's Fried Chicken has been a Hampton favorite for decades. A lunchtime line forms outside the window even on the hottest days.

The former Westinghouse factory that once produced the bestselling Micarta laminate sits abandoned behind a chain link fence on the outskirts of Hampton in late 2023. *Photos by the author.*

ABOVE LEFT: Randolph Murdaugh III during his senior year. ABOVE RIGHT: Elizabeth Jones Alexander, the future Libby Murdaugh. during her senior year at Wade Hampton High School, about 1956. BELOW: Seniors Libby Alexander and Randolph "Randy" Murdaugh III were named "Most Athletic" among Wade Hampton High School's Class of 1957. The sweethearts would marry four years later, the start of a 60-year union that produced four children, including third-born Alex Murdaugh. *Wade Hampton High School yearbook, 1957.*

Cheerleaders at Wade Hampton High School in Varnville decorate the goalposts before a football game in 1955. Libby Alexander sits in the grass, second from right. *Wade Hampton High School yearbook, 1956.*

Railroad in Hampton, 1973. *University of South Carolina Libraries, Digital Collections.*

The Murdaugh family, shortly before the murders of Maggie and Paul. From left, Buster, Paul, Maggie, and Alex. *Introduced at* State v. Murdaugh, *Andrew J. Whitaker, Charleston* Post And Courier, *pool photo.*

An entrance to Alex Murdaugh's home, Moselle, where his wife and son were shot to death the night of June 7, 2021. The 1,700-acre property in Colleton County, South Carolina, abuts the Salkehatchie River and features sections of swampland, forest, and fields. *Photo by author.*

At left stands Moselle's large shed (red roof) and, just above it, the dog kennels (silver roof). In the top right corner is the house at Moselle, where Alex initially claimed he was sleeping at the time his wife and son were slain between the shed and dog kennels. *Introduced at* State v. Murdaugh, *Andrew J. Whitaker, Charleston* Post And Courier, *pool photo*.

Moselle's dog kennels, where Paul was killed. Police believe Paul was standing in the feed room when he was shot twice with a shotgun, with fatal injuries to his chest, neck, and head. *Introduced at* State v. Murdaugh, *Joshua Boucher,* The State, *pool photo.*

Maggie Murdaugh was shot dead with an automatic rifle, falling dead under the shed roof at left. Her son, Paul, was killed a moment before, just steps away, within the feed room of the kennels to the right. *Introduced at* State v. Murdaugh, *Joshua Boucher,* The State, *pool photo.*

Calm and dignified, veteran South Carolina judge Clifton Newman oversaw Alex Murdaugh's murder trial and other legal proceedings concerning Murdaugh's many crimes. *Grace Boehm Alford, Charleston* Post And Courier, *pool photo.*

Defense attorney Richard A. "Dick" Harpootlian, standing to the left of an expert witness he was questioning, leveled a Murdaugh family semi-automatic rifle at prosecutors and said, "Tempting, but . . ." on February 21, 2023. *Jeff Blake,* The State, *pool photo.*

South Carolina lead prosecutor Creighton Waters cross-examined Alex Murdaugh on February 23, 2023. *Grace Boehm Alford, Charleston* Post And Courier, *pool photo.*

Prosecutor Creighton Waters continued his lengthy cross-examination of Alex Murdaugh for a second day on February 24, 2023. *Grace Boehm Alford, Charleston* Post And Courier, *pool photo.*

Alex Murdaugh's brother, John Marvin (left), and surviving son, Buster, attended every day of Alex's murder trial and testified when called as witnesses during Alex's defense. Alex's brother and son both said they believe Alex to be innocent of the murders of Maggie and Paul. *Andrew J. Whitaker, Charleston* Post And Courier, *pool photo.*

Alex Murdaugh is taken from the courtroom at the Colleton County Courthouse at the end of his sentencing hearing on March 3, 2021. Judge Clifton Newman sentenced the former lawyer to two life terms for the murder of his wife and son. Alex insisted to Judge Newman that he did not kill his family members. *Andrew J. Whitaker, Charleston* Post And Courier, *pool photo.*

Three years had passed since Tony Satterfield's mother, Gloria, died in 2018 from injuries sustained at Moselle, the Murdaugh family hunting compound. He had not heard much in the way of the legal claims he and his brother were pursuing through their lawyer Cory Fleming, who Alex Murdaugh had recommended to them, and he only spoke to Alex every three months or so. A few times, Tony sent Alex medical and housing bills for his mother, per Alex's instructions.

In April of 2021 he received an update, sort of, via text message from Alex. "Hey man—just checking in, been working on case and made me think about you. Hope all is good. Call me anytime I can help."

Tony was curious for more details. He replied, cheerfully, "Hey man. I'm doing good. BTW how is the case going. just curious. But how are you"

Alex was just as vague in his reply, writing, "Finally getting some movement. Still a ways to go. Doing good. Was just thinking about you and thought I'd check in. Hope to see u soon."

Alex was telling Tony lies. The settlement had already been paid, with Alex steering the bulk of it into his own fake Forge bank account and leaving a portion for Cory Fleming, his buddy and the Satterfield men's attorney. The stolen millions didn't last for long, per usual with Alex. He was still burning through money, a healthy chunk paid to his former client Eddie Smith, allegedly for pain pills. But whatever cash Alex did have stored away he wanted to keep secret for fear Mark Tinsley might try to take it. After successful treatment of his cancer in Florida, lawyer Tinsley returned to South Carolina and went back on the prowl.

Tinsley sensed Alex was guarding something he didn't want revealed. The scent of fear invigorated Tinsley, a sportsman, to pick up the trail even more. Maybe the money was hidden, guessed Tinsley. Whatever the case, his clients certainly didn't believe big shot Alex Murdaugh was hurting for money. Tinsley said he made this basic argument to the judge overseeing the boat crash lawsuit, saying essentially, "(His lawyers) say he's broke, my people have lived in Hampton their entire lives, they do not believe he's broke. If he's broke we need to open the books and let (my clients) see it."

He could not understand Alex's claims of being unable to pay. Tinsley had offered the chance for Alex to enroll in a payment plan or sign over his beach house or Moselle. These offers were declined. As the weeks ticked by Tinsley turned it over in his mind, still puzzled at the lack of interest in striking a deal, especially since the injury to the Beach family was obvious. "There's just no possibility that he could be broke . . ." Tinsley recalled thinking. "I know he's actively settling cases."

Indeed, professionally Alex had a strong start in 2021 when he delivered the closing argument in a trucking accident case that compelled the defendants to settle for $5.5 million. He and his fellow lawyer and close friend Chris Wilson each earned more than $790,000 in fees from the case, with that money initially deposited in an account belonging to Wilson's law firm. Before Wilson wrote a check to Alex's law firm and transferred Alex's share, Alex asked him to do something unusual—write the check from his trust account directly to Alex, personally. He had cleared this arrangement with the law firm's leadership, Alex said, and he wanted to put the money into a structured settlement and keep it out of sight because of the boat crash lawsuit.

These were more lies. Alex asked no one's permission to be paid this way, which was a violation of law firm policy. And he did not put the money into a structured settlement but used it to pay expenses and debts, using all the money within two months. He knew he'd have to pay the cash back eventually, when enough time passed for the law firm to notice the payment was outstanding, but Alex operated day-to-day financially, always underwater but just trying to stay off rock bottom. Certainly he was in over his head. In June 2021 he owed Palmetto State Bank $4.2 million through various loans and negative balances. And this was even after Alex and Maggie sold off their home in Hampton and moved to Moselle full-time.

Maggie was seemingly unaware of these larger financial problems. She was remodeling and making repairs to their beach house, an activity that recently introduced a rare bit of friction between the otherwise seemingly content and compatible couple. While Maggie was agonizing over choosing the perfect shade of white paint, Alex just urged her to pick any of them and move on. He was uninterested, which irritated Maggie. "She just wanted him to sit still and listen to her for ten minutes at a time," said Blanca Turrubiate-Simpson, Maggie's friend and housekeeper.

But Maggie did worry about a worst-case scenario with the lawsuit, that the family could owe up to $30 million, she confessed to Blanca. One day when Blanca was over at Moselle she was pulled aside by Maggie while Alex was sleeping. Maggie had made two cups of coffee and said she needed to talk. They went into the gun room and Maggie pulled the door behind her. Maggie confided in Blanca her fears about the family's financial situation. She said she felt like Alex was not being truthful about the lawsuit. "He doesn't tell me everything," said Maggie.

The aftermath of the boat crash, including the lawsuit, media attention, and lost friendships, were taking their toll on Maggie, provoking a lot of stress. She told Blanca she wanted the lawsuit resolved and that if she could give the Beach family everything, she would. "I'll start over. We'll start over," said Maggie. "I want it gone."

To this end, she started shopping for a new home near Hilton Head Island, where she was hoping to move and escape the hatred she felt in Hampton. "She found one house that she just loved . . . She called me and my parents to come down and take a look at it," said her sister Marian Proctor. "She really thought that they might make an offer on that house but in the end they did not. I think Alex advised her that the timing was just not right with the boat case going on."

The boat case was just one of many things on Alex's long list of problems, none of which could be easily or painlessly resolved. The list included his dependence on opioids; his potential criminal liability for his actions at the Beaufort hospital; the accumulated theft of about $9 million from his clients and law firm; his massive debt with Palmetto State Bank; and the risk of having much of this exposed should a judge rule that he must share his financial information. He also worried about Paul, who would soon face a criminal trial.

Already Paul had been somewhat ostracized for his believed role in the boat crash, allegedly harassed and subject to taunting. Some of his friendships soured. Paul and his girlfriend broke up, and he stopped socializing with the other surviving passengers. Connor Cook came to believe the Murdaughs were "trying to pin it on him." He recanted some of his previous statements to police about the accident, blaming Alex Murdaugh for persuading him not to be truthful. "I was doing what I was told," he said. The Murdaugh family's powerful reputation prevented him from telling the truth earlier, said Connor. He remained concerned about the family, he said, because of rumors of other violent behavior:

> *There's a couple of things that had happened in Hampton that I heard about . . . One was . . . that Paul had pushed his housemate down the stairs and she died and nothing ever happened. And another one, there was something that Paul was supposedly involved with a guy, got found beat up in the middle of the road that they got out of . . . I mean, just anything they get in they get out of. I've always been told that.*

Besides Paul's legal exposure, Alex was slowly saying goodbye to his parents, who were both in failing health and at the end of their lives. His mother, Libby Murdaugh, was bedridden and suffering from severe dementia. His father, Randy, was dying from a protracted battle with lung cancer. Alex was dutiful and visited often, usually during lunchtime, but it could be saddening for him to witness his parents' physical decline and watch his mother grow increasingly vacant, describing her, with love, as "a shell of her old self."

Because of their medical needs, the family employed full-time caretakers for Em and Handsome, who wanted to keep growing old within the

Murdaugh family house set atop the farmland at Almeda. This included Belinda Rast, who usually worked the night shift, from 8:00 P.M. to 8:00 A.M. and some weekends. She came to regard Miss Libby as family, she said, and observed her interact with her loved ones for years. Rast saw a different side of Paul Murdaugh, whom she credited for visiting his ailing grandparents frequently and always offering to help them. He brought ice cream to his grandmother, she said, and tried to jog her memory. "Paul had a way of having a calming effect on her." He would always remind her of the past, said Rast, before mimicking Paul: "'Grandma, you remember that whipping you give me with that fly swat?'"

But if Alex was anxious about any of this, no one could tell. Perhaps it was his alleged, gargantuan intake of opioids and other pills that balanced him in the face of so many incoming storms. As the pressure increased on a variety of fronts, Alex gathered with Maggie, Buster, Paul, and a variety of friends at the Murdaugh beach house on Edisto over Memorial Day weekend in late May 2021. He was turning fifty-three years old. At one point the crowd gathered outside around a picnic table and began singing "Happy Birthday" to Alex, while someone recorded a video. Paul, wearing a visor and white T-shirt and khaki shorts, walked out of the house with a cake topped with flaming candles in his hand. Maggie stood behind him and watched as he brought the cake to his dad, also dressed in a white T-shirt and khaki shorts. Many of Paul's friends were there, singing in the background, young men who had paid many visits to the beach house, to Moselle, or to Chechessee. Here they watched Alex and Paul interact constantly, whether working the land, shooting hogs, boating up rivers, or relaxing at the beach. Always, they said, Alex and Paul acted like the closest of friends.

Alex blew twice and extinguished the candles. He raised his arms in victory and projected an image of harmony and joy, no matter the specter of imminent financial ruin and imprisonment. "Thank you all so much," said Alex, smiling. He turned to Maggie and added, "Thank you, baby."

It was a banner day for the Murdaugh law firm, though no one finalized a settlement, won a trial, or was elected to a judgeship. Instead, on this day in June 1983, during the 41st annual Hampton County Watermelon Festival, glory was earned outside the courtroom, on a field of competition, when the children of some of the Lowcountry's top lawyers spat slimy watermelon seeds out their mouths as far as they could.

There were rules for such a contest. Seed spitters could not bring their own seeds, and could not spit with a straw, pipe, or tube. Spitters must stand in place when ejecting a seed, and any method of spitting was possible, whether flung from the tongue or puffed out between puckered lips, etc. Anyone who swallowed a seed while preparing to spit would be given one additional seed. Lastly, anyone could enter the contest, so long as they were American.

While the lawyers at Murdaugh, Peters, Parker & Eltzroth dominated the local legal scene, their progeny gathered up the ribbons at Hampton County's big shindig. Among the winners in the youth divisions of seed spitting was fifteen-year-old Alex Murdaugh and twelve-year-old John Marvin Murdaugh, both sons of lawyer and assistant solicitor Randolph "Randy" Murdaugh III. In the kid's division, the five-year-old twins of Johnny Parker and his wife spat their way to victory. None of the minors, however, slung a seed farther than forty-two-year-old John Wesley Alls, the grand champion who spat a watermelon seed twenty-two feet and four inches—the length of four men.

The Murdaugh boys had a good showing in 1983, but two years earlier it was their older sister Lynn who shined at the Watermelon Festival when she competed in the Miss Coastal Empire pageant. Lynn followed in the footsteps of her mother, Libby, who herself tried for the crown at the 1955 festival, when the runway for beauty queens was an aisle in the auditorium of Hampton Elementary School. Eight years later, after Libby had married

Randy, the Murdaughs hosted one of the Watermelon Festival's celebrity guests, thirteen-year-old British-born actress Angela Cartwright of the hit television show *Lost in Space*. Cartwright sat on an ottoman in the Murdaugh home in June 1963, sipping milk and sharing her opinions. She judged South Carolina "very quaint" and said, "I'd like to live here. But I think I'd like LA better."

Two years later, Hampton County was visited by someone who truly went to outer space and had in fact gone twice. Astronaut Virgil I. "Gus" Grissom came to Hampton County's famous hootenanny in 1965 with his boss Jim Webb, leader of the National Aeronautics and Space Administration. The spaceman stopped to address a crowd in Estill, an agricultural hub in Hampton County, making for an intriguing interaction between men who plow the Earth and men who escape it. Somehow they all found common ground. Grissom and Webb stood atop a wooden platform beside the railroad and under a live oak tree, where "they received the cheers of farmers in their best store-bought clothes and women in gay bonnets and exuberant children. There was fried chicken, and Brunswick stew and slaw, and talk of the moon and Mars and the universe beyond . . ." wrote the *New York Times*, who sent a reporter to tag along and profile the spacemen's host, Mendel Rivers, the Lowcountry's longtime congressman.

Rivers never missed a melon festival. He began his first campaign for Congress back in 1940 by glad-handing at the second Hampton County Watermelon Festival. He was one of the first politicians to realize that there's no better chance to meet the people of Hampton than during the annual salute to King Melon. He also organized Watermelon Day each year at the US Capitol, arranging for hundreds of melons to be trucked to Washington, DC, and shared with his colleagues. Years after Rivers died in 1970, the Hampton County Watermelon Festival remained a thriving annual tradition. Patrick Tyler, former editor of the *Hampton County Guardian*, described the days-long party as "the bedrock of Hampton

County culture . . . it would be impossible not to attend the Watermelon
Festival in Hampton."

A melon-munching festival was a decidedly quaint event in the 1970s
and 1980s, at least in comparison to rock concerts like Woodstock, disco
nightclubs like Studio 54, and the advent of music television. In Hampton
things were more homespun. The watermelon festival glorified the simple
life available in Hampton and the idea that everything one could need and
want could be found between the swamps.

Hampton's selling points were emphasized in essays written by eighth
grade students at Hampton Elementary in 1976. Tasked with making a
pitch for their town, most students emphasized the many ways people could
busy themselves in Hampton. As Jim Lawrence wrote:

> *We have two shopping centers for your convenience and they both
> have parking lots. We have a pool hall, a game room, lots of gas sta-
> tions, two swimming pools, three stop lights and three parks. You'll
> catch up on all the gossip in this little town and you know every-
> body. We have a swamp converted to a lake for your enjoyment . . .
> We also have lots of Little League sports for your kids. We also have
> a Hardee's, where the burgers are charco-broiled.*

Another eighth grader, Kerry Johnson, touted Hampton as "exciting"
but also peaceful. "Hey, bored homeowners, how would you like to live in
a beautiful but small town?" wrote Johnson. "Come down and take a tour
of Hampton. Talk to the friendly police and ask them about the crime rate.
I'm sure they will tell you it isn't high."

Hampton was regarded by many of its inhabitants as a refuge from an
overcomplicated world, a place where good manners mattered and evil
very rarely visited. The Coosawhatchie and Salkehatchie swamps seemed
to buffer Hampton from so many influences, even sometimes seeming to
prevent the infiltration of time. A century after its founding, Hampton

remained perpetually old-fashioned, apparently incapable of modernizing, forever destined to be an anachronism. Even when the Westinghouse factory was going gangbusters making Micarta and employing more than 4,000 people at its facilities, Hampton was irredeemably small-town in its ways, and in some regards almost too cute, such as the fact that when residents wanted to use the town tennis courts at night, they had to call the police department first and ask for a cop to turn on the lights. Or that when Hampton County's female jailer retired in 1972 at age seventy-eight after thirty-five years of working and living at the jail, she was replaced by another woman who also lived with her family in the jailer's apartment on the first floor of the small building, beneath the cells.

This young new jailer, Ida Belger Ferguson, brought a hippie vibe to the century-old brick building. She dressed in sporty red pantsuits and gathered her long brown hair in a ponytail. She placed exotic houseplants and bulbs throughout her quarters, including a night-blooming cereus and rare varieties of amaryllis. Outside she kept a noisy peacock who strutted around the jail yard in princely fashion. It was important for Ferguson to enjoy her surroundings since her job only allowed her eight hours away from the jail each week.

The jailer's job was full of surprises. Once an inmate sabotaged the plumbing and flooded the first floor where she lived with her husband and two kids. Another time an inmate hung himself within a cell with a bedsheet. One female inmate tried to smuggle a pistol into the jail by concealing it within her bra. Then there was the man who rang the doorbell at 5:00 one morning and said, "I'm drunk. Please lock me up."

Not every criminal was so polite. The rise in violent crime across the country in the 1970s did not spare the Lowcountry. Among the more shocking crimes in the 14th Judicial Circuit was the attempted robbery of legendary sportsman and hedonist Harry Cram, an incident that ended with two Marines lying dead in Cram's home, a bullet in each of their foreheads. Cram, whose marriage to Ruth Vaux ended soon after she met

Buster Murdaugh back during World War II, was still living in Bluffton in 1976, but no longer at his Foot Point Plantation. Instead, he, his wife, and a son lived on his forty-acre Potato Island in the May River. On the night of September 10, two Marines clad in diving gear swam across the May River to the island, snuck into the house and assaulted Cram's adult son. They marched him to the door of Cram's bedroom and held him at knifepoint as they called for Cram and waited for him to appear. When Cram stepped out his son ducked. The expert marksman shot each of the Marines in the head with his pistol.

The way Cram coolly dispatched the Marines further burnished his reputation. Beyond being a vaunted huntsman and a rich and romantic roughneck, Cram was now also a Lowcountry version of the folk hero William Tell, though Cram did Tell one better. While legend says that Tell shot a single apple off his son's head, Cram plugged two people standing above his own boy.

A coroner's jury cleared Cram of any wrongdoing. This spared Cram much additional interaction with Buster, who was somehow still solicitor some thirty years after he helped ruin Cram's marriage.

A year after Cram killed the intruders on his island, another shocking homicide occurred, this time right in Varnville, when a seventy-three-year-old widow was found dead in her home. Buster and Randy together prosecuted a twenty-one-year-old man for the killing, rape, and robbery of the elderly woman, asking a jury to give him the death penalty. The man was found guilty but spared execution, in part because his lawyers argued that the woman was already dead before her corpse was sexually assaulted. He received a term of life imprisonment for murder and robbery.

Just as that murder trial was starting, another Lowcountry woman was sexually assaulted and killed, this time on rural St. Helena Island in Beaufort County. A few months later, police arrested four White youths from Pennsylvania for murdering the thirty-three-year-old Black woman. The group had traveled by car to South Carolina where they picked up the woman as a hitchhiker before killing her and leaving her body in the woods. Buster, an emotionally hardened veteran of scores of murder cases, was especially disturbed by the details of this murder, which featured mutilation, sexual assault, and asphyxiation. As Buster told one lawyer, "She's God's child. I'm gonna fry them."

Two of the suspects—John Plath, twenty-three, and John Arnold, twenty-two—were tried for murder while their two female companions, ages seventeen and eleven, were given immunity from prosecution in exchange for information and testimony. During his opening statement at Plath and Arnold's trial in 1979, Solicitor Murdaugh warned the jury, "This is going to be a right gory case, but it's my duty to present all the facts . . . This is as cold-blooded a killing as has ever been performed in Beaufort County or the State of South Carolina."

Buster called the seventeen-year-old girlfriend of defendant Plath to the witness stand to testify about the attack she helped perpetrate. She detailed the unconscionable abuse heaped upon the poor murder victim. She told how the victim had asked to leave but Plath told her, "You ain't going nowhere," before he and others slapped her and kicked her to the ground. From there the group kicked the woman some more, made her strip naked, and made her perform oral sex on Plath and his girlfriend while beating the woman with a belt. Plath urinated in the woman's mouth and made her swallow.

Then they tried to kill the woman. Plath stabbed her multiple times and then mused aloud about using a pocketknife to make a necklace from the woman's genitals. When the woman failed to die from stab wounds the group from Pennsylvania slashed her neck with a broken bottle then strangled her slowly with a garden hose that was found nearby in a pile of trash. After pulling on the hose wrapped around her neck for twenty minutes, and stomping on her throat, the woman died. Plath marveled at her resilience with a racial slur and Arnold desecrated her by carving KKK into her body in an effort to mislead police.

As Plath's girlfriend related the details of the strangulation from the witness stand, the solicitor instructed the young woman to wrap a section of garden hose around his neck to demonstrate just how she and the others strangled their victim. Buster left the hose coiled around his neck as he paced back and forth before the jurors seated in the jury box, saying, "I'm going to leave it here because we're still going to be talking about it," as he continued to question the witness. When Plath's girlfriend described the victim's final moments, Murdaugh laid down on the courtroom floor in simulation of the expiring woman. The hose was looped around his neck, and the witness pulled on one end and a sheriff's deputy on the other, playacting the final moments of the murder. "Don't get between me and the jury," Buster shouted when the witness or deputy wandered in front of his collapsed body.

Thanks to Buster's histrionics the jury convicted both men of murder and recommended the death penalty, which Judge Clyde Eltzroth imposed despite his own religious objection. After the trial, he put a hand on the shoulders of one of the defense attorneys for the convicted murderers and told him, in a comforting tone, "You can't make chicken soup out of chicken shit." The convictions affirmed people's faith in Solicitor Murdaugh, but the recurrence of horrific crimes began to spook the people of Hampton and elsewhere. In the 1970s many Lowcountry residents felt compelled to lock their doors for fear of theft and violent crime. Martha Bee Anderson, keeping watch over town from her home at the end of Lee Avenue, lamented the good old days, when Hampton residents didn't have to always be on guard. As she wrote in her "Around the Clock" column in 1972:

> *It mattered not if that home was a palace or a shack, locking up was simply a blooming nuisance and quite unnecessary. Sad for us all, times have changed . . . Almost everybody is locking doors these days because widespread crime is reaching out into the remotest corners of the nation.*

Whether due to a mother's intuition or the instincts honed by a veteran newswoman, Martha Bee had a hunch that tragedy would someday strike much closer to home in the Lowcountry. Peaceful country living, she complained, was being eroded by a wave of crime. There wasn't much to do but to lock up tight, though Martha Bee fretted that wouldn't be enough:

> *One has the uneasy feeling that IT, the dreaded, could indeed happen here. For as long as many of us can remember, the prevailing feeling used to be the opposite. That weird, horrifying happenings in the headlines were from far, far away places, happening to far away people.*

———

Behind the birthday smiles was a secret—Maggie had found more of Alex's pills, the pills Alex had promised to give up. Almost a month before the Memorial Day weekend visit in late May 2021, Maggie had found a stash of unfamiliar medication. She used her cell phone to search the names of the pills, typing "white pill 30 on one side rp" into a search box and discovering it was an opioid. She did the same with another pill, which turned out to be a sedative that eases anxiety and general withdrawal symptoms, but which can become addictive and is sometimes used recreationally. Maggie told Paul about this discovery, who in turn called his father and left him a phone message. "I am still in EB (Edisto Beach) because when you get here we have to talk," said Paul. "Mom found several bags of pills in your computer bag."

Maggie had found a partner in Paul, someone with whom she could combat Alex's ongoing addiction to pain pills. Maggie called Paul her "little detective," said her sister Marian Proctor, to whom Maggie confided her worries over Alex's continual relapses of drug use and how Paul had become critical to holding him in check. "He was always looking to make sure his dad was behaving," said Proctor. "If there were pills in the house that his dad was taking that he wasn't supposed to, Paul was determined that he would find them."

Alex apologized profusely to his family. "I am very sorry that I do this to all of you. I love you," he wrote to Maggie the day after Paul called him. She did not reply. Alex told Paul he would go to a rehabilitation center as soon as they resolved the criminal charges regarding the boat crash. The dependency embarrassed him. "You don't have a real high self-esteem when you're an addict," Alex later admitted. He said he felt like he was feeding or fighting his urges for "as long as I can remember."

Alex's drug problem was supposedly so long running that it was hard to keep track of all the times he disappointed his loved ones. "Mags found pills. Paul Paul found pills. Bus found pills. It was an ongoing battle for me," said Alex, using family nicknames. Paul and Maggie in particular did not trust him, at least not when it came to his drug abuse. "They had been watching me like a hawk for years," Murdaugh said. The discovery of pills before Memorial Day weekend, he said, "was just one occurrence where I let them down."

Alex said opioids sometimes caused him a side effect of paranoia, and usually a deep breath would rid himself of any unreasonable worries. But Alex had plenty to fret about legitimately, even without a chemical catalyst. He was on constant guard to prevent his many schemes from unraveling, a task that proved more challenging by the day. One of his law partners had recently seen lawyer Chris Wilson and asked him about the delay in sending the money from the recent settlement for the trucking case. This prompted Wilson to check in with Alex, asking if everything was okay. Alex assured him all was well and he would resolve the mix-up.

But instead of resolving the issue he muddied the water. He insisted to the firm's chief financial officer, Jeanne Seckinger, that the missing money was in Chris Wilson's trust account. Yet Alex didn't know that behind the scenes, Wilson's paralegal had told the Hampton law firm that Alex had already been paid. Seckinger decided to let the issue rest and see if the money was indeed on its way from Wilson's trust account. Nonetheless, Seckinger felt like she was being deceived. She suggested to law partner Ronnie Crosby that Alex might be hiding the money because of the boat crash, a tactic the law firm did not wish to support.

At home Alex was under increased scrutiny, too. Maggie found more pills on May 26, just before Memorial Day weekend, and again researched the code printed on the side of the medication. This time her hyper-vigilance was unwarranted; it was a nonprescription, nighttime cold and flu medication. But her suspicions remained high.

The next weekend, in early June, Maggie and Alex traveled to Columbia for the weekend to meet with Buster and his girlfriend and watch college baseball. Alex missed some of the games because he was laid up sick in a hotel room from opioid withdrawal. He texted his family just before noon on Sunday morning, asking if they were in their seats at the ball field. He told them he had extended his checkout until 1:00 P.M. and would see them soon thereafter. "I'm dreading it," he wrote. "See you in a little bit." Maggie sympathetically warned Alex that while the ball field wasn't particularly crowded, it was "not the place to come if you don't feel well. Very hot and muggy. We are inside sitting at the bar. Very nice indoors." Alex tried to heed her warning and sleep in even later, but the hotel declined to offer another extension. "They are making me leave, so I'll see you all in a few," Alex texted in an update.

On the way back home to Moselle after the game, Alex and Maggie paid a visit to Alex's parents about 9:00 P.M., delivering Alex's dad a special gift of Krispy Kreme donuts they had picked up in Columbia. Randy was sleeping and missed his visitors. When he woke up later that night Handsome and a caretaker remarked to reach other that it was unusual for Alex and Maggie to come over so late. Randy, in poor health, tried a bit of raspberry donut before protesting, "I just can't eat the rest."

On Monday morning Alex slept late, or at least stayed in bed. Maggie got an early start, driving to a doctor's appointment in Charleston and also to oversee maintenance work at the beach house on Edisto Island. Just after 7:00 A.M. she texted Blanca Turrubiate-Simpson, "will u stop by store and bring Alex Capri suns he like orange and pineapple flavor plus mountain cooler ty I'll pay u back." Given her busy day and the distances she was driving, she had hoped to spend the night at the beach house and keep supervising the workmen.

Alex, meanwhile, arrived at the law office just before 1:00 P.M. Within an hour he was confronted by Seckinger, who found him upstairs leaning against a file cabinet. Alex greeted her with a dirty look, asking, "What do you need now?" Seckinger was annoyed. The money had still not arrived from Wilson's trust account. She told him they could talk in his office.

Behind closed doors Alex's demeanor softened considerably as he made assurances to Seckinger and swore the firm would get the money. As they talked he received a text message from his brother telling him and his family members that the family patriarch had been admitted to a hospital in Savannah and that doctors were trying to determine if Randy's difficulty breathing was attributable to his lung cancer, which meant his condition was terminal, or pneumonia, which left limited room for hope. This medical update broke up the meeting, as Jeanne assumed Alex was going to be with his father. They would figure out the missing money later.

But Alex did not go see his father. His father was not coming home to Almeda that day, as originally expected, and the visitor's policy at the Savannah hospital was restrictive on account of coronavirus precautions. Besides, he had other things on his mind, like the prying eyes of Mark Tinsley. Jeanne was surprised to receive a call from Alex at 4:00 P.M. that same day in which he asked for information about his retirement account balance. Alex said he needed the number to prepare for a court hearing about the boat crash lawsuit scheduled for Friday, when Tinsley would argue for access to his financial information.

At the same time Alex made his financial inquiry, Maggie texted with Blanca from a doctor's office waiting room, sharing her father-in-law's uncertain prognosis. She seemed inclined to return to Moselle, as Alex had requested. "Ty I'm waiting at dr," Maggie texted Blanca close to 4:00 P.M. "Alex wanted me to come home I had to leave door open at Edisto but trust Mexican's [*sic*] to shut and lock for me."

Maggie seemed worried about her husband just as much as her father-in-law in the hospital. She spoke to her sister about it, who encouraged her to return home and support Alex, knowing how close he was to his father. Maggie also expressed more of her concern to Blanca, writing, "Alex is about to die hope he doesn't go down there to sleep Alex needs to take care of himself as well." Thirty seconds later she wrote to Alex and confirmed she would return that night to Moselle, telling her husband, "I will be home to see u in a few hours." She then replied to more well wishes from Blanca, writing, "I am scared for [Handsome] and Alex and all of us."

While Maggie made a fateful decision to return to Moselle and agonized with Blanca over Alex's well-being, Alex took a break from crunching the numbers of his personal finances to trade text messages with his buddies. He had been distracted by an image of three women in bikinis atop a boat that popped up on his phone. "Lena in the middle," said the text message from his friend, who worked at the true Forge Consulting in Columbia. He included a fire emoji.

"U ole dog!!" wrote Alex in return. "Where is Lena now?"

Lena was up north, came the reply. And she was getting married.

Alex checked in with Maggie about the same time via text, asking about her doctor's appointment. Paul was meanwhile planning to spend the night at Moselle, too. Paul had originally hoped to replant a sunflower field with a friend at Moselle that day, though those plans were postponed. Maggie texted him just before dinnertime after he tried to call her, writing, "U ok getting little foot massage then I'm headed home."

"Yeah," said Paul.

"Love u and Blanca cooked u dinner," wrote Maggie.

"What did she make," Paul replied a few minutes later.

"Country fried steak and Mac n cheese," said Maggie.

Paul had worked at his uncle John Marvin Murdaugh's equipment rental business that day and texted with one friend about attending a weekend golf tournament. He traded messages with a woman about obtaining a residential lease and then sent another buddy an image of a hot tub for sale. Before going to Moselle, he stopped by the home of his uncle, John Marvin, and played with his young cousins outside in the yard. Then he went on his way, heading off to Moselle by way of Almeda, where he would switch a car before driving home to see his parents.

Alex was waiting for Paul when he arrived about 7:00 P.M., and the two rode the property together for an hour or so. Alex said they checked the feed plots and ponds, as well as fired a pistol a few times. Paul recorded a video on his phone of his father next to a young tree that was bending over badly. Paul laughed heartily at the floppy, top-heavy tree, conceding failure, but Alex wasn't giving up. "It's better than it was, ain't it," said Alex, dressed in a blue short-sleeved shirt, khaki pants and leather loafers. Paul shared it with some friends, to which one replied, "Damn man needs some straps o[n] it," and another said, "He's got the magic touch."

Maggie got home about 8:00 P.M. and the three Murdaughs had dinner together, eating the food prepared by Blanca. His stomach full, Alex laid down for a short nap on the couch. When he awoke a short while later, a little after 9:00 P.M., he decided to visit his mother over at Almeda. Maggie and Paul were not in the house so he called Maggie twice but she did not answer. Then he sent her a text message, writing, "Going to check on Em be rite back." He assumed they had gone down to the kennels to see the dogs, but he did not drive the short distance down there to confirm their location. Instead he just piloted his car out the main gates and off to his parents' house.

He called a handful of friends and family on the twenty-minute drive to Almeda. He visited with his mother and the caretaker on duty that evening, watched television with the women, and then headed home, making more phone calls. Upon returning to the house at Moselle, he noticed Maggie and Paul were still not there. This time he drove down to the kennels. Darkness obscured a gruesome scene only partially revealed by his headlights. Paul lay sprawled outside a feed room adjacent to the dog kennels. His face was intact, but his head was missing. The remains of his brain sat a short distance away, the skull formerly surrounding it obliterated. He had been shot twice with a shotgun. About twelve steps away was the body of Maggie. Her killer had shot her five times with an AR-15-type assault rifle. The weapon blew holes through different parts of her body. One of the final shots blasted apart her brain, too.

Shotgun shells and bullet cartridges littered the scene. Bullet fragments and shotgun pellets were embedded in walls. Body tissue, blood, and hair coated the feed room ceiling. Alex checked each of his loved ones' bodies for signs of life before calling 911 at 10:06 P.M. on June 7, 2021. "I've been up to it now, it's bad," Alex told a dispatcher in a deeply strained voice. "My wife and my son . . . they're on the ground, out at my kennels . . . neither one of them's moving."

CHAPTER SEVEN

END OF THE LINE

Something was on the side of the road. The Hampton woman's car chugged up the highway, alongside the railroad tracks. It was midday in the heat of the summer and she was passing through Almeda past Randolph "Buster" Murdaugh Jr.'s farm. As she drew closer to town she could see the scene more clearly—*someone* was in the road ahead, lying on the shoulder of the highway with part of his body in the lane of traffic. The woman pulled over on the roadside and parked the car.

As the woman approached the man she saw he was not wearing any shoes or shirt, just a pair of cutoff jean shorts. A blazing sun bore down on the highway, baking the man's tender body on the asphalt. The woman could see he was alive but passed out. He needed help. Not only was half his body on the edge of road, the other half was atop a fire ant pile he had disturbed, and what seemed like thousands of ants were exacting revenge on the scorched skin of the invader who had collapsed on their colony.

The woman pulled the man completely off the road. He didn't really wake up. She then went to the nearest payphone and dialed Hampton's big law firm—Peters, Murdaugh, Parker, Eltzroth & Detrick—and asked to speak with Randolph "Randy" Murdaugh III. When Randy got on the line the woman explained she was calling because she had found his uncle, Johnny Glenn Murdaugh, passed out drunk on the side of the road. Randy listened but offered little reaction. He seemed annoyed and asked no questions, not even where his uncle was found. "Okay, thanks for calling," he said, ready to hang up the phone.

"You don't understand," the woman protested. "His feet were in the highway." She emphasized to Randy the helpless state Johnny was in—exceedingly intoxicated and ravaged by fire ants. "Should I call an ambulance?" she asked. "No, I'm coming," said Randy, clearly annoyed by the inconvenience caused by Uncle Johnny.

Randy had grown tired of the mess that was Johnny Glenn Murdaugh, much like his father, Buster. Buster told family friend Sam Crews that his brother was "the least reliable man in America." Johnny's stepdaughter Sheryl Polk McKinney says Buster always kept his brother at a distance. "Buster didn't want to be bothered by him," said Sheryl. Now his son Randy was acting the same way.

Not too long ago, the relationship had been much closer between Johnny and Randy. That was evident in the aftermath of Sheryl and her brother once secretly poisoning Johnny in a bid to end his abuse. Sheryl and her sibling dissolved tablets of roach poison in hot water and then spiked Johnny's liquor with the toxic solution. Johnny fell severely ill after ingesting it, but, to the children's disappointment, he did not die. Randy arrived at the house to nurse his uncle through episodes of vomiting and pain. "He came and paced with him all night and fed him coffee," said Sheryl. Years later, Sheryl confessed the poisoning to Randy. He didn't care, replying, "I figured either your momma did it or something happened."

As Sheryl got older, she suspected that Johnny told some of his friends about their sexual relationship. They would touch her in very familiar ways, she said, treating her like a pet and making her feel uncomfortable. His group of confidantes included his nephew, Randy, who Sheryl said was at that time very close to his uncle. One day, when she was a girl living next door to Buster and his family in Varnville, before they moved to the old doctor's house in Almeda, Randy, a seventeen-year-old high school student, came over to play with Sheryl. He gave her a nickel for washing the tires of his Jeep. Then he invited her next door to his family's home, to see the playground his father Buster had built for his little sister. The eight-year-old girl was elated; she thought Randy the "cat's pajamas" and was flattered the high schooler paid any attention to her. Randy then took Sheryl by the hand and led her into the woods behind their houses, where, according to Sheryl, "he put his hands in my pants," and sexually assaulted her. That incident was followed by another. Sheryl said that sometime after he fingered her, Randy brought Sheryl to an upstairs room at his home and exposed himself. Sheryl said he had her sit beside him on a bed and give him a hand job while his sister played nearby. The episode was quick, she said, and that was the last time they had any sexual contact.

When Sheryl was sixteen she left home to go and live with assorted girlfriends. She was married two years later and saw the Murdaugh family less frequently. But there were still memorable occasions when her path crossed with the family. Sheryl saw Randy occasionally at the counter of Stanley's Drug Store where she worked during high school in the 1960s, making coffee and sandwiches. The pharmacy was a hangout for Hampton lawyers, and one day Sheryl witnessed Randy and his friends heckle a Black man who had sat at the counter and placed an order, laughing and ridiculing him to the point he left the drug store without any food.

As a young adult, Sheryl once returned to the old Dr. Tuten house in Almeda that was the scene of so many bad memories. Her longtime tormentor, Johnny, had moved out of the old wooden house to a new small brick home on the property. Sheryl wanted to get some family dishware from the old house and tried to get inside. Strangely, all the doors and windows were nailed shut from the inside.

Sheryl, perplexed and now curious, climbed atop a small roof above the kitchen door and climbed through an upstairs window that had not been nailed shut. Once inside, she walked down the stairs and instantly understood why almost every opening was sealed—the house was concealing a giant moonshine operation. Her mother's old coal stove formed part of a still and copper pipes ran across the kitchen. The house was full of bags of grain and sugar, as well as scores of empty milk jugs.

When Sheryl came back to the house two weeks later to gather more belongings, all the moonshine equipment was gone. And soon after that, she said, the old house was demolished, the past erased, at least the visible reminders. But memories of Johnny and his insatiable and unrestrained lust would forever remain embedded in Sheryl's mind, still fresh and vivid seventy years later.

There was always some sort of dark intrigue occurring at the Almeda property. A moonshine factory in the old house. Farmhands disappearing. Pets going splat. Corpses supposedly being plowed into the ground between the pecan trees. Little children and their mother terrorized and abused, again and again and again.

When she was a kid, said Sheryl, Buster sometimes came over to talk to Johnny. The brothers would reliably stand by Buster's farm truck, out of earshot of anyone else. Sheryl did not perceive them as equals, but rather that Buster called the shots and Johnny performed the dirty work. She wondered what Buster told Johnny, and how much he knew about what happened at the farm.

When Buster was gone, Johnny would grumble about the general debt his brother owed him. He complained to Sheryl that nobody loved him, that he'd been mistreated all his life, and that his father told him, "You weren't born right," the harsh words able to be interpreted literally or figuratively.

But Johnny might not have felt so badly if he realized Buster at least treated everyone this way. Buster was always hustling, always looking for advantage, always considering the way he might come out on top, even heading into old age. As one Hampton County woman who knew him said, "Mr. Buster was all about Mr. Buster."

By 1980 Buster was more entrenched than ever as solicitor. He notched his eleventh consecutive election victory, a feat regarded as routine. No one dared challenge Buster anymore, the post was his to keep or cede as he pleased. Retiring state senator James Harrelson of Walterboro said he would have liked to become solicitor except he would have no chance running against Buster, "the most competent, most able prosecutor in the State of South Carolina."

Buster could breathe easy having survived so many scandals, some of which were now decades old. There had been the formal accusations of income tax evasion and bootlegging, clients' accusations of stealing, the close association to an adoption scandal, whispers of so much additional wrongdoing on a near-daily basis . . . none of it derailed his career. Few people, if any, had served as prosecutor for so long. Like an alligator sinking into soft mud, Buster embedded himself in the Lowcountry, daring someone to enter the muck and dislodge him. "Mr. Buster was pretty much the king," said one woman. "Whatever he said, went."

This woman refused to hail the swamp king. She judged Buster an entitled person who expected things done for him and done quickly. He was arrogant, she said, abusing the public trust each time he shamelessly threw criminal indictments in the trash can, saying, "Don't worry about it no more." He was also plain rude. He once pushed a heavy door into her, she said, and no apology was extended. Instead, the solicitor told her, "You should have got out of the damn way."

The unspoken bargain Buster offered was this: tolerate me because you might need me. He thought this a very fair exchange. Few people were bold enough to deny him. Through either instinct or experience, people knew it was wiser to please Buster than court his displeasure. Accordingly, Buster continued to receive the red-carpet treatment and place of honor almost everywhere he went within the five-county domain, especially at down-home, out-of-the-way places where like pool halls, fry shacks, and seafood vendors, food and drink never being far from the solicitor's mind.

Even though Rigdon's Fried Chicken wasn't open on Saturdays, Buster would often call in an order of food anyway so he could bring the Hampton delicacy up to the capital, Columbia, to eat before the Gamecocks football game. Amon Rigdon said he didn't mind cooking special orders for the solicitor. The restaurant owner was friendly with Buster, but Rigdon did not act too familiar, not wanting to seem like he was looking to gain something. But when someone once threatened to sue the fry cook, Rigdon did mention the potential lawsuit to Buster. The solicitor responded reassuringly with his familiar phrase: "Don't worry about it."

"And that was the last I heard of it," said Rigdon. "He was a powerful rascal . . . If he told you something, you could take it to the bank."

In the 1980s, Buster began retreating to his own private marsh island in the middle of Beaufort County, close to the big Broad River. There were two small, modest houses on the property, a few docks, and not much else, the chief attractions being the view of the marsh and deepwater access to the creek and nearby rivers. The houses overlooked the wide and winding Chechessee Creek, which ran along one side of the island, as well as sprawling marshlands. A short causeway connected the mainland and the creekside getaway, which the Murdaugh family came to call by a few names: river house, Chechessee, and Buster's Island. The solicitor liked his hideaways. Beyond the river house and his farmland in Almeda, Buster had previously owned, or at least used, a house on Hilton Head Island, a farm in Georgia, and a cottage on Edisto Beach.

But while Buster eventually let most of those properties go, his own island proved a keeper—a place he would enjoy until his death, especially on the days when people like the loyal Lowcountry SLED agent would arrive bearing gifts of island essentials, fulfilling Buster's demands for fresh-caught shrimp, ice, and booze. Somehow these requests for free food, beer, and handles of hard alcohol never became tiresome to Buster's lackeys. Somehow, in Buster's favor economy, it all got sorted out.

Buster often invited his friends and family to his island. One weekend in late January 1983, just after celebrating his sixty-eighth birthday, Buster visited the river house with his wife, Gladys. Tagging along was his fourteen-year-old grandson Alex, and one of his friends. On Sunday afternoon the boys motored an aluminum boat away from the dock, up the creek, and into the even wider Chechessee River. They carried with them a small-bore shotgun. While floating on the river in the boat, Alex was handing the loaded and cocked shotgun to his friend when it discharged. Ammunition fired out of the gun, ricocheted off the metal boat bottom, and lodged into the knee of Alex's friend. The boys were soon motoring back to land and then were on their way to the emergency room, where Alex's friend had two shotgun slugs removed from the surface of his skin.

The teenager was back in school the next day. But other, similar incidents and accidents involving the Murdaughs did not end so happily in the years to come. This was the first of at least three boat trips originating from Buster's Island to end in tragedy, each of these journeys a little more calamitous than the last. This was also not the last time Alex Murdaugh fired a gun into another person.

———

Twenty minutes after Alex Murdaugh's call to 911, Colleton County sheriff's deputy Sergeant Daniel Greene arrived at Moselle and parked his vehicle near the dog kennels. A large man in a bright white T-shirt was in the distance, illuminated by car headlights, pacing across a grassy area close to two bodies on the ground. Greene noticed large pools of blood beneath each person.

As the deputy approached, Alex Murdaugh explained that he had grabbed a shotgun from the house for protection and that it was now leaning against his vehicle. He allowed Greene, who was carrying a flashlight in his hands, to frisk him for additional weapons. "It's bad, it's bad, I checked their pulses," said Alex, beginning to cry.

Alex had just hung up with the 911 dispatcher, with whom he had been sharing his suspicions of who might have shot his family. "He's been being threatened for months and months and months. He's been hit several times . . ." Alex said on the phone.

Now, as he stood near his wife's body, he almost immediately continued sharing his theory to police. "This is a long story, my son was in a boat wreck months back," said Alex within a minute of the deputy arriving to Moselle. "He's been getting threats, most of it's been benign stuff we didn't take serious. You know, he's been getting, like, punched. I know there's, I know that's what it is."

Alex explained his whereabouts that night and how he had gone to visit his mother. He came home to find Maggie and Paul on the ground. "I left, I don't know what time, I can go back on my phone and tell you the exact times—Did you check," said Alex, changing the subject abruptly.

"Did I check what," asked Greene, gently.

"Did you check them?" asked Alex.

"We got medical guys, that's what they're gonna do," said Greene.

"What are they doing?" said Alex, growing impatient and annoyed. "Can they hurry?"

No matter how fast the ambulance raced down the dark, rural roads of Colleton County, Maggie and Paul could not be saved. Alex knew this, asking a minute or so later as he called his brother, Randy, "They are dead, aren't they?"

"Yessir, that's what it looks like," said Greene.

As more county police arrived sheriff's deputies walked the crime scene, making sure no armed suspects were lurking in the dark. Greene noticed fresh tire tracks in wet grass and a lot of water on the concrete pads of the kennels, as if someone had recently used the hose hanging sloppily nearby. There was a dead chicken atop a dog crate. He and colleagues searched for footprints, spent ammunition, and other clues. An officer stepped into the small feed shed at the end of the kennels where Paul had fallen out the doorway.

Police lifted Paul to see if a weapon was underneath his body but saw nothing, and placed him back on the ground as he was found, with his hands beneath him. A cell phone was resting outside a pocket on the seat of his shorts, as if someone had placed it there. Emergency personnel then placed pink sheets over each of the bodies, shielding them from view from Alex and his friends and family, who were arriving at Moselle to offer support.

About that time the Colleton County sheriff asked SLED to take over the case, given the Murdaugh family's long association with local law enforcement. State police crime technicians and investigators were soon en route, driving to Moselle from all parts of the Lowcountry and Columbia. Until they arrived local police would continue securing and processing the crime scene. Already Colleton County sheriff's deputies had found spent 12-gauge shotgun shells and .300 Blackout rifle cartridges on the ground near the bodies.

As the police combed the scene, Alex's brothers and law partners and friends like Chief Greg Alexander and Chris Wilson began arriving to offer support and help. Alex was a broken man, they said, listening to him cry out, "Look at what they did! Look at what they did to them," and, "The fucking boat wreck! The fucking boat wreck!" His law partner Mark Ball said Alex was "in pieces." When Wilson arrived at Moselle he hugged Alex around the neck and cried with him. "He was destroyed," said Wilson. Alex was "just whimpering, trying to be gracious to people."

SLED agents and evidence technicians arrived on the scene. Alex submitted to a test for gunshot residue on his hands and clothing and consented to record a video interview with police, requesting that his friend and law partner, Danny Henderson, be present. As it started to rain after midnight, Alex got into the front passenger seat of a police vehicle belonging to SLED Special Agent David Owen, who moments earlier had been appointed lead investigator. Owen sat in the driver's seat while Henderson and Detective Laura Rutland of the sheriff's office sat in the rear seats. While the interview with Alex started in the car, the family, friends, and law partners that had arrived at Moselle headed to the house to console each other and keep dry.

"I hate to have to do this," said Owen, damp from the rain.

"I understand, I totally understand . . ." said Alex, who was sniffling often and staring ahead, rarely making eye contact with the SLED agent. "Don't have any problem with it."

"So, just start at the top, take your time," said Owen, who listened as Alex detailed the night's events. He described finding the bodies of Maggie and Paul and how he tried to turn each of them over trying to find a pulse. When he turned Paul over his son's cell phone popped out of a rear pocket on his shorts. Alex fiddled with the phone for a bit, he said, before placing it on Paul.

Alex told of the "wonderful" relationships he had with his wife and son. He mentioned that Paul had been the target of "vile" online attacks since the boat crash and had been "punched and hit and attacked a lot," though he was short on specifics. Alex said he admired how Paul handled this hostility, gushing, "I've never been prouder of him . . . Paul is a wonderful, wonderful kid. He can do almost anything and can get along with everybody."

Alex talked about the phone calls and text message he made that night trying to reach Maggie. He told the police there were no surveillance or hunting cameras in the vicinity of the sheds, and said that the family owned more than twenty guns, almost all kept in their hunting room, including pistols, shotguns, and rifles. "All kinds," said Alex. "You name it, across the board we have 'em."

After a half-hour of questioning, Owen signaled he was done asking questions for now. "Thank you all for everything you all are doing," Alex said to Owen and Rutland just before his phone started ringing. He answered it and learned his son Buster would soon be arriving at Moselle. Alex began to bawl, prompting Owen to reach over and comfort him by putting a hand on his shoulder. A moment later, after Alex calmed down, everyone in the car shook hands. Owen accompanied Alex to the bedroom in the main house, where he collected Alex's shirt, shorts, and shoes in evidence bags after Alex changed into fresh attire. At first glance his clothes seemed conspicuously clean given his claims of having handled two bloody dead bodies.

Having obtained a search warrant, other agents were walking through the house, looking for evidence, including 12-gauge shotguns and rifles chambered to fire .300 Blackout ammunition. With the help of some of the lawyers who were milling around in the gun room, SLED agents found and seized a handful of shotguns as well as one black .300 Blackout rifle. A colleague of theirs examined Alex's vehicle and found stains that tested presumptive for blood; she had the entire seat belt assembly from the driver's seat removed and taken to the state police lab for analysis.

As dawn loomed Alex, John Marvin, Buster, and his girlfriend left Moselle for the Murdaugh home at Almeda to try and catch a few hours of sleep. The sheriff's office and SLED prepared a joint statement released to the media about the killings. Despite not yet making any arrests for the double murder, the police insisted, bewilderingly, "At this time, there is no danger to the public."

As the sun rose on June 8, 2021, police returned en masse to Moselle to search for evidence and canvass the area. They sifted through the household trash at Moselle, finding empty ammunition boxes and a financial statement with a $1,021 purchase from the luxury goods store Gucci circled in pen. The police searched the property in daylight, finding additional bullet casings. They spoke with neighbors and collected surveillance footage from nearby properties, which was then reviewed for clues.

At midday SLED interviewed Rogan Gibson, a friend of Paul Murdaugh's whose dog, Cash, was staying in the Murdaugh's kennels for the week. Gibson said he spoke with Paul by phone about 8:40 P.M. when Paul went down to the kennels and noticed the chocolate-colored Labrador Retriever's tail was in need of possible medical attention. Paul called Gibson and described the condition of Cash's tail, but Gibson asked if he could show him via video call instead. He heard dogs in the background, as well as the voices of Alex and Maggie, or at least people who sounded just like them. This detail intrigued SLED investigators.

As Gibson told investigators, before Paul hung up he warned Gibson that the poor cellular reception at Moselle might thwart the video call. If so, he said, he'd send photos or a video to him when he could. Paul's intuition was correct; they couldn't establish a successful call. Gibson waited for a video from Paul. It did not arrive. He texted him: "See if you can get a good picture of it. MaryAnn wants to send it to a girl we know that's a vet. Tell him to sit and stay and he shouldn't move around to much."

Paul did not respond. Gibson called him three times over the next forty-five minutes. No answer. Gibson texted Ms. Maggie, "Tell Paul to call me." Ms. Maggie stayed mum. Gibson tried Paul again by phone and sent him another text message that said, "Yo." None of these communications were returned.

Though investigators found Paul's cell phone in plain sight atop his slain body, his device being handled and placed there by his father, Maggie's cell phone was still missing. This came to the attention of John Marvin Murdaugh, who had returned to Moselle the day after his loved ones' deaths. He soon brought Buster's phone to the police, and it indicated that Maggie's phone was just down the road. A few minutes later they discovered her phone in the brush on the side of the road, about a quarter mile from the house at Moselle. Police seized the device and placed it in airplane mode. Notably, they did not power the phone off or place it in a Faraday bag, which is a law enforcement tool designed to shield the device from receiving new signals that might corrupt or overwrite existing data.

This was a lot to coordinate, and SLED soon convened a meeting of about twenty-five investigators to brief them on the killings. Among the speakers at the meeting were Solicitor Isaac "Duffie" Stone III, who succeeded Randolph "Randy" Murdaugh III in office fifteen years earlier, in 2006, as well as Special Agent David Owen. The straightforward, mild-mannered investigator grew up on the edge of the Lowcountry in Orangeburg, a small city about an hour's drive from Hampton. He had worked in law enforcement for twenty-five years, the last six with SLED in their regional Lowcountry office, which was based out of Walterboro. One prosecutor in the state attorney general's office described Owen as a "grounded" and talented investigator, someone who could relate to people he interviewed and use their information to inform complex cases.

At the time of the killings at Moselle, Owen and every other SLED employee took orders from Chief Mark A. Keel, who worked from an office at headquarters in Columbia. Keel had worked for SLED for forty years and had served as chief for the last decade. Keel had done it all at SLED, working narcotics and intelligence units; serving on the SWAT, hostage negotiation, and bloodhound tracking teams; providing protection for politicians via executive detail; flying helicopters; and even getting a law degree while remaining a part-time agent, a perk afforded him that rubbed some other rank-and-file agents the wrong way. Some of these critics said Keel was just as focused on climbing the ladder as he was on making cases. Others described him admiringly as a go-getter who knew how to play politics and as someone who stabilized SLED after a previous period of cost-cutting and reduction of mission.

Keel, who had grown up close to Hampton in Barnwell, had eyed the chief's job since he joined SLED in 1979, stating this goal out loud to other agents. He was a no-nonsense leader with an impressive record, earning the endorsement of two governors and the support of many lawmakers whom he lobbied to fund state law enforcement needs. He spent much less time courting the media, only holding press conferences a handful of times as chief and rarely granting interview requests, which limited transparency at the state police force, especially over mistakes. Said one former SLED agent: "He's smart enough to keep his mouth shut."

Despite projecting a humorless, tough-guy stance, agents knew him to "cry at the drop of a hat," when addressing officers under his charge, said another former SLED agent, with Keel frequently moved by the nobility of police service and the perils and pressures that accompany the job. But apart from the occasional emotional episode, Keel overwhelmingly had the reputation of a by-the-book administrator, the type of officer who would overzealously write a book of tickets in a single day and who wouldn't hesitate to issue a citation to his own mother. As the Murdaugh case began, Keel was said to exercise an iron grip on the double murder investigation, guarding closely against leaks to the media. This vigilance indicated an awareness that SLED's reputation, and Keel's own legacy, would be shaped significantly by the outcome of this case.

Three days after the murder, half a dozen SLED vehicles rolled onto land owned by John Marvin Murdaugh and drove toward his hunting cabin. Inside the building were John Marvin and his brothers, his nephew Buster, and a number of Alex and Randy's law partners. Each of the brothers and Buster had agreed to be formally interviewed by SLED, Alex for the second time. In an effort to ensure their recollections were independent, SLED directed the Murdaugh men into different SLED vehicles and then began the interviews simultaneously.

Alex found himself back inside the car of Special Agent David Owen. Once again, Owen was in the driver's seat and Alex was riding shotgun. Alex was wearing a golf shirt and khaki pants, and he brought a drink with him into the car. He was also chewing tobacco, and during the interview opened the car's passenger door to lean out the car and spit onto the grass.

Right away Owen asked Alex if he'd consent to a cell phone extraction, in which the police would download all the digital contents of Alex's phone, including his call logs, text messages, emails, search histories, location information, and so on. Alex handed over his phone without hesitation, not even bothering to look at his new attorney, Jim Griffin, who was sitting in the back seat beside another SLED officer. Griffin, a former federal prosecutor practicing out of Columbia, was, until a few days earlier, representing Paul Murdaugh in his boating under the influence case. That criminal case would soon be dismissed on account of Paul's death.

For this second interview, Owen asked Alex to tell him about his entire day on Monday, when his wife and son were killed. Alex's memory of his activities three days earlier was less than crisp. He spoke of other people's behavior and his general routine, but had trouble detailing his own actions. As he told Owen:

> *Monday morning, uhhh, you know, what'd I do Monday morning? Umm, my wife and my older son had gone to the baseball games that weekend. Umm, uhh, you know, I really can't remember what I did Monday morning. I know I went to work. But, you know, I think I was dragging a little bit from the weekend, and, but, I went to work, umm, I usually mess around on my farm and then I go to work. Umm, I was at work, umm, huh, you know.*

An electronic log at the law firm would reveal, later, that Alex did not arrive at the office until that afternoon, walking through the law firm doors at 12:38 P.M. He did not mention to SLED his confrontation with Jeanne Seckinger and the law firm's concern for the missing money. Alex's story was also exceedingly vague and lazy. Alex continued to babble about his day, and said, "Umm, uhh, you know, I mean I was just at my office doing [legal work]. I'm sure I could go back and probably recreate some specifics if you need me to, but, I can't, like, sit here and recall on the top of my head exactly what I was working on."

Alex then did name a case he said he reviewed, and then mentioned, too, that he spent part of that Monday preparing for the upcoming hearing for the boat crash lawsuit in which he and other family members were named as defendants. Alex then spoke of returning to Moselle in the evening and meeting Paul to tour the property. "We knocked around, for, you know, just doing things that we liked to do out there," said Alex. "You know, we're riding around, looking at, um, um, food plots, looking you know, looking, looking for hogs, little bit of target shooting, just bullshitting."

Alex segued into speaking about Paul and his habit of living across the state, keeping an apartment in Columbia, and also clothes at Moselle, on Edisto Beach, and at friends' places in Charleston, too. But Owen wanted to know more about Alex firing a gun.

"Just out of curiosity—target practice—what did you all shoot?" asked Owen.

"Just a little bottle," said Alex, misunderstanding Owen for a second. "You mean what gun? . . . A .22 Magnum . . . I think he shot two times and I shot one time."

Alex then told of meeting Maggie back at the house and eating dinner together as a family, minus Buster, who was living on his own in another part of the state. At this point in the interview Alex stopped the storytelling and said to Owen and his SLED colleague, "I don't know how much detail y'all want . . ."

"The more detail the better, sir," Owen replied.

After dinner Maggie went to the kennels, said Alex, and Paul left the house, too. He stayed put at the house. "I was watching TV, looking at my phone, and I actually fell asleep on the couch," said Alex.

Alex said he couldn't remember when he woke up, and suggested SLED check his text message activity to establish a timeline. He told Owen about hearing strange noises outside when he woke up, and he wondered if it could have been Maggie and Paul returning or possibly a "wild cat" that was known to lurk around the house at Moselle. "I'm just throwing that out there because it was in my mind," he said. Alex could not offer Owen the names of any potential suspects who might have had a grudge against Maggie or Paul. He suggested Owen ask Paul's friends about the bullying he suffered in the wake of the boat crash, when people, according to Alex, would accost Paul and say, "You little piece of shit, were you driving that boat?"

Owen didn't latch onto these ideas of wild cats and anonymous boat crash vigilantes, and he told Alex it was unlikely a stranger came to an unfamiliar property at night with a hope to ambush people. Absent other leads, Owen said he needed to "look within and then start working my way out."

"So you feel that it's not random," said Alex. "You feel like it's intentional, I mean, planned."

"I don't know what to feel right now," said Owen. "And I hate to say that. I don't know what to feel right now."

Owen said he hoped to gather more clues from the evidence collected two days earlier, all of which was being rushed for analysis at the state police lab. As he detailed some of this investigative work Alex interjected. "I wanna tell you one thing while I'm thinking about it," said Alex. "Paul was really an incredibly intuitive little dude. He was like a little detective."

The relevancy of this statement was not obvious. Owen nonetheless used the remark to ask more about Paul, inquiring whether Alex knew the password to open Paul's cell phone. Alex said he did not know, and he doubted anyone else did, either. "I can tell you that he was super super super secretive with that . . . cell phone . . ." he said. "It would surprise me greatly if somebody knows it."

Owen's SLED colleague then confirmed with Alex that the last time he saw Paul and Maggie alive "was when you all were eating supper."

"Yessir," said Alex, indicating his wife and son traveled to the dog kennels without him.

As the interview wound down the SLED agents asked Alex if he would submit to a buccal swab, which entails having a Q-tip dragged across the inside of one's cheek to obtain a DNA sample. "Do I need to spit out my tobacco?" he asked, consenting to the test.

"It might be best," said Owen.

Police were wrapping up their work, but still needed to extract data from John Marvin's cell phone. But before that happened the Murdaugh brothers and Buster were told to hurry over to Almeda on account of a sudden decline in health of Randolph "Randy" Murdaugh III. The interviews were over.

The family patriarch and longtime solicitor died that day. Now the Murdaugh family had three loved ones to lay to rest.

———

Anticipation was high the night of June 9, 1980. So were some of the marijuana smugglers who arrived that day on Hilton Head Island. Their intoxication was more than an occupational hazard—they needed drugs to calm their nerves, and pot was hardly the only illicit substance they consumed. The men were about to attempt the biggest smuggling operation of their lives.

The Lowcountry had long been a smuggler's paradise, containing countless waterways and little police presence. In the 1970s Hilton Head Island was awash with a group of hippie outlaws who came to be known as the "gentlemen smugglers." These beach bums exuded good vibes, shied away from violence, and possessed a savviness and sophistication uncommon to many career criminals. These smugglers used the same creeks and inlets as maritime scofflaws from previous eras, including pirates and rumrunners, repeatedly steering sailboats and shrimp boats south to Jamaica and Colombia, where they packed their holds with as many marijuana bales as they could squeeze inside. Then the smugglers sailed or motored home, dodging the Cuban and American navies, the United States Coast Guard, and bad weather before slipping into an isolated Eastern seaboard inlet and pulling up to a secluded dock.

Oftentimes these smugglers sailed home to the Palmetto State to offload their cargo under moonlight, hauling pot bales off the boats, along a dock, and then into waiting trucks. Occasionally smugglers packed big airplanes full of tons of pot in South America, too, and then flew them to isolated airstrips within the interior of the Lowcountry, near places like Yemassee and Allendale. The cargo coming into Hilton Head this night was a little different. A kingpin living on Hilton Head Island arranged for 30,000 pounds of Lebanese hashish to be sailed across the Mediterranean Sea and Atlantic Ocean and arrive off South Carolina shores. Now he and his hired hands just needed to transfer it from the sailboat to land. While two large sportfishing boats began ferrying sacks of hashish to an abandoned oyster factory nearby, the kingpin ordered a decoy boat to zoom conspicuously in the sound behind Hilton Head Island. The ploy worked, and soon two wildlife officers on patrol started chasing a speedboat at full throttle as it tore across the water in the dark.

The speedboat was fast, but the wildlife officers' boats were faster. Unable to outrun the police, the boat driver undertook evasive maneuvers, first maniacally steering under docks along the back of the island before ditching his vessel at a marina and running off into the night, leaving the boat and a companion behind for the police to collect. Meanwhile the hashish had been moved ashore, packed into vans, and sent rolling down the highway.

Though the pot smuggling was rampant in the Lowcountry, local arrests were rare. It was not until the federal investigation Operation Jackpot commenced in 1982 that the government began rounding up scores of smugglers, including the kingpins who eventually abandoned their beachside homes on Hilton Head Island and scattered across the world in attempts to avoid capture. This was the rare instance of Randolph "Buster" Murdaugh being out of control. The solicitor's office had nothing to do with Operation Jackpot, an investigation that led to the indictment of more than 100 people, many of them residents of the Lowcountry.

Buster might not have earned many convictions of marijuana smugglers, but he did get himself their decoy speedboat. Soon after the decoy boat was seized by the police, Buster and the wildlife commission were approached by Hilton Head Island lawyer Walter Czura, who was working on behalf of a marijuana kingpin, though he didn't disclose that. Czura told Buster he wanted to get the boat back for his anonymous client. Buster said no problem, just "tell him to pop in and say hello."

Both Buster and Czura knew the client was never going to pay a visit. From the beginning, the discussion was a "legal farce," said Czura. Every time he tried to reclaim the boat, Buster or his son Randolph "Randy" Murdaugh III, acting as an assistant solicitor, just repeated the same invitation to Czura's client: "Tell them to come on by." It ended up as a game between Czura and the Murdaughs, one that the Murdaughs were going to win. "That charade went on for months," said Czura. "It was totally absurd what was going on. They enjoyed it and I enjoyed it."

Czura wasn't getting the boat back for his client, either, because Buster had other ideas for the sporty Boston Whaler speedboat. Nine months after the boat was seized, upon a motion filed by Buster, a judge ordered the boat be "turned over" to joint custody between the state wildlife commission and the solicitor's office. Murdaugh's legal maneuver was not only bold, it was precocious. In the coming years federal prosecutors waging America's "War on Drugs," including the task force members of Operation Jackpot, would rely heavily on the tactic of seizing suspected drug smugglers' cars, boats, real estate, and cash in an effort to cripple their operations and dent their finances.

A legal title for the boat was soon issued in the name of both the wildlife commission and the solicitor, though it's unknown who took possession of the boat and how it was used. In any case, more than a year later, in August 1982, Buster applied for a new boat title, this time in the name of the solicitor alone, with the wildlife commission being listed as the boat's seller. Then, a month or so later, Buster visited a boat dealer and traded the twenty-two-foot 1979 Boston Whaler and its outboard motors for a 1982 fifteen-foot Boston Whaler with a seventy-horsepower motor. Buster, who paid an additional $640 for the new boat and equipment, according to receipts, initially applied for title to the new boat in his own name, though his name was then crossed out on the form and replaced with "Solicitor,

14th Judicial Circuit," and then amended two years later to read, "Office of the Solicitor of the 14th Judicial Circuit."

It's unknown why Buster traded the boat, but the investigator employed by the solicitor's office told Czura that the solicitor ran the seized boat aground on an oyster bank and "tore that hull up." He also said Buster would take the boat out on the water to drink beer with buddies, toss the empty cans in the water, and then shoot the floating targets with powerful, semiautomatic rifles. According to Czura, there was "zero" legitimate law enforcement use of the seized boat. And at some point the new boat owned by the solicitor of the 14th Judicial Circuit ended up tied to a dock at Buster's Island.

Though Buster took the kingpin's boat for himself, the Murdaughs were otherwise aiding accused marijuana smugglers in the early 1980s, even while a federal drug task force operated in the Lowcountry and President Ronald Reagan reinvigorated the United States' War on Drugs. Randy and his alleged half-brother Roberts Vaux, a lawyer on Hilton Head Island, together represented a reputed Lowcountry marijuana smuggler charged with federal income tax evasion charges. The client, a man who owned an airplane that inexplicably contained fuel tanks large enough to fly south of the Caribbean, was convicted of the tax charges and lost a subsequent appeal, too, unable to offer a satisfactory explanation of how he made so much money.

Buster and Randy also worked with Vaux to help Czura, who found himself accused of marijuana smuggling soon after he tried to reclaim the decoy boat from the hashish venture. The lawyer heard the news from fellow Hilton Head Island lawyer Vaux, who called Czura at his law office to tell him that he'd heard Czura's name on the news. Later the men drove over to Buster's Island, where Czura received legal counsel from Buster and two of his children, Randy and Vaux. Like many people, Czura believed the resemblance between Buster and Vaux to be striking. Beyond the physical similarity, a relationship existed between Buster and Vaux that, while not officially or typically father-son, showed signs of closeness. "It was so clear with the way he helped Roberts" that Buster was his father, said Czura, who once worked for Vaux as a law clerk. Vaux, who was hired to be an assistant solicitor in the 1980s alongside Buster and Randy, is close-lipped about his bloodline and relationships, stating, "I will not discuss private family matters."

When Czura and Vaux arrived to meet Randy and Buster at the island, Randy told Czura, "Walter, hand me a dollar." Czura handed him a bill. Randy then told Czura they now had an agreement and their conversations were shielded by attorney-client privilege.

Czura related his involvement with marijuana smugglers to Buster, Randy, and Vaux, who soon began discussing how to craft the best legal strategy and defense. Buster mentioned how he once similarly faced federal charges regarding an alleged illegal whiskey conspiracy. This kind of problem could be taken care of in state court, he said, but the feds were different, not interested in cooperating. Randy and Buster wondered nonetheless if they could make some calls on Czura's behalf. Czura was semi-astonished, realizing, "They're trying to help me get out of this."

The help and support the Murdaughs provided to Czura seemed mostly motivated by friendship. The assorted family members had mentored Czura as a young lawyer, considering him "part of the tribe," said Czura, who remembered the Murdaugh family as a whole emphasizing the importance of loyalty and staying true to one's word. "It was very flattering to me. Very odd, but flattering," said Czura. "I was very appreciative."

Yet part of the motivation, too, Czura said he surmised, was the deep grudge Buster held against the federal government and his resentment of their investigations within his five-county jurisdiction. Operation Jackpot was revealing that the smuggling occurring in Buster's backyard was frequent, blatant, and long-running, embarrassing the solicitor. In the case of Czura, who was disbarred after pleading guilty to a pot smuggling charge, Buster stood on the side of his friend, not the efforts of federal law enforcement.

Buster always had a disregard for rules he didn't enforce himself, but as he got older he developed an outright contempt for any version of the law not his own. Damn convention, social norms, legal precedent, a moral code, a personal ethos, or a judge's orders, little stopped Buster from doing what he wanted to do.

During one fall term of court, Buster allegedly faked a medical emergency in order to go deer hunting. A judge had declined to delay court for the occasion, so Buster grabbed his chest and fell to the ground in the courtroom, prompting paramedics to rush to the courthouse and place him on a stretcher, said retired SLED agent Jim McClary. When the solicitor was wheeled outside to the ambulance, his condition suddenly improved. He stood up and walked away, said McClary, before going off to hunt.

Other times he bolted out the door of the courtroom after a SLED agent whispered in his ear, telling him a chase was underway and the SLED dogs were being driven down from Columbia to track the suspect. Like his father, Buster rarely, if ever, missed a manhunt. Upon these abrupt departures Randy or another assistant solicitor would step in for Buster and continue prosecuting the cases before the court.

Buster curried favor with judges, hosting them for cooks and hunts, and toasting them at banquets. But that didn't mean he always got his way and treated them kindly. Once when a judge denied Buster something in court the solicitor responded by staring down the judge, seething as he abruptly picked up a box of criminal indictments and announced he wouldn't be calling any cases. "Ladies and gentlemen, you all can go home, court's over," said the solicitor, incensed.

Another time in court Buster kept talking, loudly, with an associate while court was in progress, said Beaufort lawyer Mike Macloskie. It was distracting, going beyond the quiet, clipped conversations that normally took place between lawyers in the courtroom. Judge Clyde Eltzroth finally tried to rein in his former law partner and mentor. He rapped his pen—Buster kept talking. He banged his fist down—Buster kept talking. The judge banged his fist down again, this time with force, and asked the solicitor to please quiet down. Buster kept on speaking to his colleague, asking, loudly, "Is that white-headed old son of a bitch talking to me?"

Buster's wrath extended to so many people. He was once seen greeting people in a crowd when the solicitor stopped suddenly and removed his hand from someone's grip. "Wait a minute, I hate you," he told the nemesis he belatedly recognized, *un*shaking his hand.

At another date he attended a funeral and asked Dayle Blackmon at the solicitor's office to give him a ride. She was perplexed; Buster didn't even like the deceased person. She asked why he was going. "I want to make sure that son of a bitch is in that coffin," replied Buster.

Sometimes Buster's friends bore the brunt of his grouchiness. One day the highway patrol communicated via police dispatch that they had a "relay" for Mr. Buster, and asked if local law enforcement officers could deliver it to the solicitor on Buster's Island. And so a package was passed among a variety of policemen, crisscrossing the state and Lowcountry as it was relayed from one patrol vehicle to the next, until it reached Dayle Blackmon's husband, Jasper County sheriff Randy Blackmon, who had agreed to run the final leg. He arrived at the island just about sunset, a little after 8:30 P.M. The sheriff presented the long-traveled relay to Buster—a bunch of small, homegrown cucumbers just perfect for pickling.

Randy Blackmon knew Buster loved to make bread and butter pickles, yet Buster did not look pleased to see him when the solicitor opened the door. "Do you know what damn time it is?" asked the annoyed solicitor, proceeding to berate the sheriff for showing up after his bedtime and waking him up. The tongue lashing was so searing the sheriff decided just about everything could wait until the next day with Buster.

In the courtroom Buster was more discreet with his scolding. Once during a criminal term of court in Jasper County, Randy Blackmon took exception to something Buster said or did, grimacing in response. Buster took notice and motioned for the sheriff to come close. Buster then grabbed hold of Blackmon's earlobe and pulled the sheriff's head down to his own. "It's your job to make the case, it's my job to dispose of it," said Buster. "Do you understand?"

Other days the solicitor was considerably more lighthearted, and often inappropriate. The Blackmons witnessed Buster say many outrageous things, such as when Buster and Randy Blackmon were in court in Jasper County, seated on each side of a nightclub owner facing drug charges. The woman was wearing bright yellow patent leather heels that caught the solicitor's eye. "Those sure are some nice, fine high-heel shoes you're wearing," said Buster.

"Thank you, solicitor," said the woman.

"If I were you," he told her, "I'd stick them right up the sheriff's ass."

Once Buster spied a court reporter with a typewriter on her lap and remarked, apropos of nothing, "I bet that's the hardest thing she ever had between her legs." Another time a different woman caught his attention. He noticed her sexually, but fantasized about the verdict she might render in place of her body. "Who's that big-tittied woman?" he asked. "She'd be good on a jury."

It was often difficult to tell whether Buster was serious or joking. Buster once complained to a judge that a defense attorney allowed a chart to be inappropriately seen by the jury. "Your honor, that's highly improper," said the solicitor. "That's like something I would have done." Beaufort lawyer Macloskie said Buster once appeared unexpectedly in federal court to advise a fellow attorney during juror selection. The judge was not too pleased to see Buster, telling him, "I better not catch you fixing one of my juries."

"Don't worry, judge," said Buster. "You can't catch me."

Buster's wit could be amusing, but his interactions consistently betrayed a corrosiveness that was unsettling when fully appreciated. Macloskie might laugh at a story about his old friend, Buster, but he might also reflect, "Well, that ain't funny." Macloskie acknowledged the solicitor was sometimes crooked, fixing juries and dropping criminal charges in exchange for money or a favor. "Buster was flawed," he said, "there's no question about it."

Buster said and did so many semi-scandalous things on an everyday basis that almost any bad behavior seemed semi-plausible. One Lowcountry lawyer said he only believed about half of Buster's boasts, and that was enough to keep him stunned. "Buster would tell you things stone-cold sober that Adolf Hitler would not admit drunk," quipped the lawyer. Among Buster's more shocking claims was that he hired two Black men to kill pregnant Ruth Vaux before she revealed to Buster's wife, Gladys, that she was carrying Buster's child. The men took the money but never pulled a trigger, said the lawyer.

Buster told another man much of the same, that he solicited the killing of his mistress and unborn son. This confession occurred during a car ride, when Buster began spilling secrets by drunkenly disclosing his affair with Ruth Vaux in 1945 and claiming paternity of Roberts Vaux. This was a shocking disclosure on its own, but then Buster added that he had once asked a Black man in a liquor store to shoot Ruth as she sat on his porch and confessed their romantic affair to Gladys. The solicitor promised the man he would not spend one day in jail.

In this version of the murder conspiracy the plot also fizzled, supposedly because Buster's hastily hired hitman could not attempt a shot at Ruth Vaux without endangering Gladys. When the would-be killer told Buster this, Buster claimed to have acknowledged that he did not wish for Gladys to get caught in a crossfire, no matter how badly he wanted Ruth's lips sealed. Conspiring to kill his mistress and their child in utero was one thing, but to sacrifice his wife to cover up his own sins was, even for a predator like Buster, a step too far.

———

In the wake of the murders of Maggie and Paul the law firm locked its doors. The employees watched for unfamiliar characters and warned each other to stay inside when a suspicious car circled the block. The atmosphere at the law firm was "very scary," said the law firm's chief financial officer, Jeanne Seckinger. "Nothing happened at work that week . . . nobody knew what was going on." Her colleague Annette Griswold said the firm was especially protective of Alex and his brother, fearing that someone may have a vendetta against the entire family. "We were in complete Momma Bear mode" for Alex and Randy, said Griswold. "We were scared for them."

The Hampton community was scared and stunned as well. Hundreds of people showed up for the Murdaugh family members' funerals, first for Maggie and Paul, then for Randolph "Randy" Murdaugh III a few days later. Uniformed law enforcement officers were noticeably present, standing at attention to pay their respects, provide security, and keep out the media. The unsolved killings had become a national news story overnight; the general public was astonished that so much tragedy was befalling such a prominent family.

Ten days after Maggie and Paul were shot to death, Alex's brothers appeared in an ABC News interview that aired on the morning television show *Good Morning America*. Randolph "Randy" Murdaugh IV and John Marvin Murdaugh said they were at a loss to think of who might have targeted their family. The men denied that anyone in their family acted improperly in the aftermath of the 2019 boat crash and said the media narrative establishing the Murdaughs as an influential Southern clan was incorrect. "I see words like 'dynasty' used, and 'power,' and I don't know exactly how people use those words, but we're just regular people, and we're hurting just like they would be hurting if this had happened to them," said Randy.

Alex in particular was hurting, said his brothers. "He's upright and looks strong and making his way and then, then he just breaks down," said John Marvin.

"It changes you as a family, and I can't imagine the horror my brother is experiencing," said Randy. "The person that did this is out there."

Randy spoke to SLED often about the open murder case in the weeks after the crime. He and Alex's law partner Mark Ball said he, too, was often trying to make sense of what happened that night at Moselle. Yet Alex would not become a little detective himself, leaving it to police to find the killers and scrounge up clues. He failed to make a list of the firearms he owned, as requested by police, making it more difficult for investigators to determine which weapons exactly were used to blow apart his wife and son. Some people were struck that Alex didn't seem appropriately concerned for Buster's safety, either, given a killer was on the loose. "Everybody was afraid and Alex didn't seem to be afraid," said Maggie's sister Marian Proctor.

When Alex called SLED agent David Owen in midsummer, it was to ask if he could have his personal vehicle returned to him. Owen said no. Besides missing a seatbelt, the Chevrolet Suburban was inoperable. Unknown to Alex, police removed the computer and navigation systems from the vehicle and provided them to the FBI. Experts were using the devices to develop a computer program that could interpret trip data and produce a timeline of Alex starting and stopping his car that night.

Owen and Murdaugh agreed to meet later in the summer, after Alex returned from a vacation with his in-laws to Florida. Despite the conspicuous absence of Maggie and Paul, who had been dead for weeks, Alex did not display much interest in solving the crime when visiting and vacationing with Maggie's family, either. Instead he was preoccupied with posthumously clearing Paul of any wrongdoing in the fatal 2019 boat crash and getting Buster reenrolled at law school. "I thought that was so strange because my number one goal was to find out who killed my sister and Paul," said Proctor. "We never talked about finding the person who could have done it . . . I don't know how he could have thought of anything else." On the limited occasions they did discuss the killings, Alex told Proctor that he felt "whoever did it had thought about it for a really long time."

When he returned home, Alex appeared to sink into a prolonged state of grief, inspiring worry among his loved ones and law firm colleagues. His workload decreased dramatically and his presence in the office was spotty. Sometimes he'd arrive at the office merely to read sympathy cards and cry at his desk. His behavior was erratic, inspiring pity. Consequently the confusion with Alex regarding the missing money was forgotten by employees of the law firm for the time being, its resolution indefinitely delayed. Similarly, proceedings in the boat crash lawsuit were disrupted on account of the Murdaugh deaths, delaying a potential order from a judge compelling Alex to share his finances.

Yet while Alex appeared to wallow in grief and struggled to resume legal work, he made sure to complete a few key tasks after the killings, some of which involved one of his mother's caretakers, Mushelle "Shelly" Smith, who worked the occasional night shift at Almeda. Smith was working the night Maggie and Paul were slain and spoke with Alex as he visited his mother. She remembers Alex visiting for twenty minutes, though when she saw Alex during a funeral reception for his father just six days after the murder, he initiated conversation with her and oddly insisted he had visited for twice as long. "If someone asks you, I was here for thirty to forty minutes," he said. The conversation so unsettled Smith she called her brother, a local police officer, to relay the story. Alex also offered her help getting work and paying for her upcoming wedding.

A few days later Shelly saw Alex again. At 6:30 one morning, as her night shift was coming to a close, she heard a knocking on the side of the house. It was Alex, asking to be let inside. When he entered he was carrying what appeared to be a blue plastic tarp, which was balled up between his hands. He went upstairs, not explaining his actions, and then went outside, where Shelly observed him moving assorted trucks and all-terrain vehicles, though her vantage point from the house was sometimes obstructed by tents and other vehicles still on site from the funeral reception. This was strange; Alex never visited his parents' house that early.

Alex made time for squaring away a few pressing financial issues, too. He borrowed $250,000 from his law partner John E. Parker, as well as more money from Palmetto State Bank, where childhood friend Russell Laffitte helped him secure a rushed second mortgage of $750,000 on his beach house to make supposed improvements to the property. This million dollars left Alex's bank accounts nearly as soon as the money arrived. About $400,000 was applied to his Palmetto State Bank checking account to erase a massive overdraft. Then Alex sent the remaining $600,000 to Chris Wilson as a partial repayment of the $792,000 in fees he had previously been paid directly from the trucking case the friends had handled together. Alex explained to Wilson he had bungled investing the money properly in annuities and couldn't immediately retrieve the additional $192,000 he owed him. Alex persuaded Wilson to loan him the money and send the full amount to Alex's law firm, putting an end to that inquiry.

But now he had new debts to satisfy, millions of dollars in stolen funds to potentially answer for, and another interview with police looming. Alex Murdaugh and his friend and fellow lawyer Cory Fleming visited SLED's office in Walterboro the morning of August 11, 2021, to meet with Special Agent David Owen. The men sat in a conference room, where Fleming quickly became combative when Owen posed questions, telling the investigator Alex was looking to learn information, not provide it. "I'm not comfortable with you asking him questions as a suspect," he said, asking if SLED did consider Alex a suspect.

Owen replied calmly that every homicide investigation begins with the people who found the bodies. Until these people can be cleared of wrong-doing, Owen said, they cannot exit the circle of suspicion. At this point, said Owen, "I cannot get Alex out." Fleming relented and said that sounded reasonable, although he scoffed at law enforcement believing any of the many rumors circulating about the Murdaughs and their possible culpability in a variety of unnatural deaths. "I don't read it, but, uh, everybody in the United States of America has an opinion on this case, and because

I know everybody I know it's a bunch of bullshit," said Fleming. "I can't imagine you all are going to be asking about nonsense on the Internet."

But Alex said he had no reservations about Owen asking him questions—"Anything to help!"—and the third and final session between the men began. Like twice before, Alex told Owen he did not accompany Maggie and Paul to the kennels, stating, "I stayed on the couch and I dozed off." After plowing this familiar ground, the interview took a few turns. Owen showed Alex the video Paul took and shared with friends the evening he died, in which Alex is standing next to the bending tree, dressed in a blue shirt, khaki pants, and leather boat shoes. When did you change into the white T-shirt, shorts, and sneakers, Owen wanted to know.

"I'm not sure, you know, it would have been . . . it would have been, what time of day was that, I would have thought I'd already changed," said Alex, before answering, finally, "I guess I changed when I got back to the house."

The interview lasted for more than an hour. Owen mentioned that Paul's friend Rogan Gibson said he heard Alex in the background when Paul talked with him by phone from the kennels, moments before Paul was believed to have been killed. This surprised Alex. Owen mentioned, too, that the investigation had so far failed to yield any foreign DNA or fingerprints. Any impressions of tire treads or footwear were obliterated by rainfall. In sum, SLED had identified no one to consider as a suspect beyond the man who found his family members dead on the ground. Finally, just before Alex left, Owen sprung a final, unexpected question, resulting in a tense exchange that capped their conversations together.

"Did you kill Maggie?" asked Owen.

"No!" said Alex, stunned. "Did I kill my wife?"

"Yessir."

"No, David!"

"Do you know who did?"

"No, I do NOT know who did."

"Did you kill Paul?"

"No, I did NOT kill Paul."

"Do you know who did?"

"No, sir, I do NOT know who did. Do you think I killed Maggie?"

At this query Agent Owen moved his hands, making a more-or-less-type motion. "I have to go where the evidence and the facts take me," he said.

"I understand that," said Alex. "Do you think I killed Paul?"

"I have to go where the evidence and the facts take me, and I don't have anything that points to anyone else at this time."

"So does that mean that I am a suspect?"

"You are still in this."

———

The letters flooded into the governor's office from the Lowcountry. They came from at least five town councils, two county councils, a bar association, and the local state representative and state senator. They all asked for the same thing: please appoint Randolph "Randy" Murdaugh III the next solicitor of South Carolina's 14th Judicial Circuit. God help the governor if he didn't choose Randy to replace his father, who was due to retire at the end of 1986 after more than forty-six years as solicitor.

Randolph "Buster" Murdaugh Jr. claimed the form letters signed by so many local politicians did not originate from his office, that their distribution was coordinated by others. He would soon turn seventy-two years old—the mandatory retirement age for South Carolina solicitors. It seemed natural to him that his son would take his place. Randy had been following Buster to work at courthouses since the boy could walk. He had also been a part-time solicitor for the last twenty-two years, trying criminal cases alongside his father since graduating from law school. The governor gave Randy the nod, not having much of a choice; no one else dared ask for the office. Just before he assumed control in 1987, the new solicitor offered what, in his mind at least, was reassurance to the public, saying, "I expect things not to be a whole lot different from what they are now."

Indeed, before he even took office Randolph announced he'd be hiring his father as a part-time solicitor, completing an exchange of their roles. "I know I am going to need him and want him to be here," said Randy. "My father and I have a fine relationship, always have . . . He amazes me. He's definitely one of a kind in a courtroom. I learn something new from him every time I see him."

Buster left office on a high note, feted at his retirement dinner by Governor Carroll A. Campbell Jr., who said Buster's departure from elected office is the "ending of an era . . . a dynasty . . . the changing of the guard." A few years earlier, upon Buster's fortieth year in office, Campbell stopped by that dinner party, too, along with more than 700 other people, all paying $10 for a barbecue dinner and the chance to hear speaker after speaker praise Hampton's forever solicitor. Buster was used to this sort of thing. In 1985 he attended a law enforcement banquet in honor of the scandal-prone Hampton County sheriff Rudy Loadholt. Somehow Murdaugh became the center of attention, and the sheriff began lauding Buster for never letting him down when he needed help. "I consider Mr. Murdaugh one of my best friends," said Loadholt. "When you've got a problem, go to Big Daddy and he'll take care of it for you."

Buster offered his own remarks that night and, for whatever reason, felt inspired to go on the warpath. He chastised the Hampton newspaper for its negative coverage of Loadholt and then told the sheriff to "ignore anybody who criticizes you." He complained of another sheriff and a local politician both being constant drunks. He demeaned another sheriff because he was a Republican. He stated he remained friends with yet another sheriff who had recently been removed from office for misconduct. After all that he told of how the one local official makes him "hold his nose and vomit every time I see him." The charm was wearing thin with Buster.

Rather than fade away quietly after his retirement, Buster remained fully engaged, working in the solicitor's office and then rejoining the law

firm. Business was booming at the practice started by his father. As Buster
boasted in testimony to a state legislative commission:

> *You can't draw much—you legislators have made it where we can't*
> *draw but about $8,000 a year as an assistant [solicitor] drawing*
> *retirement [pay]; so I started practicing law again and I found out*
> *it's more lucrative than it was when I quit practicing to take full-*
> *time solicitor. I've got a bunch of young boys in the office that are*
> *making me an awful lot of money.*

The success of the old family firm further emboldened Buster. In his final
years practicing law he could be as impudent as ever, realizing he rarely
suffered the consequences of anything he said or did. He instructed shop-
lifting charges be dropped against one suspect who he needed as a witness
for a slip-and-fall civil lawsuit, said former prosecutor Jared Newman. He
became infuriated when a state trooper refused to drop an open container
charge against his grandson, Alex, his lip quivering over the lack of cooperation, according to another lawyer. Once this same lawyer defended a
client on drunk driving charges. When he saw that assistant solicitor Buster
Murdaugh would be prosecuting the case he said, "It scared the hell out of
me." But this version of Buster wasn't interested in seriously practicing law.
During a jury trial he trotted out one of his tired arguments, telling the
jury that if they didn't convict the defendant they might as well just hang
a big sign outside of town that says, WE LOVE DRUNK DRIVERS.

The judge stopped the trial and called Buster and the defense lawyer
to the bench. The judge asked why Buster would repeat the same type of
argument for which he had been twice overturned by the South Carolina
Supreme Court, most recently in 1981 when the state supreme court overturned Buster's hard-earned death penalty sentences of John Plath and
John Arnold, who were convicted of the brutal murder of a hitchhiker in
Beaufort County. The court found Buster's argument improperly appealed

to "personal prejudice," and in its decision made a point to note "the same solicitor made an almost identical mistake twenty years ago in State v. Davis," referencing the overturned conviction and death penalty of the White Marine accused of raping an older Black woman in Beaufort in 1959.

Explaining himself to the judge presiding over the drunk driving case, Buster said he just could not help himself. As he and the opposing lawyer walked back to the lawyers' tables, Buster said to him, "Okay, man, you've got a winner now," knowing he had poisoned the case, perhaps even by design.

Inevitably, even hard-charging Buster Murdaugh slowed down. Sheryl McKinney, who finished her career as a municipal judge in Hampton County municipalities, said she was working as a clerk at the magistrate's office in Hampton County in the late 1990s when Buster unexpectedly asked to see her. He was very old and relied on a walker to move. He had attached a spit cup to the walker to collect the tobacco juice that still streamed out his mouth.

"I came to tell you something before I die," said Buster. "I want to apologize to you for what Johnny Glenn did to you all."

Sheryl was stunned. Buster's brother had been dead for ten years, and she had been free of his clutches for much longer than that. She did not expect to see Buster that day, and she did not expect him to ever acknowledge her suffering from long ago. Sheryl began to cry as Buster started scooting away. "Couldn't do anything about it then and can't do anything about it now," he said in parting, not bothering to hear any reply Sheryl might make.

In 1997 Gladys Murdaugh died. Buster was heartbroken to the point he lost his sense of humor. He would not last long without her. Half a year after his wife's death Buster was in the hospital in Hampton, close to the end himself. His friend Mike Macloskie paid him a visit. Randy was in the room and the men hugged and cried. Buster didn't look too good. The fight had finally left him. "That's the only time I saw Buster scared," said Macloskie. "There was no power in that face at all. It was all fear." Buster died a day or two later, on February 5, 1998, at the age of eighty-three.

Buster was a creature of the swamps he ruled, slippery and hard to catch, unafraid to roll in the mud, nasty when cornered, and ruthless on the hunt. His friend Macloskie reflected that Buster was part of a loose group of men who "didn't control what happened in South Carolina, but they had a lot to do with it.

"If he had been born any earlier, someone would have killed him," said Macloskie. "If he was born any later, they'd have locked his ass up."

———

On May 10, 1998, Diaz Scoggins had one hell of a Mother's Day. She woke to learn her twenty-two-year-old son, Jimmy Carroll, had been injured early that morning in a boat accident on the Chechessee River. Emergency responders first rushed him by ambulance to Beaufort Memorial Hospital. There doctors discovered Carroll's head and brain injuries to be much more severe than anticipated and immediately arranged for the man to be transferred by helicopter to Savannah Memorial hospital, across the state line in Georgia.

The night before Carroll had gone to a party hosted by the Murdaugh family on Buster's Island. Buster had died three months earlier, and his surviving family opted to keep the property and continue enjoying the outpost in the marsh. Carroll came to the party about 10:30 P.M. with four friends, including Brent Evans and John Rhodes Jr., who had been invited to the party earlier that day when Rhodes encountered Buster's grandson, John Marvin Murdaugh, while boating.

The friends mingled with the hundred or so other guests and each consumed a handful of alcoholic drinks. "The party was going good," Evans later told police. "There were a lot of people there I haven't seen in a while." As it approached 2:00 A.M., the friends readied to leave. Though they had arrived by car, Rhodes asked John Marvin Murdaugh if he could borrow a boat to travel to his family home on a nearby creek about five miles away.

John Marvin agreed and walked with Rhodes, Evans, Carroll, and two other friends down a boat dock to a fifteen-foot Boston Whaler. The men loaded a cooler with beer aboard and started the boat's outboard motor. They let the seventy-horsepower motor warm up while John Marvin, under a full moon, offered some pointers on the boat's use. Life preservers were on board, he told Rhodes, but the boat's navigation lights, which are required by state law when operating in darkness, were broken. Before saying goodbye, John Marvin handed the boaters a cell phone and a flashlight to help them on their journey, just in case.

With Rhodes at the helm, the boat motored away from the dock and out of the creek, soon hitting nearly full speed as it traveled up the Chechessee River. Each of the other men had staked out a spot on the boat, with Carroll, a former high school quarterback, standing at the bow. The boat soon passed under a bridge and the adjacent Lemon Island Marina at a brisk pace. Moments later Rhodes slowed the boat to half throttle and began to cruise at about twenty to twenty-five miles per hour. Carroll, in one of his final memories from that night, remembers his buddy Rhodes yelling to him, "Sit down, Jim, we're fixing to hit some shallow water."

The boat borrowed from the Murdaughs was approaching the appropriately named Hazzard Creek, which the boaters knew to be wide but shallow, especially at low tide, and that its shoals or mudbars could shift location. Evans had years of experience in the creek and had scraped bottom before. It could be difficult to navigate, he said, as you "have to be able to go right through in the right place."

As the young men cruised up the creek Evans suggested that Rhodes, also an experienced local boater, "go left some." The advice came too late. Suddenly the boat's hull or propeller struck something below the water, likely muddy river bottom, instantly halting the vessel. All the men lurched forward. One friend "flew" between Evans and himself, said Rhodes, who stuck out his arm in an attempt to grab him. Carroll fell out of the boat entirely, tumbling over the starboard side of the bow. Yet as soon as the boat stopped the vessel started forward again, clearing the obstacle and cruising through open water. The collision, said Rhodes, was over before he could even ease up on the throttle.

As the friends onboard collected themselves, they realized they were a man down. Rhodes turned the boat around and spotted Carroll in the distance, about 100 yards away in shallow water. They motored toward him and soon realized the former athlete was struggling to stand and, according to Evans, was "walking around in sort of a daze." What's more, Carroll was bleeding heavily on his forehead and the right side of his face.

Realizing Carroll's injuries were severe, his friends laid him down in the boat. They stripped off their shirts and blanketed Carroll in an effort to keep him warm, the garments soon becoming soaked with saltwater and blood. The friends conversed with Carroll, who remained conscious and coherent, and Evans attempted calling 911 on the cell phone. Seeking the quickest way to emergency aid, Rhodes drove the boat back toward the marina and bridge they had passed after leaving Buster's Island. While two friends attended to Carroll, Rhodes and Evans threw the alcohol in the cooler overboard, with Rhodes later stating that he was fearful "that we may be taken to jail because of the beers."

"I know and understand that this should not have happened," he told police, "but at the time I was in shock and all I was thinking and concerned about was Jim's safety."

As the friends neared the bridge and Lemon Island Marina they spotted a boat in the distance—it was John Marvin, who had decided to take a late-night cruise with a friend on board the family boat *Guilty Verdict*. As the boats rendezvoused John Marvin became aware of Carroll's injury and immediately called for help.

"Mayday, mayday . . . Coast Guard Savannah, Coast Guard Savannah, this is *Guilty Verdict*. Ah, come back please . . ." said Murdaugh, speaking calmly as he attempted to establish contact via radio. "We've got an injured passenger on the Chechessee River. We need some help at Lemon Island

Marina. If you could call someone and an ambulance we need some help, please."

As Murdaugh repeatedly asked for an ambulance, he and Rhodes piloted each of their boats to the marina. Dispatchers asked the boaters' location and the extent of Carroll's injuries, directing the men to apply pressure to the wound on his forehead.

"Could you tell me what's wrong with the subject. I want to know what happened to him and what kind of condition is he in," said one emergency official via radio.

"We have a guy that has, has a cut on his forehead and its pretty serious," John Marvin replied. "If you can get an ambulance here it'd be great."

Minutes later the boats reached the marina. Rhodes beached his boat near the landing and Evans jumped out and ran to the top of the ramp, where he called 911 again on the cell phone. Once emergency workers arrived Carroll walked to the ambulance, with Rhodes supporting him on one side and an emergency medical technician on the other. The ambulance departed with Carroll at 3:26 A.M., taking him to the local hospital in Beaufort, where it was discovered that Carroll had experienced severe trauma to his head. Carroll was flown to the Savannah hospital where he underwent a lobotomy to remove his brain's left frontal lobe.

Back at the marina and boat landing, police arrived and began asking the men questions about Carroll's injury. The police performed a sobriety test on the driver of the boat, Rhodes, evaluating his speech, balance, and gaze. Rhodes passed the test. Their questions exhausted for the time being, law enforcement officers gave the stranded men a ride back to Buster's Island, leaving the fifteen-foot Boston Whaler and *Guilty Verdict* tied to a dock beside the boat ramp.

In the aftermath of the accident, investigators with the South Carolina Department of Natural Resources visited the crash site in daylight, examined the blood-streaked boat, and interviewed the witnesses to the accident. They determined the boat was owned by the 14th Circuit Solicitor's

Office, the vessel obtained years earlier when Buster Murdaugh traded it for the speedboat seized from marijuana smugglers. Despite the severity of the young man's injury, the presence of empty beer cans on board the boat, and the fact that the boat owned by the solicitor's office was being operated by friends of the solicitor's son, the investigation file shows no record of any interview with Solicitor Randolph Murdaugh III, any of his employees, or any family members aside from John Marvin.

Some of the investigators' reports contain conflicting information. A man named Wiley Bell was not listed as being a passenger in a preliminary report of the accident, and investigator D. Allen Trapp notes in one report that boat passenger Travis Reynolds said, "there was talk among the group w/ John (Marvin) Murdock (sic) taking an active part to get stories straight and possibly omit some of the people on board."

Bell's fellow boaters did mention his presence on the boat in interviews days after the accident, though assorted people referred to Wiley Bell as Wylie Bell, Willie Bell, and Wylie Garbade. The latter surname appears elsewhere in the boat accident reports. Investigator Trapp noted in a memorandum that he was assigned the case on account of a "request from (Department of Natural Resources) District Nine Captain D. Henry Garbade" due to Carroll's serious injuries. Garbade said he is unaware of Mr. Bell and has no known relationship to him.

There are no records indicating Bell was interviewed by law enforcement. Every other man aboard the Boston Whaler was interviewed, including the injured Carroll, who investigators visited as he convalesced at his family's home a month and a half after the accident. Carroll was unable to provide investigators with a written account of the accident because of his injuries, which investigators described as "severe trauma to head." Part of the accident reports include a list of unanswered questions written by investigator Trapp, including, "Where's Wylie Bell?"

Ultimately the department decided the boat's driver, John Rhodes, broke no laws that contributed to the accident. He was charged, however, for safety violations, including operating a boat without running lights, a fire extinguisher, or enough lifejackets or personal flotation devices. He paid $225 in fines.

More than twenty years after the accident, few people wish to discuss how Carroll was injured. One limited exception is the passenger Reynolds, who shared a written statement about that night.

"I will only tell you this," said Reynolds. "If it weren't for John Marvin Murdaugh on the night of the accident, Jim Carroll would probably be dead. John Marvin got the EMS services there within minutes of the accident happening. We didn't have a radio on the boat with us and cell phones weren't a big thing then. John Marvin was our guardian angel that night."

The boat's location since the accident is unknown. A spokesman for the 14th Circuit solicitor says the office has not owned a boat since at least 2006, just after Randolph Murdaugh III retired from public office.

When it comes to Jim Carroll, investigators determined he likely fell forward over the bow of the boat when the vessel momentarily slowed as the bottom of its hull or outboard motor cut through a mud flat. As the boat quickly regained its speed investigators concluded Carroll was run over and struck in the forehead by the bottom of the outboard motor. Carroll's life has never been the same since the accident and the emergency surgery on his brain.

His mother Diaz Scoggins said her family has struggled in the long, still-rippling wake of the accident, especially her son. Carroll does not remember being injured, she said, and can only recall a few things immediately afterward. His injuries can prompt personality changes and poor behavior. While her son has worked occasionally as a landscaper since his injury, Carroll has difficulty finding and keeping other jobs, she said, often due to unreliability. More than twenty-five years after the accident, Carroll is still prone to headaches. About once a week, said Scoggins, the headaches become so debilitating that Carroll is bedridden.

Though Scoggins doesn't suffer the physical pain her son endures, the emotional toll has been heavy. "I think about it every day," she says of the accident. Not that she's asking for pity. Even in her darkest hour, she said, she never feared she would lose her boy. "My faith kicked in, and I was protected from that."

It always could be worse. "He's upright," she said.

———

Alex walked out of SLED's Lowcountry office a free man. State police investigators may have had their suspicions about the widower, but agents were nowhere near making an arrest. Suspicion fell on Alex only by default, by virtue of the fact that he discovered his loved one's bodies. SLED had found nothing that linked him, or anyone else, to the killings.

It wasn't for lack of trying. Police obtained phone records and DNA samples from several people in the Murdaugh's orbit, including caretakers employed at Moselle, two men associated with the boat crash, and Alex's alleged opioid supplier Curtis Edward Smith. None became a suspect. SLED used all-terrain vehicles to search Moselle and sent its divers into the property's shallow ponds, where they walked on their hands and knees in pursuit of murder weapons. They searched nearby swamps and creeks, too, but never found a discarded shotgun or rifle. Once a tip came in from a man who briefly pulled what he believed to be a shotgun out of a creek using a magnet and string, the object slipping back beneath the surface before he could grab it. When SLED divers arrived they recovered the supposed firearm, which turned out to be a metal pipe that looked like a shotgun barrel. Law enforcement was not unaware of the challenge they faced in recovering any missing weapons. If there's a place to dump some guns, it's in the South Carolina Lowcountry, said state prosecutor Creighton Waters. "There's a swamp every fifteen feet in Hampton County and the ocean nearby."

Waters worked at the state attorney general's office in Columbia and had been following the Murdaugh murder case from afar since the day after the killings, when a SLED officer called him as a courtesy and told him Paul Murdaugh and his mother had been killed. As the chief attorney for the state grand jury, Waters was familiar with the Murdaugh family, given the investigation already underway into Lowcountry police officers' actions in the aftermath of the boat crash involving Paul. In the middle of August, however, he was suddenly placed in charge of prosecuting the double-homicide case after the 14th Circuit solicitor recused his office, stepping away because volunteer assistant solicitor Alex Murdaugh was plausibly involved in the killings of his family members.

Waters had worked as a prosecutor in the attorney general's office for more than twenty years, never tiring of the work. As a young man, he had ambitions to be a criminal defense lawyer, where he was "going to get all the innocent people out of jail." But after a clerkship and other legal experience, Waters changed his mind. "I realized along the way that most of them were freaking guilty," he said. "So I decided to become a prosecutor instead."

Waters gave off the vibe of a spirited and buttoned-up Boy Scout, self-assured in his mission of stamping out wrongdoing in South Carolina, including malfeasance in its legal community. A law degree, he said, isn't a license to abuse the legal system and engage in gamesmanship at the expense of the truth. Though indictments couldn't change the past, he believed criminal accountability could affect the future. "Misconduct can lead to a unique opportunity to make things better," the prosecutor once said while seated in a conference room within the attorney general's office. "We believe that around here."

Waters was once more rebellious in nature. He grew up in Columbia, the son of a lawyer and a Women's and Gender Studies professor, and in high school was a smart kid with long hair and a small mustache who smoked cigarettes and played in a rock band by the name of Sludge Muffin. When Sludge Muffin crumbled Waters moved on to new bands, including Due Process in college and Zero Tolerance in law school—names that foretold his destiny as a prosecutor. He earned undergraduate and law degrees from the University of South Carolina, trailing Alex Murdaugh by two years. Though his personality was sober in court, Waters cut loose on stage even into his fifties, playing guitar in two bands.

While Waters acquainted himself with the case, injecting fresh enthusiasm into the investigation, Alex was buckling. His friends and coworkers witnessed his deterioration. By late summer 2021, more than two months after the murders, Alex was barely coming to the law firm. When he did come to work, he often fell asleep in his office chair, the sleeping pills and other medications he consumed, and exhaustion, finally kicking in. He was sleeping among the houses of loved ones, keeping an extended closet of clothing across Hampton and the Lowcountry, much like Paul did. He never spent a night at Moselle after the murders and instead paid his friend and housekeeper Blanca Turrubiate-Simpson to live there with her husband. Taking care of the dogs and the immense property made for a lot of chores. It took more than two days to cut the grass alone.

Alex and his family were increasingly the subject of news reports and community speculation. The family of Gloria Satterfield became suspicious of Alex's repeated delays and dodges related to the wrongful death lawsuit and found their champions in lawyers Eric Bland and Ronnie Richter, who began working to uncover the methods Alex used to steal money from the heirs of his children's former nanny. Slick, smart, and eager to attract attention, Bland would soon initiate a colorful public blitz against Alex Murdaugh as he pursued money taken from his clients.

Also potentially problematic for Alex and his family was SLED's decision to open an investigation into the unsolved roadway death of Hampton teenager Stephen Smith. Two weeks after the deaths at Moselle, SLED said they decided to follow up on the state highway patrol's investigation of Smith's death due to "information gathered during the course of the double murder investigation of Paul and Maggie Murdaugh."

Money remained a problem, too—Alex never had enough. A board member of Palmetto State Bank became concerned that Alex owed the bank large sums of money but wasn't working. He and other board members became upset when they learned about Alex's huge overdraft and that Alex was extended a $750,000 mortgage in irregular fashion. Yet Alex had his defenders on the Palmetto State Bank board, including president Russell Laffitte and his father, bank chairman Charlie Laffitte, who once finally stifled dissent concerning loans to Alex by stating at a board meeting, "We've given him this, and if he comes back and wants more, we will give him some more."

Given all these things swirling about Alex in his battered state, Chris Wilson became concerned that his old friend might attempt suicide. Beyond losing a friend, Wilson would also forfeit the $192,000 he had informally loaned Alex to cover the fees owed to his law firm, there being no official record of their transaction. Wilson finally asked Alex if he'd mind recording the loan. "Bo', I hate to even ask you to do this, but can we do this?" said Wilson. Alex grabbed a pen and wrote out the details in three sentences, "nothing formal or fancy," said Wilson.

Any relief Wilson might have felt was short-lived. He soon received a phone call from a partner at the Hampton law firm with shocking news: Alex had been fired for stealing. His schemes were exposed when paralegal Annette Griswold said she went into Alex's office and disturbed a check that "floated like a feather to the ground." The $224,000 check was from Chris Wilson's law firm directly to Alex, which violated law firm rules. Instantly she and a few of her colleagues knew Alex had lied to them because he had taken the missing money. Jeanne Seckinger began looking into other cases handled by Alex and noticed troubling signs that Alex had likely stolen from a number of clients. "I'm about to throw up, you need to come over here," Seckinger said aloud to a law partner.

The law firm's partners held an emergency meeting the next morning, Friday, September 3, 2021, at one of their homes. Alex was not invited. Confronted with evidence that Alex steered clients' settlement money to his own accounts, the partners decided he must go. Danny Henderson and Randy Murdaugh were dispatched to confront Alex, who admitted to stealing from clients and abusing opioids for years. He agreed to resign that day.

The law firm, however, decided to delay the announcement of Alex's departure until the next week, on Labor Day. The firm's senior partner, John E. Parker, was getting married over Labor Day weekend, and besides, the firm would prefer to have more time to prepare for the turmoil and speculation that would no doubt follow the announcement of Alex's termination. But the law firm was not scripting this narrative. Alex had other plans, and there would be no shrinking from the bright spotlight about to be pointed Hampton's way.

After Chris Wilson was told of Alex's alleged crimes he called and called and called his longtime friend. He demanded Alex give him an explanation face-to-face. Alex resisted, and only when Wilson started driving toward the Lowcountry did Alex agree to speak with him at his mother's house in Almeda. Alex sat on the porch with Wilson and told his friend that a twenty-year addiction to opioids motivated him to steal. "I shit you up," Alex told Wilson. "I shit a lot of people up."

Alex's remorse was short-lived. After parting ways with his dejected friend at Almeda, Alex set in motion another ruse, almost as if it was instinctual for him to deceive. He arranged for Curtis Edward Smith to meet with him on a rural roadside outside of Hampton, near a church. There a gun was fired and Alex suffered a non-life-threatening gunshot wound to the head that sent him to a hospital in Savannah via helicopter. When police talked to Alex he said he had stopped to change a car tire when an unknown man drove by and shot him.

The story was suspicious. Even a passing motorist who saw Alex bloodied on the side of the road was wary, declining to stop but calling 911 to report the incident that she said seemed like a "setup." Things soon began unraveling for Alex. After an especially speedy recovery from a gunshot wound to the head, Alex left the hospital for a detox center, releasing a statement through his attorneys on September 6, 2021, that said, "I have made a lot of decisions that I truly regret. I'm resigning from my law firm and entering rehab after a long battle that has been exacerbated by these murders."

Alex's resignation and admission of addiction was shocking. No longer would he enjoy his friends and family's unreserved support. Maggie's sister, Marian Proctor, began to have doubts about Alex when she heard reports he had been stealing. Blanca and her husband moved out of Moselle after the Labor Day shooting. Alex's brother Randy, too, was disappointed in his brother and told SLED of suspicious phone calls Alex made to unknown numbers while he was in the hospital. "While I will support him in his recovery, I do not support, condone, or excuse his conduct in stealing by manipulating his most trusted relationships," Randy said in a statement, acknowledging Alex's confessed theft.

For law enforcement, too, the roadside shooting significantly changed the investigation, revealing Alex to be untrustworthy. With the involvement of his lawyers, Alex soon confessed a new version of the roadside shooting to SLED in which Alex said he arranged for Curtis Edward Smith to kill him so that his son Buster Murdaugh could collect Alex's life insurance policy. Police arrested Smith for his alleged role in Alex's fraudulent roadside scheme, but Alex's alleged drug supplier pleaded not guilty and denied shooting Alex in the head, not in malice and not even as a favor to his friend and former lawyer. "I'm innocent," Smith said a month later during a television appearance on the *Today* show. "If I'd have shot him, he'd be dead."

As Smith's appearance on a nationally televised morning show indicated, Alex's actions had initiated a media frenzy that grew more intense with every twist of the story. The day after Smith's arrest, SLED announced it had opened an investigation into the 2018 death of the Murdaugh's former housekeeper and nanny, Gloria Satterfield. Then, the next day, Alex was arrested for insurance fraud and conspiracy charges related to the roadside shooting. A judge allowed his release on bond, but a month later Alex was arrested again, this time for looting $4.3 million from an insurance settlement owed to Satterfield's sons. This time a judge denied him bond and ordered Alex jailed—an astonishing fall from grace.

Journalists and producers from near and far flooded the Lowcountry, especially Hampton County. Documentary projects began filming interviews. A podcast launched about the crimes, followed by others. The Murdaugh family soon appeared in popular tabloids, celebrity magazines, and television specials, too. All these productions and publications tried to help their audiences understand a dizzying amount of backwoods dysfunction. The online magazine *Slate* summed up the general reaction to what was unfolding in the Lowcountry with its headline on an extended explainer piece, which read: LET ME SAY THIS WITH AS MUCH SENSITIVITY AS I CAN: WOW, THAT'S A LOT OF DEAD PEOPLE AND CRIME.

Representing Alex in court, as well as to the police and to the media, were his well-regarded attorneys Jim Griffin and South Carolina state senator Richard "Dick" Harpootlian, Columbia lawyers who had worked on cases together for more than twenty years, though they weren't partners and kept separate offices. Their latest collaboration had been defending Paul Murdaugh from criminal charges related to the boat crash, but that case was dismissed soon after Paul's death. That freed the men up to defend Alex against what would turn out to be an avalanche of alleged wrongdoing.

The pair described themselves as opposites, or "fire and ice" according to Griffin. If so, Griffin was the flame, warm and amiable, while Harpootlian fulfilled the role of ice, his style cold and crass, but not ineffective. The state senator conceded he was prone to "offend" and "irritate" and that "sometimes I'm a little rough."

Both men had worked as prosecutors, with Griffin serving as a federal prosecutor and Harpootlian working locally as a deputy solicitor and solicitor. While Griffin handled more white-collar crime, Harpootlian had experience handling dozens of murder cases, including helping obtain a death penalty conviction of South Carolina serial killer Pee Wee Gaskins in 1983. A few weeks after helping send Gaskins to death row, Harpootlian left the solicitor's office to join the law firm of Gaskins's defense lawyer, Jack Swerling, a transition that infuriated the killer. Gaskins supposedly sent Harpootlian some kind of tic-tac-toe-type picture or game that depicted gruesome ways in which the former prosecutor might die, according to one of the lawyer's former employees. Harpootlian loved it, said the employee, and proudly hung it on his office wall.

The transition to private practice was a success, as Harpootlian was happy to boast in 1989. "Let me put it this way," said Harpootlian, "Six years ago, when I went into practice with Swerling, I was driving a 1970 Volkswagen, I had a 1,600-square-foot house and about four suits. Now I drive a 1988 Mercedes 420 SL. I have a 3,600-square-foot house and a lot more suits." Money was important to Harpootlian. He once joined a long-running civil case, perplexing one of the lawyers on the other side who asked him why he got involved just to prolong its resolution. Harpootlian spelled it out for him—he knew he'd signed onto a loser of a case, but he was happy to make money losing it. In Harpootlian's eyes, both he and the soon-to-be-victorious opposing lawyer were coming out ahead. "Dollars for me, dollars for you," Harpootlian told his legal colleague.

Harpootlian was cantankerous, foul-mouthed, brash, and scheming, which made him a perfect fit for the rough-and-tumble world of Palmetto State politics. Beyond being elected a solicitor in 1990 and a state senator in 2018, he was twice the chairman of the South Carolina Democratic Party as well as a prominent booster of President Joe Biden. As Harpootlian began defending Alex in late 2021, his wife, Jamie Lindler Harpootlian, was preparing to move abroad and begin serving as the US ambassador to Slovenia in the Biden administration.

One of Harpootlian's political mentors was Ernest "Fritz" Hollings, who represented South Carolina in the U.S. Senate for decades alongside Strom Thurmond. Hollings advised Harpootlian to "give it back better than he got" and "never let a punch go unreturned." But this pugnacious strategy had its limits, especially when employed against the wrong foe. Such an instance occurred in 1981, when deputy solicitor Harpootlian exchanged harsh words with police investigator John M. "Jakie" Knotts Jr. After Harpootlian uttered one insult too many, the argument culminated with Knotts knocking Harpootlian out cold, with Harpootlian collapsing to the floor, the deputy solicitor's legs sticking out an open office door. Harpootlian and Knotts downplayed their disagreement, but the conflict nonetheless sent the courthouse "abuzz" for a day, according to *The State* newspaper.

If Knotts clocked Harpootlian, he did not cork him. Harpootlian became well-known in South Carolina legal and political circles for his quick wit and sharp tongue. Sometimes he was amusing, like when, as solicitor, he said, "What's up, Doc?" to a defendant accused of impersonating a medical professional in order to perform intimate physical exams on bodybuilders. But other times he was insufferable. There wasn't a building in Columbia big enough to contain his ego, said one former law enforcement official who attended court often with Harpootlian. This person admired Harpootlian's legal ability, but found him grating in court, to the point the official wanted "to bash his fucking head in," he said. "Every fucking time."

Harpootlian wasn't the only lawyer in the Murdaugh case who could prove exasperating. In the coming months the comparatively more congenial Waters would also rankle his opposing counsel. One lawyer became so peeved at Waters that he drafted a profane message that he mistakenly shared with the prosecutor before realizing, with pure horror, his mistake. As Waters read on his phone one evening:

Creighton can eat a duck
*dick
Oh no

I don't know how that just happened. That is not what I meant to say at all.

Waters and his staff laughed at the mix-up. They would take the light moment. The case was otherwise quite dark, especially when the state of South Carolina accused Alex Murdaugh of murdering his wife and son.

CHAPTER EIGHT
THE TRIAL

E ven when Alex Murdaugh was confined to a jail cell, his problems proliferated. In the months following Alex's arrests for staging the roadside shooting and stealing the Satterfield family's money, Alex's law partners and police investigators were uncovering more and more of his alleged thefts, estimating he stole close to $9 million from clients, the law firm, and others for more than a decade. To be a free man he would have to disprove nearly 100 charges related to theft, fraud, and illicit drugs.

The Murdaugh case and its offshoots could prove overwhelming. Beyond investigating Alex and his tangle of alleged financial misdeeds, state and federal authorities charged Alex's friends Cory Fleming, Russell Laffitte, and Curtis Edward Smith for crimes that helped enable Alex's schemes. Police opened fresh inquiries into the suspicious deaths of Stephen Smith and Gloria Satterfield, both of whom would be exhumed. Investigators probed possible public corruption among police and judges friendly with Alex, and investigated suspected opioid trafficking. Police and prosecutors toiled, too, on the double murder investigation, desperate for a breakthrough. They theorized family weapons and ammunition from Moselle were used to kill Maggie and Paul, and that they died about 8:50 P.M., more than fifteen minutes before Alex left for his mother's house.

Investigators were focused on Alex, suspicious that the roadside shooting was not an act of assisted suicide but instead a desperate ploy to create the illusion that someone was stalking the Murdaugh family. They knew him to be a liar. They knew him to be at Moselle about the time when Maggie and Paul fell dead. They knew he was on the verge of financial ruin and exposure, spooked by his confrontation at the law firm over the missing money. They knew he was suffering from withdrawal from an opioid addiction, sick and agitated. Prosecutor Creighton Waters in the state attorney general's office thought this a recipe for bad things. "This guy had been on an exhausting journey of just constant fraud and staying just one step ahead of the game for over a decade and finally he was running out of time and guess what?" said Waters. "That happened to be the day that his wife and son died."

Waters had a mantra: "Find me the lie." There were plenty for police to discover, but few clues that meant Alex killed his family. Yet nine months after Maggie and Paul were shot apart beside their dog kennels, state authorities caught a break—Paul's cell phone had been unlocked.

Within a week of the killings, investigators were able to obtain data from phones belonging to Maggie, Alex, Buster, and Alex's brothers. But no one knew the passcode to Paul's phone, preventing it from being examined. Only nine months later, when Paul's phone was given to a civilian employee of the Secret Service, could investigators access this digital domain. On a whim this employee entered Paul's birthdate as the six-digit passcode—a combination that no other investigator had tried. The phone instantly unlocked!

Alex Murdaugh had warned SLED agents that Paul was "super, super, super secretive" with his cell phone, and for once he wasn't lying. Stored on Paul's phone was a short video he recorded at the kennels just moments before he died. In a clip nearly a minute long, Paul is seen entering a kennel to interact with Cash, his friend Rogan Gibson's chocolate Labrador Retriever. As Paul struggles to keep his phone's camera focused on the injured tail of the moving dog, the voices of Alex and Maggie can be heard in the background discussing the family dog, Bubba, who had captured some kind of fowl. There is a sound, too, of someone off-camera seemingly spraying water from a hose.

"Hey, he's gotta bird in his mouth," Maggie is heard to say in the background as Paul films Cash the dog.

"Bubba!" says Alex.

"Hey, Bubba," Paul adds quietly, almost to himself.

Maggie then offered her best guess as to what unfortunate creature Bubba snatched up and smothered in his jaws. "It's a guinea!" she ventured.

"It's a chicken," said Paul, speaking in a goofy voice.

"Come here, Bubba," said Alex, attempting to free the bird. "Come here, Bubba!"

A few seconds later, the video ends. This was an incredible find. The video evidence confirmed Rogan Gibson's hunch that Alex Murdaugh was not napping at the house, but instead at the kennels with Maggie and Paul just minutes before they were believed to have been killed. This video, which Paul had intended to share with Gibson, was plainly at odds with Alex's statements to police and loved ones that he never visited the kennels.

Within a few weeks, Waters was ready to make a pitch for pursuing double murder charges against Alex Murdaugh. He gathered the top brass from SLED and the South Carolina attorney general's office, including Chief Mark Keel and Attorney General Alan Wilson, and outlined the evidence against the suspect. Waters and SLED special agent David Owen narrated a forty-slide presentation titled "The Gathering Storm" that detailed the evidence against Alex, including the kennel video. Waters was cognizant of the fact it had been a year since someone slaughtered Maggie and Paul, and "cases tend not to get better with age." Waters and Owen and their colleagues had found the lie—Alex was at the kennels, not asleep on his couch cushions. Now they wanted the chance to prove that in court. Turning to the state's top cop and top prosecutor, Waters said, "Chief, General, we believe it's go time."

On July 14, 2022, a state grand jury indicted Alex Murdaugh on charges of murdering his wife, Maggie, and youngest son, Paul. A week later Murdaugh pleaded not guilty at his arraignment. His lawyers moved for a speedy trial, hoping to catch prosecutors unprepared. Waters said he was unfazed. "You want a speedy trial," he said he thought to himself, "let's do this thing." Such bravado was necessary to distract from the staggering complexities of the investigation, which was still ongoing, and the work needed to be done to prepare for trial. "We were in no way ready to start on this marathon," said Waters, "but we'd be more ready than the defense and we'd outwork them during trial."

The state attorney general's office decided against pursuing a death penalty case against Alex, the case being tenuous enough without the addition of that legal hurdle, too. Both the prosecutors and defense lawyers were satisfied to try the case in Colleton County, where the murders occurred. The Colleton County Courthouse stood in the center of the county seat, Walterboro, within a historic district with charming old wooden homes and a main street with a dated, stuck-in-time vibe and a few restaurants. Surrounding this historic core were much poorer neighborhoods and more modern development, especially close to Interstate 95, which ran along Walterboro's western edge, with two exits in town.

Walterboro branded itself as "The Front Porch of the Lowcountry," and in late January 2023, as the highly anticipated trial was due to begin, the small, Southern city of 5,000 residents began welcoming a swell of guests, including a robust contingent of media that had come to report on the trial, which would be broadcast live. Beyond having shared cameras in the courtroom, television crews set up tents housing mini studios around the courthouse square, where commentators could be filmed with the stately, historic courthouse in the background.

Colleton County's temple of justice had been built 201 years earlier atop a small hill at the western edge of Walterboro, where the ground descended into swampland. The building was stuccoed smooth and painted white and featured a pair of curved, exterior stairways leading to a columned portico that stood outside the doorway to the second-story courtroom. The courthouse's design was largely attributed to Robert Mills, a renowned South Carolina architect whose buildings include the Washington Monument.

A few subtle changes had been made at the courthouse ahead of the trial. Courthouse employees taped sheets of white paper over the transom window and sidelights surrounding the exterior doorway to the courtroom, atop the portico. This tactic was intended to thwart any video-equipped drones from filming the trial through the glass from outside. Inside the courtroom there was a bare spot on the back wall, where a portrait of Alex's grandfather, former solicitor Randolph "Buster" Murdaugh Jr., usually hung. A judge had previously ordered it removed from the courtroom for the trial. Alex's grandfather would not be around to try and help him get out of trouble this time.

The courtroom was spacious and somewhat austere, with white walls and uncomfortable wooden benches in the gallery and wooden chairs for jurors and others that one lawyer joked came with the courthouse in 1820 and then received cushions in 1920. There were touches of elegance, at least for an old Southern courthouse, including brass chandeliers with glass globes hanging beneath plaster ceiling medallions. Large windows surrounded the courtroom, though the blinds were kept drawn to shut out the rest of the world.

Presiding over Alex Murdaugh's murder trial was Judge Clifton Newman, whose restrained personality had a way of keeping attorneys in check in his court, especially if his demeanor and tone suddenly reflected a lack of amusement. The seventy-one-year-old Newman had been a judge for twenty-three years, and before that operated his own law firm, with offices in Columbia and his hometown of Kingstree, where he also worked seventeen years as a part-time solicitor. He grew up in a family of farmers in rural South Carolina and attended segregated schools before moving to Cleveland for college and law school. He moved back home to South

Carolina in 1982 as a young married lawyer and raised a family, including a daughter, Jocelyn, who followed him into law and even onto the bench, joining her father in 2016 as one of South Carolina's few Black judges. The double murder trial of Alex Murdaugh would be one of Clifton Newman's final cases, as he would soon be required to retire when he turned seventy-two, the age limit for judges and solicitors in South Carolina.

On the afternoon of January 25, 2023, Prosecutor Creighton Waters stood within the upstairs courtroom of the Colleton County Courthouse. He faced eighteen people seated in the jury box—twelve jurors and six alternates. As he began his opening statement in a hushed courtroom, Waters, dressed in a charcoal suit and wearing glasses, described how Paul Murdaugh and then Maggie Murdaugh were killed. Paul was standing in the feed room beside the dog kennels at Moselle, said Waters, when Alex Murdaugh took a shotgun and blasted a load of buckshot into his chest before firing a second load of birdshot into his shoulder, neck, and head, causing "catastrophic damage." Waters said Alex then used a .300 Blackout assault rifle to fire at his wife Maggie at close range. He shot her five times, including twice in the head.

Alex "told anyone who would listen" that he was not at the kennels, said Waters. "Told everybody that he was never there." But a video of a dog at the kennels recovered from Paul's phone says otherwise, he claimed, as Alex's voice can be heard in the background. Waters told the jury that Alex was being squeezed by a "gathering storm" of pressures when he killed his family, and then that Alex himself became "the storm." He warned the jurors that a long trial was ahead of them. "It's complicated, it's a journey, there's a lot of aspects to this case, there's a lot of factors to this case," said Waters. "But like a lot of things that are complicated, when you start to put them all together, piece them together like a puzzle, all of a sudden a picture emerges and it's really simple."

Waters was followed by Alex's lawyer Dick Harpootlian, bedecked in a blue suit and teal tie, who told the jury, first thing, that "It is our honor to represent Alex Murdaugh. Or Murdock, depending how you pronounce it." He told his client to stand up and then introduced Alex, who was wearing a blue blazer and a checkered shirt. He described him as the "loving father of Paul and the loving husband of Maggie." Not one witness will say otherwise, said Harpootlian.

The brutal ways in which Paul and Maggie were murdered is not consistent with the actions of such a devoted family man, argued Harpootlian, before giving graphic descriptions of the murders. He mentioned the second shotgun blast that killed Paul. "The gases from that shot literally exploded his head like a watermelon hit with a sledgehammer. All that was left was the front of his face, everything else was gone," said Harpootlian. "His brain exploded out of his head, hit the ceiling in the shed, and dropped to his feet. Horrendous. Horrible. Butchering."

Then he described Maggie being killed as she ran. "She falls to the ground and has one bullet that has hit her, and probably traveled up and hit her brain . . ." said Harpootlian. "She's on the ground and whoever the perpetrator was, walked up, took that AR, and put one in the back of her head. Executed. Executed."

Harpootlian said the police were sloppy and failed to properly investigate the case. "They decided, that night, he did it," said Harpootlian. "They've been pounding that square peg in the round hole . . . since June of 2021." If Alex did not tell the full truth about being at the kennels it was of no consequence, said Harpootlian, and also understandable given the "accusatory fashion" in which Alex was questioned in SLED Special Agent David Owens's car the night of the murder. "He may not have dealt all the facts, but by the way, whether he had been down to the dog pens that night or not, really didn't matter," said Harpootlian, explaining that Alex didn't have enough time, in the span of an hour or so, to kill his family, clean himself up, dispose of weapons and bloodied clothing, and visit his mother at her house about twenty minutes away. According to Harpootlian, Alex had neither the motive nor the means to kill his family that night. "Not believable," he said.

Court resumed the next day and prosecutors began questioning the first of sixty-one witnesses they would call to the stand to testify before resting their case. They began with police officers, including the first officer to arrive on the scene, whom Alex immediately told of the 2019 boat crash and how it must figure somehow into the murders. Another officer mentioned her observation of Alex's white T-shirt being particularly clean for having checked the vital signs of two bloody murder victims, implying he changed his clothes. Two other witnesses who handled the shirt mentioned it smelled freshly laundered.

Police crime scene and lab technicians spoke of Maggie's sandals making impressions in the sand as she ran along a shed in alarm before collapsing to the ground, and of finding bullet fragments and bullet casings, as well as shotgun shells and pellets at Moselle. They mentioned drops of blood found on a shotgun Alex said he grabbed from the house after finding Maggie and Paul's bodies, as well as on a steering wheel. They testified about Alex's shorts, shirt, hands, and seatbelt testing positive for gunshot residue. They described his trip to Moselle, where vehicle data from the FBI and General Motors indicated he zoomed at speeds close to eighty miles per hour on the rural roads to his mother's house.

Prosecutors called Murdaugh family employees like Shelly Smith, who said Alex tried to pressure her into lying about how long he was at the house, and Blanca Turrubiate-Simpson, who testified that Alex tried to persuade her he was not wearing the clothes she remembered him wearing the morning of the murders. The prosecution presented evidence of how a very large blue rain jacket, mistakenly identified as a tarp by Shelly when she saw Alex arrive with it to Almeda early one morning, contained high concentrations of gunshot residue. They called a variety of witnesses who testified that Alex told them he never went to the kennels, and a number of other witnesses who identified Alex as one of three voices in the background of the kennel video, along with Maggie and Paul.

Alex's friends and colleagues spoke of his betrayal. His sister-in-law Marian Proctor testified to his disinterest in solving the murders. Law firm employee Nathan Tuten told of frequently cashing checks at the bank for Alex and bringing the money to his office, where Alex was notably waiting with friends like Greg Alexander, Cory Fleming, and Chris Wilson. Lawyer Mark Tinsley detailed the pressure campaign he was enacting against Alex, and the finance chief of the law firm, Jeanne Seckinger, testified about Alex's theft and how she was seeking missing money. Alex was about to be exposed, argued the prosecution, and he killed his family to distract and buy time.

Prosecutors also showed the communications and movements of Alex, Maggie, and Paul, creating a narrative of the last day the family would be together. Jurors learned that Paul was texting with a girl about watching a movie in the moments before he died. Data from cell phones told the number of steps the Murdaughs took at Moselle that evening, who the family members called, and at what times messages were received and read. Some of this data was compelling and created suspicion against Alex, but much was also tedious and inconclusive.

Testimony from police, ballistics experts, and a pathologist who autopsied the murder victims altogether painted a picture of the murders that went like this: After Alex lured Maggie and Paul to Moselle that night, the family ate dinner and then traveled to the kennels. The kennel video records a light scene, with Maggie and Paul excited by the predicament of the poor bird in Bubba's mouth. Alex, though, sounds exhausted as he exclaims, "Come on, Bubba!" The evidence suggested that Paul and Maggie were clueless to their impending deaths. Neither saw the burst of violence coming.

Alex is believed to have lurked outside the small feed room while Paul stood inside. Alex nosed a shotgun through the open doorway and pulled the trigger. A volley of buckshot sank through Paul's chest. Paul survived, at least immediately, and stumbled toward the doorway, stepping in fast-forming puddles of his own blood, which was streaming down his arms onto the floor. Another shot rang out from a low angle, spraying steel birdshot upward into his shoulder, neck, and head. This blast of the shotgun exploded his skull and blew his brain outside his body. Paul fell forward, his dead body falling across the door threshold and out of the feed room. Prosecutors alleged Alex used Paul's favorite Benelli shotgun to kill his son, the one Alex had placed against his car when police arrived at Moselle.

Alex then took hold of Paul's other favorite weapon—a .300 Blackout rifle, likely the black replacement gun that Maggie had picked up and purchased with a check. Alex fired shots at Maggie from just a few feet away, the bullets tearing through his wife's thigh, abdomen, breast, neck, and head as she crashed to the ground, one of the bullets also tearing through her wrist and shattering her diamond bracelet. One final shot was fired as Alex stood over her, aimed into the back of her skull and brain stem. During testimony concerning the murders, Alex rocked and sniffled at the descriptions of his family members' deaths and the prosecution's allegations. Otherwise he was somewhat impassive in court and sucked on mints and candies almost constantly, as if they were opioid pills.

Prosecutors steadily built momentum as they told, witness by witness, the story of Maggie and Paul's joint demise. Yet they stumbled a bit during the testimony of SLED agent Owen. During cross-examination, defense lawyer Jim Griffin questioned Owen about alleged mistakes made by the state police agency, including Owen's erroneous assertion to the state grand jury that Alex's white T-shirt contained microscopic blood spatter. Beyond this error, which Owen said stemmed from an overlooked email that contained exculpatory lab results, Griffin cornered Owen on the fact he told Alex, and the state grand jury, that guns in Moselle's hunt room were all loaded the same way as the shotgun used to kill Paul—with one buckshot shell and one birdshot shell. This was not true, Owen admitted, but said that as a policeman he was "allowed to use trickery" when interviewing Alex. The withering cross-examination, which tarnished SLED's integrity and competence, inspired one lawyer in the courtroom to write his impression of Griffin's questioning on the back of a card. It read: "Bend over, I'll drive."

The prosecution took their lumps and moved on, not believing the damage was fatal to their case or that the police had been painted as totally untrustworthy. In a sprawling investigation like this one, prosecutors figured, jurors would not expect a total absence of errors. "Sometimes mistakes get made in good faith," Waters would later say. "Nobody falsified evidence or lied." Despite this rough patch, the prosecution made an effective, and extended, presentation of the evidence before resting their case. Now the defense would have the opportunity to explain why Alex lied about being at the kennels, and who might have really killed Maggie and Paul.

———

A visiting French writer called it the Circus. He traveled across an ocean to watch Walterboro absorb an influx of lawyers, journalists, true crime fanatics, and curious day-trippers who crammed themselves into the Colleton County Courthouse, many of the visitors lining up before dawn in the courthouse square to gain a ticket. As the trial picked up steam, the crowds grew, flooding Walterboro with so many extra cars and pedestrians that many local residents steered clear of downtown, temporarily ceding this patch of the county seat. Locals were gracious to the visitors, and most everyone polite, even the police keeping order inside and outside the courtroom. An atmosphere of general civility and goodwill existed among the locals, the authorities, the press, and other visitors, all coexisting in a cramped courthouse in a small Southern town. Yet just beneath the good manners and smiles lay a seriousness, at least among the lawyers, journalists, and police, that reflected the grim facts of the case being tried, and that two people had lost their lives.

For more than a month all eyes were on Walterboro, and the town lived up to its name as the Front Porch of the Lowcountry as it warmly welcomed guests. To accommodate so many people, local leaders arranged for food trucks to park across the street from the courthouse where they could serve up lunch each day for court attendees. Officials also arranged for a truck trailer full of impressive portable bathrooms—named the Taj Ma Stall—to be parked a block away from the courthouse to minimize crowding at the small restrooms within the historic courthouse. Users of the Taj Ma Stall were treated to a soundtrack heavy on 1980s hits, providing a jolt of jock-rock energy to court attendees sometimes fatigued from listening to hours of testimony on hard seats.

Across the street from the courthouse, too, was the Walterboro Wildlife Center, which was designated as the media hub during the trial. Seating was limited inside the courtroom, and each major news organization was granted just one reserved seat. Journalists were restricted from using electronic devices in court, so this prohibition and the limited seating split reporters into two general factions, those who sat in court each day and filled notebook after notebook by hand, waiting to publish their goods at end of day, and those who camped beneath the tents or in the nearby media center, able to report in real time while watching the television broadcast.

The lobby of the wildlife center contained aquariums full of local snakes and turtles. A small juvenile alligator sat in a central, open-air enclosure with low walls. Journalists streamed through all day while on their way to a makeshift newsroom at the back of the building within a reception hall with lots of big tables. One weekend during the trial, a wedding reception was scheduled to be held in the wildlife center, making the hall unavailable for a day and forcing some media to move to the small lobby and set up workstations and cameras beside and among the amphibians and reptiles.

While everyone else had an hour or so of freedom at lunch, the jury was confined to the courthouse and provided with a midday meal. The jury configuration had already changed a few times because of jurors needing to be excused for medical reasons. As a wave of COVID overtook jurors and many court attendees at the beginning of trial, lawyers on both sides wondered aloud to Judge Newman if the trial should be paused for fear an outbreak could cause all the jurors and alternates to be exhausted, which would result in a mistrial. But Newman decided they should press ahead without delay.

Management of the jury, as well as almost everything else at the courthouse, fell to Clerk of Court Rebecca "Becky" Hill, a friendly, upbeat administrator tasked with hosting what some people were calling the trial of the century, given the huge television audience it was attracting. The jury alone was enough of a responsibility, never mind attending to the needs of both sides of lawyers, law enforcement, the media, and the general public. Becky and her staff stayed busy but calm, a sense of Southern hospitality prevailing despite the stresses of facilitating so many constituencies.

Hill and her colleagues provided for the jurors to take smoking breaks in a tented and protected area outside the courthouse during recesses. Lunch orders would prompt headaches they became so complicated, with twelve jurors, six or so alternates, two court staff, two bus drivers for the jury, and three police officers all indicating their choice of sandwich, chips, and drink each day. Jurors had medical conditions that had to be accommodated, and at least one man needed help arranging to be away from work for so long.

The clerk managed access to the courthouse, arranging for groups of students to attend portions of the trial and learn firsthand about government and the legal system. Hill forged friendships with numerous reporters and other attendees and seemed universally liked, always gracious and bubbly and prepared. Even prickly Dick Harpootlian lavished the clerk with praise, telling Judge Newman a week into trial that Hill was exceeding all expectations:

> *Your honor can I just make one brief comment . . . And I've talked to all of us over here. We want to thank the clerk of court for her*

assistance. Every time we need something, she has been there for us . . . We feel like we have been treated extraordinarily well by all court personnel. And I want to put on the record, since there seems to be a national media interest here, I've tried many cases in many jurisdictions and I've never been treated at this level of courtesy and understanding. Thank you.

From the prosecutor's table Creighton Waters agreed with his opponent's sentiments. "I absolutely echo that," said the lead prosecutor. "Everybody's been great. Absolutely."

Judge Newman looked semi-amused and decided to join in. "Okay. I echo that as well. Very good," he said. "Bring the jury."

Harpootlian's tribute was as feel-good a moment one can hope for in a murder trial, yet the warm feelings between the defense lawyer and the clerk of court would not last beyond the end of the trial.

Each day brought new surprises. A false bomb threat was called into the courthouse one day, forcing Judge Newman to halt trial in the middle of a witness's testimony. "Ladies and gentlemen, we have to evacuate the building at this time. We'll be in recess until we discover what's going on," said Newman, spurring people to stream out the seldom-used doors at the rear of the courtroom, where they stepped out onto the portico and walked down one of the double staircases to the courthouse square below. Another day, a rumor went around the courthouse that novelist John Grisham was in attendance, though it turned out to be the mayor of Walterboro, who did bear a physical resemblance to the famous author. It was up for debate which was more riveting, Grisham's bestselling fictional legal thrillers or the abominable, real-life actions of Alex Murdaugh.

A version of Grisham crashed the proceedings, too, when police confiscated a copy of his book *The Judge's List* that Alex's family attempted to pass to him across the courtroom bar. For that offense, as well as for generally communicating and interacting with the defendant, Judge Newman warned Alex's family through the clerk of court, and required that they be moved a few rows back from Alex. Alex, too, got caught at least once with contraband, but a sharp-eyed police officer prevented him from leaving the courtroom with the mint candies he was permitted to enjoy while seated at the defense table during trial.

Alex's surviving son, Buster, and his girlfriend attended the trial every day, as did Alex's sister Lynn and brother John Marvin. Other family attended less regularly, such as Alex's other brother, Randy Murdaugh IV. For the most part the family was stoic while watching the trial, and John Marvin Murdaugh would even flash a smile and offer a greeting to strangers during court recesses. But the friendly behavior masked a world of pain. Day after day, the Murdaugh family had to listen to how one of their own turned on his loved ones and plugged their bodies with steel and lead. Prosecutor Creighton Waters said the Murdaugh family's predicament inspired sympathy among him and his colleagues, even when two of the Murdaughs took the stand as defense witnesses. "There's a family there trying to stop themselves from being ripped apart, and we were sensitive to that," said Waters. "We understand how difficult this is."

Similarly, Waters and other prosecutors had to handle other interactions with increased sensitivity, too, particularly the questioning of emotionally fragile and anxious witnesses. Much energy was spent among Waters's staff to keep the supply of witnesses steady or otherwise the prosecution would suffer the judge's displeasure. "Judge Newman likes for a witness to be walking up while another is stepping down," said Waters. Everyday kinks in the plan needed to be resolved, such as when the death of Agent Owen's mother caused the postponement of his testimony for a day. It was a tough stretch for the lead investigator. One day the special agent lost his mom, the next he endured Griffin's aggressive cross-examination. Waters gave him high marks. "He came and did his job. He was a professional and a trooper."

The trial, watched daily by an ever-growing television audience, was stressful enough without the addition of personal sorrow. Every evening, said Waters, he looked forward to hearing Judge Newman say, "We'll be in recess." This meant he could return to the privacy of his hotel room to nap for a moment or call family and friends. He would often make himself some soup at night and gulp bottles of water he picked up for free at the hotel, as many as seven a night, having denied himself much to drink during the day. On Saturdays he rested at the hotel and washed his laundry and ironed his shirts. The Hampton Inn & Suites in Walterboro became a home away from home for Waters, his refuge during the trial. He made friends with two women on the breakfast crew at the hotel, and he was soon the recipient of gourmet waffles topped with strawberries and chocolate sauce.

The defense team was eating well, too, enjoying salmon and chicken dinners cooked by a personal chef at a gated, 500-acre plantation on the outskirts of Walterboro. Their rented compound contained five separate homes, including a lakeside manor house, where they would retreat to rest and hatch the next day's plan for court. To hear the defense tell it, the police and other officials were sloppy and lazy, not bothering to properly search the crime scene or search for suspects beyond Alex Murdaugh. In presenting their case they called fourteen witnesses to the stand, some of whom badmouthed the police investigation and others of whom cast doubt on the prosecution's theories of how Maggie and Paul were killed. The defense cast doubt on the expertise of the county coroner, who, in place of using a thermometer, estimated Maggie and Paul's time of death by placing his hands inside the victims' armpits to gauge their body temperatures.

The defense also highlighted the fact that SLED failed to take steps, such as using a Faraday bag, to protect Maggie's phone from losing GPS information that could have clarified her location and activity before she was killed. Additionally, defense witnesses faulted SLED and local police for permitting so many people onto the crime scene that night, both near the kennels and at Moselle's main house, where some visitors cleaned rooms and took showers. One witness called by the defense, Alex's former law partner Mark Ball, said law enforcement was very polite and accommodating the night of the murders—"Probably too much." They were also incompetent, he thought, allowing cars to keep "piling in" to Moselle and failing to protect Paul's body from rainwater running off the edge of the shed roof. "It pissed me off," he said of having to watch Paul's blood wash across the ground during the rainstorm.

The defense called a handful of expert witnesses to the stand to poke holes in SLED's police work, the autopsies of Maggie and Paul, and the prosecution's interpretation of the evidence as to how the shootings occurred. One was from Georgia, two were from North Carolina, and two were from Connecticut, but none were from South Carolina. The prosecution, meanwhile, had previously called two charismatic witnesses to relate details of the shooting who both lived within an hour of the jurors' homes in Walterboro, pathologist Dr. Ellen Riemer of Charleston, and crime scene reconstruction expert and sheriff's deputy Kenny Kinsey of Orangeburg. Moreover, most of the defense's out-of-state expert witnesses offered alternate interpretations of evidence that was unconvincing, with some of these theories ridiculed by prosecutors during cross-examination.

At other times, it was the lawyers stealing the show. During one witness's testimony regarding his analysis of the shooting scene, Dick Harpootlian picked up Buster Murdaugh's .300 Blackout AR-style rifle, pointed it toward the prosecutor's table, and said, "Tempting, but . . ." Previously, while cross-examining another shooting scene expert, he leveled the shotgun suspected of killing his former client, Paul, at co-counsel Phillip Barber. "Mr. Barber in the interest of justice, has allowed me to point the shotgun at him," Harpootlian announced to the courtroom. He was similarly sassy with journalists at the trial, suggesting to some that they "get a fucking life." Similarly profane was defense lawyer Jim Griffin, who was chided by Judge Newman one morning for sharing on social media a *Washington Post* opinion column titled ALEX MURDAUGH TRIAL REVEALS A SLOPPY INVESTIGATION. In response Griffin stated he would not share or post anything else until the trial was over. Later, while leaving the courthouse during a recess, someone asked him about the judge's scolding. "Fuck that shit!" he said in response.

The defense called Buster Murdaugh to the stand, who spoke of some of the challenges facing his family, including Paul's boat crash and his father's on-and-off struggle with opioids. John Marvin Murdaugh took the stand, too, and spoke about the warm relationship that existed between Alex and Maggie, as well as his fondness for his nephew Paul, whose remains he personally cleaned up the morning after Paul's murder. "I saw blood, I saw brains, I saw pieces of skull, I saw tissue," he testified. "And when I say brains it could just be tissue. I don't know what I saw, it was just terrible.

"I felt like I owed him, and I just started cleaning, and I promise you, no mother, father, aunt, or uncle should ever have to see and do what I did that day. It's the hardest thing I've ever been through in my life," said John Marvin, crying. "I told Paul I loved him, and I promised him I'd find out who did this."

The testimony of these Murdaugh men, however, was mere prelude to the main act, when Alex Murdaugh took the stand to explain his actions on the night Maggie and Paul were killed. His lawyer Jim Griffin immediately picked up a shotgun and a rifle and asked Alex if he used those weapons to kill Maggie and Paul. "No, I did not," said Alex. "I didn't shoot my wife or my son any time, ever."

Alex did, however, confess to deceiving police about his presence at the kennels. His drug addiction caused him to occasionally become paranoid, he said, and he already harbored a distrust for SLED based on the charges against Paul as well as SLED's previous investigation of his friend, Yemassee police chief Greg Alexander, that Alex and his father felt was so wrong. Alex said he also mistakenly confused David Owen with the SLED agent who investigated Alexander, who was also named David. The end result, he said, was he told a false story, and then had to repeat these falsehoods to be consistent. "I lied about being down there," said

Alex, "and I'm so sorry that I did." Part of his paranoia, too, Alex explained, came from him having illicit opioid pills in his pocket while he was being interviewed in a police car.

Alex testified that after dinner Paul and Maggie headed to the kennels while he stayed behind at the house, not wanting to get sweaty outside. But then he changed his mind and joined them, arriving via golf cart to find a chaotic scene at the kennels, with two dogs loose chasing chickens and guinea hens. Bubba proudly pranced around with a dazed bird in his jaws until Alex removed the chicken from his mouth and placed it atop a crate, where it died. Then he returned home for a short nap on the couch before driving to his mother's house. After that, he said, he returned to find Maggie and Paul dead on the ground, and he called 911.

As Alex spoke he used cute nicknames to describe Maggie and Paul, nicknames that no one else had used for the entire trial. Maggie became Mags and Paul became Paul Paul, or was it Paw Paw or Pau Pau? Print journalists were at a loss when it came to the proper spelling, though Alex listed his son in his phone as Paul Paul. Alex may not have invented the nicknames outright, but the frequency in which he used the nicknames struck many observers as forced. Alex also went on at length about any number of items, providing great detail about the layout of his parents' house at Almeda and what each room was used for, or listing all the people that attended a weekend event, as if that was the true question at the heart of the entire inquiry, and as if anyone cared. The babbling allowed him to avoid providing precise details. He did not have to lock himself into any solid account of the facts that could be challenged.

Under questioning from Griffin, Alex denied feeling financial pressure around the time of the murders, mentioning he could sell the beach house or Moselle to raise money. Alex also said he didn't think he would be forced to share full financial records with lawyer Mark Tinsley, at least not at this point in the boat crash lawsuit. He even downplayed the health condition of his father, who died three days later, believing he merely had pneumonia rather than worsening symptoms of cancer. Nothing was amiss on June 7, 2021, said Alex.

Lead prosecutor Creighton Waters believed differently, that Alex's life was absolutely falling apart on the day he allegedly shot Maggie and Paul. As he cross-examined Alex over two days, Waters covered a tremendous amount of ground, discussing many of Alex's fraud victims, his connections to law enforcement, the 2019 boat crash and its aftermath, the roadside shooting, and his family history. At one point Waters told Alex, "I know you want to get through it quicker but we're not."

Waters dwelled on the fact that the first time Alex admitted to being at the kennels was a few minutes earlier, when he was questioned by his lawyer. Waters's questioning established that Alex had lied for a long time to a lot of people, suggesting his newest version of events is merely his newest lie. Waters's questioning also made clear that even now, after laying his hand on a Bible and swearing to tell the truth, he had difficulty giving a straight story. Alex couldn't remember when he started stealing. He couldn't estimate how many opioids he consumed a day. He couldn't answer where money went without records in front of him. He couldn't remember why he borrowed money from underage clients instead of obtaining a traditional bank loan. In Alex's limited recollections, everything was fuzzy and the facts were always loose. When Waters asked Alex if he borrowed a million dollars from his underage clients Alex offered one of his typically ambiguous and unhelpful answers, replying, "If that's what the records say, I don't dispute it, (but) that's not what I thought."

Waters spent much time questioning Alex about his actions after the killings, and how his cell phone suggests he was frantic, a "busy bee" moving around the property with seeming urgency, according to step counts contained on his phone, as well as speeding to and from his mother's house. Waters stated that the murders and the roadside shooting were similar for the fact that they distracted attention and generated sympathy for Alex, at least briefly. "When accountability is at your door, Mr. Murdaugh, bad things happen, isn't that true?" said Waters.

"For the first time in your life of privilege and prominence and wealth, when you were facing accountability, each time suddenly you became a victim . . . Shame for you is an extraordinary provocation . . . isn't it?"

Waters then began to ask about a long list of people and if Alex had deceived them. Alex admitted to lying to his wife, his sons, his brothers, his in-laws, his friends, his law partners and coworkers, his clients, and more. "Do you know why people lie, Mr. Murdaugh," asked Waters, not waiting for an answer. "Because they've done something wrong."

After Alex finished testifying the defense soon rested. The prosecution mounted a brief rebuttal case, calling repeat witnesses to explain again exactly how Maggie and Paul were killed, but the testimony was becoming repetitive. With this finished, the judge, at the suggestion of the defense team, ordered the jury be taken to Moselle before closing arguments, to see the kennels and shed where Maggie and Paul died as well as their home and the surrounding property. The judge visited the property at the same time as the jurors, as did Colleton County Clerk of Court Becky Hill. She recounted that moment in a book she wrote and published soon after the trial:

> While the jurors viewed the Moselle property, we all could hear and see Alex's story was impossible. Some of us either from the courthouse, law enforcement, or jury at Moselle had an epiphany and shared our thoughts with our eyes. At that moment, many of us standing there knew. I knew and they knew that Alex was guilty.

The jurors returned to hear closing arguments from each side, which again focused on themes and facts that by now had become familiar. But before the jurors were sent off to deliberate, Judge Newman announced he was removing a juror for allegedly discussing the case, a violation of the judge's orders. He had received a complaint about the juror and preliminary interviews by SLED agents seemed to confirm possible inappropriate communications. The judge dismissed the juror, telling her his decision and reasoning in open court. Before she was escorted out of the courthouse, she asked if she could retrieve some items left in the jury room, namely a purse, a bottle of water, and a dozen eggs. Laughter erupted around the courtroom at the mention of the eggs, the audience delighted by the absurdity of the request. As the outgoing juror explained, another juror brought in eggs from their farm as a gift, and she didn't want to leave without them. "We get a lot of interesting things," said Judge Newman, "but now a dozen eggs."

A new juror was sworn in, leaving just a single alternate. These seven men and five women deliberated for a mere three hours before coming to a unanimous decision just before 7:00 P.M. on March 2, 2021. The judge, jury, lawyers, Murdaugh family, and media all gathered hurriedly in the courtroom to listen to the clerk of court read Alex's fate: Guilty on all counts.

Alex Murdaugh turned red-faced as he was handcuffed and led out of the courtroom. His family all looked downcast. He would be back in court in the morning to receive his sentence.

Outside the courthouse, a man in a black robe with a white scarf stood in the square holding a big white sign with red letters that said JUSTICE. The Reverend Raymond Johnson was shouting, thanking God for answering his prayers. "He could not outsmart God, he thought he was smooth," said Johnson. "Thank you, Jesus."

The Reverend began to shuffle and dance, moved by the Holy Spirit.

"Mama dies. Son died. Daddy's supposed to protect his wife and child," said Johnson. "How wicked can you get?"

———

Alligators rest in plain sight in Southern swamps, unafraid of most other creatures. Few animals are foolish enough to pick a fight with the toothy beasts, and the smarter swamp critters give gators a wide berth, just in case the dragon-like creatures happen to be hungry. Alligators are often tranquil, but in an instant they can become swift, vicious, and lethal. That is how they thrive. They are hardwired to exploit opportunity.

For a century assorted members of the Murdaugh family ruled the swamp and controlled much of the Lowcountry. Alex seemingly undid their legacy in an instant, but the family foundation had never been stable and always rested on soggy soil, their power more precarious than appreciated. But compared to his forefathers, Alex's misdeeds were too egregious and long-running to be ignored. His evil acts—the stealing and lying and killing—seemed more natural to him than practicing law and trying to play the outdated role prescribed for him even before birth—to be a bigshot and to do what he wanted, without consequence.

A few months after Alex's conviction, lead prosecutor Creighton Waters reflected on the trial fondly, no doubt in part because he and his team in the South Carolina Attorney General's Office achieved a conviction in the high-profile case. But his reminiscing was also inspired by the intimacy of the trial, a proceeding that offered a chance to purge the Lowcountry and drag a century of accumulated sins out of the muck and into the sunlight.

"It will never happen again that all of us will all be in the same room again. It just won't," said Waters. "And that is a little sad because we made a lot of friends down there. And when you go through something like that there's a connection you know you will always have."

But Waters might be mistaken. Six months after Alex Murdaugh was convicted, his attorneys filed for a new trial, accusing the clerk of court of jury tampering, including having private discussions with jurors and steering them to convict Alex. Apart from that there remained unresolved charges against several of Alex's accused accomplices and open investigations into the suspicious deaths of Stephen Smith and Gloria Satterfield, as well as drug-running and public corruption. Waters would at least be seeing many familiar faces in South Carolina courthouses in the coming months and years. Only time would tell whether higher courts would sanction the way Alex Murdaugh was poached from the swamp, or if he deserved another murder trial, or if weapons and bloody clothing would ever be found. Rumors abound about what happened to the missing clothing and rifle. Some guess it was all dropped in the ocean, others suggest it was tucked inside a coffin beside Alex's late father and now sits underground. Another claim is that particular police took away the soiled clothing and weapons shortly after the murders, and also brought Alex a fresh change of clothes. Without anyone finding the clothes and weapons, such claims mostly remain speculative.

During a sentencing hearing for Alex Murdaugh on March 3, 2021, Newman spoke more than at any point during the trial, finally sharing some of his impressions after five intense weeks of testimony and argument. He reflected on the fates of other criminal defendants affected by the Murdaugh family and thought Murdaugh to be fortunate that his life was spared:

> *I don't question at all the decision of the state not to pursue the death penalty. But as I sit here in this courtroom and look around at the many portraits of judges and other court officials and reflect on the fact that over the past century, your family, including you, have been prosecuting people here in this courtroom and many have received the death penalty, probably for lesser conduct.*

Newman said Alex told incredible stories, and persisted in telling them, even though almost no one believed him. The judge wondered if Alex believed his own lies. "Within your own soul, you have to deal with that," said Newman, invoking the ghosts of his wife and son. "And I know you have to see Paul and Maggie during the nighttime when you're attempting to go to sleep. I'm sure they come and visit you."

"All day and every night," said Alex, offering a rare glimpse into his soul.

"I'm sure," said Newman. "And they will continue to do so. And reflect on the last time they looked you in the eyes, as you looked the jury in the eyes."

At another point in his commentary, Judge Newman offered an observation that the truth in these cases proved too painful, too ugly, for any person to admit:

> *As I've presided over murder cases over the past twenty-two years, I have yet to find a defendant who could go there, back to that moment in time, when they decided to pull the trigger or otherwise murder someone. I have not been able to get anyone, even those who have confessed, to go back and explain to me what happened at that moment in time when they opted to pull the trigger. When they opted to commit the most heinous crimes known to man.*

Judge Newman would not achieve that breakthrough with Alex. The defendant asserted his innocence for a final time, stating to the judge, "I will tell you again. I respect this court, but I am innocent. I would never under any circumstances hurt my wife, Maggie, and I would never under any circumstances hurt my son Paul Paul."

Newman wasn't interested in arguing. Just before sentencing Alex Murdaugh to two consecutive life terms in prison, he told the killer, "It might not have been you. It might have been the monster you become when you take fifteen, twenty, thirty, forty, fifty, sixty opioid pills . . . We'll leave it at that."

The veteran judge did not expect to find truth in the swamp. Up above treetops shut out sunlight. Down below blackwater pools swirled with sediment. All around sprawled the dark mire of Hampton County, saturated with sin and secrecy, desperate for a cleansing rain.

CODA

Once again, Alex Murdaugh appeared before Judge Clifton Newman. Nine months had passed since Newman sentenced the former lawyer to a pair of life terms in South Carolina prisons for the double murder of his wife and son. Now Alex was back in court awaiting punishment for some of his other crimes, namely the theft of millions of dollars from his legal clients and law partners. He had agreed to a plea deal with South Carolina prosecutors in order to resolve more than one hundred charges relating to fraud and theft and drug trafficking. The plea deal, which Judge Newman was being asked to approve, required Alex to plead guilty to twenty-two of these charges and serve a twenty-seven-year prison sentence.

Alex was dressed in an orange prison jumpsuit, with handcuffs and chains wrapped around his waist, wrists, and ankles. People eyed him from their seats in an upstairs courtroom at the Beaufort County Courthouse on November 28, 2023. Among the crowd were some of Alex's victims and their representatives. One by one they stood before a microphone that afternoon and addressed the man who had so brazenly deceived them. Among the first to speak was Ginger Hadwin, the sister of Gloria Satterfield, the longtime housekeeper and nanny to the Murdaugh family whose death Alex exploited for millions of dollars. Hadwin said she was appalled to know Alex stole from so many desperate people, including the children of a woman who died in a car crash involving an alleged drunk driver.

"They lost a mother and you stole every dime from them?" said Hadwin. "I just don't understand. Did you not have a soul?"

Hadwin had grown up with Alex and been his schoolmate. Her sister worked for him and his family for two decades. Yet despite this familiarity, she had been deceived entirely by Alex. "You are not the person that I thought I knew," said Hadwin, casting Alex as an anomaly. ". . . You come from a good family but you wasted your life."

A few speakers later, lawyer Mark Tinsley addressed Alex. Since Alex's murder trial ended in March 2023 Tinsley had helped negotiate an $18.5 million settlement between victims of the 2019 boat crash involving Paul Murdaugh and a convenience store chain that sold some of the underage victims alcohol. Though Tinsley had done well for his clients, his harsh words to Alex in the Beaufort courtroom did not betray much satisfaction or relief. Tinsley challenged the notion that Alex was haunted by visions of his victims:

> *Alex, you're a broken person. I don't think you're gonna lie in bed at night and have people come to you. I don't think that those people matter. And I don't know when that happened, but clearly it happened, where you matter more, and I feel bad for you as a result of that. I knew Paul and Maggie. I knew you. A lot of people thought they knew you. Clearly we didn't. I don't think you've always been this way, but somewhere along the way, you became broken.*

Tinsley doubted Alex's supposed remorse. He also accused him of hiding money. In his opinion, Alex had hardly come clean. "If he wants to be accountable, if he wants to be contrite, he ought to tell these people where their money is," said Tinsley. "That's not gonna happen. The same as he's not gonna lie in bed at night and think about the wrongs and feel sorry for what he did."

Next came Jordan "J. J." Jinks, one of Alex's oldest friends who once hired Alex to represent him after a car accident. Jinks became emotional as he began his remarks, recalling old times with the Murdaugh clan and their friends. "I've got a lot of intimate, intimate stuff that I could say," Jinks told Alex. "You remember all those wildlife hunts I had for law enforcement? Your entire family was the guest of honor. Mr. Buster, Judge Eltzroth insisted on me taking care of them for the day."

Like almost everyone else, Jinks said he was blindsided by the revelations of Alex's crimes, and doubly shocked to find that he was among his friend's many victims—defrauded of $150,000. "Boy I gave you my all," Jinks told Alex. "The money you stole from me, you could have asked me for it and I would have gave it to you, that's how I felt about you and your family. You didn't have to steal it from me, man." Jinks noted the irony of a discussion he once had with Alex about a potential settlement related to the car accident, when Alex warned, "Don't spend all this money foolishly."

Like Hadwin, Jinks was disgusted to learn Alex stole from children and the severely disabled. He wondered why Alex would stoop so low. "I didn't want to come up here and bash you," said Jinks, "but I gotta ask you, 'What kind of animal are you?'" Though all of Alex's known crimes were now years old, Jinks was still processing the enormity of his longtime buddy's wrongdoing. "When all this came about Paul, Paul and Maggie, I couldn't believe it. I didn't believe it," Jinks told Alex. "But after sitting here today and hearing some of the devious things that you did to people, these victims here—changed my mind, bro. Once again, I ask you, 'What kind of animal are you?'"

When Jinks finished speaking, Alex was allowed to make his own address. He held court for nearly fifty minutes. Despite an imminent twenty-seven-year prison sentence and being called soulless and an animal by longtime friends, Alex seemed buoyant. He was quick to acknowledge the "terrible things" he did, but also eager to make corrections and take advantage of having the last word. "One more thing, J. J., going back . . . ,"

Alex said to his friend just a few minutes into his commentary. "You are absolutely right about everything you said, but you are dead wrong about one thing: I would never hurt Maggie and I would never hurt Paul and it is important to me that you know that."

Alex left it at that, declining to explain himself or disclose anything else regarding his family members' still-mysterious deaths. Instead, he awkwardly moved on and began expressing regret to a long list of people. First, he apologized to his many financial victims, including some of the people who had addressed him directly moments earlier. He apologized to his son Buster, whom Alex complained suffered from a variety of baseless accusations because of the publicity surrounding his own criminal cases. "I am so sorry that I let you down. I am so sorry that I have not been able to be with you during such hard times," Alex said to his son, who was absent from the courtroom. "I am so sorry that I did so many things that are so contradictory to every single thing Mom and I ever taught you and Paul."

Alex then extended the apology to all his family members, whom he also addressed in absentia. "I am so sorry that I let each of you down," said Alex. "I am so sorry that I humiliated each of you. I am so sorry that I destroyed our family's reputation with these terrible things that I have done." At this point Alex dwelled on his heritage for a moment longer, on the family tradition he failed to fulfill and the family legacy he sullied. "I am so sorry that my actions that I'm pleading guilty to here today somehow made people on social media and in the media think that it's okay to falsely attack two of the three best men that I've ever known," said Alex, "and that's my father and my grandfather."

He proceeded to repeat the familiar Murdaugh mythology, describing Randolph "Buster" Murdaugh Jr. and Randolph "Randy" Murdaugh III as "two men who spent their life in service, helping others. Two men fully and wholly committed to justice. Two men who were most honest and most decent, and if they were here today, two men that would be devastated by what I have done." This was a simplistic take on the Murdaugh family, one in which a line of illustrious lawyers and community saviors was interrupted by Alex, the evil exception. Alex was now spinning this fiction himself, exaggerating the distinction between him and his forefathers, leaning on lore instead of a full set of facts. It was a talent and habit he came by naturally, an inherited instinct to recast the past for future advantage. Even as he admitted massive fraud and accepted a twenty-seven-year prison term he was seeking to escape accountability and change the narrative elsewhere, asking the courts to overturn his convictions for murdering his wife and son.

Stunningly, these convictions were in jeopardy. In September 2023, six months after the murder trial ended, Alex's lawyers filed claims of jury tampering by court official Rebecca "Becky" Hill and asked that their client be granted a new trial. For five intense weeks, Hill was the center of attention during the hoopla surrounding Alex Murdaugh's murder trial. As the county clerk of court she administered the courthouse and tended to the needs of many people associated with the trial, including prosecutors, police, defense lawyers, witnesses, the Murdaugh family, the courthouse staff, the media, and the jury. She seemed to be friends with everyone. Beyond being publicly praised in court by defense lawyer Richard "Dick" Harpootlian, Hill was thanked in a post-trial press conference by South Carolina attorney general Alan Wilson, who revealed he had a pet name for the clerk of court—Becky Boo.

In the months after trial, though, Alex's defense team soured on Hill, ultimately alleging that she told jurors not to believe Alex's claims on the witness stand and pressured them to quickly reach a verdict. Alex's defense lawyers accused Hill of other bad behavior, such as soliciting jurors' thoughts on Alex's culpability, inappropriately e-mailing prosecutors and witnesses, engineering the removal of a juror who may have voted to acquit Alex, and taking actions designed to boost sales of a book she quickly co-wrote about her experience at the trial. Hill denied these charges, but other events soon came to cloud her reputation and further the intrigue surrounding her behavior.

First, her thirty-four-year-old son, Jeffrey, was arrested on a wiretapping charge on November 21, 2023, accused of secretly listening to a supervisor's phone conversation. He was fired that day from his job as Colleton County's technology director and police also reportedly seized a cell phone belonging to Becky Hill. A few weeks after that, Becky Hill was reported to be the subject of an ethics complaint that accused her of using her position for personal gain. And then, in late December, sales of Hill's books were stopped after she admitted to plagiarizing a portion of her book, using a draft of a news reporter's article about the murder trial without attribution.

As these allegations swirled, South Carolina's Supreme Court announced Alex would have the chance to press his case for a retrial. In December the court appointed a retired chief justice of the South Carolina Supreme Court to handle all future matters related to Alex's murder conviction and his request for a new trial. This judge promptly scheduled hearings for January 2024 to hear evidence of the alleged jury tampering.

The courts seemed to think there might be more to learn. But would a murder retrial set the record straight, or further muddy the swampwaters? Had Alex, by telling so many lies, obliterated any hope of establishing the truth? Yet perhaps there are still chapters to write in the Murdaugh saga, especially if Alex cared to untangle his elaborately woven web. As his older brother Randolph "Randy" Murdaugh IV stated in a rare public comment soon after Alex's murder conviction, "He knows more than what he's saying. He's not telling the truth, in my opinion, about everything there."

"The not knowing," said Randy, "is the worst thing there is."

WORKS CITED

Newspapers
The Augusta Herald, Augusta, GA.
The Beaufort Gazette, Beaufort, SC.
The Carolina Morning News, Beaufort, SC.
The Charleston Mercury, Charleston, SC.
The Charlotte Observer, Charlotte, NC.
The Hampton County Guardian, Hampton, SC.
The Island News, Beaufort, SC.
The Island Packet, Hilton Head Island, SC.
The News and Courier, Charleston, SC.
The New York Times, New York, NY.
The State, Columbia, SC.
The Savannah Morning News, Savannah, GA.
The Washington Post, Washington, DC.

Books, theses, and pamphlets
Cash, Wilbur J. *Mind of the South*. New York: Alfred A. Knopf, 1941.
Conroy, Pat. *The Death of Santini: The Story of a Father and His Son*. New York: Doubleday, 2013.
Conroy, Pat and Suzanne Williamson Pollak. *The Pat Conroy Cookbook*. New York: Doubleday, 2004.
Conyngham, David P. *Sherman's March Through the South: With Sketches and Incidents of the Campaign*. New York: Sheldon and Company, 1865.
Cuthbert, Robert B. and Stephen G. Hoffius, eds. *Northern Money, Southern Land: The Plantation Sketches of Chlotilde R. Martin*. Columbia: University of South Carolina Press, 2009.
Edgar, Walter B., ed. *The South Carolina Encyclopedia*, Columbia: University of South Carolina Press, 2006.
Elliott, William. *Carolina Sports by Land and Water; Including Incidents of Devil-fishing, Wild-Cat, Deer and Bear Hunting, etc*. Columbia: University of South Carolina Press, 1994.
Garnet And Black. College yearbooks, assorted years, the University of South Carolina Digital Collections.

Hill, Rebecca and Neil Gordon. *Behind the Doors of Justice*. Naples, FL: Wind River Media LLC, 2023.

"Judicial Hellholes 2004." Washington, DC: American Tort Reform Foundation, 2004.

Laurie, Pete and David Chamberlain. *The South Carolina Aquarium Guide to Aquatic Habitats of South Carolina*. Columbia: University of South Carolina Press, 2003.

Lockhart, Matthew Allen. "From Rice Fields to Duck Marshes: Sport Hunters and Environmental Change on the South Carolina Coast, 1890–1950." Doctoral dissertation. Columbia: University of South Carolina Scholar Commons, 2017.

Marscher, Fran Heyward. *Remembering the Way It Was at Hilton Head, Bluffton and Daufuskie*. Charleston, SC: The History Press, 2005.

Marscher, Fran Heyward. *Remembering the Way It Was, Volume Two: More Stories from Hilton Head, Bluffton and Daufuskie*. Charleston, SC: The History Press, 2007.

McTeer, J. E. *Adventure in the Woods and Waters of the Low Country*. Beaufort, SC: Beaufort Book Co., 1972.

McTeer, J. E. *High Sheriff of the Low Country*. Beaufort, SC: JEM Company, 1970.

Rossignol, Rosalyn. *My Ghost Has a Name: Memoir of a Murder*. Columbia: University of South Carolina Press, 2018.

Rowland, Lawrence S. and Stephen S. Wise. *Bridging the Sea Islands' Past and Present, 1893–2006: The History of Beaufort County, South Carolina, Volume 3*. Columbia: University of South Carolina Press, 2015.

Sherman, William T. *Memoirs of General W. T. Sherman, Volume II, Part 4, 1889*, published online by Project Gutenberg.

South Carolina: The WPA Guide to the Palmetto State. Columbia: University of South Carolina Press, 1988.

Williams, Rose-Marie Eltzroth, ed. *Railroads and Sawmills: Varnville, S.C., 1872–1997*. Varnville Community Council, 1998.

Winn, J. Murry. *Growing Up in Hampton County*. Bemidji, MN: Focus Publishing, 2013.

Woods, Baynard. *Coffin Point: The Strange Cases of Ed McTeer, Witchdoctor Sheriff*. Montgomery, Ala.: River City Publishing, 2010.

Magazine articles and other articles

"A Rich Do-Gooder Named Winthrop Turns Detective to Solve a Brutal Murder." *People* 1974.

Dickey, Gary C. "A Heritage in the Law: Randolph Murdaugh Jr. '38."
    Carolina Lawyer vol. IX, 1989, University of South Carolina School of
    Law.

Edmunds, Emma. "Slouching Toward Bluffton." *Atlanta Weekly* June 27, 1982.

Eisenstaedt, Alfred, "Life Spends a Day at Yemassee Junction." *Life* May 1942.

Freedman, Michael. "Home Court Advantage," *Forbes* June 10, 2002.

Hunt, Morton M. "Damage Suits—A Primrose Path to Immorality." *Harper's
    Magazine*, Jan. 1959, reprinted in *The Hampton County Guardian*.

Mathis-Lilley, Ben. "Let Me Say This with As Much Sensitivity As I Can:
    Wow, That's a Lot of Dead People and Crime." *Slate* Sept. 16, 2021.

"South Carolina's Growing Wild Hog Problem: Recommendations for
    Management and Control." https://www.dnr.sc.gov/wildlife/hog/pdf
    /wildhogwhitepaper.pdf.

"Third Parties: Southern Revolt." *Time*, Oct. 11, 1948.

Televisions shows, podcasts and docuseries

Good Morning America, ABC.

Murdaugh Murders: A Southern Scandal, Netflix, 2023.

Murdaugh Murders Podcast, https://murdaughmurderspodcast.com/.

Today, NBC.

Museums and libraries

Beaufort County Library, the Beaufort District Collection, Beaufort, SC.

Charleston County Library, the South Carolina Room, Charleston, SC.

Colleton County Library, Walterboro, SC.

Hampton County Library, Hampton, SC.

Hampton County Museum, Hampton, SC.

Hampton Museum and Visitors Center, Hampton, SC.

Marlene and Nathan Addlestone Library, College of Charleston, Charleston,
    SC.

Nimitz Library, Special Collections, United States Naval Academy, Annapolis,
    MD.

South Carolina Law Enforcement Officers Hall of Fame, Columbia, SC.

South Carolina Supreme Court Library, Columbia, SC.

Walker Local and Family History Center, Richland Library, Columbia, SC.

NOTES

Chapter 1

p. 2   "Bright as day": testimony of W. W. Bartlett during Hampton County coroner's inquest of Randolph Murdaugh Sr., July 19, 1940; coroner's inquest records at the Hampton County Courthouse in Hampton, SC.

p. 9   "Oh, what a tangled web": testimony of Alex Murdaugh, *State of South Carolina v. Richard Alexander Murdaugh*, Feb. 23, 2023.

p. 11   "About half a mile": Bartlett testimony.

p. 12   "Community life at Hampton": *South Carolina: The WPA Guide to the Palmetto State*, Columbia: University of South Carolina Press, 1988, 454.

p. 13   "Redeemed South Carolina": Walter B. Edgar, *The South Carolina Encyclopedia*, Columbia: University of South Carolina Press, 2006; "Red Shirts," 782.

p. 14   "*Times were exceedingly difficult*": "Hampton County Emerges from Trials of War," *The Hampton County Guardian*, Oct. 23, 1963.

p. 15   "This county was formed": letter to the editor of *The Hampton County Guardian* from George Warren, Feb. 9, 1921.

p. 15   "When the general rose": "Hampton County Emerges from Trials of War," *The Hampton County Guardian*, Oct. 23, 1963.

p. 16   "Hampton seems . . . in a class": "Beauty of Town Seen by Woman," *The Hampton County Guardian*, April 5, 1922.

p. 16   "Like having a cooling poultice": Chlotilde R. Martin, "Lowcountry Gossip," *The News and Courier* [Charleston, SC], Nov. 24, 1935.

p. 17   "Pretty, old town": "Hampton County's Condition Good Says *Morning News*," *The Hampton County Guardian*, March 11, 1925.

p. 17   "Nobody hurries in Hampton": "Hampton Nothing if Not Individual Says *Herald*," *The Hampton County Guardian*, Aug. 22, 1928.

p. 17   "It is not a young": ibid.

p. 17   "Distressingly healthy": "Newspaper Man Thinks Well of the Town of Varnville," *The Hampton County Guardian*, May 11, 1921.

p. 17   "Lack of work": "Hampton Has Entered Contest," *The Hampton County Guardian*, July 26, 1916.

p. 17   "Like balm to a storm-tossed": "Hampton Nothing if Not Individual Says Herald," *The Hampton County Guardian*, Aug. 22, 1928.

p. 18   "Good-sized swamp": "A Little Touch Now and Then," *The Hampton County Guardian*, Dec. 1, 1920.

p. 18   "Caught like rats": "Hampton Jail Denounced As Dangerous Fire Trap," *The Hampton County Guardian*, June 11, 1924.

p. 18   "Shameful thing for a civilized community": "County Officials Are Severely Criticised," *The Hampton County Guardian*, June 18, 1918.

p. 19   "You folks in Hampton County": "Strong Charge Made by Jurist," *The Hampton County Guardian*, June 4, 1924.

p. 19   "Disgrace to the county": "The Court House," *The Hampton County Guardian*, Oct. 8, 1924.

p. 19   "Unsafe, uncomfortable . . . and an eyesore": "County Court House Unsafe Says Moxon," *The Hampton County Guardian*, April 16, 1924.

p. 21   "Less talk about crops": *South Carolina: The WPA Guide to the Palmetto State*, 454.

p. 21   "The price doesn't matter": Chlotilde R. Martin, "Lowcountry Gossip," *The News and Courier* [Charleston, SC], Nov. 24, 1935.

p. 23   "Mitral heart murmur": admission and medical records of Randolph Murdaugh Sr., the United States Naval Academy.

p. 23   "One of the most apt": "Murdaugh Joins Carolina Squad," *The State*, Sept. 2, 1934.

p. 23   "Otherwise known as 'Buster,'": *The Garnet and Black* yearbook, University of South Carolina, 1908, 25.

p. 23   "Proficient": list of graduates from the University of South Carolina School of Law, *The News and Courier* [Charleston, SC], June 9, 1910.

p. 24   *"Buster," or "Old Hatchet Face"*: *The Garnet and Black* yearbook, University of South Carolina 1910, 67.

p. 24   "Charming and accomplished": "Marriages at Hampton," *The News and Courier* [Charleston, SC], March 27, 1914.

p. 25   "Quite surprised": "Varnville Department," *The Hampton County Guardian*, Dec. 3, 1919.

p. 26   "Faithful, fearless, and competent": campaign advertisement for Randolph Murdaugh Sr., *The Hampton County Guardian*, June 30, 1920.

p. 26   "Has no entangling connections": campaign advertisement for R. M. Jefferies, *The Hampton County Guardian*, Sept. 8, 1920.

p. 26   "Mr. Murdaugh enjoys a large": campaign ad for Heber R. Padgett, *The Hampton County Guardian*, Aug. 18, 1920.

p. 28   "Un-American": "Jury Convicts Negro Slayer," *The Hampton County Guardian*, Feb. 7, 1923.

p. 29   "One of the hardest working": "Political Pot Begins to Boil," *The Hampton County Guardian*, March 12, 1924.

p. 29   "Will you take him on": interview with Jim Moss, July 25, 2023.

p. 31   "His real forte": ibid.

p. 32   "Burst her bubble": interview with an anonymous source.

p. 32   "It was on": interview with an anonymous source.

p. 33   "Beat the hell": interview with an anonymous source.

p. 33   "God, Randy is such": interview with an anonymous source.

p. 33   "He could do what other people": interview with an anonymous source.

p. 34   "Alex is the reason": interview with an anonymous source.

p. 34   "Spiritual founder": the website of Kappa Alpha Order (https://www .kappaalphaorder.org/about/history/robert-e-lee/).

p. 34   "The highlight of the spring": *The Garnet and Black* yearbook, University of South Carolina, 1960, 304.

p. 35   "Was always broken": interview with an anonymous source.

p. 35   "One-horse farm": testimony of Ben Heyward, *State of South Carolina v. Benjamin Heyward* (1940), South Carolina Supreme Court Library.

p. 36   "Colored houses": testimony of Hubert W. Randall, *State of South Carolina v. Benjamin Heyward* (1940), South Carolina Supreme Court Library.

p. 36   "Are you Willie Heyward": testimony of Willie Heyward, *State of South Carolina v. Willie Heyward* (1932), records of Beaufort County, SC.

p. 39   "Ginger cake": "$400 Reward Offered for Murderers," *The Beaufort Gazette*, Jan. 29, 1925.

p. 40   "Curious spectacle": Chlotilde R. Martin, "Lowcountry Gossip," *The News and Courier* [Charleston, SC], July 5, 1933.

p. 41   "What would you do": Baynard Woods, *Coffin Point: The Strange Cases of Ed McTeer, Witchdoctor Sheriff,* River City Publishing, Montgomery, Ala., 2010, 34.

p. 43   "Willie, there is a car": testimony of Willie Heyward, *State of South Carolina v. Willie Heyward* (1932), records of Beaufort County, SC.

p. 45   "He stops everywhere to talk": testimony of Russell Laffitte, *United States v. Russell Lucius Laffitte,* Nov. 18, 2022.

p. 45   "I don't think": Gary C. Dickey, "A Heritage in the Law: Randolph Murdaugh Jr. '38," *Carolina Lawyer,* University of South Carolina School of Law, vol. IX, 1989, 5.

p. 45   "When he talked, everyone listened": interview with an anonymous source.

p. 45   "I could hear him": testimony of Russell Laffitte, *United States v. Russell Lucius Laffitte,* Nov. 18, 2022.

p. 46   "They were the law": ibid.

p. 47   "Tell my grandaddy": interview with Mike Macloskie, July 25, 2023.

p. 48   "It is said that Coach Laval": "Young Murdaugh Like Dad in
         Football," *The Hampton County Guardian*, Oct. 10, 1934.

p. 48   "Busted hell": Dickey, 5.

p. 49   "Although a prosecuting attorney": "Murdaugh unopposed," *The State*,
         June 29, 1936.

p. 49   "Their presence would have": "Just a minute!" *The State*, Dec. 12, 1935.

p. 51   "When I left to go": Dickey, 5.

p. 51   "It was during this period": J. W. DeLoach, "The Requiem," *The
         Hampton County Guardian*, Sept. 21, 1977.

p. 52   "A long trail": J. E. McTeer, *High Sheriff of the Low Country*, JEM
         Company 1970, 42.

p. 53   "Mobsters": Lawrence S. Rowland and Stephen S. Wise, *Bridging the
         Sea Islands' Past and Present, 1893–2006: The History of Beaufort County,
         South Carolina, Volume 3*, Columbia: University of South Carolina
         Press, 2015, 265.

p. 54   "In fact his own people": "Negro Lynched by Unknown Parties," *The
         Hampton County Guardian*, May 26, 1920.

p. 55   "We have an unfortunate situation": "Guardian Gives World
         Opinion," *The Hampton County Guardian*, Nov. 24, 1926.

p. 56   "I will say": "Action Called for by Johnson," *The Hampton County
         Guardian*, Jan. 26, 1927.

p. 56   "Disgrace": "A Shameful Record," *The Hampton County Guardian*,
         May 14, 1930.

p. 57   "I would like to state": arraignment of Ben Heyward, Fall 1939,
         records of Beaufort County, SC.

p. 58   "Despite the fact": "Solicitor Is Stricken As Court Opens," *The
         Hampton County Guardian*, Feb. 22, 1939.

p. 58   "Here is hoping": letter from J. D. Mars to Randolph Murdaugh,
         Feb. 21, 1940, records of Beaufort County, SC.

p. 59   "If Mr. Carden had presented": testimony of Ben Heyward, *State of
         South Carolina v. Benjamin Heyward* (1940), South Carolina Supreme
         Court Library.

p. 60   "The prosecution was brilliantly handled": "Beaufort Negro Is
         Sentenced," *The Hampton County Guardian*, March 13, 1940.

Chapter 2

p. 63   "Wonderful in their way": "Expert in Forestry Writes of Cypress," *The
         Hampton County Guardian*, Feb. 21, 1923.

p. 63   "Such dismal swamps are frequent": David P. Conyngham, *Sherman's
         March Through the South: With Sketches and Incidents of the Campaign*,
         New York: Sheldon and Company, 1865, 319.

p. 64   "Cut up by an infinite": William T. Sherman, *Memoirs of General W. T. Sherman, Volume II, Part 4*, 1889, published online by Project Gutenberg, chapter XXII.

p. 64   "A dense marsh": Conyngham, 305.

p. 65   *"Fishing and hunting were fun"*: J. Murry Winn, *Growing Up in Hampton County*, Bemidji, MN: Focus Publishing, 2013, 18.

p. 65   "The gentleman of all poisonous snakes": J. E. McTeer, *Adventure in the Woods and Waters of the Low Country*, Beaufort, SC: Beaufort Book Co., Inc., 1972, 91.

p. 66   "One of a kind": "His death is like a library burning down," *Savannah Morning News*, electronic edition, Feb. 6, 1998.

p. 67   "Well, that's Buster's circuit": interview of Randy Blackmon, Oct. 4, 2022.

p. 67   "He had absolute control": "His death is like a library burning down," *Savannah Morning News*, electronic edition, Feb. 6, 1998.

p. 67   "Dominated": "Murdaugh Legacy Is One of Service," *The Hampton County Guardian*, Feb. 12, 1998.

p. 68   "He never failed": ibid.

p. 68   "Personally, as a Black man": "Benjamin Praises Buster Murdaugh," *The Hampton County Guardian*, Feb. 12, 1998.

p. 68   "Best known as a plaintiff's attorney": obituary of Randolph "Buster" Murdaugh Jr., who died Feb. 5, 1998.

p. 68   "Treated everybody with respect": "Murdaugh Legacy Is One of Service," *The Hampton County Guardian*, Feb. 12, 1998.

p. 68   "The most outstanding trial lawyer": ibid.

p. 69   "Automatic": interview with Ronnie Crosby, May 11, 2023.

p. 70   "The last vestige of normalcy": interview with an anonymous source.

p. 70   "Experienced": campaign advertisement for Walton J. McLeod Jr. in *The Hampton County Guardian*, Aug. 21, 1940.

p. 70   "Aggressive": campaign advertisement for Randolph "Buster" Murdaugh Jr. in *The Hampton County Guardian*, Aug. 21, 1940.

p. 71   "Every-one a fair deal": ibid.

p. 71   "Nobody in Hampton": Chlotilde R. Martin, "Lowcountry Gossip," *The News and Courier* [Charleston, SC], Nov. 24, 1935.

p. 72   *"We have not always had"*: "Just Hampton," *The Hampton County Guardian*, Nov. 18, 1931.

p. 73   "Times were not always good": Rose-Marie Eltzroth Williams, *Railroads and Sawmills: Varnville, S.C., 1872–1997*, Varnville Community Council, 1998.

p. 73   "We crowded as many people": Winn, 8.

p. 75   "Heroic adventure": "Expert in Forestry Writes of Cypress," *The Hampton County Guardian*, Feb. 21, 1923.

p. 77   "Odds and ends of lumber": "Lightsey Brothers Makers of Miley," *The Hampton County Guardian*, Jan. 29, 1930.

p. 78   "Low, white rambling bungalow": *Northern Money, Southern Land: The Plantation Sketches of Chlotilde R. Martin*, edited by Robert B. Cuthbert and Stephen G. Hoffius, Columbia, University of South Carolina Press, 2009.

p. 79   "When you get in trouble": interview with Patricia Moore, July 14, 2022.

p. 79   "My father and I": "Changing of the Guard," *The Hampton County Guardian*, Dec. 24, 1986.

p. 80   "I've never tried to compete": ibid.

p. 80   "I've never wanted to do": "Like Father, Like Son," *The State*, Dec. 30, 1986.

p. 80   "The purpose of prosecution": Dickey, 6.

p. 81   "It always gave me": ibid.

p. 81   "I need a favor": interview with an anonymous source.

p. 82   *"When you wake up Monday"*: Rosalyn Rossignol, *My Ghost Has a Name: Memoir of a Murder*, Columbia, University of South Carolina Press, 2018.

p. 83   "He used personality": testimony of Jeanne Seckinger, *State v. Murdaugh*, Feb. 7, 2023.

p. 83   "They eat what they kill": testimony of Jeanne Seckinger, *United States of America v. Russell Lucius Laffitte*, Nov. 9, 2022.

p. 85   "We don't live": Michael Freedman, "Home Court Advantage," *Forbes*, June 10, 2002.

p. 85   "I didn't have but two": interview with an anonymous source.

p. 85   "Big stick": interview with an anonymous source.

p. 86   "The trip was made": "Personals," *The Hampton County Guardian*, July 30, 1941.

p. 86   "Unselfish and untiring efforts": "General Sessions Court Convenes at Hampton," *The Hampton County Guardian*, Feb. 23, 1944.

p. 86   "Your Honor, please": Fran Heyward Marscher, *Remembering the Way It Was, Volume Two: More Stories from Hilton Head, Bluffton and Dafauskie*, Charleston, SC: The History Press, 2007, 90.

p. 87   "The atmosphere at said crossing": complaint of *Randolph Murdaugh Jr. v. Charleston & Western Carolina Railway Company*, Sept. 30, 1940, records of Hampton County, SC.

p. 87   "It was just a clear night": testimony of W. W. Bartlett during Hampton County coroner's inquest of Randolph Murdaugh Sr., July 19, 1940, records of Hampton County, SC.

p. 87   "It was very clear": testimony of C. T. Billiter during Hampton
         County coroner's inquest of Randolph Murdaugh Sr., July 19, 1940,
         records of Hampton County, SC.

p. 87   "A proper lookout for travelers": complaint of *Randolph Murdaugh Jr.
         v. Charleston & Western Carolina Railway Company*, Sept. 30, 1940,
         records of Hampton County, SC.

p. 87   "I had no idea": testimony of W. W. Bartlett during Hampton County
         coroner's inquest of Randolph Murdaugh Sr., July 19, 1940, records of
         Hampton County, SC.

p. 87   "I mentioned something": testimony of C. T. Billiter during Hampton
         County coroner's inquest of Randolph Murdaugh Sr., July 19, 1940,
         records of Hampton County, SC.

p. 87   "Did all within his power": complaint of *Randolph Murdaugh Jr. v.
         Charleston & Western Carolina Railway Company*, Sept. 30, 1940,
         records of Hampton County, SC.

p. 88   "If (Randolph Sr.) had": testimony of C. T. Billiter during Hampton
         County coroner's inquest of Randolph Murdaugh Sr., July 19, 1940,
         records of Hampton County, SC.

p. 88   "He was 100 percent country": testimony of Alex Murdaugh, *State v.
         Murdaugh*, Feb. 23, 2023.

p. 89   "Little Dylan Klebold": interview with Kim Brant, April 19, 2023.

p. 89   "Ever since . . . I've always pushed": interview with Ronnie Crosby,
         May 11, 2023.

p. 89   "Friendly and cheerful every time": interview with Kim Brant,
         April 19, 2023.

p. 90   "It was almost like": interview with Ronnie Crosby, May 11, 2023.

p. 90   "She didn't grow up": testimony of Alex Murdaugh, *State v. Murdaugh*,
         Feb. 23, 2023.

p. 90   "She made the best": testimony of Marian Proctor, *State v. Murdaugh*,
         Feb. 14, 2023.

p. 90   "She never took not working": testimony of Alex Murdaugh, *State v.
         Murdaugh*, Feb. 23, 2023.

p. 90   "She wasn't sitting around": interview with an anonymous source.

p. 91   "Her pregnancies were so hard": testimony of Alex Murdaugh, *State v.
         Murdaugh*, Feb. 23, 2023.

p. 91   "Very much a lady": interview with Ronnie Crosby, May 11, 2023.

p. 91   "Free spirit": testimony of Marian Proctor, *State v. Murdaugh*, Feb. 14,
         2023.

p. 91   "She had this little playful look": testimony of Alex Murdaugh, *State
         v. Murdaugh*, Feb. 23, 2023.

p. 91   "They had a comfortable life": testimony of Marian Proctor, *State v. Murdaugh*, Feb. 14, 2023.

p. 92   "Maggie, she always had": interview with an anonymous source.

p. 92   "Great second fiddle": interview with an anonymous source.

p. 92   "Yeah, I think the death penalty": Marscher, 88.

p. 93   "In Beaufort yesterday": "Lawyers Form Bar Association," *The Hampton County Guardian*, July 2, 1947.

p. 94   "You can well realize": "Solicitor Murdaugh Charges Politics Governs Pardons," *The News and Courier* [Charleston, SC], Jan. 9, 1945.

p. 95   "I have great respect": McTeer, *High Sheriff of the Low Country*, 63.

p. 95   "I moved the court": Marscher, 89.

p. 96   "*The city desk*": Tom O'Connor, "The Time Has Come . . ." *The Hampton County Guardian*, Jan. 28, 1948.

p. 97   "Pure meanness": "Colleton Resident Held in Slaying of Aged Sister," *The News and Courier* [Charleston, SC], April 9, 1949.

p. 97   "When you've got a crime": Marscher, 88.

p. 99   "Dull normal": "Hampton Youth Found Sane by State Doctors," *The News and Courier* [Charleston, SC], March 30, 1951.

p. 99   "Deliberate and cold-blooded": "Mixon Gets Life in Death of Parents," *The State*, June 7, 1951.

p. 99   "I did care about them": ibid.

p. 99   "Just killed his old lady": "Jury Finds Bowers Guilty," *The News and Courier* [Charleston, SC], Oct. 12, 1950.

p. 100   "When he has whiskey": ibid.

p. 100   "Just another murder case": "Estill Citizens Demand Speedy Trial As Authorities Find Bowers Is Now Sane," *The Hampton County Guardian*, Aug. 9, 1950.

p. 100   "Raising the devil and fussing": "Jury Finds Bowers Guilty," *The News and Courier* [Charleston, SC], Oct. 12, 1950.

p. 101   "*Sometimes I'd think*": Marscher, 89.

Chapter 3

p. 102   "I just missed three weeks": *Northern Money, Southern Land*, 68.

p. 103   "It was the funniest thing": Fran Heyward Marscher, *Remembering the Way It Was at Hilton Head, Bluffton & Daufuskie*. Charleston, SC: The History Press, 2005, 78.

p. 103   "They were jealous of me": ibid, 79.

p. 103   "At the end of nowhere": *Northern Money, Southern Land*, 66.

p. 103   "Real home": ibid, 67.

p. 103   "Shoot the eye out": Emma Edmunds, "Slouching Toward Bluffton," *Atlanta Weekly*, June 27, 1982.

p. 103 "Constant surprise": "Harry Cram Is Wed in Ridgeland," *The Hampton County Guardian*, Oct. 28, 1936.

p. 103 "A figure out of": Fran Heyward Marscher, *Remembering the Way It Was*, 77.

p. 103 "Where the guests rode hard": "Local Legend Harry Cram Dies," *The Island Packet* [Hilton Head Island, SC], May 22, 1997.

p. 104 "Telling Harry Cram stories": "Slouching Towards Bluffton," 18.

p. 104 "You have to remember": Jim Littlejohn, "Lowcountry Lore," *Carolina Morning News* [Beaufort, SC], Aug. 26, 2002.

p. 104 "Went through every suit": "Slouching Towards Bluffton," 21.

p. 104 "I've never seen daddy": "Local Legend Harry Cram Dies," *The Island Packet* [Hilton Head Island, SC], May 22, 1997.

p. 104 "Whatever it is": *Northern Money, Southern Land*, 67.

p. 105 "Harry always lived differently": Fran Heyward Marscher, *Remembering the Way It Was*, 80.

p. 105 "I hear these wild stories": "Slouching Towards Bluffton," 21.

p. 105 "Mister Harry": unpublished story "Mister Harry" by Roger Pinckney.

p. 105 "Booze!": Undated question-and-answer interview with Harry Cram reprinted from the *Bluffton Eccentric* newspaper.

p. 106 "I only fired two shots": ibid.

p. 107 "You'd have to be an idiot": interview with an anonymous source.

p. 107 "You know Roberts Vaux": interview with an anonymous source.

p. 107 "Wasn't discussed and wasn't denied": interview with an anonymous source.

p. 108 "The drunker I got": interview with an anonymous source.

p. 110 "I saw a vehicle coming": Witness statements and other details are included in the South Carolina Highway Patrol's Multidisciplinary Accident Investigation Team (MAIT) report on the fatal collision involving Stevie McAlhaney in Hampton County on March 9, 2007.

p. 110 "I waz runing speed": ibid.

p. 110 "Hey, STOP": ibid.

p. 111 "If it were not": ibid.

p. 111 "The Honda Civic": ibid.

p. 111 "Oh my God": ibid.

p. 111 "We can't see anything": ibid.

p. 111 "I approached the car": ibid.

p. 112 "One of the finest": "Charges pending in fatal wreck," *The Hampton County Guardian*, March 15, 2007.

p. 112 "He was relaxed": ibid.

p. 112 "To lift my face out": letter to the editor of *The Hampton County Guardian* from Cam Mixson, unknown date.

p. 112   "I certainly do not mean": ibid.

p. 113   "Illegally stopped": South Carolina Highway Patrol report from
Corporal T. M. Bell, March 10, 2007.

p. 113   "Might have created": South Carolina Highway Patrol MAIT report
concerning fatal collision involving Stevie McAlhaney.

p. 113   "Ten to fourteen years": "Charges are filed in fatal crash," *The Hampton
County Guardian*, March 29, 2007.

p. 113   "We believe Manigo": ibid.

p. 114   "When he knew Cameron Mixson": complaint of *Linda J. McAlhaney
v. Richard Mixson*, filed June 17, 2008, in Hampton County, SC.

p. 115   "Very good at reading people": testimony of Ronnie Crosby, *State v.
Murdaugh*, Feb. 7, 2023.

p. 115   "Tasmanian Devil": testimony of Annette Griswold, *State v.
Murdaugh*, Feb. 8, 2023.

p. 115   "Always loud, always busy": testimony of Jeanne Seckinger, *State v.
Murdaugh*, Feb. 7, 2023.

p. 115   "It'd aggravate the hell": testimony of Mark Ball, *State v. Murdaugh*,
Feb. 22, 2023.

p. 115   "I never thought Alex worked": interview with an anonymous source.

p. 116   "Not self-aware": interview with an anonymous source.

p. 116   "He never listened to anyone": interview with an anonymous source.

p. 116   "He had friends": interview with an anonymous source.

p. 116   "They're sorry you got": interview with an anonymous source.

p. 116   "Bo', you know what": interview with an anonymous source.

p. 117   "Alex Murdaugh has": letter from Fourteenth Circuit Solicitor
Duffie Stone to the South Carolina attorney general, July 27,
2007, obtained via Freedom of Information request to the attorney
general's office.

p. 118   "There appears to be": email from South Carolina Assistant Deputy
Attorney General David Stumbo to the Hampton County clerk of
court, Aug. 4, 2011, records of *State of South Carolina v. Jerome Manigo*,
Hampton County Courthouse.

p. 118   "These people are just hard headed": email from South Carolina
Assistant Deputy Attorney General David Stumbo to a colleague,
June 24, 2011, obtained via Freedom of Information request to the
attorney general's office.

p. 119   "There was never any justice": interview with Cam Mixson, April 27,
2023.

p. 120   "Fair, polite but firm": "Attorney's [sic] Explain Cram-Murdaugh
Case," *The Hampton County Guardian*, Feb. 16, 1949.

p. 121   "Interesting if somewhat complicated reading": "Hot Words Are Exchanged in Records of Murdaugh-Cram Suit and Cross-Suit," *The News and Courier* [Charleston, SC], Feb. 8, 1949.

p. 121   "He made a studied effort": ibid.

p. 121   "The cows were gone": interview with an anonymous source.

p. 121   "Wild and unruly": "Hot Words Are Exchanged in Records of Murdaugh-Cram Suit and Cross-Suit," *The News and Courier* [Charleston, SC], Feb. 8, 1949.

p. 121   "Mr. Boulware, Murdaugh's attorney": "Attorney's [sic] Explain Cram-Murdaugh Case," *The Hampton County Guardian*, Feb. 16, 1949.

p. 122   "Reputable lawyers make it": ibid.

p. 123   "I will welcome": "Murdaugh Would Welcome Bar Hearing," *The News and Courier* [Charleston, SC], Aug. 3, 1949.

p. 124   "I welcomed a full": "Murdaugh Charges Dismissed by Bar," *The Hampton County Guardian*, Oct. 5, 1949.

p. 124   "Law enforcement solicitor": "Murdaugh Legacy Is One of Service," *The Hampton County Guardian*, Feb. 12, 1998.

p. 125   "My reaction to your work": letter to Randolph "Buster" Murdaugh Jr. from Judge J. Frank Eatmon, of Kingstree, SC, May 21, 1951; Murdaugh records at the Hampton Museum and Visitor's Center, Hampton, SC.

p. 125   "I remember a time": Dickey, 5.

p. 128   "Intimidation factor": interview with anonymous source.

p. 128   "He helped people": interview with Jared Newman.

p. 128   "Genteel": interview with Travis Medlock, Dec. 12, 2022.

p. 128   "You just thanked them": interview with William Humphries, March 2023.

p. 128   "They didn't advertise it": interview with Dayle and Randy Blackmon, Nov. 21, 2022.

p. 129   "Fun-loving": interview with an anonymous source.

p. 129   "My wife who is": interview with an anonymous source.

p. 129   "We've got to do something": interview with Kim Brant, April 19, 2023.

p. 130   "More full of shit": interview with an anonymous source.

p. 130   "Accidental solicitor": interview with Jared Newman, Oct. 5, 2022.

p. 130   "The best thing": interview with Dayle and Randy Blackmon, Nov. 21, 2022.

p. 131   "There's two types of bitches": ibid.

p. 131   "Solicitor's probation"; Dickey, 6.

p. 132   "I know your wife": interview with Jared Newman, Oct. 5, 2022.

p. 132   "If y'all believe that": Rossignol, 217.

p. 133   "You have to have": interview with Jared Newman, Oct. 5, 2022.

p. 133   "Could talk to a fence post": testimony of Mark Ball, *State v. Murdaugh*, Feb. 22, 2023.

p. 134   "Likable, boisterous personality": interview with Dayle and Randy Blackmon, Nov. 21, 2022.

p. 134   "Always very respectable": ibid.

p. 134   "It was a very informal process": testimony of Alex Murdaugh, *State v. Murdaugh*, Feb. 23, 2023.

p. 135   "*Possum is good*": "Festival Takes on Patriotic Theme with Flags, Band Music, Soldiers," *The Hampton County Guardian*, July 23, 1941.

p. 136   "It takes a ton of guts": "History of the Chitlin Strut," *The Hampton County Guardian*, Nov. 21, 1973.

p. 136   "Frolicsome fun": "Melon Festival Becomes Traditional and Bigger and Better Every Year," *The Hampton County Guardian*, June 24, 1959.

p. 136   "Beautiful girls and beautiful watermelons": ibid.

p. 136   "Flop": "Melon Harvest Again Attracts Visitors," *The Hampton County Guardian*, July 7, 1948.

p. 137   "For memories in technicolor": "Melon Festival Becomes Traditional and Bigger and Better Every Year," *The Hampton County Guardian*, June 24, 1959.

p. 137   "I have the gift of creation": "Pictures Tumble from His Fingers," *The Hampton County Guardian*, July 13, 1955, reprinted from the English newspaper *The Stratford Express*.

p. 76   "Strangely enough": "Expert in Forestry Writes of Cypress," *The Hampton County Guardian*, Feb. 21, 1923.

p. 139   "Too shallow and obstructed": Pete Laurie and David Chamberlain, *The South Carolina Aquarium Guide to Aquatic Habitats of South Carolina*, Columbia: University of South Carolina Press, 2003, 108.

p. 139   "Some people think": Harry Lightsey, "You Can Come Home Again," *The Hampton County Guardian*, Aug. 19, 1970.

p. 140   "Within it all": ibid.

p. 141   "Getting something done": "Colleton Magistrate Says He Got Payoff on Bootleg Whiskey," *The News and Courier* [Charleston, SC], Sept. 23, 1956.

p. 142   "You see what I'm up against": ibid.

p. 142   "Friendly raids": "Murdaugh Named in New Charges," *The News and Courier* [Charleston, SC], Sept. 2, 1956.

p. 142   "I wish I could": "Colleton Case Witness Cites $500 'Payoff'," *The News and Courier* [Charleston, SC], Sept. 22, 1956.

p. 142   "Share": ibid.

p. 143 "The *News and Courier*": ibid.

p. 143 "An injustice has been done": "Solicitor Posts Bond Pending Liquor Case," *The Hampton County Guardian*, June 20, 1956.

p. 143 "Champion of youth": "Murdaugh Posts Whisky Case Bond," June 16, 1956.

p. 144 "However much his method": "Solicitor Cleared in Tax Case," *The News and Courier* [Charleston, SC], Sept. 9, 1955.

p. 144 "A law enforcement officer": "The Proper Respect for Law," *The Beaufort Gazette*, June 7, 1956.

p. 145 "I wish to reiterate to you": "Murdaugh Asserts Charges Are False," *The Hampton County Guardian*, Sept. 12, 1956.

p. 145 "These lawyers down here": "Defendant Changes His Plea As Colleton Whisky Case Opens," *The News and Courier* [Charleston, SC], Sept. 18, 1956.

p. 145 "For God's sake keep quiet": "Colleton Case Witness Cites $500 'Payoff'," *The News and Courier* [Charleston, SC], Sept. 22, 1956.

p. 146 "I've known Clifton": "Jurors May Present Verdict in Colleton County Case Tonight," *The News and Courier* [Charleston, SC], Sept. 29, 1956.

p. 146 "And yet, you defended him": "Battle of Wits Marks Murdaugh Court Appearance," *The News and Courier* [Charleston, SC], Sept. 28, 1956.

p. 146 "Now you two lawyers quit": ibid.

p. 146 "I call the solicitor": "Jury May Get Colleton Case Tomorrow," *The News and Courier* [Charleston, SC], Sept. 27, 1956.

p. 146 "Cesspool of lawlessness": "Murdaugh, 2 Others Acquitted; Thompson, 16 Others Acquitted," *The News and Courier* [Charleston, SC], Oct. 2,1956.

p. 147 "The top control": "Jurors May Present Verdict in Colleton County Case Tonight," *The News and Courier* [Charleston, SC], Sept. 29, 1956.

p. 148 "This is really 'old grudge week'": ibid.

p. 148 "Do you believe": "Jurors Postpone Colleton County Case Deliberation," *The News and Courier* [Charleston, SC], Sept. 30, 1956.

p. 148 "I'm sure that there isn't": ibid.

p. 148 "Each government witness": ibid.

p. 148 "Are you going to": ibid.

p. 149 "Not guilty"; "Murdaugh, 2 Others Acquitted; Thompson, 16 Others Acquitted," *The News and Courier* [Charleston, SC], Oct. 2,1956.

p. 149 "I appreciate from the bottom": David Lauderdale, "A whiskey conspiracy: How 'Righteous Randolph' Murdaugh almost became 'Bootlegging Buster,'" *The Island Packet* [Hilton Head Island, SC], updated May 19, 2022.

NOTES

p. 149 *"I can't get involved"*: "Although Freed, Murdaugh Castigated by U.S. Judge," *The News and Courier* [Charleston, SC], Oct. 3, 1956.

p. 150 "We are delighted": "Allendale Jurors Laud Solicitor Murdaugh," *The News and Courier* [Charleston, SC], Oct. 23, 1956.

p. 150 "as unwarranted and uncalled for": "On Butting in," a letter to the editor of *The News and Courier* [Charleston, SC] by M. T. Laffitte, Oct. 7, 1956.

p. 151 "They are attempting to prosecute": "Murdaugh on Trial in Tampering Case," *The News and Courier* [Charleston, SC], Dec. 5, 1957.

p. 151 "Odd": United States Attorneys Bulletin of Nov. 9, 1956.

p. 151 "Get even with Murdaugh": "Battle of Wits Marks Murdaugh Court Appearance," *The News and Courier* [Charleston, SC], Sept. 28, 1956.

p. 152 "I'm not doing so well": ibid.

p. 152 "Publicly castigated": United States Attorneys Bulletin of Nov. 9, 1956.

p. 153 "The second invasion": Matthew Allen Lockhart, "From Rice Fields to Duck Marshes: Sport Hunters and Environmental Change on the South Carolina Coast, 1890–1950," University of South Carolina Scholar Commons, 2017, 23.

p. 154 "Not Maggie's favorite place": testimony of Marian Proctor, Feb. 14, 2023.

p. 155 *"You may fool"*: from the poem "The Man in the Glass," unknown author, a framed copy of which was found in the Murdaughs' house at Moselle.

p. 157 "Alex had a POA": interview with Ronnie Crosby, May 11, 2023.

p. 157 "Obsessed": testimony of Ronnie Crosby, *State v. Murdaugh*, Feb. 8, 2023.

p. 157 "Hog dogs": ibid.

p. 157 "Rude awakening": "South Carolina's Growing Wild Hog Problem: Recommendations for Management and Control," https://www.dnr.sc.gov/wildlife/hog/pdf/wildhogwhitepaper.pdf.

p. 158 "Pretty much an expert": testimony of Ronnie Crosby, *State v. Murdaugh*, Feb. 28, 2023.

p. 158 "Scourge": testimony of Mark Ball, *State v. Murdaugh*, Feb. 28, 2023.

p. 158 "They got where they were": testimony of Ronnie Crosby, *State v. Murdaugh*, Feb. 7, 2023.

p. 158 "There remains a wide expanse": William Elliott, *Carolina Sports by Land and Water; Including Incidents of Devil-fishing, Wild-Cat, Deer & Bear Hunting etc.*, Columbia: University of South Carolina Press, 1994, 152.

p. 159   "For the same reason": Wilbur J. Cash, *Mind of the South*, New York: Alfred A. Knopf, 1941.

p. 160   "The bream, flat fish": *South Carolina: The WPA Guide to the Palmetto State*, 327.

Chapter 4

p. 161   "Unwarranted and entirely uncalled for": "Murdaugh Blasts at Judge on Castigation in U.S. Court," *The News and Courier* [Charleston, SC], Oct. 4, 1956.

p. 162   "When the federal government": ibid.

p. 162   "Segregation in education": *Briggs v. Elliott*, 98 F. Supp. 529, Eastern District South Carolina. 1951.

p. 163   "You don't believe": "Jasper Grand Jury Is Challenged Again," *The News and Courier* [Charleston, SC], May 18, 1954.

p. 164   "If I will have to": "Konfesses to Konfusions," *The Hampton County Guardian*, Nov. 27, 1957.

p. 164   "A trap": "Integration—A Trap," *The Hampton County Guardian*, Oct. 23, 1963.

p. 164   "People are forgetting all reason": letter to the editor of *The Hampton County Guardian* from R. A. Kinard, Oct. 9, 1963.

p. 165   "I never want to see": Martha Bee Anderson, "Around the Clock" column, *The Hampton County Guardian*, March 23, 1960.

p. 165   "No Integration": "'No Integration' Convention Keynote," *The Hampton County Guardian*, March 7, 1956.

p. 165   "There's not enough troops": "Third Parties: Southern Revolt," *Time*, Oct. 11, 1948.

p. 166   "It wasn't to my advantage": "Essie Mae's Story," interview of Essie Mae Washington by WLTX News, Columbia, SC, Dec. 15, 2003.

p. 166   "God never would have put": letter to the editor of *The Hampton County Guardian* from R. A. Kinard, Oct. 9, 1963.

p. 167   "An interracial rape case": McTeer, 59.

p. 167   "Overpowering sex urge": "White Youth Guilty of Rape of Negro," *The News and Courier* [Charleston, SC], June 30, 1959.

p. 167   "Got pleasure out of using": ibid.

p. 168   "Israel, as many colored women": *State of South Carolina v. Israel Sharpe*, 239 S.C. 258 (1961).

p. 169   "Must be removed from society": "Court Considers Appeal for New Trial of Marine," *The News and Courier* [Charleston], Oct. 10, 1961.

p. 169   "We white people": "Second Interracial Trial: Negro Is Found Guilty in Beaufort Rape Case," July 1, 1959.

p. 170 "Forever set it clear": ibid.

p. 170 "The two verdicts rendered": ibid.

p. 171 "Big dogs": testimony of Chris Wilson, *State of South Carolina v. Richard Alexander Murdaugh*, Feb. 9, 2023.

p. 171 "They took business": interview with an anonymous source.

p. 172 "Conversations with local attorneys": "Judicial Hellholes 2004," American Tort Reform Foundation, 21.

p. 173 "We got to know": interview with Amon Rigdon, April 24, 2023.

p. 174 "I think they were worse": interview with an anonymous source.

p. 174 "Home field advantage": interview with an anonymous source.

p. 175 "Other than being somewhat ruthless": interview with an anonymous source.

p. 175 "What are you supposed to do": ibid.

p. 177 "Pine and blood": testimony of Alania Plyler Spohn, *United States v. Russell Lucius Laffitte*, Nov. 14, 2022.

p. 179 "I looked up to him": testimony of Arthur Badger, *United States v. Russell Lucius Laffitte*, Nov. 16, 2022.

p. 182 "I want it to be": testimony of Annette Griswold, *State of South Carolina v. Richard Alexander Murdaugh*, Feb. 8, 2023.

p. 182 "I was so worried": ibid.

p. 183 "He just wasn't": testimony of Mark Ball, *State of South Carolina v. Richard Alexander Murdaugh*, Feb. 22, 2023.

p. 184 "*The feeling among the troops*": Conyngham, 310.

p. 184 "*In Georgia few houses*": Conyngham, 311.

p. 185 "I slept on the floor": William T. Sherman, *Memoirs of General W. T. Sherman, Volume II, Part 4*, 1889, published online by Project Gutenberg, Chapter XXII.

p. 185 "Spartan State . . . that had hatched": Conyngham, 301.

p. 185 "Her cities are in ruins": ibid.

p. 186 "Briar patch bank": "Famous Old Banking House Is Sold; Laffitte Acquires Loan & Exchange," *The Hampton County Guardian*, July 13, 1955.

p. 186 "Unreconstructed banker": ibid.

p. 187 "I want to wish": ibid.

p. 189 "Our Lowcountry has no money": "Hiott Convicted of Manslaughter," *The Hampton County Guardian*, June 7, 1939.

p. 189 "Micarta had been like": "Micarta Goes Around the World Spreading the Name of Hampton," *The Hampton County Guardian*, March 25, 1959.

p. 189 "I think the numbers": interview with Alan Young, Dec. 13, 2022.

p. 191   "National pastime . . . Cherished traditions": Morton M. Hunt, "Damage Suits—A Primrose Path to Immorality," *Harper's Magazine*, January 1959, as reprinted in *The Hampton County Guardian*.

p. 191   "As long as we condone": Martha Bee Anderson, "Around the Clock" column, *The Hampton County Guardian*, Oct. 4, 1954.

p. 192   "It started one night": deposition of Anthony K. Cook, Dec. 20, 2019, as part of *Beach V. Parker, Inc. et al.*, Hampton County, SC.

p. 193   "(Paul) loved to tear stuff up": ibid.

p. 193   "When he goes to point": ibid.

p. 193   "Always had problems with DNR": deposition of Connor M. Cook, Jan. 13, 2020, as part of *Beach V. Parker, Inc. et al.*, Hampton County, SC.

p. 193   "He never disciplined them": interview with an anonymous source.

p. 194   "If Paul wasn't a sociopath": interview with an anonymous source.

p. 194   "*I picked this picture*": photography blog posts from 2016 attributed to Buster Murdaugh were published on https://bustermurdaugh.word press.com/.

p. 197   "Pack a punch": interview with an anonymous source.

p. 197   "She seemed to be fine": testimony of Marian Proctor, *State v. Murdaugh*, Feb. 14, 2023.

p. 198   "They'd leave a gun": testimony of Mark Ball, *State v. Murdaugh*, Feb. 22, 2023.

p. 198   "Of course, in classic, Alex": testimony of Ronnie Crosby, *State v. Murdaugh*, Feb. 2023.

p. 198   "I had to smile": testimony of John Marvin Murdaugh, *State v. Murdaugh*, Feb. 27, 2023.

p. 199   "I don't know what": testimony of Ronnie Crosby, *State v. Murdaugh*, Feb. 2023.

p. 199   "I could have picked": testimony of Mark Ball, *State v. Murdaugh*, Feb. 22, 2023.

p. 200   "People are saying I hit": interview with an anonymous source.

p. 200   "He was laid out": "Mother of slain H.C. teen states possible 'hate crime,'" *The Hampton County Guardian*, Nov. 24, 2015.

p. 200   "I was going down": 911 call from motorist reporting the body of Stephen Smith being spotted in the road, Hampton County, SC, July 8, 2015, 3:39 A.M.

p. 201   "I saw no vehicle debris": South Carolina Highway Patrol MAIT report concerning death of Stephen Smith, 4.

p. 201   "Heated": South Carolina Highway Patrol MAIT report concerning death of Stephen Smith, 25.

p. 202   *"I heard that"*: Portions of South Carolina Highway Patrol investigator Todd Proctor's interviews regarding the death of Stephen Smith were published on assorted episodes of the *Murdaugh Murders* podcast.

p. 207   "Crazy as hell": interview with an anonymous source.

p. 207   "Few marbles loose": interview with an anonymous source.

p. 207   "A screw loose": interview with an anonymous source.

p. 207   "Don't worry about the dog": interview with an anonymous source.

p. 208   "No scooterbootin'": interview with an anonymous source.

p. 208   "You are not allowed": interview with an anonymous source.

p. 209   "C'mon, pard, let's have a drink": interview with an anonymous source.

p. 209   "The pretty little girls": interview with an anonymous source.

p. 209   "My housekeeper has fallen": 911 call from Maggie Murdaugh reporting a fall suffered by Gloria Satterfield, Colleton County, SC, Feb. 2, 2018, 2015, 9:34 A.M.

p. 211   "As if something bad happened": "Documents, audio released in Gloria Satterfield death investigation," WCBD-TV, Charleston, SC, May 8, 2023.

p. 211   "Let me go after": testimony of Tony Satterfield, *State v. Murdaugh*, Feb. 3, 2023.

p. 212   "Very particular": testimony of Dale Davis, *State v. Murdaugh*, Feb. 14, 2023.

p. 212   "Laid back": ibid.

p. 213   "To the moon": interview with an anonymous source.

p. 213   "She'd wear that": interview with an anonymous source.

p. 213   "Catty": interview with Kim Brant, April 19, 2023.

p. 213   "Grinning his ass off": interview with an anonymous source.

p. 214   "Whatever I was doing": testimony of Alex Murdaugh, *State v. Murdaugh*, Feb. 24, 2023.

p. 216   "A railroad junction": Alfred Eisenstaedt, "Life Spends a Day at Yemassee Junction," *Life*, May 1942.

p. 218   "Murdaugh passed the bar exam": Rossignol 102.

p. 218   "Deception was indicated": SLED polygraph examination of Gregory Alexander, Sept. 21, 2010.

p. 218   *"During the post test interview"*: ibid.

p. 218   "We have full faith": "Yemassee Police Captain Indicted," *Bluffton Today*, May 31, 2012.

p. 219   "The charges against Greg Alexander": testimony of Alex Murdaugh, *State v. Murdaugh*, Feb. 24, 2023.

Chapter 5

p. 220   "Sport coat justice": interview with Walter Czura, July 25, 2023.

p. 221 "Justice was served": ibid.

p. 221 "Just his way of life": interview with Lewis Pitts, Jan. 21, 2022.

p. 221 "It was more than": interview with Dayle and Randy Blackmon, Nov. 21, 2022.

p. 222 "He won't have no worms": interview with an anonymous source.

p. 222 "You got along with him": interview with Duane Swygert, June 1, 2022.

p. 222 "You don't want to cross": interview with an anonymous source.

p. 223 "You might end up": interview with an anonymous source.

p. 223 "If Buster wanted you": interview with Duane Swygert, June 1, 2022.

p. 223 "No necktie": interview with Lewis Pitts, Jan. 21, 2022.

p. 224 "Listening constantly to desperate situations": Sammy Fretwell, "Crusading Lawyer Who Fought for 'the Little Guy,' Including SRS Workers, Dies at 75," *The State*, March 11, 2020.

p. 224 "Nightmare of injustice": interview with Lewis Pitts, Jan. 21, 2022.

p. 225 "I just want you": interview with Mike Macloskie, July 25, 2023.

p. 225 "If you wanted to be": interview with Bill Humphries, March 2023.

p. 225 "I'll mail yours": interview with Sam Crews, April 26, 2023.

p. 225 "Man to see": Patra Taylor, "On the Edge: A Lowcountry Legend Opens Up About His Past . . . and His Future, Part One," *The Charleston Mercury*, May 2023.

p. 226 "The cock of the walk": Pat Conroy, *The Death of Santini: The Story of a Father and His Son*, New York: Doubleday, 2013.

p. 232 "Your honor, the state": interview with Jared Newman, Oct. 5, 2022.

p. 232 "Would the two defendants": Dickey, 6.

p. 233 "This is where Johnny": John Monk and Cody Dulaney, "Powerful SC Family Faces Scrutiny Following Boat Crash That Killed 19-Year-Old Woman," *The State*, April 5, 2019, updated Sept. 29, 2021.

p. 233 "Slap you on the back": interview with Alan Young, Dec. 13, 2022.

p. 233 "It ain't personal": interview with Dayle and Randy Blackmon, Nov. 21, 2022.

p. 234 "If he ever needed something": interview with an anonymous source.

p. 234 "A cult following of Buster": interview with an anonymous source.

p. 234 "We feel Mr. Murdaugh": "Grand Jury Backs Murdaugh Election," *The Hampton County Guardian*, Feb. 17, 1960.

p. 234 "You would have thought": interview with an anonymous source.

p. 235 "Playing bartender": interview with an anonymous source.

p. 235 "If we get stopped": interview with an anonymous source.

p. 235 "What color car": interview with Jared Newman, Oct. 5, 2022.

p. 236 "He went far enough": interview with an anonymous source.

p. 236 "Careful, you might want": interview with Jim McClary, Dec. 12, 2022.

p. 236   "I don't want the officer": interview with an anonymous source.

p. 236   "Governors come and go": interview with an anonymous source.

p. 237   "If you could benefit him": interview with an anonymous source.

p. 237   "You're gonna get a call": interview with an anonymous source.

p. 237   "It's alright to know them": interview with an anonymous source.

p. 237   "If you ever got": interview with an anonymous source.

p. 237   "Benevolent crook": interview with Bill Humphries, March 2023.

p. 238   "I want to be": interview with an anonymous source.

p. 238   "It wasn't good": interview with Mike Macloskie, July 25, 2023.

p. 239   "You're damn right": Dayle and Randy Blackmon, Nov. 21, 2022.

p. 239   "All my life": interview with an anonymous source.

p. 239   "There was an acute awareness": interview with an anonymous source.

p. 240   "The camaraderie and the gossip": Pat Conroy, Suzanne Williamson Pollak, *The Pat Conroy Cookbook*, New York: Doubleday, 2004.

p. 241   "I wouldn't eat one": ibid.

p. 241   "I never have left": ibid.

p. 242   "A beautiful shot": Unless otherwise noted, quotations concerning the fatal boat crash on Archers Creek on Feb. 24, 2019, are contained in a South Carolina Department of Natural Resources investigative file.

p. 243   "Very weird": deposition of Morgan Doughty, Jan. 6, 2020, as part of *Beach V. Parker, Inc. et al.*, Hampton County, SC.

p. 244   "Just being Timmy": deposition of Connor M. Cook.

p. 247   "(It will) be all right": ibid.

p. 247   "He's a crazy drunk": deposition of Morgan Doughty.

p. 247   "No one could operate": deposition of Connor M. Cook.

p. 248   "Make that mistake": deposition of Anthony K. Cook, Dec. 20, 2019, as part of *Beach V. Parker, Inc. et al.*, Hampton County, SC.

p. 249   "Fixing to make it home": deposition of Connor M. Cook.

p. 249   "CONNOR! CONNOR!": South Carolina Department of Natural Resources investigative file concerning the fatal boat crash on Archers Creek on Feb. 24, 2019.

p. 250   "The pity of it is": "The Painful Truth," *The Beaufort Gazette*, Oct. 4, 1956.

p. 251   "Larger than is justified": order of Judge J. A. Spruill Jr., *George T. Rodgers v. Howard P. Cooper*, Beaufort County, SC, Jan. 6, 1964.

p. 251   "Severe emotional and mental strain": personal papers of *Beaufort Gazette* publisher Howard Cooper, courtesy of his son Brent Cooper.

p. 251   "You were stupid": ibid.

p. 252   "Community reaction terrific": ibid.

p. 252   "It was literally like waking": deposition of Anthony K. Cook.

p. 253   "MALLORY!": South Carolina Department of Natural Resources investigative file concerning the fatal boat crash on Archers Creek on Feb. 24, 2019.

p. 253   "Shut up": ibid.

p. 253   "Nine-one-one": 911 call from Connor Cook reporting a boat crash on Archers Creek, Beaufort County, SC, Feb. 24, 2019, 2:26 A.M.

p. 254   "Sit right here": police dashcam recording of Beaufort County Deputy Sheriff Stephen Domino.

p. 257   "It would be hard": *State v. Davis*, 122 S.E.2d 633 (S.C. 1961).

p. 258   "The most vivid memory": email to author from Travis Medlock, Feb. 7, 2023.

p. 259   "I signed some of them": "Investigation Spreads: Adoption Records Probed, Colleton Court Clerk Says," *The News and Courier* [Charleston], March 9, 1963.

p. 259   "I didn't know": "Case for Private Adoptions," *The State*, March 1, 1984.

p. 261   "Buster could get a baby": interview with Alan Young, Dec. 13, 2022.

p. 261   "Pretty little girls": interview with an anonymous source.

p. 261   "Crazy": interview with Sheryl McKinney, Aug. 19, 2023.

p. 265   "Weird, corny, teen drama movie": unless otherwise noted hospital and accident scene statements are found in the South Carolina Department of Natural Resources investigative file concerning the fatal boat crash on Archers Creek on Feb. 24, 2019.

p. 267   "That everything was going": deposition of Connor M. Cook.

p. 270   "Can you feel that heat": police dashcam recording of Beaufort County Deputy Sheriff Stephen Domino.

p. 272   "I don't know why": "County Jail Warden a Happy Hostess," *The Hampton County Guardian*, Sept. 10, 1969.

p. 272   "Sometimes a drunk"; ibid.

p. 273   "Handy in fights": "Tom O'Connor," *The Hampton County Guardian*, Dec. 31, 1969, reprinting of a tribute from *The News and Courier* [Charleston].

p. 273   "My son came home": "The Time Has Come" column, *The Hampton County Guardian*, Jan. 5, 1972, reprint of a column from January 1968.

p. 274   "*There was somewhere in me*": ibid.

p. 274   "Through the years": "The Time Has Come" column, *The Hampton County Guardian*, July 12, 1967.

p. 276   "Slobbering": Sheryl McKinney's statements come from interviews, Dec. 7, 2022; May 20, 2023; and Aug. 19, 2023.

Chapter 6

p. 280   "Each taking a turn": "Changing of the Guard," *The Hampton County Guardian*, Dec. 24, 1986.

p. 280   "We must not permit": Martha Bee Anderson, "Around the Clock" column, *The Hampton County Guardian*, July 18, 1973.

p. 281   "Sadly, the 'blushing pink'": Martha Bee Anderson, "Around the Clock" column, *The Hampton County Guardian*, Feb. 27, 1974.

p. 281   "Look at those sections": Martha Bee Anderson, "Around the Clock" column, *The Hampton County Guardian*, Sept. 25, 1974.

p. 281   "She had a strong bent": interview with Patrick Tyler, April 19, 2023.

p. 281   "She was talking": ibid.

p. 282   "She reminded you": ibid.

p. 282   *"It is no great contribution"*: "Our Hampton County Courthouse," *The Hampton County Guardian*, Jan. 31, 1973.

p. 283   "Is a small price to pay": "Court of General Sessions Convened," *The Hampton County Guardian*, June 16, 1971.

p. 283   "It will tax": "More Indictments Pursued in Case," *The Hampton County Guardian*, May 29, 1974.

p. 284   "I was appalled": "A Rich Do-Gooder Named Winthrop Turns Detective to Solve a Brutal Murder," *People*, 1974.

p. 285   "A good boy": "Retaliation Hinted in Slaying of a Black", *The New York Times*, Dec. 11, 1972.

p. 285   "The Youmans case": "A Rich Do-Gooder Named Winthrop Turns Detective to Solve a Brutal Murder," *People*, 1974.

p. 286   "We think we know": "'70 Slaying Spurs N.A.A.C.P. Inquiry," *The New York Times*, Sept. 10, 1973.

p. 286   "It seems right strange": "Youmans Case: Five Indicted by Grand Jury," *The Hampton County Guardian*, April 24, 1974.

p. 286   "Corrupt or paralyzed": "Four Years Is Too Long," *The Hampton County Guardian*, March 27, 1974.

p. 286   "I'm not saying": "A Rich Do-Gooder Named Winthrop Turns Detective to Solve a Brutal Murder," *People*, 1974.

p. 287   *"I hadn't heard anyone"*: "Youmans Case: Five Indicted by Grand Jury," *The Hampton County Guardian*, April 24, 1974.

p. 287   *"(My uncles) think"*: "A Rich Do-Gooder Named Winthrop Turns Detective to Solve a Brutal Murder," *People*, 1974.

p. 288   "It's no wonder": "Evidence Hearing Stumps Defense, Prosecution," *The Hampton County Guardian*, June 12, 1973.

p. 288   "Professional do-gooder": "Attempted Bribes Hit Murder Case," *The Hampton County Guardian*, May 15, 1974.

p. 288   "The point is Mr. Winthrop": "Evidence Hearing Stumps Defense, Prosecution," *The Hampton County Guardian*, June 12, 1973.

p. 288   "We resent one side": ibid.

p. 289   "They talk about sacrificial lambs": "Youmans Murder: Trial Clears Fairfax Five," *The Hampton County Guardian*, July 17, 1974.

p. 289   "Frankly, I don't think": ibid.

p. 289   "I know how you can": ibid.

p. 290   "How did I ever manage": interview with Patrick Tyler, April 19, 2023.

p. 290   "That's when I started": *Murdaugh Murders: A Southern Scandal*, Netflix, 2023.

p. 291   "They say the good ones": "Community Says Goodbye to Mallory Beach: Teen Who Was Always Kind with the Biggest Smile," *The Island Packet* [Hilton Head Island, SC], Sept. 29, 2021.

p. 291   "Gripped the Lowcountry": David Lauderdale, "Lowcountry SC Wants Justice in Fatal Boat Wreck," *The Island Packet* [Hilton Head Island, SC], March 8, 2019.

p. 292   "It's definitely an uneasy feeling": testimony of Buster Murdaugh, *State v. Murdaugh*, Feb. 21, 2023.

p. 292   "Devastating blow": testimony of Marian Proctor, *State v. Murdaugh*, Feb. 14, 2023.

p. 293   "None of us thought": testimony of Buster Murdaugh, *State v. Murdaugh*, Feb. 21, 2023.

p. 293   "He's not leaving the state": "Man Pleads Not Guilty in Deadly Boat Crash in Beaufort County," WSAV.com, May 6, 2019.

p. 294   "Line in the sand": testimony of Mark Tinsley, *State v. Murdaugh*, Feb. 6, 2023.

p. 294   "He was always going": testimony of Mark Tinsley, *State v. Murdaugh*, Feb. 9, 2023.

p. 296   "Classic Southern boss's suit": interview with Patrick Tyler, April 19, 2023.

p. 296   "Moving like a great white": ibid.

p. 296   "He was in business": interview with an anonymous source.

p. 296   "*It would be incongruous*": "Full Time Solicitor?" *The News and Courier* [Charleston], Nov. 5, 1975.

p. 298   "I always thought": "Rodney Peeples Installed As Second District Judge," *The Hampton County Guardian*, Dec. 11, 1974.

p. 298   "He didn't come up easy": "Judge Eltzroth Dies at 93," *The Hampton County Guardian*, Nov. 10, 2014.

p. 298   "The brother that I didn't": "Eltzroth Takes Oath As Judge," *The Hampton County Guardian*, Aug. 20, 1975.

p. 298 "It wouldn't bother me": "Eltzroth to Seek 14th Judgeship," *The Hampton County Guardian*, March 27, 1974.

p. 300 "We are seeing how many": "Quail purchased for plantation," *The State*, Oct. 30, 1971.

p. 300 "Mistakes of the head": "Candidates for Court Bench Certified by Commission," *The News and Courier* [Charleston], May 1, 1975.

p. 300 "Whether I did things right": "Quiet 14th Circuit Judges Race Heating Up," *The News and Courier* [Charleston], Dec. 26, 1974.

p. 300 "TEEN-AGE HEADQUARTERS": Wade Hampton High School yearbook, Hampton County, SC, 1957.

p. 301 "Captivating but highly volatile person": "Tribute to the Late Horace Charles Parker Sr.," *The Hampton County Guardian*, June 8, 1966.

p. 302 "Oozing": interview with an anonymous source.

p. 302 "Johnny taught me a lesson": interview with Travis Medlock, Dec. 12, 2022.

p. 303 "Johnny's a nice guy": interview with an anonymous source.

p. 303 "No matter what you do": "R. Murdaugh III Speaks at Banquet," *The Hampton County Guardian*, Jan. 28, 1976.

p. 303 "How can you tell": interview with Jared Newman, Oct. 5, 2022.

p. 303 "Oh, you know Libby, huh": interview with an anonymous source.

p. 304 "She used the power": interview with an anonymous source.

p. 304 "Batshit crazy": interview with an anonymous source.

p. 304 "Crazy as a shithouse rat": interview with an anonymous source.

p. 304 "Only public building with character": J. W. DeLoach, "The Requiem," *The Hampton County Guardian*, Sept. 21, 1977.

p. 305 "Machines were hooked up": Libby Murdaugh, "Let Her Die," *The Hampton County Guardian*, Oct. 5, 1977.

p. 306 "Small but powerful group": Linda M. Gallagher, "Don't Give Up the Ship!: Let Her Live!" *The Hampton County Guardian*, Oct. 12, 1977.

p. 307 "You ain't seen nothing": interview with an anonymous source.

p. 308 "Having the time": interview with Dayle and Randy Blackmon, Nov. 21, 2022.

p. 308 "He had a grand time": interview with an anonymous source.

p. 308 "I became happily married again": interview with Dayle and Randy Blackmon, Nov. 21, 2022.

p. 308 "He put the fear": ibid.

p. 309 "Hey man—just checking in": Tony Satterfield read text messages between him and Alex during his testimony in *State v. Murdaugh*, Feb. 9, 2023.

p. 309 "(His lawyers) say he's broke": testimony of Mark Tinsley, *State v. Murdaugh*, Feb. 6, 2023.

p. 311   "She just wanted him": testimony of Blanca Turrubiate-Simpson, *State v. Murdaugh*, Feb. 10, 2023.

p. 311   "He doesn't tell me everything": ibid.

p. 311   "She found one house": testimony of Marian Proctor, *State v. Murdaugh*, Feb. 14, 2023.

p. 312   "Trying to pin it": deposition of Connor M. Cook.

p. 312   "I was doing": ibid.

p. 312   *"There's a couple"*: ibid.

p. 312   "A shell of her old": testimony of Alex Murdaugh, *State v. Murdaugh*, Feb. 23, 2023.

p. 313   "Paul had a way": testimony of Belinda Rast, *State v. Murdaugh*, Feb. 10, 2023.

p. 313   "Thank you all so much": video of Murdaugh family and friends celebrating Alex's 51st at Edisto Beach in May 2021, as introduced in the trial of testimony of *State v. Murdaugh*.

p. 315   "Very quaint": "Teen-Age Star Has Idol, Too," *News and Courier* [Charleston, SC], June 26, 1966.

p. 315   "They received the cheers": "Rivers Delivers," *The New York Times Magazine*, Aug. 29, 1965.

p. 315   "The bedrock of Hampton County": interview with Patrick Tyler April 19, 2023.

p. 316   *"We have two shopping centers"*: "Hampton: The Place to Live," Dec. 29, 1976.

p. 316   "Exciting": ibid.

p. 317   "I'm drunk. Please lock me up:" "Attractive Lady Jailer Carries On 20-Year Tradition for County," *The Hampton County Guardian*, July 30, 1975.

p. 319   "She's God's child": interview with anonymous source.

p. 319   "This is going to be": Scott Graber, "Facts of Gardner Case Twice Lead to Death Sentence," *The Island News* [Beaufort, SC], Feb. 20, 2020.

p. 319   "You ain't going nowhere": *Arnold v. State*, 309 S.C. 157 (1992) 420 S.E.2d 834.

p. 320   "I'm going to leave": Scott Graber, "Facts of Gardner Case Twice Lead to Death Sentence," *The Island News* [Beaufort, SC], Feb. 20, 2020.

p. 320   "Don't get between": ibid.

p. 320   "You can't make chicken soup": "We All Played Our Roles but Outcome Was Already Decided," *The Island News* [Beaufort, SC], Feb. 26, 2020.

p. 320   *"It mattered not"*: Martha Bee Anderson, "Around the Clock" column, March 22, 1972.

p. 321   "White pill 30": testimony of SLED special agent Peter Rudofski, *State v. Murdaugh*, Feb. 17, 2023.

p. 321   "I am still in EB": ibid.

p. 321   "Little detective": testimony of Marian Proctor, *State v. Murdaugh*, Feb. 14, 2023.

p. 322   "I am very sorry": unless otherwise noted, family communications in the final weeks Maggie Murdaugh and Paul Murdaugh were alive are contained in a SLED investigative report titled "Murdaugh Murders Timeline of Events" and were disclosed during the testimony of SLED special agent Peter Rudofski, *State v. Murdaugh*, Feb. 17, 2023.

p. 322   "You don't have": testimony of Alex Murdaugh, *State v. Murdaugh*, Feb. 24, 2023.

p. 322   "Mags found pills": ibid.

p. 323   "I'm dreading it": ibid.

p. 323   "I just can't eat": testimony of Belinda Rast, *State v. Murdaugh*, Feb. 10, 2023.

p. 324   "What do you need now": testimony of Jeanne Seckinger.

p. 325   "Ty I'm waiting": "Murdaugh Murders Timeline of Events," SLED report.

p. 325   "Alex is about to die": ibid.

p. 326   "It's better than it was": a video filmed by Paul Murdaugh on his phone was introduced during the testimony of Heidi Galore, *State v. Murdaugh*, Feb. 2, 2023.

p. 327   "I've been up to it": 911 call from Alex Murdaugh at Moselle, Colleton County, SC, June 7, 2021, 10:06 P.M.

Chapter 7

p. 329   "Okay, thanks for calling": interview with anonymous source.

p. 329   "The least reliable man": interview with Sam Crews, March 22, 2023.

p. 329   "Buster didn't want": interview with Sheryl McKinney, Dec. 7, 2022.

p. 331   "Mr. Buster was all about": interview with anonymous source.

p. 332   "The most competent": "Harrelson Thinking," *The Hampton County Guardian*, Aug. 11, 1976.

p. 332   "Mr. Buster was pretty much": interview with anonymous source.

p. 332   "Don't worry about it": interview with anonymous source.

p. 333   "We're going to": interview with Jared Newman, Oct. 5, 2022.

p. 334   "It's bad, it's bad": Alex's initial statements to police at the murder scene were recorded by the dashcam of Sergeant Daniel Greene, of Colleton County Sheriff's Department, June 7, 2021.

p. 336   "Look at what they did": testimony of Mark Ball, *State v. Murdaugh*, Feb. 22, 2023.

p. 336   "The fucking boat wreck": testimony of Nolen Tuten, *State v. Murdaugh*, Feb. 23, 2023.

p. 336   "In pieces": testimony of Mark Ball, *State v. Murdaugh*, Feb. 22, 2023.

p. 336   "He was destroyed": testimony of Chris Wilson, *State v. Murdaugh*, Feb. 9, 2023.

p. 337   "I hate to have to": SLED interview of Alex Murdaugh, June 8, 2021.

p. 338   "At this time": statement from the Colleton County Sheriff's Office, June 8, 2021.

p. 339   "See if you can": "Murdaugh Murders Timeline of Events," report by SLED.

p. 340   "Grounded": interview with Creighton Waters, May 9, 2023.

p. 341   "He's smart enough": interview with anonymous source.

p. 341   "Cry at the drop": interview with Jim McClary, Dec. 12, 2022.

p. 342   *"Monday morning, uhhh"*: SLED interview of Alex Murdaugh, June 10, 2021.

p. 347   "Tell him to pop in": interview with Walter Czura, July 25, 2023.

p. 347   "Turned over": order of resident judge (signature illegible), *State v. John Thomas*, Beaufort County, SC, March 2, 1981.

p. 349   "It was so clear": interview with Walter Czura, July 25, 2023.

p. 349   "I will not discuss": message from Roberts Vaux to author, March 24, 2023.

p. 349   "Walter, hand me": interview with Walter Czura, July 25, 2023.

p. 350   "Ladies and gentlemen": interview with anonymous source.

p. 351   "Is that white-headed": interview with Mike Macloskie, July 25, 2023.

p. 351   "Wait a minute": interview with Jared Newman, Oct. 5, 2022.

p. 351   "I want to make sure": interview with Dayle and Randy Blackmon, Nov. 21, 2022.

p. 351   "Relay": ibid.

p. 351   "Do you know": ibid.

p. 352   "It's your job": interview of Randy Blackmon, Oct. 4, 2022.

p. 352   "Those sure are some nice": interview with Dayle and Randy Blackmon, Nov. 21, 2022.

p. 352   "I bet that's the hardest": ibid.

p. 352   "Who's that big-tittied woman": ibid.

p. 352   "Your honor, that's highly improper": interview with anonymous source.

p. 352   "I better not catch you": interview with Mike Macloskie, July 25, 2023.

p. 353   "Well, that ain't funny": ibid.

p. 353   "Buster would tell you": interview with anonymous source.

p. 354   "Very scary": testimony of Jeanne Seckinger, *State v. Murdaugh*, Feb. 7, 2023.

p. 354 "We were in complete": testimony of Annette Griswold, *State v. Murdaugh*, Feb. 8, 2023.

p. 354 "I see words like": *Good Morning America*, ABC, June 17, 2021.

p. 354 "He's upright and looks strong": ibid.

p. 355 "Everybody was afraid": testimony of Marian Proctor, *State v. Murdaugh*, Feb. 14, 2023.

p. 355 "I thought that was": ibid.

p. 356 "If someone asks you": testimony of Mushelle "Shelly" Smith, *State v. Murdaugh*, Feb. 6, 2023.

p. 357 "I'm not comfortable": SLED interview of Alex Murdaugh, Aug. 11, 2021.

p. 360 "I expect things": "Changing of the Guard," *The Hampton County Guardian*, Dec. 24, 1986.

p. 360 "I know I am going": ibid.

p. 360 "My father and I": ibid.

p. 360 "Ending of an era": ibid.

p. 360 "I consider Mr. Murdaugh": "Generous Portions of Praise Heaped on Sheriff Loadholt at Appreciation Dinner: 'Big Daddy' Leads Lauding," *The Hampton County Guardian*, Jan. 23, 1985.

p. 360 "Ignore anybody who criticizes you": ibid.

p. 361 "*You can't draw much*": testimony of Buster Murdaugh during a hearing of South Carolina's Judicial Screening Committee composed of state legislators, either late 1990 or early 1991, scstatehouse.gov.

p. 361 "It scared the hell out": interview with anonymous source.

p. 361 "WE LOVE DRUNK DRIVERS": interview with anonymous source.

p. 362 "Personal prejudice": *State of South Carolina v. Plath*, 277 S.C. 126 (1981) 284 S.E.2d 221.

p. 362 "Okay, man, you've got": interview with anonymous source.

p. 362 "I came to tell you": interview with Sheryl McKinney, May 20, 2023.

p. 362 "That's the only time": interview with Mike Macloskie, July 25, 2023.

p. 363 "The party was going good": unless otherwise noted, statements of those involved in the Beaufort County boat crash on May 10, 1998, are from a South Carolina Department of Natural Resources investigative file on the incident.

p. 365 "Mayday, mayday . . . Coast Guard Savannah": Recording of distress call placed by John Marvin Murdaugh to the U.S. Coast Guard, May 10, 1998, records of South Carolina Department of Natural Resources.

p. 368 "I will only tell you": message from Travis Reynolds to the author, Aug. 22, 2022.

p. 368 "I think about it": interview with Diaz Scoggins, May 4, 2022.

p. 369   "There's a swamp every fifteen": interview with Creighton Waters, May 9, 2023.

p. 370   "Going to get": interview of state prosecutors in *State v. Murdaugh*, WCIV, ABC, April 3, 2023.

p. 370   "Misconduct can lead": interview with Creighton Waters, May 9, 2023.

p. 371   "Information gathered during the course": "SLED releases statement, provides new details on Stephen Smith murder investigation," *The Greenville News*, March 23, 2023.

p. 372   "We've given him this": testimony of Norris Laffitte, *United States v. Laffitte*, Nov. 8, 2022.

p. 372   "Bo', I hate to even": testimony of Chris Wilson, *State v. Murdaugh*, Feb. 9, 2023.

p. 372   "Floated like a feather": testimony of Annette Griswold, *State v. Murdaugh*, Feb. 8, 2023.

p. 372   "I'm about to throw up": testimony of Jeanne Seckinger, *State v. Murdaugh*, Feb. 7, 2023.

p. 373   "I shit you up": testimony of Chris Wilson, *State v. Murdaugh*, Feb. 9, 2023.

p. 373   "Setup": 911 call made by motorist in Hampton County, SC, Sept. 4, 2021.

p. 374   "I have made a lot": public statement of Alex Murdaugh, Sept. 6, 2021.

p. 374   "While I will support him": Michael M. DeWitt, "Randy Murdaugh Issues Statement on Recent Events Involving His Brother Alex Murdaugh," *The Hampton County Guardian*, Sept. 8, 2023.

p. 374   "I'm innocent": *Today* interview with Curtis Edward Smith, NBC, Oct. 4, 2021.

p. 375   "LET ME SAY THIS": Ben Mathis-Lilley "Let Me Say This with as Much Sensitivity as I Can: Wow, That's a Lot of Dead People and Crime," *Slate*, Sept. 16, 2021.

p. 375   "Fire and ice": John Monk, "Who Are Alex Murdaugh's Attorneys? What to Know About Longtime SC Legal Bulldog Duo," *The State*, Jan. 25, 2023.

p. 375   "Offend": opening statement by defense lawyer Dick Harpootlian, *State v. Murdaugh*, Jan. 25, 2023.

p. 376   "Let me put it": John Monk: "Mr. Murder Looms Large in SC Courts," *The Charlotte Observer*, April 16, 1989.

p. 376   "Dollars for me": interview with an anonymous source.

p. 376   "Give it back better": John Monk: "Mr. Murder Looms Large in SC Courts," *The Charlotte Observer*, April 16, 1989.

p. 377   "Abuzz": "Periscope: Harpootlian, Knotts Clash," *The State*, Feb. 12, 1981.

p. 377   "What's up, Doc": interview with an anonymous source.

p. 377   "To bash his fucking head": interview with an anonymous source.

p. 377   "*Creighton can eat a duck*": text messages to Creighton Waters from an unidentified lawyer on June 3, 2022, as shared by Waters one year later on X.

Chapter 8

p. 380   "This guy had been": interview of state prosecutors in *State v. Murdaugh*, WCIV, ABC, April 3, 2023.

p. 380   "Find me the lie": interview with Creighton Waters, May 9, 2023.

p. 380   "Super, super, super secretive": SLED interview of Alex Murdaugh, June 10, 2021.

p. 381   "Hey, he's gotta bird" unsent video taken by Paul Murdaugh on his phone, 8:44 P.M., June 7, 2021.

p. 381   "Cases tend not to get": interview with Creighton Waters, May 9, 2023.

p. 381   "Chief, general, we believe": ibid.

p. 382   "You want a speedy trial": ibid.

p. 384   "Catastrophic damage": opening statement by prosecutor Creighton Waters, *State v. Murdaugh*, Jan. 25, 2023.

p. 384   "It is our honor": opening statement by defense lawyer Dick Harpootlian, *State v. Murdaugh*, Jan. 25, 2023.

p. 388   "Allowed to use trickery": testimony of David Owen, *State v. Murdaugh*, Feb. 15, 2023.

p. 389   "Bend over, I'll drive": jottings of a lawyer in attendance of the trial.

p. 389   "Sometimes mistakes get made": interview with Creighton Waters, May 9, 2023.

p. 391   "Your honor can I just": statement of Dick Harpootlian, *State v. Murdaugh*, Jan. 31, 2023.

p. 392   "Ladies and gentlemen": statement of Judge Clifton Newman, *State v. Murdaugh*, Feb. 8, 2023.

p. 393   "There's a family there": interview with Creighton Waters, May 9, 2023.

p. 393   "Judge Newman likes": ibid.

p. 393   "He came and did": ibid.

p. 394   "We'll be in recess": interview of state prosecutors in *State v. Murdaugh*, WCIV, ABC, April 3, 2023.

p. 395   "Probably too much": testimony of Mark Ball, *State v. Murdaugh*, Feb. 22, 2023.

p. 395   "Piling in": ibid.

p. 395   "It pissed me off": ibid.

p. 395   "Tempting, but": statement by Dick Harpootlian during testimony of
Mike Sutton, *State v. Murdaugh*, Feb. 21, 2023.

p. 395   "Mr. Barber in the interest": Feb. 16, 2023.

p. 395   "Get a fucking life": comment from Harpootlian to author, Jan. 27,
2023.

p. 395   "ALEX MURDAUGH TRIAL REVEALS": Kathleen Parker, "Alex
Murdaugh Trial Reveals a Sloppy Investigation," *The Washington Post*,
Feb. 17, 2023.

p. 396   "Fuck that shit": statement by Jim Griffin outside of Colleton County
Courthouse, per two witnesses and acquaintances of the author.

p. 396   "I saw blood": testimony of John Marvin Murdaugh, *State v.
Murdaugh*, Feb. 27, 2023.

p. 396   "No, I did not": testimony of Alex Murdaugh, *State v. Murdaugh*,
Feb. 23, 2023.

p. 399   *"While the jurors viewed"*: Rebecca Hill, *Behind the Doors of Justice*,
Wind River Media LLC, 2023.

p. 400   "We get a lot": comment of Judge Clifton Newman, *State v. Murdaugh*,
March 2, 2023.

p. 400   "He could not": the author observed and spoke with the Reverend
Raymond Johnson, who demonstrated outside the Colleton County
Courthouse the night Alex Murdaugh was found guilty.

p. 401   "It will never happen again": interview of state prosecutors in *State v.
Murdaugh*, WCIV, ABC, April 3, 2023.

p. 402   *"I don't question"*: Judge Newman and Alex Murdaugh conversed
during the sentencing hearing of *State v. Murdaugh*, March 3, 2023.

CODA

p. 406   "They lost a mother": All quotations in the coda, unless otherwise
noted, are from Alex Murdaugh's financial crimes sentencing hearing
on November 28, 2023, in the Beaufort County Courthouse, in
Beaufort, South Carolina.

p. 410   "He knows more": Nicholas Bogel-Burroughs, "Breaking Silence,
Murdaugh Brother Says 'Not Knowing Is The Worst Thing,'" *The New
York Times*, March 6, 2023.

A NOTE FROM THE AUTHOR

For two years I lived a second life in Hampton County. Once a week or so I'd leave my home on the South Carolina coast and drive inland for two hours, across a number of rivers and swamps, to arrive in one of the Palmetto State's most isolated sections. I often felt, as I left Charleston behind, that I was piloting a time machine as much as an automobile. There is little overlap between these places.

On most mornings I headed straight to the Hampton library, where I hid away in a small room, possibly a repurposed closet, to read old issues of the *Hampton County Guardian* on a microfilm machine. I'd break for lunch, usually buying a sandwich and coffee at Juliennes on Lee Avenue or fried chicken and iced tea at Rigdon's, the popular cinder block fry shack beside the railroad, catty-corner from the shuttered laminate factory. Then I'd make a round of phone calls from my truck and begin an afternoon spree of door-knocking, driving across the Lowcountry to run down people on my ever-growing list of potential sources, all of whom I wanted to ask a simple, initial question: Would you like to talk?

Most people did not want to talk. On the days I struck out, at least in the short term, I headed back to the library, where the microfilm machine was at least always willing to shine a light on the past, both literally and figuratively, with its small projector bulb. On these days I communed with the town's ghosts as much as I conversed with living residents, quickly scanning each newspaper page for items of interest. Like the newspaper microfilm, the history of Hampton County and the Murdaugh family unspooled slowly for me, its details often fuzzy and its stories sometimes incomplete. There was a hefty amount of rumor to constantly sort through, some of it unlikely, some of it plausible, and all of it a challenge to confirm.

Sometimes when driving home from Hampton at dusk I'd become seized by sadness. The same landscape that seemed enchanting in the morning, at first light, now seemed threatening and heavy. I saw the trees and fields and rivers differently after a day's work in the Hampton library, where I fast forwarded through years of community tragedies, absorbing, in rapid-fire fashion, week after week of grim headlines that screamed so many different ways in which people unexpectedly died. I felt glum after conducting certain interviews, too, after spending hours with a source in their living room or cabin or law office or plantation house, listening to stories that made me shake my head in disbelief and disgust. After these conversations the forests and swamps no longer seemed serene but instead complicit, concealing all sorts of crimes.

Most of my interviews took place in person in the Lowcountry, but others occurred in other parts of South Carolina and North Carolina, and some were conducted by telephone and email. I'd like to thank everyone who spoke with me, especially those people who allowed me to quote them by name. I'd also like to thank all the librarians and archivists who facilitated my research, and to acknowledge the talents and smarts of William "Jack" Ross, who assisted me with newspaper research, as well as the wonderful work of literary agent Jessica Papin and editor Jessica Case.

Beyond the newspaper in Hampton County, the archives of the Charleston *News and Courier* and Columbia's *The State* newspaper proved crucial resources. I also relied on police reports, legal documents, and Freedom of Information requests to tell this story, as well as my experiences attending the banking crimes trial of Russell Laffitte in federal court in Charleston in November 2022 and the murder trial of Alex Murdaugh, which started in the Colleton County Courthouse in Walterboro in January 2023.